UNITY AND STRUGGLE

Amilcar Cabral

UNITY AND STRUGGLE

Speeches and Writings

Texts selected by the PAIGC
Translated by Michael Wolfers

MONTHLY REVIEW PRESS
NEW YORK AND LONDON

Copyright © 1979 by the PAIGC

Library of Congress Cataloging in Publication Data
Cabral, Amilcar.
  Unity and struggle.
  "These texts amount to some two-thirds of the French
edition of his work that was published by François
Maspero in 1975."
    1. National liberation movements – Guinea Bissau –
Collected works. 2. Guinea-Bissau – Politics and
government – Collected works. 3. Cape Verde Islands –
Politics and government – Collected works. 4. National
liberation movements – Cape Verde Islands – Collected works.
5. Partido Africano da Independência da Guiné e Cabo
Verde – Collected works. I. Partido Africano da
Independência da Guiné e Cabo Verde. II. Title.
DT613.75.C335   320.9'66'5702   79-2337
ISBN 978-0-85345-625-4

Manufactured in the United States of America
10 9 8 7 6 5 4 3 2 1

Contents

PART 1   The Weapon of Theory

WRITINGS OF YOUTH

MAN AND LAND

PORTUGUESE COLONIAL DOMINATION

PARTY PRINCIPLES AND POLITICAL PRACTICE

PART 2   Revolutionary Practice

Abbreviations

CLSTP (Comité de Libertação de São Tomé e Principe) Committee (later Movement) for the Liberation of São Tomé and Principe

CONCP (Conferência das Organizações Nacionalistas das Colónias Portuguesas) Conference of the Nationalist Organizations of the Portuguese Colonies

CUF (Companhia União Fabril)

FRELIMO (Frente de Libertação de Moçambique) Mozambique Liberation Front

MPLA (Movimento Popular de Libertação de Angola) Popular Movement for the Liberation of Angola

OAU Organization of African Unity

PAIGC or PAI (Partido Africano da Independência da Guiné e Cabo Verde) African Party for the Independence of Guiné and Cape Verde

PIDE (Policia Internacional e de Defesa do Estado) International Police for the Defence of the State (created for Portugal by the Salazar regime, extended to Africa after 1954).

Introduction

When Africans of Portugal's empire began at last to make their voices heard in the world outside their barricaded colonies, soon after the middle of the 1950s, they found few to listen to them and fewer still to understand the importance of what they were proposing to do. The outside world, they learned, knew little of Portugal itself, let alone of 'Portuguese Africa'; and, knowing little, cared even less.

Yet these Africans and their companions in struggle, fewer than twenty years later, had moved into the very heart and centre of the world's attention. And no wonder: for, whether greatly admired or as greatly hated, they were seen by their own efforts to have wrecked the forty-year-old dictatorship of Fascist Portugal and destroyed the Portuguese empire. They were seen to have radically changed the balance of African power and influence in decisive areas of the continent, and above all in relation to the racist regimes of the far south and the various African agents of those regimes. They were seen to have built powerful movements of revolutionary challenge and changed the course of African history. And all this they were seen to have done in territories where a more or less complete 'colonial silence' and stagnation had previously reigned.

How was this possible among populations reputed to be among the most 'backward' in all Africa: populations having only one or two per cent of literate persons, possessing almost no access of any kind to modern technology, or to modern ideas, or to modern forms of organization, and meanwhile suffering from the most repressive of all the colonial regimes? How could it be done?

It may be too soon for history's definitive answers. But just as the importance of what these Africans achieved is now very clear, whether in relation to their own territories or to the more general issues of anti-colonial and post-colonial change, so are some of the reasons for their success. Among these were the absolute intransigence of the Fascist regime and the consequences of this intransigence for the thought and practice of African nationalists who had to meet and overcome it; the efficacy of that thought and practice as it developed in largely peasant societies; the international links that were forged with governments and groups willing to give material and moral aid to these nationalists; the fact that Lisbon was obliged to fight wars in three territories at the same time, and to fight them, moreover, on the self-defeating principles of Fascism; and other reasons deriving from these or added to these.

But history's definitive analysis will go beyond these instrumental reasons for a remarkable success. It will ask and answer other and more decisive questions. Who were the men and women who conceived the possibility of liberation, back in the dark days of its beginning in these territories? Who forged the instruments, learned to use them, taught others to use them, led these struggles through every kind of mental ambush and physical barrier? What were their ideas, what was their morality? Whose were the keys that could unlock that seemingly unpassable door to freedom, to any useful unity and progress, and trample on its fortifications? How far can others use the same keys?

These are the questions, no doubt, that matter most to a world still sorely needing keys of this kind; and, happily, these questions can be largely answered by the record as we have it even now. That is what this book is about. These long and difficult campaigns for anti-colonial and post-colonial liberation and development in the African empire of the Portuguese – in Angola, Cape Verde, Guinea-Bissau, Mozambique, São Tomé – produced a number of outstanding revolutionary thinkers who proved able to live their thought in their practice, and who, in doing that, have displayed a rare and often decisive talent for *explanation* in writing and the spoken word. Among these thinkers, and even at the head of them, was Amilcar Cabral, the author of the writing in this book. Murdered by the agents of Portuguese Fascism in 1973, his work lives after him and is there for inspection. A supreme educator in the widest sense of the word, Cabral can be recognized even now as being among the great figures of our time. We need not wait for history's judgement to tell us that. The evidence is available. Among this evidence are the texts that follow here.

It would be easy to write of him as a person and a friend, though it would also be difficult: easy because of his simplicity and sympathy, his directness, his love of life, his enduring interest in everyone and everything that came his way; and yet difficult, too, because of the depth and complexity of his thought and meditation. Suffice it here to say that he was loved as well as followed, and he was both because he was large hearted, entirely committed, devoted to his people's progress. But of course you can be devoted and still reach wrong conclusions. Cabral was also loved and followed because events repeatedly proved that he could and did reach right conclusions. The imperfections that were as natural to him as to any other vivid human being were outmatched, it was seen, by intellectual and moral power in all that mattered most, in whatever could be decisive. And he asked of no one what he would not do himself.

When in 1956 he launched his revolutionary party – the PAIGC, Partido Africano da Independência da Guiné e Cabo Verde – he had five trusted companions and no more. Long before he was killed, the PAIGC had become a national movement of overwhelming power and influence. When he first set out to win support in Europe during 1960, he had to travel under an assumed name, Abel Djassi, and found not many to welcome him. Long before his death in 1973 the meetings he addressed in Europe and outside Europe were attended by thousands, governments asked his advice, other governments listened to him, the United Nations gave him its platform, and a wide audience in many countries looked to him for leadership. He took all this fame in his stride, having no self-indulgence for big words or big claims, and replied that hard work and hard thought in his people's cause, holding nothing back, were the only factors that could count.

But if one had to define a single influential aspect of Cabral's approach, perhaps it would be his insistence on the study of reality. 'Do not confuse the reality you live in with the ideas you have in your head', was a favourite theme in his seminars for party militants. Your ideas may be good, even excellent, but they will be useless ideas unless they spring from and interweave with the reality you live in. What is necessary is to see into and beyond appearances: to free yourself from the sticky grasp of 'received opinions', whether academic or otherwise. Only through a principled study of reality, of the strictly *here* and *now*, can a theory of revolutionary change be integrated with its practice to the point where the two become inseparable. This is what he taught. But the manifest fact that he practised what he taught in all that mattered most, in whatever could be decisive, was another factor that convinced.

There are many stories about his habit of linking the everyday scene, the banal scene you take for granted and barely even see, with the intellectual groundwork of an overall theory of society: of a theory, that is, always riveted to the reality of time and place. One might even say that this habit was amongst his most persuasive gifts as an educator. Well known in Guinea-Bissau, for example, is what he one day said after watching a boy of eleven in a dugout canoe. This was a scene that those who were with him had known a thousand times, as he had, or as often acted it themselves: the boy in the canoe balancing his body against the thrust of his paddle so as to keep the lip of the wood above the tide, working across the ocean creek, swinging to approach the shore, deciding how to land beyond the current's clutch, then stowing the paddle and leaping ashore where the mud was firmest. What could anyone say about any of that: save perhaps, if you were an educated 'doctor' from Lisbon, that here was another aspect of Africa's 'backwardness', of Africa's 'cultural void'? But Cabal passed no such comment. He talked instead of the skills required to use that excavated log of wood, and said: 'You see. Environment, they say, is formative of culture. If that is so, then ours is a highly cultivated people.' And he proceeded, while the boy danced up the mud and vanished amid the mangrove trunks, to draw appropriate conclusions from the dialectical interplay of culture and environment. The texts that follow here display this approach at many levels and in many circumstances. For this reason, among others, they go far to explain the major influence of his thought in three concentric fields: at home in Guinea-Bissau and Cape Verde; in the wider African scene; and in the world outside Africa. They are not by any means all that he wrote or spoke for publication. Selected by the editorial care of the National Council of Culture of the Republic of Guinea-Bissau, these texts amount to some two-thirds of the French edition of his work that was published by François Maspero in 1975. But even the Maspero edition, though running to six hundred pages, is far from complete, for this greatly gifted man found time and need to write copiously; and many of his reflections, statements, directives and informal lectures for internal use remain in PAIGC archives.

A full history of the national liberation struggle of the PAIGC will one day take account of all his writings. They will be found to accompany every phase and critical decision of the period before war was launched in January 1963, as well as of the ten years that followed till his death. They include dozens of letters and directives. Their 'guides to action' range from a detailed analysis of helicopters and how to shoot them down to a long series of operational orders to troops in the field. Their notes from internal lectures and seminar discussions cover a multitude of everyday events and aspects of ideological development within the PAIGC. Perhaps above all, they deal repeatedly with the necessary bases of revolutionary democracy, whether in the liberation of women, in anti-élitist education, in a decentralised system of public health, and, as the essential guarantee of all such gains, in the building of participatory political structures at and from the grass roots.

But the texts presented here are likely to be seen as Cabral's most influential work in theoretical and practical exposition. They can be said to fall into two connected parts: the texts written or spoken (but taped and then transcribed) for his own internal audience, the militants of the PAIGC and all who were active in its ranks; and, secondly, the texts conceived with an external audience chiefly in mind. One may note in passing that no contradiction will be found to arise between these two: what Cabral said at home was the same in content as what he said abroad, even if the form was often very different. His argument abroad, and he was often a brilliant publicist, was invariably the truth that he drew from his study of reality at home: the same truth, with the same conclusions, that he expounded in the forests of his homeland. So that these texts may better be seen as I think Cabral would have seen them: as texts concerned for different purposes with a theory of effective action for determined ends; and, secondly, as texts concerned for the same purposes with the practice of that theory. Given their range and diversity, the reader will find his or her own preferences. But a few comments on them may be useful here.

Whether for an internal or external audience they will be found to be all of a piece in another important sense. Each in its own way has Cabral's insistence on looking squarely into the particular reality of time and place, on inspecting this reality in its parts and in its whole, and then on drawing from it the lessons that can be useful to progress. Such was his practice. As to his theory, evolving over all the years of struggle from soon after the Second World War, its development and nature emerge with an especial clarity from two or three of the 'external' texts (made abroad, that is, but then used by the PAIGC at home): for example, his 1966 address on 'Presuppositions and objectives of national liberation in relation to social structure', perhaps the chief text which established Cabral as an original thinker in the Marxist tradition (Item 14), and a lecture of 1970 on 'National Liberation and Culture' (Item 15) which offers another insight, opened this time on the cultural implications of liberation struggle, into the critical subtlety of his thought.

The opening pair of items make a very effective introduction to reading Cabral. Two poems indicate something of the underlying passion of his sense of self-identity with the situation into which he was born in Guinea-Bissau, at Bafata where forest and savannah meet, and grew to manhood in the sister land of the Cape Verde archipelago, where his father was a teacher at Santa Caterina on the island of Santiago, and, not incidentally for Cabral's youthful development, a fervent defender of Cape Verdian folklore and popular culture. But the next item here is altogether of a different sort. It is not a bit poetic. It consists of extracts from the through-going agricultural survey of Guinea-Bissau that Cabral made when, briefly in colonial service as an agricultural engineer before the early onset of the struggle, he studied his own country at the grass roots and came to know it better than anyone else. The survey took him two years to complete, and the Portuguese ignored it. But for him these facts and findings were to provide the foundations of his theory of anti-colonial revolution and post-colonial development in Guinea-Bissau. When he spoke of these matters afterwards, he did so from an intimate and even unique knowledge of his country's peoples and their cultures, problems, ways of life.

Item 3 is the pamphlet that he wrote in London, in French for English translation, during a stay of many weeks during 1960, and at a time when he considered, as did his comrades from other Portuguese colonies, that they must study this 'outside world' they had to come to grips with, but also begin to make their voices heard in it. Here one may find, at least in outline, many of the chief arguments that later years would develop in more detail; and one finds them, characteristically again, not only for his own country but also for Angola, Mozambique and São Tomé. Cabral concentrated on the problems of his own people, but he never forgot that these problems and his people belonged to a wider world.

With Items 4 to 12 we find him again among his own people, and intimately so. These nine texts were selected from numerous tape recordings of an extended seminar given by him to an assembly of leading militants during November 1969, when the armed struggle against colonial rule was nearly seven years old but still far from ended. These lectures and replies to discussion were spoken in the creole of Guinea-Bissau (a language combining an indigenous syntax, drawn from other local languages such as Pepel and Manjaco, with Portuguese words and usages), and were given extempore or from a minimum of notes. That is why their style is so informal and easy-going; but they will be read profitably for their style as well as for their content. Better perhaps than in any other African texts from any source, here one may see just what the intellectual promotion and development of a liberation movement must entail: the patient discussion of terms, the advance of the argument from stage to stage, the continued emphasis on a principled inspection of the reality within which one lives and upon which one must work.

Again we are far from slogans or facile statements of denunciation or triumph. A gathering of political workers and fighters, many at an early stage of literacy or not yet of any literacy, almost none with any habit of learning from books, all but a handful knowing no more than a purely local experience, is drawn into a prolonged debate on the theory of what has to be done. Each has to understand and measure the part of his own task in that theory, and yet perceive the wider connexions. Perhaps it is this last emphasis that explains why the overall effect is repeatedly one of wide application: here are problems which concern us all, even though our circumstances seem altogether different. A reading of these nine texts, holding in mind the conditions under which they emerged, the audience, and the conjuncture of the year 1969, can tell one much about the whole struggle in the Portuguese colonies and even, or so it appears to me, about the universal aspects of any liberation struggle conducted so as to succeed.

But practice, Cabral used to say, comes before theory. Closely linked to these texts of 1969 are eight others of four years earlier, Items 25-32. Gathered under the heading of 'general watchwords', these are concerned above all with practice. Conceived in 1964 and written in 1965 into a booklet called *Palavras Gerais* for strictly internal use, they march together with the theory of national liberation, of the politics of liberation, which Cabral and his leading companions had already begun to elaborate. Concisely and even curtly and never in the least ambiguously, these directives define the action and approach that Cabral considered vital to success. They became from the time of their issue within the PAIGC, in November 1965, the 'book of reference' for every militant, whether by direct reading or by reading aloud to those who could not read. Downright as always with him, critical and self-critical, sparing no private corners of doubt or evasion, they form one of the most instructive manuals of practical revolution – of revolution, that is, specific to its time and place – to have reached us from any source.

An historian will be especially impressed by these directives of 1965. At a stage when the PAIGC was still weak in the number of its trained militants, when its political organization in liberated areas had yet to move beyond initial phases, and when its fighting organization was still in relative infancy, Cabral lays down a programme for development, a series of targets to be achieved, a guide to reaching them, and a style of behaviour (whether individual or collective), that will steer the PAIGC through all its problems to the end of the war and beyond. This is what events will prove; but the foresight is extraordinary. Much will be taken further in the years that follow. Yet already the characteristic tones are here, the tones that will afterwards be recognized across the world. 'Hide nothing from our people . . tell no lies. . . claim no easy victories': but all the time explain, discuss, debate, argue, learn and above all *lead.* It is here in the general directives, as in the seminar texts of 1969, that one may well be reaching the true genius of this man.

He enlarged on the experience of his party, on the lessons it had accepted, the mistakes it had made, the successes it had won, in many other documents. Occasionally he was willing to build all this into a general framework of analysis and prescription, as for example in his Havana address of 1966 and his Syracuse lecture of 1970, already mentioned. At other times, as in his UN speech printed as Item 34, he preferred to enlarge on the particular circumstances of the PAIGC in Guinea-Bissau and Cape Verde, and on the necessary stages of its growth and development. He did this, too, in many communiqués and notably in annual reviews of progress (Items 23 and 24).

But a selection aiming to be comprehensive at least in offering the diversity of his writing has to show many aspects of the problems that he faced. One of these aspects arose from his concern with history: with the theme that African history, stopped by colonial intrusion, could embark once more upon its own development only through the awakened conscious-ness and objective gains of a struggle such as the PAIGC had launched. This insistence on the absolute need for revolutionary change from the colonial or neo-colonial condition did not lead him, however, into denying the earlier achievements of African nationalism. On the contrary, it was the pioneers of African nationalism who had opened the way (Item 13), and now, partly thanks to them, it was for others to press further.

Nor did his insistence on the need for revolutionary struggle ever lead him into any acceptance of violence for its own sake. Anti-colonial counter-violence was necessary in Guinea-Bissau, as in other colonies so situated. But this counter-violence, for Cabral, still remained the particular *political* form which any progress must demand. Power did not come from the barrel of a gun in any primary sense: power came, and must come, always from the consistent application of a just political analysis and programme across the whole field of effort, including the military field. He raised an army, led and taught it how to fight, gave it detailed orders, supervised its every major action; but he did all this, by the habit of his practice, through a process of collective political discussion. Counter-violence was unavoidable, but it was still a monster to be used with care, kept firmly on a guiding rein, and never preferred to non-violent action if that could yield the same results. All through its years of toughest fighting, the PAIGC was repeatedly offered as a partner for Portugal as soon as Portugal shed its Fascism, surrendered its empire, and turned towards the future. Items 17 to 20 are four texts which illustrate Cabral's general position that armed warfare should be always an extension of political warfare.

And it had its due effect. In April 1974 the Portuguese officers of the Movimento das Forças Armadas (MFA) overthrew the dictatorship on the dual slogan of 'Decolonization and Democratization'. Some of the most active of these officers, as they bore witness then or later, had learned their politics of liberation from the example of the PAIGC. 'The colonised peoples and the people of Portugal are allies', declared the assembly of the MFA officers of Guinea-Bissau in a unanimous statement of June 1974: 'The struggle for national liberation has contributed powerfully to the overthrow of fascism and, in large degree, has lain at the base of the MFA whose officers have learned in Africa the horrors of a fruitless war, and so have understood the roots of the evils which afflict the society of Portugal.' And it may well be thought that these words enshrine one of Cabral's greatest victories, though sadly a posthumous one.

The acid test of a revolutionary leader has to lie in his effectiveness. By the time of his death in January 1973 the policies he had shaped with his companions had very obviously won the war: the end came sooner than expected, but delay would have made no essential difference. Then what about the peace that followed? This is a story that still unfolds. Yet the manner of its unfolding from the time when fighting ceased early in 1974, and Portugal conceded independence in September 1974, and the new Republic took command of its dual heritage – its heritage of socio-political development within the liberated areas but of colonial ruin outside them – and began to live in peace, shows at every essential point the value and effectiveness of the policies and programmes shaped under Cabral's leadership for the future.

Whether in Guinea-Bissau or its sister republic of Cape Verde, these policies and programmes were then applied in style as in content, and were found to meet the challenges of peace and reconstruction. Increasingly, towards the end of his life he had begun to turn his mind to those challenges. But if the precise conclusions that he reached with his companions are present in these wartime texts only by implication, they will be found, written large and clear, in the analytical reviews issued by the PAIGC since the war ended: for example, in the *Relatório geral* offered by Aristides Pereira,

Cabral's successor as secretary-general, to the third congress of PAIGC in November 1977.

There, for example, one may find the reflection of one of his firmest beliefs: that further progress in any African development must require a steady advance towards new and organic unities of thought and action. The building of independent nations must be the prelude to the building of larger constellations of independence. And this, too, he saw as the necessary evolution of an African history which regains command of itself and is therefore able, with due time and effort, to move forward into a fully post-colonial society. With due time and effort: for this process, in his thinking, could never be achieved by any extension of the colonial heritage, whether political or economic or cultural. It would come, on the contrary, only through a continued process of social and structural revolution capable of drawing whole peoples into an arena of active participation: an arena thereby freed of old servitudes, old inferiorities, old miseries. Then, but only then, would Africa realize its potentials.

'My own view', he said in 1967, 'is that there are no real conflicts between the peoples of Africa. There are only conflicts between their élites. When the peoples take power into their own hands, as they will with the march of events in this continent, there will remain no great obstacles to effective African solidarity.' But having said this he at once came down, as he always did, to the cases that he knew himself. For it could be no good talking about any theory of social change unless this theory, he was careful to insist, stood firmly on a known and practical reality. Progress, to mean anything, had to be in the here and in the now. So he went on, in that conversation of 1967, to show that a real and practical process of developing solidarity of thought and action was now in fact at work among the previously divided peoples of his own country, Balanta, Manjaco, Mandinga and the rest. Yet if mass participation in social and cultural change could bring this unifying process into motion within one country, why should it not be able to bring it into motion between different countries? Specifically in his own case, it could and would do this between Guinea-Bissau and Cape Verde. And ten years later, in 1977, the *Relatório geral* of Aristides Pereira, reporting for the PAIGC, was able to list the practical ways in which a unifying process had indeed been set in motion between those two countries.

Cabral gave his life for the liberation that he served, and he had to give it long before his time and when he was still in the full zest and vigour of his work. What else he gave is displayed at least in the outline of its manifold mastery of revolutionary thought and action in the pages of this book. They can only suggest the spendour of the man himself. But they are the record of him that we have. It is a record that will count in Africa, and outside Africa, beyond our time.

Basil Davidson

Biographical notes*

Only a little while ago, just a few years, Amilcar Cabral's name was among those that angry youth in Europe and America were hurling in defiance at the establishment of the societies under challenge. They went onto the streets and proclaimed their faith in a new world, when they brandished like a weapon portraits of Che Guevara, the Latin American, and of Amilcar Cabral, the African. These two men, although very different, were the Revolution.

If Che's life story was fairly well known, that of Cabral, although still living and at the peak of activity, was much less so. For the young challenging the old world, Cabral was undeniable evidence of Africa's struggle against anachronistic colonialism – the natural outcome when society was justifiably called in question – and therefore of struggle against modern imperialism which sought the same aims as colonialism by much more formidable means.

In Africa Cabral's name was already spontaneously linked with those of Nkrumah and Lumumba. In fact in the tragic history of revolutionary Africa, so many of whose leaders have left only a faint memory, three great figures stand out indisputably: Kwame Nkrumah, the visionary; Patrice Lumumba, the martyr; Amilcar Cabral, the unifier. As a unifier and mobilizer, he was both a theoretician and a man of action indefatigably in pursuit of reality, by revealing the deep roots, fundamental causes, so often blurred in the tumult of revolutionary action. For Guineans and Cape Verdians, he is the founder of the nation and the guide: his watchwords remain binding and current as specific targets that two peoples born out of a common history are engaged in fulfilling. But how did this son of the Cape Verdians, kept out of the stream of time by obsolete colonialism and isolated from the world on a remote island in the Atlantic, become that man of international dimension?

Amilcar Cabral was born on 12 September 1924 at Bafata in Guiné.The civil registers suggest that his father, Juvenal Cabral, had given him his forename in memory of the great African who made the Roman empire shake – spelling it Hamilcar†.

---

*These notes are based largely on an unpublished work: *Amilcar Cabral – Essai de biographie politique.*

† Hamilton Barca, the Carthaginian general who, like his son Hannibal, fought in the Punic Wars. Cabral's father records in his memoirs, *Memórias e reflexões* (Praia, 1947), that *his* father had named him Juvenal after the classical Latin poet. *(Translator's note.)*

Juvenal Cabral, an 'obscure non-graduate schoolmaster', had been teaching since 1913 in various regions of Guiné, notably at Cacine and Geba. He came from a farming family on the Cape Verde island of Santiago which also numbered teachers and priests, the learned, as they were then described. Amilcar Cabral's mother, Dona Iva Pinhel Évora, had been born into a humble family on the same island. Santiago was regularly hit by drought which Juvenal believed was a disaster the causes of which were in no way supernatural and could therefore be combated. As for so many other Cape Verdians, the drought and the ensuing famine altered Juvenal's fate which he expected to resemble that of the learned in his family, if not to be brighter.

Up to the age of seven, Amilcar was educated by his parents, and doubtless his father passed on to him some of the characteristics he developed: a taste for study, generosity and love of his country. In 1931 Amilcar and his mother went to Cape Verde, where his father joined them in the following year. The family had a brief period of relative prosperity which allowed the boy to begin highly rewarding study.

Beyond the Cape Verde archipelago, which seemed to be forgotten by history, the world was experiencing violent tremors, a prelude to the cataclysm which very soon would spare no one and nothing. The Second World War would accelerate exploitation of the human and natural resources of what was not yet known as the Third World. The Cape Verdians, like others under colonialism, had no other role or purpose than production to supply to the 'Metropole' what the latter delivered to the countries at war. This veritable pillage was aggravated by the expected drought that struck Cape Verde and from 1941 to 1948 caused fifty thousand deaths. In the Cabral family what would they talk about except the highly catastrophic events about which the father had original ideas and for the drought proposed rational remedies using agricultural techniques, such as tree planting and irrigation, and political measures, such as 'reorganization' of large landholdings. But the family were soon without means and the mother, Dona Iva, was wearing herself out at her sewing machine and later as a labourer in the fish-packing station.

Amilcar, who had gone to primary school at Praia, attended the Infante Don Henrique secondary school at Mindelo on the island of São Vicente. Like many adolescents, he was awakened to life through poetry. Its lyricism brought him the discovery of the magnificent beauty and harsh reality of the archipelago. Those islands at the world's end, symbolizing paradise for so many lovers and poets, are for the islanders who drag out their wretchedness there no more than a version of hell. Their dream then: escape. And Amilcar in adolescence shared that obsession: witness the dramatic story he wrote shortly before his eighteenth birthday: *Fidemar* (Son of the sea). He portrayed his hero as 'a revolutionary' who claimed the right of all 'to liberty and life' and who finished up departing from his island in the hope of returning strengthened in order to liberate it. 'One day the sea will take possession of the land. . . '

But the echo of the din of world war, albeit muted, reached Cape Verde. Amilcar could not be insensible to it. He wrote a reflective text 'Today and tomorrow', in which he explained his concept of the world, and this was later to be published in the bulletin of the House of Empire Students in Lisbon.* He was convinced that men, despite and through their struggles and suffering, were moving towards a future of 'happiness and life'. He declared: 'On earth there is a single people to which all nations belong.'

In 1944, when his secondary schooling had been completed with distinction, he returned to Praia, the capital of Cape Verde, where he worked at the national printing press. For a year, too long for him, he champed at the bit in an atmosphere of mediocre bureaucracy. Amilcar, however, continued to devote himself to literature and he entrusted to João de Deus Lopes da Silva (brother of the writer Baltazar), commander of the sailing boat 'Nossa Senhora dos Anjos', one of his poems (See Item 1) which was to be published in a weekly in the Azores:

ISLAND:
endless hills of red soil
   – rough soil –
cragged rocks masking the horizons
sea at the four corners holding fast our anguish!

In the autumn of 1945, with great difficulty Cabral secured a university scholarship and left for Lisbon. He had decided to become an agricultural engineer.

When Amilcar arrived in Europe, the war had ended with the victory of the Allies over Fascism. But in Lisbon this was by no means evident. The Iberian peninsula had to wait thirty years to achieve the democracy that was much talked about in the Portuguese capital. The streets were lively; the Portuguese people, like any other, do not have a vocation for oppression. For a while they demonstrated openly. Repression speedily re-established 'order'.

It was in this climate that Cabral became familiar with Portuguese resistance to Fascism. From his entry to the Higher Institute of Agronomy (in the 1945 – 46 academic year), he took part in the struggles for student demands. One of his contemporaries, later to become his first wife, Dona Maria Helena Vilhena Rodrigues, has recalled:

> I have known Amilcar since my first year in agronomy in 1945. Classes began in November but he arrived in the following month. There were a lot of students in that year: two hundred and twenty, including two hundred boys and twenty girls exactly. I did not belong to his set but I remember perfectly seeing

*Vol. II. No. 11. Lisbon (May – December, 1949).

him among other colleagues. As he was the *only* black, that was very obvious .
. . Amilcar did not take the entrance examinations to the university. He was
distinguished right off in the first general mathematics tests, with one of the
highest scores. Everyone was talking about him, praising his brightness and on
top of this he was attractive and relaxed. . . . As far as his political activities are
concerned, I remember that my colleagues were collecting signatures for
enrolment in anti-fascist student democratic movements. At meetings he used
to lead the discussion, since he expressed himself very well.

. . . At the start of the third year, in October, we found ourselves in the same
class again and this time in a single set of twenty-five students who had passed
the examinations.

But if Amilcar was determined to succeed at his studying, he also enlarged
the field of his general culture. An indicator of the concerns which moved
him is this poem dating from 1946 and submitted to the *Seara Nova* review
which rejected it:

> . . . No, poetry,
> Do not hide yourself away in the grottoes of my being
> espouse life
> Break the invisible bars of my prison
> open the gates of my being through and through
> and leave. . .
> In the struggle (life is struggle)
> men outside call you
> and you, Poetry, you are a man too.
> Love the poems of the whole world,
> – love men –
> Deliver the poems for all races,
> for all things,
> whelm your body with all the bodies of the world,
> whelm yourself with me . . .
> Leave, poetry:
> take my arms to bind the world
> give me your arms to bind life
> My poetry is me.

One might guess that the identity established between *being* and poetry is
not a gratuitous image.

In the still colonized continents, and particularly in Africa, the first
cracklings of the international conflagration that shook the old world were
being felt. In Algeria and in Madagascar; in Asia, the peoples of Indochina
were making it understood that they were determined to realize their
independence; China was turned upside down by revolution. Amilcar, who
took an enthusiastic part in debates and in organizing anti-fascist student
groups, saw his adolescent beliefs confirmed. But if he was convinced that he
must and would struggle for the achievement of the 'world of his dreams', he
felt the call of his land, Africa. He said this and wrote it. Within a year of

being in Europe he felt an irresistible need to return, faithful to himself, to the image of the romantic hero he had foretold. 'I live life intensely and I draw from it experiences that have given me a direction, a life I must follow whatever personal sacrifices it asks of me. That is the purpose of my life.' In fact he was a man of his time and the time was one of awakening of consciousness in Africa, for intellectuals who at that juncture, in 1949, expressed the profound hopes of their peoples.

It was the great era of the affirmation of differences, of cultural reclaim, of the defiance of those who, after admittance to the privileged enclosure of the alma mater of the dominant world, called it in question and thus opened the way to the challenge of that very world. Amilcar, with other African students in Lisbon, absorbed this message through reading poets and writers from the French colonies published in Paris where an informal movement brought European and African intellecturals more or less together in agreement to denounce that pestilence of history, shame of the twentieth century – colonialism.

Among the books which then circulated in the small group of African students featured Léopold Sédar Senghor's *Anthologie de la Nouvelle Poésie Nègre et Malgache de Langue Française* (Paris, 1948). Amilcar displayed boundless enthusiasm on reading these poems:

> . . . Things I had not even dreamed of, marvellous poetry written by blacks from all parts of the French world, poetry that speaks of Africa, slaves, men, life and human hopes. . . Sublime. . . infinitely human. . . The book brings me much and, among the many things, the certainty that the black man is in the process of awakening throughout the world.

For sensitive Africans, for Cabral, it was obviously not a matter of a hypothetical return to some imaginary purity, nor of voluntary integration into the so-called modern society (product of the slave trade, of insane exploitation of slave descendants), but of re-entry into history of men freed from all the servitudes and from systematic ideas that had only served to restrict life and to retard human accomplishment. For him, this colossal task, the only one worthy of faith and sacrifice, was everyone's concern. As he saw it, the task was first and foremost a concern of Africans.

At the end of the academic year in 1949, he returned for holidays to Cape Verde, firmly set on putting his ideas into practice. And, first, to reveal Cape Verde to the Cape Verdians: the only possible introduction to liberty and knowledge of Africa and the world. On 8 September, he began a series of radio talks on geophysical aspects of the archipelago, 'Some thoughts on the subject of rains'. It was an opportunity for Cabral to talk about the essential. He argued with conviction that Cape Verdians had the means of taking charge of their own destiny. A student, he turned himself into a teacher, calling on 'those with knowledge to enlighten those who do not know'. He launched into his topic quickly and dealt with the basic question: the Cape

Verdians have the means to live from their land, they must therefore organize themselves to take account of their realities. The broadcasts were soon banned by the colonial authorities.

'*To bring the reality of the archipelago home to the Cape Verdians themselves. . .*' This first venture in politico-cultural teaching achieved by Cabral in Santiago in 1949 already had an analogy in Luanda of the same period, with the movement *Vamos descobrir Angola* (Let's discover Angola), launched by a group of young intellectuals around the poet Viriato da Cruz. But it was in Lisbon, at the heart of colonial Fascism, that the first project for collective engagement by the men in political battles was to ripen. From his entry to the university, Amilcar Cabral was intimately tied to the group of students born in the Portuguese colonies. By their *class* origin, the latter were objectively drawn from humble stock, from an urban *petty bourgeoisie.* The more sensitive elements were aroused by the tangible facts of colonial exploitation operating at the level of the mass of the people and whose effects, albeit to a lesser degree, they experienced in their material and social lives. Those who had reached the advanced training institutes (often at the cost of enormous financial sacrifices made by their families and by virtue of jockeying for *assimilado* vacancies) bore the stigmata of revolt. Their consciousness of the *negation of the colonized man* came at the same time from their objective material situation and from the aggression to which their cultural personality as Africans was subjected. Armed with a privileged education, these *assimilados* were faced with a dilemma: either to struggle for their self-advancement in the framework of colonial society or to arm themselves culturally to challenge and destroy the system of domination. In other words, it was a matter of choosing between two views of life: either individual ascent by accepting the system's rules, or total rejection, in effect breaking away in order to open the way to freedom for the strata most oppressed by colonialism. Around these ideas was built and progressively sharpened the definition of unity for nationalists from the Portuguese colonies, the content of their ideology, and the form their combat should take.

But we are talking of the threshold of 1950: the number of intellectuals able to speak the liberation language 'for all those who have no voice' was derisory. However, this kernel of students in Portugal was engaged in feverish activity on two complementary levels. First came ideological and political training, extended into the absorption of knowledge in all fields, and the training was acquired in the crucible of more or less clandestine meetings, through reading Marxist works, or through personal contacts. The logical outcome of this was militant participation in Portuguese democratic youth organizations – MUD Juvenil (Democratic Unity Movement Youth), Peace Movement. The second level of activity lay around the safeguarding of identity, or to use Cabral's phrase the struggle for the 're-Africanization of minds'. At the same time as this *group of students* became acutely conscious of their specific situation as assimilated and colonized persons, rationalized their feelings and searched for anchorage points in African culture to revive it, they were receptive to analogous experiences worked out in the universe of oppression. Hence the absorption of currents of the American *new negro*, of *negritude* seen through Léopold Sédar Senghor's famous anthology, contacts established with the *Présence Africaine* review, and a quest for information about the growth of struggles in Africa. Agostinho Neto was expressing in his poems this moment of certainty.

This profound quest for African identity could not be limited to the simple level of individual awakening or solitary reading: it found a natural extension in efforts to unify diverse elements of the African community in Portugal, while establishing lasting contact with the kernels of embryonic political organizations in the colonies. That is why the group of students tried to take over Africa House to make it the headquarters for their activities. When they failed in this endeavour, they organized seamen in the 'Club Maritimo', and to meet the demands of their own search for identity they formed the Centre of African Studies.* In this context, Cabral disclosed his ideas on land use, the typical systems of cultivation practised by the black African, the advantages and disadvantages of the itinerant system (shifting cultivation and rotation). More and more concern about cultural questions overflowed into the area of political organization. At this point it was realized that there was a scale of values between commitment to Portuguese democratic groupings and organizational autonomy. Some African students were still active in the Portuguese structures (MUD Juvenil, Peace Movement) and represented the colonial peoples there, but it appeared on examination that it was essential to break away from the static notion of reciprocal effects between the struggle against Fascism and against colonialism.

But to return to Amilcar Cabral's career. When his university course was completed at the end of the 1949-50 academic year (with 15 points out of 16), he took courses in the following year as an Agronomy Engineer and a Colonial Agronomy Engineer (with 18 points out of 19). He was a trainee member of the soil study team at Santarém (the agronomy centre in Portugal) when he was hit by the harsh news of the death of his father, Juvenal Cabral. He had already made a *political* decision to return to Guiné and he set off for Bissau where he was put under contract by the Provincial Department for Agricultural and Forestry Services of Portuguese Guiné. It was the starting-point for a new phase that was to have a decisive effect in the future. So when agronomy engineer Cabral disembarked in Bissau at the age of twenty-eight, his countrymen were in the presence of a man determined to deliver the great political battles.

*The author who played a part in the conception and organization of this Centre puts the date of the first working meeting as 21 October 1951.

Here was an African moulded in the crucible of an island region of the continent, who had experienced the drama of famine and understood perfectly the dual nature of the Portuguese regime – in the colonies and the metropolis. Above all he was *invested* by his contemporaries with the task of achieving in the peculiar circumstances of Guiné the *bringing to concious-ness* of the mass of the people. Much later he said:*

It was after the Second World War that a need to struggle to put an end to colonial domination was born and grew in people's thoughts. At that period, a group of students from the Portuguese colonies began to seek how to *re-become* Africans, for the cunning of the Portuguese had always lain in not allowing us to be Africans in order to turn us into second-class Portuguese. Anyone who had the luck to go to school was used by the Portuguese as an agent, as an individual who would disown Africa to serve the colonialists. So our work lay in searching out again our African roots. And that was so wonderful, so useful and laden with consequences that even today the founders of that group are all leaders of liberation movements in the Portuguese colonies.
. . . Then one after another we returned to our countries and met others who thought as we did, and we sought to awaken in each person's mind the sense of freedom. It was not at all easy.
So it is not by chance that I went to Guiné. It was not material hardship that drove me back to my native land. Everything had been calculated, step by step. I had enormous potential for working in any of the other Portuguese colonies, or even in Portugal; I gave up a good position in the Lisbon agronomy centre, as a researcher, for a post as an Engineer second-class in Guiné.
. . . It was thus to follow a calculation, the idea of doing something, to make a contribution to arousing the people for struggle against the Portuguese. And I did this from the first day I set foot in Guiné.

The *political* plan was clear. But he still had to uncover the social ground of the struggle.

Cabral in Bissau was in an exceptionally strategic position to bring his plan to fruition. An African revolutionary has rarely been as well placed as the Engineer (this was how his countrymen used to address him) to create the instrument for socio-economic transformation of his country's town and countryside.

The first political problem he had to solve was that of the milieu in which to form the revolutionary kernel. He approached his former comrades at secondary school – Cape Verdians with a fairly established social position in Guiné. He asked them to take a stand. The majority took fright. Those rare few who responded positively were twenty years later to become the leaders of Guinea-Bissau and Cape Verde. But, exposing theory to reality, he received a more responsive hearing among workers at the experimental agriculture unit – Pessubé Grange – and thanks to them enlarged his

*Talk to the Seminar for PAIGC Cadres: Evolution and Prospects of the Struggle, 1969.

contacts in the townships of Bissau, Pilun and Pepel Territory. It seemed clear to him then, and would remain his principal watchword, that the key to liberty was unity of the Cape Verdians and the Guineans who had been divided by the colonial system.

Instructed to plan and execute the agricultural census of Guiné from 1953 (See Item 2), he accomplished this task with such ability and such an acute sense of professional understanding that his report is considered even today as the primary source for overall information on Guinean agriculture. For him it was above all an opportunity to grasp at the roots and in scientific form the characteristics of economic exploitation, and through contacts with the growers to understand historical, racial and cultural data about ethnic groups (a factor of diversity and of unity), and finally to identify the basic, essential motivations for the struggle against colonial domination.

In 1954, the year of Dien Bien Phu and of the Algerian rising, he tried to set up a sports association open to all Guineans without exception. This popular springboard had been used for evidently political purposes elsewhere in Africa and successfully. The Portuguese steadfastly refused, just as they had banned the broadcasts from Praia. The Governor, in his wisdom, indicated to Cabral that the latter's presence was unwelcome in Guiné. But he would be allowed on application to return once a year for a brief stay to visit his family. It was 1955.

This imposed transfer was to enable Cabral to enrich his dual scientific and political experience, since he was to be found in that year as a collaborator with two of his former teachers in 'studies concerning soil technology in certain regions of Angola' and at the head of the Soil Studies Team of the Cassequel Agricultural Company. During his spells in the colony of Angola and between tours of the countryside and missions on the plantations, Engineer Cabral took an active part in the hatching of the political structures that constituted the MPLA. As he was present on two battlegrounds (not forgetting his journey through São Tomé), his life and work were henceforth dedicated to drawing up a strategy for unitary struggle against Portuguese colonialism.

The path Cabral followed, as can now be seen, was direct, a 'royal road' one might say, without much winding. He fully lived the revolutionary activity with which he identified and advanced towards the target he had set himself. Time was racing by but the hour had not yet struck. For sure, Cabral's companions – Aristides Pereira, Luiz Cabral, Abilio Duarte, among others – who had stayed in Guiné had not stopped for a moment to act. The group developed in circumstances that were always dangerous, and they undertook the fight to take over commanding positions in the union of employees in trade and industry in Guiné. There was a long way still to go.

During an authorized visit to his family Cabral, drawing up a balance-sheet of the country's general situation with his first colleagues, directed the meeting at which the historic decision was taken: the founding of Partido

Africano da Independência – União dos Povos de Guiné e Cabo Verde. Six people attended: Amilcar Cabral, Aristides Pereira, Luiz Cabral, Julio de Almeida, Elisée Turpin and Fernando Fortes. The meeting occurred at nightfall on 19 September 1956. This was the line adopted:

> The time has come to prepare our people to take on a decisive epoch of their history – that of the struggle for national liberation; it will only succeed by mobilizing all the offspring of our motherlands without distinction as to sex, tribe and colour. It will be the struggle of all Guineans and Cape Verdians dedicated to the search for happiness for all the offspring of these two countries. But to engage in this struggle our people need direction. It is the Party which must be organized in a clandestine manner with the aim of eluding police vigilance by the colonialists.

This Party – PAI – was of course kept strictly secret. As its existence was known only to the militants, one would find no *written* trace of the date of its appearance inside or outside the frontiers of Guiné and Cape Verde. The PAI really came out of clandestinity at the moment when the African political context and particularly the option taken by the Republic of Guinea enabled the general secretariat to find a base there.

Meanwhile Amilcar Cabral exercised intense activity during the four years from the birth of the Party to the establishment of its external delegation in Conakry. He still carried out his duties at the head of plant protection and soil study teams which led him to divide his time on triangular journeys: Portugal–Angola–Guiné. Cabral made a brief stop in Paris, in November 1957, to take part in the 'consultative study meeting for the development of the struggle against Portuguese colonialism', and revived this flame in Lisbon with the creation of MAC (Anti-colonialist Movement), and put in a discreet appearance in Accra for the Pan-African sessions. He was en route for Luanda when the Pidjiguiti massacre occurred.

In seeking to express the people's hopes in colonial Guiné and to identify the social driving forces for the struggle for liberty, the first militants had begun by securing the adherence of some elements both of the petty bourgeoisie and more significantly of the most exploited labouring strata in the wage economy – seamen in the port of Bissau, small craftsmen, the fringe of the 'lumpenproletariat'. They had formed the conclusion (which later they were to regard as mistaken) that the social basis for the struggle lay in assembling the mass of labourers in the marketing centres. This is why the first active kernels of party militants had with determination pursued recruitment of workers in Bissau, Bolama, Bafata. When, at the end of July 1959, the first seamen's strikes had been successfully initiated, some militants regarded this initiative and the meeting of their demands as a victory for the correctness of the Party's line.

But this belief lasted only a few days. In fact on 3 August 1959 the little quay at Pidjiguiti was the stage for a tragic event: the massacre of fifty African workers. They are the ones who wrote with their blood one of the most shining pages in the great book of PAIGC history. In gunning down the seamen, the agents of colonial Fascism were aiming not only at stifling the raising of demands by these workers but also at dismantling the structure of the Party, whose influence was obviously making itself felt on a national level. Directly threatened at the nerve centre of their economic interests, the colonialists clearly understood that down there on the Pidjiguiti quay had occurred – in Cabral's words – 'the first organized demonstration of the political consciousness of the mass of labourers, in particular those from Bissau.' So the *internal* factor that was deciding the criminal reaction of the direct enemy in his stronghold demanded likewise on the Party's side a *line of action* able to prevent repression going unpunished. Cabral was to devote himself to the task of readjusting PAI's political strategy.

In September 1959 Cabral returned for a last time to Bissau for the meeting he was to judge the most decisive 'because there it was agreed to mobilize and organize the peasant masses . . . principal physical force of the national liberation struggle' and, notably, 'to struggle for the acquisition of the indispensable means in order to pursue the struggle to victory'. It was during this meeting that the decision was taken, for obvious reasons, to transfer the Party general secretariat abroad to Conakry. Direct action had not yet come. But the new world was knocking at the gates of Guiné. In Conakry, where under trying circumstances PAI was to establish its sanctuary, Sékou Touré, at the head of the Democratic Party of Guinea, had a year before established unanimity by opposing a categorical 'No' to any form of neo-colonialism. It was a great moment in the history of Africa and an event – the *external* factor – that was to accelerate the liberation of Guinea-Bissau. The PAI was to make good use of it; it would be confirmed in Africa. That is why Amilcar Cabral was a delegate to Tunis where in January 1960 the second All-African People's Organization conference was held and proclaimed the coming year as Africa's Year – during which Patrice Emery Lumumba, the Congolese leader, was to burn like a flaming meteor. Immediately afterwards, Cabral was in London where he drafted the pamphlet *The Facts about Portugal's African Colonies* (see Item 3), and then in Conakry in May of the same year.

The hot spot in international news in 1960 was Africa which aroused the anxiety of the great powers, the enthusiasm of young people throughout the world and the interest of peoples freed from colonization. The world was entering a phase in which the acceleration of positive events in the field of liberation struggle seemingly foretold a transformation in the sinister plans and blind obstinacy of colonial Fascism. The nationalists in Guiné and Angola were not the only ones to think that the *decolonization* movement at the level of the main imperialist powers would also reach 'the little Lusitanian house' and that the winds of history would likewise sweep the

Portuguese colonies from the map of the oppressed regions of the world. These nationalists were convinced that international pressure, as a sequel to resolutions approved by the United Nations, would oblige the Lisbon government to negotiate the transfer of power with their movements. Inspired by a political concern with putting responsibility where it belonged, they had at the head of their organizations taken certain initiatives in the prospect of a peaceful solution to the conflict between them and colonialism. So a PAIGC memorandum to the Portuguese government on 15 November 1960 (see Item 19) contained twelve proposals whose immediate fulfilment would lead to peaceful elimination of Portuguese colonial domination.

But the leaders of these organizations did not cherish illusions about the reaction of the direct enemy. From Conakry, they drew up requests for material support from countries willing to supply it to them in a spirit of fighting solidarity: the socialist countries. So it was that in August 1960 Amilcar Cabral led a delegation of his Party to the People's Republic of China which granted the first substantial practical aid to PAI and to MPLA. On his return, he chaired a clandestine meeting of PAI held in Dakar from 1 to 8 October 1960 during which a decision was reached on 'preparing the final phase of liberation from Portuguese colonialism'. On this occasion PAI adopted the set of initials PAIGC – Partido Africano da Independência da Guiné e Cabo Verde. The establishment of CONCP (Conferência das Organizações Nacionalistas das Colónias Portuguesas) at Casablanca on 18 April 1961, thanks to the decisive support of the Kingdom of Morocco, further enlarged the potential for acquiring varied support on an international scale.

Since the meeting on 19 September 1959, the Party had begun the active (and possibly most difficult) phase of preparing the mass of the people for decisive collision with the repressive machinery of the colonial state, with the prospect of a long battle for total independence. While giving priority to mobilizing the labouring strata in the countryside, the Party had also stepped up appeals for a stand to be taken by other professional strata and categories in Guiné and Cape Verde – civil servants, traders, soldiers, young people (see Items 16 – 18). Cabral, through various messages and direct contacts, demonstrated the urgency of eliminating colonialism and the certainty of triumph for the cause of national independence. It was in the framework of the immense task of mobilizing the labouring population in the countryside, in colonized Guiné, that young PAIGC militants showed the extent of their political commitment. It had not been easy to convince the peasantry that they had an objective interest in joining the national liberation struggle, when their outlook was limited to a simple understanding of the difference between the price and value of their produce. To turn the peasantry into the principal physical force, Amilcar Cabral personally undertook direction of the training of the first mobilizers who, with the benefit of his profound knowledge of the special circumstances and behaviour of the mass of the people, were able to spread the Party's new ideas into the heart of the villages. The Party owes the support and adherence of the population in Guinean territory on the eve of the launching of armed struggle to these militants, shaped by Amilcar Cabral, the political instructor. Today one can appreciate in all its historic dimension the importance that Cabral attached to the task of training men.

Came the dawn of 4 February 1961, when a handful of MPLA militants mounted an attack on the prisons in Luanda. This eruption into history by Angola strengthened the determination of PAIGC to commit itself to the path of arms. On 3 August 1961, in commemoration of the second anniversary of Pidjiguiti, PAIGC published to the world (see Item 21) the proclamation which records in the annals of history 'the date of the passage of our national revolution from the phase of political struggle to that of national insurrection, to direct action against the colonialist forces...' At the very moment when successful ambushes were being mounted against the colonialist forces, PAIGC on 13 October 1961 addressed an open letter to the Portuguese Government (see Item 20) putting the dilemma before it: either the colonial Fascist power should reconsider its position, by agreeing to the application of the principle of self-determination and independence, or the Party would fulfil its historic task, 'developing our national liberation struggle, answering with violence the violence of the Portuguese colonialist forces and by all the means possible completely eliminating colonial domination from Guiné and Cape Verde.' It was in this direction that Cabral successively declared to the United Nations Special Committee on Territories under Portuguese Administration and to the Fourth Committee of the General Assembly (see Item 34):

> Rejecting the idea of begging for freedom which is incompatible with the dignity and sacred right of our people to be free and independent, we reaffirm here our steadfast determination, no matter what sacrifices are involved, to eliminate colonial domination from our country and to win for our people the opportunity to build in peace their progress and happiness.

Cabral was to spend ten years keeping his promise to his followers and to himself 'to arouse the people for struggle against the Portuguese'. During these ten years he became an agitator, promoter, inspirer, propagandist and messenger of the Revolution.

But now he was finding himself faced with problems such as few revolutionaries have known, problems which always had to be solved quickly and without real precedent since each people has its own genius, its own culture. He was to be confronted unsparingly, this time in the heat of actions of war, by impatience, improvisation and by combatants' dreams. There too he was to behave indefatigably as the unifier. In the logical sequence of the efforts undertaken by militants in the country's interior at the level of political mobilization and the transport of weapons to the very heart of the villages, a PAIGC commando unit attacked the barracks at Tite on 23 January 1963, so marking the real beginning of armed struggle.

Military successes by the combatants had the effect on the one hand of strengthening the guerrilla bases politically and on the other of paralyzing economic exploitation by the colonial power. Sabotage of land communications infrastructures forced the enemy to fight on the run and to shut themselves up in some town centres in the south and centre-south of the country. By the end of six months of armed struggle, all the areas to the south of the Geba and Corubal had been liberated. So obvious and spectacular were these military successes that the Portuguese Defence Minister had publicly to confirm the extent of the guerrilla action, with a conservative estimate that 15 per cent of national territory was occupied and controlled by PAIGC combatants.

The enemy, in their own words, were experiencing an 'uncomfortable and disagreeable situation'. The combatants had inflicted considerable casualties on the colonial troops, liberated the entire forest zone of Oio, and totally dominated the triangle of routes Mansoa-Mansaba-Bissorã, thus upsetting the communications system between Bissau and the interior of the country. A journalist in *The Times* was certainly inspired when he predicted then that Guinea-Bissau would become 'the Achilles heel of Portuguese colonial policy'. The course of the most important episodes of this struggle, and the nature of its advances or reverses, have been described many times. There is therefore no need here to dwell on the chronology of the war that pitted the people of Guiné against Portuguese colonial power. We should rather recall this essential fact: the national liberation struggle waged by PAIGC began to have the force of example for Africa. During ten years Amilcar Cabral was definitively to embody the hopes of all oppressed peoples. But as he was fighting on a particular ground, the Secretary-general of PAIGC first exerted his energy in understanding the special situation of war, while broadening the field of his analyses to the march of history in the Third World. So in the period that extended to the end of the decade, Cabral stamped the seal of his personality on two important events on the internal level: at Cassaca in the liberated areas of the south from 13 to 17 February 1964 he chaired the first PAIGC Congress which achieved a decisive transformation in the struggle; in the sequel to the directives drafted in 1965 (see Items 25–32) he guided the seminar for Party cadres held from 19 to 24 November 1969 (see Items 4-12).

On the international level, we find him successively in Italy, from 1 to 3 May 1964, at the Frantz Fanon Centre in Milan discussing class struggle in the underdeveloped countries dominated by imperialism, then in Havana in January 1966, at the Tricontinental Conference, during which he presented his famous speech on 'Presuppositions and objectives of national liberation in relation to social structure' (see Item 14). It is likewise worth mentioning his remarkable statements to the United Nations Human Rights Commission in 1968 and 1969, as well as his active participation in the conference in support of the peoples of the Portuguese colonies held in Khartoum in January 1969.

One might say that Cabral's ideological and political standing was established in the eyes of PAIGC militants and combatants in the storm zones during the period we have briefly outlined. This was the effect of political and intellectual maturity of a leader in permanent contact with a reality undergoing profound change. In fact the victory won in the battle for Como and the decisions taken by the Cassaca Congress strengthened the Party which was reorganized from top to bottom, and the decisions led to the forming of a regular army. The development of activity in the justice, health and education departments, and the setting up of 'People's Stores' in the liberated areas, all endowed PAIGC with the character of a Party-State and consolidated the attributes of sovereignty of the people of Guiné over the major part of national territory. Spectacular results were recorded on the military side. The creation of the first regular army units initiated a process of a break in the balance of power, revealing Cabral's acute sense of strategy: to diversify initiatives against enemy forces and gradually to adopt more sophisticated fighting methods. In regard to the military situation at the end of 1968, the colonial power was fully aware that the war would be lost. A period then began when the Portuguese would speed up the subtle manoeuvres around a 'better Guiné' policy, draw up invasion plans against the PAIGC *sanctuary,* and in short prepare the new policy of *reconquest.* Cabral, always alert to enemy tactics, would once again show his great capacity for the analysis of all circumstances and would devise the appropriate strategy. But these were to be the last three years of his life.

When one considers the principal activities undertaken by Cabral, one is struck by the variegated character of his mind and the international dimension of his ideas. At Syracuse University in the United States on 20 February 1970 he delivered a memorial lecture to Eduardo Mondlane, the President of FRELIMO, on the theme of 'national liberation and culture' (see Item 15). Then in Washington he sustained a tough debate before the House Subcommittee on African Affairs in Congress on the aims of PAIGC's struggle. In Moscow in April Cabral took part in the commemoration of the centenary of Lenin's birth, and in June he was one of the architects of the success of the Conference in support of the peoples of the Portuguese colonies, held in Rome, which ended with the audience granted by Pope Paul VI to the leaders of three nationalist movements – MPLA, FRELIMO and PAIGC.

The range of Cabral's activity was equally broad in 1971: in Stockholm in April he denounced the famine situation in Cape Verde; in Addis Ababa in June he spoke at the eighth summit of the OAU on behalf of the African liberation movements; and in October he fulfilled a mission to provide information and to make diplomatic contacts in several European capitals –

Helsinki, Dublin and London.   In 1972 Amilcar Cabral received political recognition (the Gamal Abdel Nasser and Joliot-Curie medals) and academic recognition (an honorary doctorate in juridical science from Lincoln University in the United States and an honorary degree in political and social science from the Institute of African Studies in the Soviet Academy of Sciences) – these were awarded for his personal contribution to the cause of people's liberation and for his intellectual contribution to progress in the social sciences. The same year saw PAIGC record significant successes at the international level. Once more Cabral was its spokesman in Addis Ababa in February at the Security Council, meeting in Africa for the first time, and at the OAU summit held in Rabat in June, and then in October before the Fourth Committee of the United Nations General Assembly (see Item 34).

But a criminal plot was being hatched in the offices of the sinister PIDE that had as its target the Secretary-general of PAIGC. The irreversible nature of the liberation struggle in Guiné and Cape Verde had been demonstrated beyond doubt by the progress made in the political, military and reconstruction fields internally, and by diplomatic victories externally. To meet this situation and faced with the prospect of military defeat, the Lisbon government set in train the first plan aimed at depriving PAIGC of its most secure rear base by direct aggression against the Republic of Guinea. Cabral regarded the failure of imperialist and Portuguese joint aggression on 22 November 1970 as a 'fruitful victory for Africa' (see Item 23) and commented:

> The criminal figure of Portuguese colonialism, defeated and isolated before world opinion, was thus more clearly defined than ever as a historical aberration which it is vital and urgent to eliminate by all the necessary means.

Again it was Cabral who led his Party to take all the advantages of the failure of the Portuguese. He multiplied the directives on the ground in order to consolidate the State developing in the liberated areas and to raise the level of politico-military and national reconstruction work. In June 1971 the PAIGC armed forces for the first time succeeded in attacking within the space of a few months all the military garrisons in the remaining occupied urban centres, including Bissau. In the same year the Supreme Council of the Struggle, during a meeting held from 7 to 17 August, took a decision which was to have an epoch-making effect: to create the first People's National Assembly of Guiné, thus giving the people of that country an essential instrument of sovereignty.

Cabral had already noted in earlier statements that there was a crucial contradiction to be resolved in his country: while the people had since 1968 possessed political, judicial and administrative, military, social and cultural institutions – hence a State – and were free and sovereign over more than two-thirds of national territory, they did not yet have *juridical personality* at the international level. Cabral inspired and promoted all the initiatives that were to bring the United Nations Special Mission, at the invitation of the PAIGC Secretary-general, to visit the liberated areas in the south from 2 to 8 April 1972. Through meetings, rallies and inquiries of the local population and after observing the actual facts of the transformation achieved in these areas, the United Nations Special Mission concluded that the struggle for national liberation continued to progress and that Portugal no longer exercised any effective administrative control over vast areas of Guiné (Bissau); that PAIGC was the sole legitimate representative of the interests of the people of Guiné and Cape Verde. Other UN bodies took the same view: the Decolonization Committee at its Conakry session on 13 April 1972, and later the General Assembly on 14 November formally recognized PAIGC as the sole, genuine and legitimate representative of the people of Guiné and Cape Verde. Finally the Security Council on 22 November unanimously voted on a resolution condemning Portuguese colonialism and demanding that the Lisbon government end the colonial war, withdraw its troops and enter into negotiations with the national liberation movements.

The democratic process of general elections in the liberated areas had meanwhile culminated in the constitution of Regional Councils which met and elected from among their members 120 representatives to the People's National Assembly. Cabral, who personally announced the news of the partial results of these elections for African and international public opinion, made it clearly understood that a decision of great historical import was imminent (see Item 35). And on 1 January 1973, in his last message to militants (see Item 36) – his political testament – he declared unequivocally:

> In the course of this coming year and as soon as it is conveniently possible we shall call a meeting of our People's National Assembly in Guiné, so that it can fulfil the first historic mission incumbent on it: the proclamation of the existence of our state, the creation of an executive for this state and the promulgation of a fundamental law – that of the first constitution in our history – which will be the basis of the active existence of our African nation.

Events were to decide differently: he was not present at the proclamation of the State of Guinea-Bissau.

Cabral, in a far-sighted document, had already foreseen the plan the Portuguese had in mind to carry out through their African agents and in several phases with the aim of destroying the Party from *within* and of eliminating its main leaders. Cabral's successor as Secretary-general of PAIGC, Aristides Pereira, recalled in the report to PAIGC 3rd Congress (held in Bissau in September 1977):

> In Africa and in the progressive world, nobody was unaware of the international dimension to the thought of Amilcar Cabral, the craftsman of the

victories that definitively turned the African people of Guiné and Cape Verde into *subject and author* of their own history. Our armed struggle for liberation was marked as one of the most advanced in the general framework of the struggle of oppressed peoples against colonialism and imperialism. That is why the ferocity of the criminal face of the Portuguese colonialists had to strike and the *architect* of our building, the *strategist* of our military successes, the *diplomatist* of our initiatives in the international field, and finally at the leader who by his intelligence and by his generosity had shaped the singular character of the war in Guinea-Bissau. An attempt at all costs to bar the way to the march of our struggle and, above all, to prevent the triumph of its *example,* by virtue of economic interests at stake in Angola and in Mozambique – this was the principal motive that guided the carrying out of the sinister plans of the Portuguese colonialist government.

The exemplary destiny of Amilcar Cabral was to be brutally cut short on the tragic night of 20 January 1973.

But Amilcar Cabral's life story had already become history: the history of Africa, of our age – that of the peoples committed to the winning of their freedoms. In Guinea-Bissau, his thought and action remain the living reference point for his colleagues and for a people confronted today with the tasks of national reconstruction. Amilcar Cabral's name will always be among those that youth can hurl in defiance at the old world.

Mário de Andrade
Bissau

PART 1
The Weapon of Theory

WRITINGS OF YOUTH

1. Two poems

Island[1]

You live – sleeping mother –
naked and forgotten,
dry,
battered by the winds,
to the sound of melodies without melody
of the waters which hold us fast . . .

Island:
your mountains and your valleys
did not sense the times pass,
and stayed in the world of your dreams
   – the dreams of your sons –
to cry out to the winds passing,
and the birds flying, free
your anguish!

ISLAND:
endless hills of red soil
   – rough soil –
cragged rocks masking the horizons
sea at the four corners holding fast our anguish!

Return[2]

Old Mama, come and listen with me
to the beating of the rain there at your gate.
It is a beating of a friend
that throbs within my heart.

The friendly rain, Old Mama, the rain
which for so long has not beaten like this. . .
I heard it said that the Old City,
   – the whole Island –
had in scant days become a garden. . .

[1]Published in the weekly *A Ilha* (The Island) Ponta Delgada, Azores, 22 July 1946.
[2]*Cape Verde – Propaganda and Information Bulletin,* 1,2 (November, 1949).

They say that the countryside has turned verdant,
a most beautiful colour, because it is the colour of hope.
The land, now, is truly Cape Verde –
    – It is the storm becalmed. . .

Come with me, Old Mama, come,
gather your strength to reach the gate.
The friendly rain has already come to greet you
and is beating within my heart.

MAN AND LAND

2. Agricultural Census of Guiné[1] (1953 estimate)
IV Final comments

'The results of the census are shown in 471 tables included in this report. The comments which follow are an attempt to synthesize these results.

1. Number of agricultural holdings

Guiné has 85 478 indigenous agricultural holdings. This is the number of indigenous families which make their living from agricultural activity.

a) By Councils, Circles and Administrative Districts

Among the Councils and Circles, Mansoa has the highest number of agricultural holdings – 19 538 – which corresponds to the fact that it has the highest population. The Councils and Circles are ranged in the following way for the number of agricultural holdings in descending order: Mansoa, Cacheu, Bafata, Gabu, Farim, Bissau, Fulacunda, Catio, S. Domingos, Bijagos and Bolama.

As for Administrative Districts, Bissorã has the highest number of agricultural holdings – 9481. This District has more agricultural holdings than the majority of Circles.

[1]*Boletim Cultural da Guiné Portuguesa,* Bissau, XI, 43 (1956), 7–246.

b) By peoples or tribes

The most populous tribes have the highest number of agricultural holdings. So the holdings of the Balanta people (29 198), Fula (19 637), Manjaco (9762), Pepel (5205) and Mancanha (2959) together make up 91·25 per cent of the total.

2. Cultivated areas and crops

The true cultivated area is 410 801 hectares, that is 12·21 per cent of the surface area of Guiné (3 363 700 hectares), minus the part under water. Crops cover an area of 482 177 hectares, with a multiple cropped area of 71 376 hectares.

a) By Councils, Circles and Administrative Districts

Mansoa, Gabu, Bafata and Farim have the largest cultivated areas (with an absolute figure of more than 50 000 hectares), followed in descending order by Fulacunda, Bissau, S. Domingos, Catio and Bolama.

If the cultivated area is considered as a proportion of the surface area (minus the part under water) of each Council or Circle, the administrative units can be ranged in the following (descending) order: Mansoa (17·08 per cent), Bafata (11·36 per cent), Bolama (9·57 per cent), S. Domingos (9·37 per cent), Gabu (7·91 per cent), Fulacunda (5·42 per cent) and Catio (5·01 per cent). For the reasons already given, the true cultivated area of the Bijagos Circle is not known.

As for Administrative Districts, Bissorã (42 136 hectares), Mansaba (32 916 hectares), Bafata-Sede (27 764 hectares) and Cacheu-Sede (25 716 hectares) have the largest cultivated areas (with an absolute figure of more than 20 000 hectares). These figures are higher than the equivalents in the majority of the Circles and Councils: Bissorã has a cultivated area more than double that of the Circles of S. Domingos, Fulacunda, and Catio and that of Bissau Council. As the surface area of each Administrative District is not known, it is possible to make a comparison of the respective cultivated area with the total surface area in each of them.

The largest cultivated areas generally correspond to the largest multiple cropped areas.

b) By people or tribes

The Balanta tribe (30·07 per cent), Fula (28·61 per cent), Mandinga (15·69 per cent) and Manjaco (12·62 per cent) have the largest share of cultivated area, making up 86·99 per cent of the overall total. They are followed, in descending order, by the Mancanha people (3·36 per cent), Pepel (2·89 per cent), Beafada (1·62 per cent), Felupe (1·53 per cent), Mansoanca (0·86 per cent), Balanta-Mané (0·76 per cent), Baiote (0·46 per cent), Bijago and Nalu (0·44 per cent), Pajadinca (0·20 per cent), Sosso (0·18 per cent), Saracole (0·13 per cent), Cassanga (0·11 per cent) and Banhum (0·03 per cent). In other words: there are in Guiné about twenty-five different tribes (1950 Population Census), of whom only a quarter have almost the whole of the cultivated area, with four peoples particularly prominent (Balanta, Fula, Mandinga and Manjaco).

The largest cultivated areas correspond generally to the largest multiple cropped areas. The Fula people who have the largest area under crops do not, however, cultivate the largest true area (the Balanta people do this), as the former practise intensive multiple-cropping (31 811 hectares). The Mandinga people also show this characteristic.

c) By crops

Rice (Oryza spp., 25·86 per cent), groundnuts (Arachis hipogaea, 21·78 per cent), millet (Pennisetum spp., 15·95 per cent) and sorghum (Sorghum spp., 10·97 per cent) are the crops which take up the largest areas (with a figure above 50 000 hectares). Then follows, in descending order, *fundo* (Digitaria sp.), upland rice (Oryza spp.), maize (Zea mays), manioc (Manihot utilissima), bean varieties, cotton (Gossypium spp.), other food crops, sugar cane (Saccharum spp.) and sesame (Sesamum indicum). In other words: rice (floodplain and upland, 31·72 per cent), cereals (Zea, Pennisetum and Sorghum, 32·07 per cent) and groundnuts (21·78 per cent) take up 85·57 per cent of the area for crops. They are, accordingly, the main crops. If the purpose of these main crops – consumption or export – is considered, it is seen that the food crops, including *fundo* (Digitaria sp.) take up 70·73 per cent of the total area, and cash crops (groundnuts for export) 21·78 per cent.

Other crops, which may be regarded as secondary, take up 7·94 per cent of the total area, with 6·55 per cent as food crops and 1·34 per cent for cash crops.

d) By crops by tribes

Taking into consideration only the main crops (rice, cereals and groundnuts), it is seen that the Balanta people provide about half the area for floodplain rice (47·16 per cent) the Manjaco people (14·30 per cent), Fula (12·27 per cent) and Mandinga (10·53 per cent) follow. For upland rice, the largest shares come from the Manjaco people (27·95 per cent), Mandinga (21·29 per cent) and Beafada (7·11 per cent). The Fula people have the largest share of the area taken by cereals – sorghum or *milho cavalo* (44·21 per cent), millet (42·15 per cent) and Brazilian maize (53·73 per cent). The

Mandinga people follow with 23·23 per cent, 17·59 per cent and 25·86 per cent respectively, and the Balanta with 16·54 per cent, 21·92 per cent and 10·39 per cent respectively. The Fula people also have the largest share of the area taken by groundnuts (36·04 per cent). The Balanta people follow (24·99 per cent) and the Mandinga (21·58 per cent). These three peoples have 82·61 per cent of the area for groundnuts.

If the distribution of crops within the area cultivated by each people is now considered, it is seen that with the exception of Bijago and Banhum and those peoples who do not cultivate groundnuts (Baiote, Cassanga and Felupe), all the others devote to groundnuts more than ten per cent of the area under crops. The highest percentages are shown by the Balanta-Mané people (28·45 per cent), Sosso (27·62 per cent), Mandinga (27·28 per cent), Mancanha (26·72) and Fula (25·34 per cent).

The Baiote people and Felupe cultivate rice (floodplain and upland) almost exclusively and devote to this plant 99·27 per cent and 90·89 per cent respectively of the total area under crops. They are followed by the Nalu people (75·05 per cent), Bijago (72·43 per cent), Sosso (66·49 per cent), Pepel (60·61 per cent), Beafada (56·88 per cent), Balanta (45·24 per cent) and Manjaco (44·72 per cent).

The peoples who devote to cereals (sorghum, millet and Brazilian maize) the highest percentages of the area under crops are the Saracole (53·40 per cent), Pajadinca (51·48 per cent), Fula (46·56 per cent), Mandinga (38·80 per cent), Banhum (37·94 per cent) and Mansoanca (34·62 per cent).

As for *fundo*, the Saracole, Mancanha and Balanta peoples devote the largest areas to this, with 16·43 per cent, 13·86 per cent and 9·87 per cent respectively of the total area under crops. The peoples who keep the largest areas for beans are the Mancanha, Bijago (Mancanha-Bijago) and Manjaco with 12·76 per cent, 7·55 per cent and 7·02 per cent respectively of the total area under crops.

In respect of production per unit of area, it is observed that this is generally low, in the light of the areas taken by each crop. But despite this and because of the broad extent of the cultivated areas, it is seen that some crops reach a considerable global production figure. This is the case for the main crops: floodplain rice – 90 247 tons; groundnuts – 63 975 tons; cereals (sorghum, millet and Brazilian maize) – 49 796 tons; upland rice – 10 050 tons.

The following comments refer essentially to the main crops:

a) By Councils, Circles and Administrative Districts

The Circles of Mansoa (28 547 tons), Catio (15 294 tons), Cacheu (12 821 tons) and Fulacunda (8445 tons) have the largest share of rice production. Among Administrative Districts, Bissorã (10 575 tons), Bedanda (7008 tons), Catio-Sede (6264 tons), Binar (5947 tons), Mansoa-Sede (5331 tons), Nhacra (4998 tons) and Cacheu-Sede (4992 tons) produce most rice. Catio and Fulacunda show the highest average yield for this crop.

Gabu (19 183 tons), Farim (12 655 tons), Bafata (12 428 tons) and Mansoa (10 155 tons) are the regions with the largest share of groundnuts production. Gabu, Bafata and Farim show the highest average yield for this crop.

Among Administrative Districts, Mansaba (7513 tons), Gabu-Sede (6296 tons), Bissorã (6207 tons), Bafata-Sede (6159 tons), Pirada (4579 tons), Contubo (3535 tons) and Sonaco (3303 tons) produce most groundnuts.

Gabu and Bafata are the highest producers of cereals, with 18 430 tons and 12 366 tons respectively. Farim and Mansoa follow. The yield is higher in the first two regions. They are also the Districts of those administrative zones which produce the largest quantity of these items (sorghum, millet and Brazilian maize).

b) By peoples or tribes

The Balanta people supply 61·01 per cent of the total production of floodplain rice. They are followed by the Manjaco people (12·06 per cent), Fula (7·06 per cent), Mandinga (6·90 per cent) and Pepel (5·01 per cent). For upland rice production, the main suppliers are the Manjaco people (26·08 per cent), Fula (21·88 per cent) and Mandinga (19·19 per cent), and the share of the remaining peoples is minute. The highest average yields are those attained by the Balanta people, Pepel and Manjaco.

The Fula people supply nearly half the groundnuts production (43·61 per cent), followed by the Mandinga people (22·71 per cent), Balanta (17·92 per cent), Manjaco (7·58 per cent), Mancanha (3·80 per cent) and Balanta-Mané(1·24 per cent). The share of the remaining peoples is insignificant. The highest average yields are those attained by the Fula people and Mandinga.

The Fula and Mandinga peoples supply more than two-thirds of the cereal production, with the first of these claiming more than fifty per cent. If the share of these two peoples is added to that of the Balanta, it is seen that almost the entire production of cereals (sorghum, millet and Brazilian maize) is due to them. The highest average yields are those attained by the Fula people and Mandinga.

c) By crops

The production per unit of area is, as was stated, generally low. For all the crops studied, yield varies not only from region to region, but also with the farmers. It does not make sense, therefore, to establish a general average (over the whole of Guiné) of production for each crop.

The main crops (rice, groundnuts and cereals) are those which give the highest yields.

For floodplain rice the highest averages (1800 kilograms) are found in the Catio region and are attained by the Balanta people. The lowest averages (300 to 600 kilograms) are found in the Bafata, Gabu and Farim regions, and are attained by the Islamized peoples (Fula, Mandinga, etc.) Between these extremes lie the averages of the remaining regions, attained by other peoples.

For groundnuts, the highest averages (700 to 900 kilograms) are attained in the Farim, Bafata and Gabu regions by the Islamized peoples (mainly Fula and Mandinga). The lowest averages (300 to 450 kilograms) are attained in the Bolama, Fulacunda and Bissau regions. Between these extremes lie the averages of the remaining regions.

For cereals (sorghum, millet and Brazilian maize), the highest averages (400 to 600 kilograms) are attained by the Fula people and Mandinga in the Gabu and Bafata regions. In the remaining regions the average yield (150 to 300 kilograms) is always below the earlier figures, no matter who the farmers are.

It should be pointed out that in some cases the production of the crops in question achieves noteworthy yields, if the conditions under which they are grown are taken into consideration. So one can see rice production varying between 2500 and 3000 kilograms per hectare (Bedanda region), groundnuts between 1500 and 2000 kilograms per hectare (Nova Lamego region) and cereals between 700 and 1200 kilograms per hectare (Gabu region).

Under present conditions of Guinean agriculture, it is not possible to establish the yield for each species cultivated. Various investigations were made, however, in the hope of finding out, albeit approximately, the order of this characteristic. From the information obtained, it can be concluded that rice is the crop which gives the best return to the indigenous farmer, while groundnuts give him the least return per unit of area.

3. Perennial crops; number of bushes

The character of tilling of fruit-bearing species in indigenous agriculture has already been mentioned. It is clear that the tilling of these bushes by the indigenous farmer cannot be treated as cultivation from the technical point of view. One can point out, as an exception to the general rule, the case of kolas and some other species (bananas and citrus) in the south of Guiné (Cacine and Cubisseque), which are already cultivated with a certain regularity, and on some holdings form genuine orchards.

Fruit trees are always close to or in villages and are generally scattered or in small clumps. They total 1 210 702 bushes, of which 820 884 are already bearing and 389 818 have not yet come into fruit. As will be seen, the great majority comprise bananas, mangoes and papayas.

a) By Councils, Circles and Administrative Districts

In respect to the total number of bushes (bearing and not bearing), the Councils and Circles are ranged in the following way in descending order: Farim, Cacheu, Bafata, Mansoa, Catio, Gabu, Fulacunda, Bissau, S. Domingos and Bolama. Among Administrative Districts, Mansaba, Bafata-Sede and Bissorã show the highest number of bushes, followed by Cacine, Gabu-Sede, Cacheu-Sede and Piche.

b) By peoples or tribes

In relation to trees bearing fruit, the Mandinga people (27·40 per cent), Fula (20·74 per cent), Balanta (16·88 per cent) and Manjaco (12·11 per cent) show the highest number of bushes. The Nalu people (5·22 per cent), Pepel (4·57 per cent), Mancanha (3·74 per cent), Beafada (3·55 per cent) and Felupe (2·90 per cent) follow, and the share of each of the remaining peoples is insignificant. In relation to the total number of bushes which have not begun bearing, the descending order for tribes is as follows: Fula (30·20 per cent), Mandinga (19·54 per cent), Manjaco (18·13 per cent), Balanta (12·40 per cent), Nalu (5·56 per cent), Beafada (4·37 per cent), Mancanha (2·86 per cent), Felupe (2·12 per cent), Pepel (2·08 per cent), and the share of each of the remaining peoples is minute.

But the real value of these figures becomes clear only when the share of each people in respect of the various fruit species is considered.

c) By crops

Bananas (39·03 per cent), mangoes (26·88 per cent) and papayas (13·60 per cent) comprise, as has been said, the great majority of the total of trees bearing fruit (about eighty per cent). Then follow oranges (6·38 per cent), cashews (6·19 per cent) and lemons (4·64 per cent). As for bushes not yet bearing fruit, bananas take pride of place with 50·14 per cent of the total, followed by the bushes mentioned above as the most common.

d) By crops by tribes

The Balanta people have the highest number of mangoes (fruit bearing, 33·26 per cent; not bearing, 37·65 per cent), followed by Mandinga (19·84 per cent and 18·87 per cent), Fula (16·71 per cent and 12·31 per cent) and Manjaco (8·90 per cent and 20·30 per cent). These peoples also have most bananas, papayas and citrus. The Fula people have more than fifty per cent of the total of tangerines.

As for kola – the richest of the bushes mentioned – it is the Nalu people who have the highest number (fruit bearing, 46·57 per cent, not bearing, 34·96 per cent), followed by Beafada (18·92 per cent and 19·66 per cent),

Fula (16·61 per cent and 25·12 per cent) and Mandinga (10·14 per cent and 9·10 per cent). The Balanta and Mancanha peoples have the highest number of cashews.

As for distribution of the various species by people, it is seen that mangoes, bananas and papayas are the most common. Exceptions are the Nalu and Cassanga peoples: the former have a larger showing of kolas and the latter of oranges.

4. Burning off and fallow; nurseries

Burning off had affected an area of 75 670 hectares in 1953, while at the end of the previous farming year 43 275 hectares of cultivated ground had been left fallow. The total fallow can be expressed as approximately four-sevenths of the total burned-off area.

a) By Councils, Circles and Administrative Districts

Mansoa (13 871 hectares), Bafata (13 643 hectares), Gabu (12 354 hectares), Farim (11 246 hectares) and Cacheu (11 122 hectares) are the regions with the largest burned-off areas. S. Domingos (5275 hectares) and Fulacunda (4459 hectares) follow. The first five regions have the largest areas in fallow and the widest differentials burned off – fallow. The Circle of Cacheu shows the widest differential burned off – fallow (7460 hectares). Catio shows the narrowest (16 hectares), with fallow land more extensive than burned-off in Bissau and Bolama (297 hectares and 10 hectares respectively).

Bissorã, Bafata-sede, Mansaba and Gabu-Sede are the Districts with the largest areas burned off and left fallow.

b) By peoples or tribes

The Fula people (burned off 30·72 per cent; fallow 32·00 per cent), Mandinga (18·57 per cent and 19·95 per cent), Balanta (17·88 per cent and 20·66 per cent) and Manjaco (16·80 per cent and 12·40 per cent) have the greatest areas burned off and left fallow. The Mancanha people (3·39 per cent and 2·41 per cent), Beafada (3·21 per cent and 3·90 per cent) and Mansoanca (2·52 per cent and 3·87 per cent) follow.

It is found that all the peoples practise burning off and leaving fallow, with the exception of Banhum (burning off without fallow) and Sosso (fallow without burning off).

Nurseries intended for the floodplain rice crop take up an area of 18 453 hectares.

Circles and Councils can be ranged in respect of areas used for nurseries in the following descending order: Mansoa, Cacheu, Bafata, Gabu, Fulacunda, Catio, Bissau, Farim, S. Domingos, Bijagos (two Districts only) and Boloma. Mansoa, with the largest area provides about one-third of the total.

The Balanta people have the largest share (about 51 per cent of the total), followed by Fula (14·8 per cent), Manjaco (11 per cent), Mandinga (8·6 per cent) and Pepel (5·8 per cent). The shares of the remaining peoples only rarely (Beafada, Felupe and Nalu) go higher than one per cent of the total area, with nil returns for Banhum and Cassanga peoples.

5. Conclusions

a Analysis of the area cultivated and the number of structural units per people shows that the following peoples cultivate the largest average area per agricultural holding: Mandinga (6·601 hectares), Cassanga (6·291 hectares), Mancanha (6·108 hectares) and Fula and Mandinga (5·985 hectares). The Bijago tribe (1·664 hectares), Baiote (1·967 hectares) and Pepel (2·286 hectares) cultivate the smallest average areas per structural unit. Between these extremes lie the remaining peoples, with a cultivated area close to the general average (4·805 hectares per agricultural holding).

The figures mentioned, as they relate to the whole of Guiné, do not make clear variations in the characteristic under study. It should be noted that, for a given people, the area cultivated per structural unit varies quite frequently from region to region. However the averages shown are as nearly as possible an index of the reality.

Through the census, it has been found that the average number of units of labour per agricultural holding and by tribe varies between three and seven, and the Islamized peoples have the highest averages. In the light of this fact and in view of the rudimentary nature of indigenous technique (notably in regard to farm implements) the following question arises: will it be viable to increase substantially the area cultivated per indigenous agricultural holding in the current technical, economic and social conditions of agriculture in Guiné?

It is arguable that this is viable for the tribes which show the smallest area cultivated per structural unit, and for some agricultural holdings of other peoples. But it can be asserted that generally speaking it would be difficult or practically impossible, on an indigenous agricultural holding, to increase substantially the area cultivated on the basis solely of the tools and the hands currently available.

b The true cultivated area represents 12·21 per cent of the surface area of Guiné, minus the part under water. With the inclusion of areas lying fallow, which can be regarded as part of the agricultural holding, the total area for crops amounts to 13·5 per cent of that surface area.

This figure is low in comparison with the effectively cultivable area. If one accepts the advantage and the need to retain for forestry about 50 per cent of the total surface area of Guiné, 50 per cent remains available for crops. Within the latter 50 per cent, it has to be admitted that only 30 per cent might be economically cultivable, or about one million hectares. It can be seen, on hypotheses advanced on the basis of knowledge of the environment, that only about 41 per cent of the total cultivable area is cultivated. Another question therefore arises: will it be viable to put under cultivation the remaining 59 per cent of effectively cultivable area? Viability depends fundamentally on factors of a technical and social nature. Technique founded on scientific knowledge of the environment (the physical and human environment), supported by research and experimentation and with concomitant progressive improvement of living conditions for the indigenous farmer, could achieve this objective.

c Rice, cereals and groundnuts are the main crops and take up 85·57 per cent of the area under crops.

Rice is the most beneficial crop for the indigenous farmer, and is cultivated by all the peoples of Guiné. It currently takes up about 30 per cent of the area under crops. If one applies this percentage to the total cultivable area, it is seen that only about 45 per cent of the ground where rice can be grown economically is cultivated. The future of this crop in Guiné is certain.

The cereals (mainly sorghum and millet) are poor foods, cultivated by nearly all the peoples of Guiné. They take up about 30 per cent of the total area. They constitute a substitute for rice in the indigenous diet and their cultivation is closely tied to that of peanuts. Because they do not require much in the way of soil fertilization, they are usually grown in ground which has undergone cultivation of groundnuts or are grown in association with the latter. Although tied to the indigenous agricultural tradition, they are crops of limited value for human diet, but they can be highly beneficial in the livestock field. The same may be said of *fundo*, which is widely used in human diet.

Groundnuts – the prime, and effectively sole, export crop – take up 21·78 per cent of the total area, and they play an increasing part in the agriculture of the peoples of Guiné. Given the characteristics of this crop (soils, dressings and yields), it is arguable that groundnuts already have a sufficient area in Guiné to guarantee high production. Before thinking of increasing the area cultivated, it is essential to solve the problem of increasing the yield. The current trend towards groundnuts as a monocrop (the association with maize does not contradict this trend) is rapidly creating the prospect of making all or nearly all of Guiné's economy dependent on production of groundnuts (or rather on the potentials for the export of groundnuts). To the technical disadvantages of a monocrop there is the additional contingent character of the value of this product, which is strictly dependent on international factors in the oil-seeds market.

Other crops, which are today of secondary importance, could play a prominent part in Guinean agriculture, so long as they were well directed in technical, economic and social aspects: manioc, sweet potato, cotton, sugar cane, Brazilian maize, beans and other food crops. It should be noted that the majority of these crops, which are familiar to all or nearly all the peoples of Guiné, offer, in addition to their nutritional value, wide potential for commercialization. The oil palm (Elaeis) is another crop of the future for Guiné.

Rational exploitation of fruit species, which are today cultivated in a sporadic and scattered way, will complete the ensemble of highly beneficial crops for Guiné. Bananas, citrus, cashews, kola, mangoes of reasonable quality and other species could come to play an important part in the Guinean agro-economy.

The existence of the crops mentioned (annuals and perennials) is shown in the figures of the Agricultural Census. Their encouragement will necessarily benefit the economy of Guiné.

d The main crops show the highest production, both as global figures and in terms of yield.

There is not a single Circle or District, village or agricultural holding which does not produce rice. To have a scrap of floodplain land is the first essential of an agricultural holding of any people. Rice cultivation, throughout Guiné, has an important objective: family sustenance. In the southern region (mainly Catio, Bedanda, Banta and Enxudé), where rice is practically the only crop and where the existence of extensive concessions creates a special situation for the indigenous farmer, the aim of providing food is overlaid with another objective: the sale of rice to the concessionary enterprises.

Out of global production, about 6238 tons are used for seed. Given the inadequate conditions in which the product is harvested and stored, it can be seen that there is considerable wastage which can be estimated at about one per cent of global production (approximately a thousand tons wasted). Exports in 1954 amounted to 1 507 169 kilograms, which corresponds to about 2300 tons of paddy. So the conclusion may be drawn that from the global production,about 80 000 tons of paddy remain for consumption, so long as one does not consider the clandestine drain over the land frontiers, the amount of which cannot be calculated. Part of the paddy (about 10 000 tons) for consumption was treated by the hulling firms. The rest is consumed in the period from when the ears begin to ripen in the floodplains until the last grain in the store is exhausted.

Groundnuts, with about the same area as rice, are found in almost all regions (relatively scanty in the south, absent from the Bijagos Circle and among the Felupe) and production has the following distribution:

		Tons[1]
Purchased for export		44 050
Purchased for oil		1 323
Used for seed		7 000
Consumed		3 000
Wasted (in harvesting and by poor storage)		4 000
Drain (hypothetical) across land frontiers		4 600
	Total	63 973

Cereals production is exclusively consumed for food. Millet is greatly in demand by the indigenous population for the preparation of fermented drinks.

The main crops and those which are currently secondary provide, as has been said, low yields and returns. The result is that one of the urgent problems of Guinean agriculture is improvement in production. The raising of production and yield of the most beneficial crops seems the first step to take in the direction of progress for indigenous agriculture in Guiné (more profitable crops, larger area cultivated, higher production, better living conditions).

e Study of the distribution of the various crops by people shows, within certain limits, the agricultural vocation of each people. This characteristic may be a useful guide to the encouragement of various crops, as it will be easier to develop the cultivation of a given species the more it is integrated into the farming habits of the people in question.

It is seen that for the Fula people, Mandinga, Mancanha and Balanta-Mané groundnuts are the crop which takes up the largest area, while for other peoples a food crop (in most cases rice) is the main activity. The Banhum people and Cassanga restrict their agriculture practically to three species: upland rice, sorghum and millet. The agriculture of the Balanta people, Fula and Mandinga shows the highest number for all Guiné of cultivated bushes. These three peoples show wide capabilities of devoting themselves to all the crops which are adaptable to the Guinean environment. There are wide differentials too in respect of fruit crops.

But agricultural vocation reflects only the traditional appearance of land use, conditioned by agro-climatic and socio-economic factors. It can be asserted that any people in Guiné have conditions to devote themselves efficiently to more diversified agriculture, so long as the latter is properly guided in technical, social and economic aspects. This fact, allied to the presence of a varied and numerous population, constitutes or will constitute a very important factor in progress for agriculture in Guiné.

[1]The first two figures are official; the figures for seed and consumption are estimates based on information collected during the Census; the figure for wastage is estimated on the basis of research by entomologists (*Boletim Cultural*, No. 30) on the Guinean groundnuts.

The burned-off areas are much more extensive than those left fallow, even though the latter include fallow in the floodplain where there is practically no burning off.

The largest areas burned off and left fallow correspond to the most productive regions for groundnuts. It is in these regions too that the differential burned off – fallow reaches the highest figures.

The largest areas burned off and left fallow correspond likewise to the peoples with the largest share in groundnuts production. It is in the agriculture of these peoples that the differential burned off – fallow reaches the highest figures.

Analysis of the figures relative to burned off, fallow and the areas taken up by the different crops shows that, for a given region or for a given people, the burned-off area, the fallow area and the differential burned off – fallow are greater in proportion with the extent of the area taken up by groundnuts in the agriculture of the region or people under consideration.

The area of nurseries for floodplain rice represents 14·7 per cent of the total area taken up by this crop. If one considers that the area of a nursery should not exceed one-fifth to one-tenth of the crop area, it is observed that in Guiné the nurseries are generally speaking poorly used. This fact arises in part from the habit of making the nursery in plots of the floodplain itself and because these plots are used as allotments for the crop after the seedlings have been removed for other plots. This means that larger areas are considered as nurseries than are strictly necessary or used as such. In addition the sowing of the nursery in the floodplain carries high risk of failure both for the seed and for the new plant.

The Balanta people, the best rice cultivators, show the largest area of nurseries (9462 hectares – 51·3 per cent of the total). They rarely sow the nursery in the floodplain and usually place it close to the compound in ground rich in organic matter. The practice of the Manjaco people and Pepel is similar, although the care taken with the nursery is less than among the Balanta. Among Fula and Mandinga, who have significant shares in rice growing, the crop is almost exclusively tended by women. Cultivation is on small plots, with inadequate preparation of the ground, and the nursery is usually placed in the floodplain itself, with all the disadvantages mentioned. The Banhum people, Cassanga, Bijago, Mansoanca, Pajadinca and Saracole, whose share of floodplain rice production is nil or very small, either do not have nursery areas or these are very reduced in relation to the total.

It must be stressed that progress in Guinean rice growing – the most promising of all crops in Guiné – demands, for any of the peoples who practise it, not only other improvements of an agronomic kind, but also a vast improvement in the conditions under which currently is carried out this fundamental stage in the cultivation of rice – the establishment of the nursery.

PORTUGUESE COLONIAL DOMINATION

3. The facts about Portugal's African colonies[1]

Eleven million Africans suffer under Portuguese colonial domination. The Portuguese colonies cover an area of about two million square kilometres (about five per cent of the entire continent and larger than the combined areas of Spain, France, Germany, Italy and England). The African population of these colonies has been enslaved by a small country, the most backward in Europe.

These two million square kilometres are rich in natural resources. The land supports agriculture and livestock breeding. The sub-soil contains iron, coal, manganese, oil, bauxite, diamonds, gold, precious metals, etc. The variety and beauty of nature offer possibilities for tourists.

Side by side with these natural riches, some of which are exploited by the colonialists, Africans live on a sub-human standard – little or no better than serfs in their own country.

Contempt for Africans

After the slave trade, armed conquest and colonial wars, there came the complete destruction of the economic and social structure of African society. The next phase was European occupation and ever-increasing European immigration into these territories. The lands and possessions of the Africans were looted. The Portuguese 'sovereignty tax' was imposed, and so were compulsory crops for agricultural produce, forced labour, the export of African workers, and total control of the collective and individual life of Africans, either by persuasion or violence.

As the size of the European population grows, so does its contempt for Africans. Africans are excluded from certain types of employment, including some of the most unskilled jobs.

Racial discrimination is either openly or hypothetically practised. Africans have been driven from the remaining fertile regions left to them in

[1]This text, written in French under the pseudonym of Abel Djassi and translated into English was published as a pamphlet by the Union of Democratic Control, with an introduction by Basil Davidson, London July 1960.

order that *colonatos* for Europeans could be built there[1]. Political, social or trade union organization is forbidden to the Africans, who do not enjoy even the most elementary human rights. When the United Nations Charter was adopted, giving all countries the right of self-determination, the Portuguese Constitution was hastily changed. The name 'colony' was replaced by 'overseas territory', thus enabling Portugal to claim that she had no colonies and could not therefore make reports on her 'African territories'.

As Africans have awakened and begun moving towards freedom and independence, efforts to control and oppress them have redoubled. A political secret police was created. The colonial army was reinforced. In Portugal, military mobilization was increased, attended by warlike manoeuvres and demonstrations of force. Air and sea bases were built in the colonies. Military observers were sent to Algeria. Strategic plans were drawn up for a war against the Africans. Political and military agreements were made with other colonial powers. New and increasingly advantageous concessions were given to non-Portuguese enterprises.

The demands of the Africans and the work of their resistance organizations, which are forced to remain underground, have resulted in severe repression. All this was and still is perpetrated in the name of 'Civilization and Christianity' by the most retrograde kind of colonial system.

Both the human and natural resources of these colonies are exploited and mortgaged at the lowest possible value. The colonialists deny the practice of Christian principles in their lack of reverence for the human being, and they do everything they can to hide the true effects of their 'civilizing influence'.

While humanity discovers its unity and strives for community of interest based on peace and the recognition of the Rights of Man, of freedom and equality of all peoples, the Portuguese colonialists prepare to launch new colonial wars.

Flimsy arguments

Portuguese colonialism can offer only flimsy arguments, devoid of human or scientific content, to justify its existence and conceal its crimes. These arguments are negated by the very facts which the Portuguese colonialists attempt to conceal. The salient arguments are as follows:

a 'Historical rights'.
Answer:
This concept, so far as 'Portuguese Africa' is concerned, was buried at the Berlin Conference in 1885 by the colonial powers, and has, in any case, never been accepted by Africans.

b The process of 'civilizing' – the real means and results of which are

[1]*Colonatos* – groups of farms reserved for European settlers.

carefully concealed by Portugal.

Answer:
This process is being carried out by an underdeveloped country, with a lower national income than, for example, Ghana, and which has not as yet been able to solve its own problems.

c The colonialist 'theory' of so-called 'assimilation'.

Answer:
This is unacceptable not only in theory but even more in practice. It is based on the racist idea of the 'incompetence or lack of dignity' of African people, and implies that African cultures and civilizations have no value.

d The idea of creating a 'multiracial society' within the colonies, legally based on the Native Statute – Portuguese *apartheid*.

Answer:
This prevents any social contact with the so-called 'civilized' population, and reduces 99 per cent of the African population to sub-human conditions.

e 'National unity' with the colonies, a concept which was hastily brought into the Portuguese Constitution as a means of avoiding the responsibilities set out in the United Nations Charter.

Answer:
This disgraceful subterfuge totally contradicts all the geographic, historic, ethnic, social and cultural facts, and it even comes into conflict with the laws prevailing in the colonies concerning their practical relationship with Portugal.

f The 'state of peace' that is claimed by Salazar to exist.

Answer:
In these colonies Africans have no political rights and cannot form trade unions. Africans do not enjoy even the most elementary human rights. Despite a vicious secret police, an inhuman colonial administration, and brutal soldiers and settlers' militia, African nationalist organizations are offering active resistance to Portuguese colonialism.

The real situation

It might be asked whether Portuguese colonialism has not done a certain amount of good in Africa. Justice is always relative. For the Africans who for five centuries have lived under Portuguese domination, Portuguese colonialism represents a reign of evil, and where evil reigns there is no place for good. As for other people, particularly those who fortunately have not known colonial domination, they will first have to acquaint themselves with all the facts before passing judgement.

Those people who really love truth and justice must overcome the barriers that Portugal sets up against visitors to these colonies. They must go there without allowing themselves to be deceived in any way and they must carefully study the real situation of the people. They must observe the whole truth of what is happening there, and then they will be able to judge the 'civilizing influence' of Portugal. When they know the truth these people cannot but realize the desperate situation of Africans in the Portuguese territories. This colonialism is in process of systematically depriving Africans of the most essential requirements for living, and has taken a heavy toll in African lives, suffering and humiliation.

Portugal is an underdeveloped country with 40 per cent illiteracy, and with one of the lowest standards of living in Europe. If she could have a 'civilizing influence' on any people, she would be accomplishing a kind of miracle. Colonialism, a historical phenomenon which is now disappearing, has never depended on miracles to keep it alive. Portugal is exercising the only kind of 'civilizing influence' she can – one that corresponds to the type of colonialism she has adopted and to her position as a colonial power whose economy, culture and civilization are backward.

Economic misery

Both the laws and the concerted action of the settlers and colonial authorities prevent Africans from owning rural or urban property.

Most African peasants have to cultivate land which is not officially recognised as belonging to them. In Angola and Mozambique nearly 70 per cent of the agricultural produce, and in Guiné the total amount, comes from the African cultivator. He is forced to sell his products to the settlers at artificially low prices imposed by the authorities, and these prices are then reduced still further by the buyers.

The most fertile areas of land, from which Africans have been systematically driven away, were used by colonial companies and are now being occupied by European *colonatos*.

In Mozambique, for example, one-fifth of the land – that is, more than half the cultivated land – is reserved for a small European minority, and includes the richest area. In Angola, more than four-fifths of the coffee plantations, bringing a higher revenue than any other product, belong to settlers who took most of the land from Africans and are now exploiting it with forced African labour. In the Quanza Valley (Angola) alone, more than 100 000 hectares (220 000 acres) of land are reserved for European settlers and colonial companies. In the island of San Tomé nearly all the cultivated land (cocoa and coffee) is in European hands, and was taken illegally by the violence of the settlers and the colonial authorities. Tens of thousands of African families (more than 14 000 families in the *colonato* de Cela of Angola) have been driven off their lands to make way for farmers from Portugal.

Colonial companies own properties which sometimes exceed hundreds of hectares. The Companhia Angolana de Agricultura, for example, owns about 250 000 hectares (550 000 acres) of which 17 000 hectares (37 400 acres) are coffee plantations. The Companhia dos Diamantes de Angola is the sole concessionary for diamond mining in that colony. Five hundred and seventy thousand Africans in Angola and Mozambique are forced to produce cotton and about 60 000 peasant families in Guiné have to grow peanuts.

While the African people live in misery, the colonial companies and the settlers amass wealth and capital most of which is taken out of the colonies. To take the year 1957 as an example – during that year a number of companies, the Sociedade de Agricultura Colonial (San Tomé), the Banco de Angola, the Companhia dos Diamantes de Angola, Comgeral Purifina, the Sociedade Agricola de Cassequel (Angola), Sena Sugar Estates (Mozambique) made a net profit which averaged about 49 per cent of their capital. This net profit alone would be sufficient to cover all the public expenditure in Cape Verde, Guiné and San Tomé during 1957 – leaving a surplus of fifty million escudos (£650 000); and this sum would also be higher than the amount spent in the same year on public education in Angola. The agricultural and commercial company Mario Cunha (Angola) owns blocks of flats in Lisbon (Portugal) which are worth hundreds of thousands of escudos and has set up two humanitarian foundations with the profits derived from the forced labour – which is really slave labour – of Africans in Angola.

In order to protect Portugal's impoverished industries, the Africans are forced to buy second-rate Portuguese products at very high prices, and to sell their products to the settler-traders at much lower prices than the latter receive on resale.

Wine is one of the most important imports of the Portuguese colonies, usually coming second to textiles.

The Africans have to pay various taxes, among them the 'sovereignty tax'. The so-called 'native tax' provides the largest single contribution to the budget of each of Portugal's colonies. Every African over fifteen must pay taxes which often exceed a quarter of his tiny annual income.

Portugal intends to turn these colonies, especially Angola and Mozambique, into so many South Africas to enable her to exploit even more fully their resources and the labour of the Africans. In order to achieve this aim, she considers the mass immigration of Europeans to be her principal task in Africa and spends large sums on this purpose.

In Angola alone, 500 million escudos (£6 250 000) are to be spent on the *colonato* de Cela to build 530 farms in an area of 40 000 hectares. This sum, largely the proceeds of African labour, is equivalent to twenty times the amount spent in Angola by the Agricultural and Forestry Services in 1957.

The setting up of each European family costs Angola one million escudos. For an African peasant family to earn that much money, it would have to live for a thousand years and work every year without stopping.

The economic backwardness of Portugal is reflected in the economic and financial life of her colonies. Portugal never has been, and never will be, capable of creating the necessary foundations for the economic advancement of her colonies. Portugal herself is lacking in these basic requirements and the less impoverished colonies, Angola and Mozambique, now face an economic crisis that Portugal cannot solve.

The social situation

Of the African population of Angola, Guiné and Mozambique, 99·7 per cent are classified as 'uncivilized' by Portuguese colonial laws, and 0·3 per cent are considered to be 'assimilated' (*assimilados*).

For an 'uncivilized' person to attain the status of *assimilado,* he has to prove his economic stability and a standard of living higher than that enjoyed by a large majority of the population of Portugal. He must live in the 'European manner', have paid all his taxes, have done his military service and know how to read and write Portuguese correctly. If the Portuguese people themselves were asked to fulfil these conditions, well over fifty per cent of the population would not have the necessary requirements for becoming 'civilized' or *assimilado.*

The so called 'uncivilized' African is treated as a chattel, and is at the mercy of the will and caprice of the colonial administration and the settlers. His situation is absolutely necessary to the existence of the Portuguese colonial system. He provides an inexhaustible supply of forced labour and labour for export. By classifying him as 'uncivilized', the law gives legal sanction to racial discrimination and provides one of the justifications for Portuguese domination in Africa.

The tiny minority of so-called 'civilized' Africans who are theoretically considered to be Portuguese citizens do not enjoy the privileges reserved for Europeans. Some find themselves in an isolated position between the mass of the African people and the settlers, and are discriminated against by the latter either in an open or a veiled manner. Most of them actually live in similar conditions to those which are legally imposed on the 'uncivilized' Africans.

Portuguese 'multi-racialism' is a myth.

It really means complete racial segregation, except for contact through work, where it furthers the interests of colonialism. With very few exceptions – such as can also be found in South Africa – there is no social contact between Africans and European families. It is only in the schools and other places outside the family environment that European children come into direct contact with the few *assimilado* children who attend schools. The children mix together in innocence, but these relationships also contain prejudices and complexes. Cinemas, cafes, bars, restaurants and so on are almost exclusively frequented by Europeans. Any African bold enough to enter one of these places must be prepared to face humiliation. In the towns of Lourenço Marques and Beira (Mozambique), Nova Lisboa and Lobito (Angola), racial segregation is openly practised.

Portuguese racism hardly existed at the beginning of the period of colonization. It was born and increased as the size of the European population grew. It is no accident that of the ten million inhabitants of Angola and Mozambique, there are only 60 000 'coloureds', and for the past half century the size of this 'coloured' population has remained almost static. Nearly all of them are illegitimate children who have been abandoned by European fathers. A mixed couple, especially an African man and a European woman, is always a target for the insults and mockery of the settlers, so much so that the very few existing couples do not usually show themselves in public.

In country districts, the Africans must suffer very miserable conditions. In the towns, the 'uncivilized' Africans live in areas which are being moved further and further from the town centres, in squalid shanty-towns such as the *musseques* in Luanda. Few houses occupied by Africans could be considered as habitable by any standards of decency. These were built by the authorities in a selected area, as is the case in South Africa. After overcoming innumerable obstacles, a few *assimilados* manage to acquire a reasonably decent home. This is only achieved by the handful of Africans who have been to university and by the ever-decreasing number who are able to gain public employment despite racialism. These people are always cited in colonialist propaganda. Most of the Europeans, however, live in *vivendas* – some of which are real colonial palaces comparable to the richest homes in Portugal.

'Uncivilized' Africans, especially in the towns, have to carry passes and obey a 9·0 p.m. curfew. A wise *assimilado* always carries his identity card which, when accepted by the authorities and settlers, is his only valid proof of being a human being.

Forced labour

Twenty thousand workers from Angola, Mozambique and the Cape Verde Islands work twelve hours a day on the settlers' farms of San Tomé, in the heart of the equatorial zone. There is forced labour for public works in Guiné, Angola, Mozambique; but in the latter two it extends as well to privately owned companies. Every year 250 000 Angolans are rented out to agricultural, mining and construction concerns. Every year 400 000 people of Mozambique are subjected to forced labour, 100 000 of whom are exported to the mines of South Africa and the Rhodesias.

This trade in forced labour provides one of Portugal's most stable sources of foreign currency. Henrique Galvão, a one-time colonial administrator who has had the courage to tell the truth, has stated that 'only the dead escape forced labour...The present situation is worse than that created by pure slavery...There are employers who have a 30 per cent mortality rate among their workers and they have never had any trouble obtaining new workers.' The Companhia Angolana dos Diamantes alone uses up to 20 000 workers a year. This new form of slavery – for it cannot be considered anything less than that – has broken up millions of African families.

The authorities who hire forced labour make a substantial yearly profit on each man rented out. Seventy-five per cent of the workers' wages are paid when they return to their place of origin. But this is paid by the authorities, not the employers, and the authorities' annual average profit is of the order of about 1500 escudos or £18 15s (£18.75) on each man, while the yearly annual net salary is 1200 escudos, or £15 15s (£15.75).

This payment is made only after all taxes have been deducted, and after the worker gives fifteen days of free labour to the State. Theoretically he is entitled to medical assistance, but in most cases this scarcely exists. He is also entitled to food, but even Portuguese technicians have established that the diet of the African worker remains deficient in nutritive value. Much forced labour is provided by children and adolescents. Apart from agricultural work, the settlers also use 'uncivilized' Africans for heavy labour and as houseboys.

The *assimilado* worker earns three or four times less than the European worker who does the same work. He is always a 'second-class' worker, even if skilled. With the exception of a few public employees and miserably paid workers, the *assimilados* are always fighting the threat of unemployment, and their adult children are mostly unemployed. Even the most unskilled jobs, such as waiter or lottery-ticket vendor, are reserved for Europeans. Africans in Angola and Mozambique are not in practice allowed to become taxi drivers or shop salesmen.

The African worker has never been allowed to defend himself. The 'uncivilized' are not allowed to organize themselves, and the *assimilados* have no voice even in Salazar's Fascist 'trade unions'. In the farms, mines and everywhere else, the work schedules are entirely dependent on the good will of the employer, leaving the African worker exposed to all the whims and sanctions of the settlers which may include beating.

Medical 'care'

Three hundred and eighty doctors 'care' for the health of eleven million people who inhabit an area of two million square kilometres. Communications in these territories are by far the worst in Africa. In the Cape Verde Islands, which have proportionately the greatest number of doctors, there is one doctor for every 10 000 people. In Angola, where the situation is better than in Guiné or Mozambique, there is one hospital for every 280 000 people, one doctor for every 20 000 people, one nurse and thirty beds for every 10 000 people.

The infant mortality rate is said to be higher than 40 per cent and in some regions may attain 80 per cent. Among Africans who died in 1956, 84 per cent of registered deaths were attributed to 'obscure or unknown causes' but these 'causes', we may note, kill only Africans. From 1940 to 1950 drought and famine in Cape Verde caused the deaths of about 40 000 people.

Literacy: 1 in 100

Catholic Missions hold a monopoly of education for the so-called 'uncivilized' Africans. According to the Agreement between Portugal and the Vatican this education must 'conform to the doctrinal dictates of the Portuguese Constitution and must take its directions from the plans and programmes issued by the local governments'. This means that 99·7 per cent of the African population is forbidden access to lay schools. Due to this Catholic monopoly, the educational influence of other Christian missions is small.

In Angola, Mozambique and Guiné, 99 per cent of the population is illiterate.

Areas larger than Portugal are totally without schools.

In 1937, 40 000 children out of a total population of about four million attended mission schools in Angola. Yet in the same year in the Belgian Congo there were 1 300 000 children at elementary school – proportionately ten times as many as in Angola.

The sons of the *assimilados* (0·3 per cent of the population) are allowed to attend official elementary schools, secondary schools and universities. But the various forms of racial discrimination practised in colonial schools, especially in Mozambique and Angola, added to the great poverty of African families, limit the number of pupils who may graduate. Only those pupils capable of making an extraordinary effort manage to finish their studies.

The secondary schools are almost exclusively attended by the sons of the settlers.

There are no universities in the colonies. About one hundred Africans are in the universities of Portugal or are prepared for university entrance – one hundred students out of a population of eleven millions.

Most elementary-school teachers and all secondary teachers are European except in Cape Verde, where Africans who have diplomas may teach at secondary level.

All Portuguese education disparages the African, his culture and civilization. African languages are forbidden in schools. The white man is always presented as a superior being and the African as an inferior. The colonial 'conquistadores' are shown as saints and heroes. As soon as African children enter elementary schools, they develop an inferiority complex. They learn to fear the white man and to feel ashamed of being Africans. African geography, history and culture are either ignored or distorted, and children are forced to study Portuguese geography and history.

Puppets and stooges

Africans have no political rights. The old structure of African political life was totally destroyed by Portuguese colonialism. The few remaining chiefdoms[1] are controlled by the colonial authorities, who use the chiefs as puppets. Most of the chiefs are put in 'command' of communities different from those to which they really belong.

In the so-called local government Council 'elected' by the Governor, there are sometimes a few members representing the African people. These men are usually Europeans. The few Africans who accept these positions, or are forced to accept them, are not entitled to intervene in any way on behalf of African interests.

On one occasion a 'coloured' Councillor was expelled from the Council in Angola for having attempted to criticize the Government. One of the very few African doctors in the colonies was invited to take his place. This doctor declined on the grounds that the only thing he knew anything about was medicine. An African priest finally took the post of Councillor after being subjected to intimidation and pressure by the Archbishop of Luanda.

In the Lisbon 'Parliament' one of 120 Deputies elected by the Government is an African. He is the 'Deputy' for San Tomé. The Deputy for Cape Verde, who is of European descent, is the leader of the Fascist political party in the colony and holds his position indefinitely. The 'representatives' for Angola, Mozambique and Guiné are Europeans closely linked to the large colonial concerns. All the 'Deputies' from the colonies enjoy the absolute confidence of the Fascist colonial government. They have nothing in common with the Africans, 99·7 per cent of whom, in any event, are not allowed to vote.

Three Africans are used as political puppets, or as synthetic samples of a non-existent product, by the Portuguese delegation to the United Nations and at other international meetings. These three men, the Negro, James Pinto Bull (Guiné), the 'coloured' Augusto Santos Lima (descendant of Cape Verdians) and the 'coloured' Julio Monteiro (Cape Verde), are considered by their countrymen as traitors. They are administrative functionaries in the well-paid service of Portuguese colonialism.

[1]Chiefdoms – *regulados* in Guiné and *sobados* in Angola and Mozambique.

All demonstrations and organizations are forbidden unless rigorously controlled by the colonial authorities. Even football clubs are exclusive. With the exception of one useless newspaper in Mozambique – the Government-controlled *Brado Africano* – no African press is permitted.

★

What the Africans want

We, the Africans of the Portuguese colonies, are fighting Portuguese colonialism to defend the rights of our peoples, to defend the true interests of people everywhere.

The Africans want Portugal to respect and rigidly adhere to the obligations set out in the UN Charter. We demand that Portugal should follow the example of Britain, France and Belgium in recognizing the right of the peoples she dominates to self-determination and independence.

The African anticolonialist organizations of the Portuguese colonies representing the legitimate aspirations of their people want to re-establish the human dignity of Africans, their freedom, and the right to determine their own future. These organizations want the people to enjoy real social development based on fruitful work and economic progress, on African unity and fraternity, on friendship and equality with all peoples, including the Portuguese people. They want peace in the service of humanity.

The African organizations fighting Portuguese colonialism believe in the use of peaceful means for achieving independence. However, we have no illusions, and since Portugal intends to use violence to defend her interests, we will be ready to answer with violence. Our organizations are vigilant. They follow closely all the diplomatic manoeuvres of Portugal. They believe that no democratic government will prejudice its own good name by continuing to ally itself with Portuguese colonialism – doomed like all other colonial regimes. They believe that the material and human wealth of their countries are part of the patrimony of humanity and should be made to serve the progress and happiness of their own people and of peoples in all countries.

The Africans of the Portuguese colonies will destroy Portuguese colonialism. It may be the last colonial regime to go, just as it is the last in terms of technical and economic development, and the last to respect the Rights of Man. But its days are surely numbered.

PARTY PRINCIPLES AND POLITICAL PRACTICE[1]

4. Unity and struggle

Let us go on with our work and talk a little to the comrades about some principles of our Party and of our struggle.

Those comrades who were aware of a document published in 1965 under the title *General Watchwords of our Party* should remember that the final part is a chapter entitled 'Apply Party principles in practice'. Obviously those watchwords dealt with fairly general principles and today we can talk about some additional principles. Everyone knows them well, but sometimes overlook that they are the foundation, the bases, the principle of our struggle. In other words, our struggle is seen in its fundamental political aspect, in its principal aspect which is the political aspect. Obviously for us to define, for example, the strategy and even the tactics we adopt in our armed struggle for liberation, other principles were stated, but these are no more than the application of our general principles to the field of armed struggle.

A first principle of our Party and our struggle, that we all know well, is: 'Unity and struggle'; which is even the motto, if you like, the theme of our Party. Unity and struggle. Obviously to study the basic meaning of this fairly simple principle we must know well what unity is and what struggle is. And we must put or treat the question of unity and the question of struggle in a particular context, that is from the geographical viewpoint and bearing in mind the society – social and economic life, etc. – of the environment in which we want to apply this principle of unity and struggle.

What is unity? We can clearly take unity in a sense which one might call static, at a standstill, as no more than a question of number. For example, if we consider the entirety of bottles in the world, one bottle is a unity. If we consider the entirety of men meeting in this hall, comrade Daniel Barreto is a unity. And so on. Is this the unity that we are interested in considering in our work when we speak of our Party principles? It is and it is not. It is to the extent that we want to transform a varied entirety of persons into a well defined entirety seeking one path. And it is not because here we must not forget that within this entirety there are diverse elements. Rather the meaning of unity that we see in our principles is the following: whatever might be the existing differences, we must be one, an entirety, to achieve a

---

[1]Nine of the main lectures delivered by Cabral in *crioulo* (a Guinean language consisting of Portuguese loanwords and other words and syntax drawn from local African languages), during a seminar for PAIGC cadres held from 19 to 24 November 1969. The lectures were tape-recorded and later transcribed into Portuguese.

given aim. This means that in our principle, unity is taken in a dynamic sense, in motion.

Let us consider, for example, a football team, which is made up of various individuals, eleven persons. Each person has his specific work to do when the football team is playing. The persons differ from each other: different temperaments; often different education, some cannot read or write, others are doctors or engineers; different religion, one might be Moslem, another Catholic, etc. They may even act differently on the political plane, one might be of one Party, another of another. One might be for the status quo, in Portugal for example, another might be for the opposition. That is, persons different from each other, each one feeling different from the other, but in the same football team. And if this football team, when it comes to playing, does not succeed in achieving a unity of all its elements, it will not be a football team. Each one can preserve his personality, his ideas, his religion, his personal problems, even a little of his style of play, but they must all obey one thing: they must act together to score goals against any opponent with whom they are playing, that is act around this specific aim of scoring the maximum number of goals against the opponent. They have to form a unity. If they do not do this, there is no football team, there is nothing. That is to show you a clear example of unity.

You see a person coming along, for example, with a basket on her head, and the person usually sells fruit. You do not know what fruits are inside the basket, but say: here she comes with a basket of fruit. There might be mangoes, bananas, papayas, guavas, etc. inside the basket. But in our thinking, she is coming with an entirety which represents a unity, one basket on her head, one basket of fruit. You know that it is a unity, whether from the point of view of number: one basket of fruit; or of objective: sale. It is all one thing, even though there are various things inside: various fruits, mangoes, bananas, papayas, etc. But the fundamental question that she is coming with fruit for sale makes it all into a single thing.

That is to give you an idea of what unity is and to tell you that the basic principle of unity lies in the difference between the items. If the latter were not different, it would not be necessary to make unity; the question of unity would not arise. So what is unity for us? What is the objective around which we must make unity in our land? Obviously we are not a football team, or a basket of fruit. We are a people, or members of a people, who at a certain stage of their history, have taken a certain course on their path, have raised certain matters in their spirit and their life, have guided their action in a certain direction, have put certain questions and have sought answers. It might all have begun with one person alone, or two, or three, or six. At a certain stage this question appeared in our midst – unity. And the Party was so far-sighted, that is, it understood this so well, that in its very theme it adopted as its main principle, as the base of everything, unity and struggle.

Now a question arises: was this unity, which arose as a necessity, because our ideas were different from the political point of view? No, we were not accustomed to dabbling in politics in our land. There was no party. But furthermore, under foreign domination – which is our case and that of other lands – a poorly developed society, like that of Guiné and Cape Verde, where there is no great difference between the positions of persons (although as we have seen there are some differences) cannot easily have very divergent political aims. This means that our question of unity was not in the sense of reuniting various different heads, different persons, from the point of view of political aims, of political programmes. In the first place because in the very structure of our society, in the very reality of our land, the differences are not so great as to provoke such differences in political aims. But in the second place and above all because with foreign domination in our land, with the total ban that always operated throughout our life on forming any party in our land, there were no different parties to have to be united, there were no different political courses which would have to be steered to the same path, to come together to form the unity.

So what was the question of unity in our land? Fundamentally it was simply this: in the first place, as everyone knows, union makes for strength. Right from the moment when there came into the heads of some sons of our soil the idea of eliminating foreign colonialist domination, there arose a question of strength, the strength necessary to be pitted against the strength of the colonialists. So, the more persons who join together, the more united we become, the better we reflect what everyone knows: union makes for strength. If I take one matchstick and want to break it, I can break it quickly. If I take two together, it is no longer quite so easy, and then with three or four, five, six, a given moment will come when I cannot break them at all. This is a simple, natural illustration that union makes for strength (and we must realize that union does not always make for strength, there are certain kinds of union which make for weakness – and this is the wonder of the world: all things have two aspects, one positive and the other negative). Those who had the idea of unity, because union makes for strength, put the question of unity into the spirit and letter of our struggle, because they knew that there was much division in our midst.

In Guiné and in Cape Verde there was division, division in *creole*, meaning contradiction. In our society, for example, any person who gives serious thought to our struggle knows that if we were all Moslems, or all Catholics, or animists believing in the *iram* spirits, it would be more simple. At least no force against the interests of our people could try to divide us on grounds of religion. But let us go on and look at the case of Cape Verde. In Cape Verde, where there are no great difficulties over religion, except for minor points of difference between Protestants and Catholics in their fine city life, there are other questions which divide persons – like, for example, that some families own land, and others do not. If everyone owned land or no one owned land, it would be more simple. The enemy, for example, the force opposing us and from which we want to liberate our land, can bring against us and to their side those who own land, on the notion that we want to take their land from them. Similarly in Guiné it can set the notables against us, on the notion that we want to take their authority from them. If there were no notables, it would be more simple; if everybody were notables, it would be more simple. This means that the question of unity arises in our land, I say it again, not because of the need to bring together persons of different political thought, but to bring together persons of different economic position, although this difference is not as great as in other lands which have a social situation of different cultures, including religion. We posed the question of unity in our land, in Guiné and in Cape Verde, in the sense of removing the enemy's potential for exploiting the contradictions there might be among our population in order to weaken the strength of ours that we must pit against that of the enemy.

So we see that unity is something we have to achieve in order to be able to do something else. If we are going to wash, for example, either by turning on a tap or washing ourselves in the river, unless we are crazy, we are not going into the water without undressing; we must first take off our clothes. It is an action we carry out, a preparation so that we can take a bath. Better still: if we want to hold a meeting in this hall, with persons seated, we must call them, set up tables, arrange pencils and pens, etc. That is, we have to arrange means to be able to hold a meeting as it should be. Unity is also a means, not an end. We might have struggled a little for unity, but if we achieve it, that does not mean the struggle is over. There are many persons in this struggle of the colonies against colonialism who up till now are still struggling merely for unity. Because, as they are unable to wage the struggle, they confuse unity with struggle. Unity is a means towards struggle, and as with all means, a little goes a long way. It is not necessary to unite all the population to struggle in a country. Are we sure that all the population are united? No, a certain degree of unity is enough. Once we have reached it, then we can struggle. Because then the ideas in the heads of these persons advance and develop and serve increasingly to achieve the aim we have in view. So you have seen more or less what is the basic idea expressed in this principle of ours – unity.

And what is struggle? Struggle is a normal condition of all living creatures in the world. All are in struggle, all struggle. For example, you are seated on chairs, I am seated on this chair. My body is exerting a force on the floor, through the bench which is above it. But if the floor did not have sufficient force to support me, I would go down below, would break through the floor. If beneath the floor there was no force, I would go on breaking through, and so on. So there is a silent struggle between the force I exert on the floor and the force of the soil which holds me up, which does not let me pass. But you all know that the earth is constantly in motion – perhaps some of you do not yet believe that the earth is rotating. If you set a plate spinning, in rotation, and if you put a coin on it, you will see that the plate throws off the coin. Anyone who uses a sling to knock out crows or sparrows with a stone, as is done in Guiné or Cape Verde, knows that once he has put the stone in the sling and swung it round a few times, it is unnecessary to cast; it is enough to release part of the sling and the stone flies out with enormous force. What is needed is good marksmanship to be able to do what one wants, to know the exact moment when the stone must be released. This means that anything which is spinning, within the space in which it is spinning, develops a force which casts things outwards. So all of us on earth, which is spinning, are constantly being repelled by a force which pushes us off the earth, which is called centrifugal force – which pushes us from the centre outwards. But there is also a further force which attracts persons to earth, and this is the force of gravity. This means that the earth, like magnetic force, attracts all bodies which are close to it, in accordance with the distance and mass of each body. We remain on earth and do not go outwards, because the force of gravity is much greater than the centrifugal force which draws us outwards. The question of sending bodies to the moon, etc., the basic question for the scientists is the following: to overcome the force of gravity. By overcoming the force of gravity, they can succeed in leaving the earth. And we know today that for a body to be launched outwards from earth, by overcoming the force of gravity, it has to travel at eleven kilometres per second. If it travels at such speed as will reach eleven kilometres per second, it has overcome the force of gravity. However, any force acting on an object can only exist if there is an opposite force. You have your hand on your face, your hand does not move the face because the face also has resistance. You do not feel it, but it is also pushing. Because the weight of it alone is a form of pushing.

In our specific case, the struggle is the following: the Portuguese colonialists have taken our land, as foreigners and as occupiers, and have exerted a force on our society, on our people. The force has operated so that they should take our destiny into their hands, has operated so that they should halt our history for us to remain tied to the history of Portugal, as if we were a wagon on their train. And they have created a series of conditions, within our land; economic, social, cultural conditions, etc. For this they had to overcome a force. During almost fifty years they waged a colonial war against our people: war against Manjaco, Pepel, Fula, Mandinga, Beafada, Balanta, Felupe, against nearly all the ethnic groups of our land in Guiné. In Cape Verde, the Portuguese colonialists found the islands deserted. At the period when the great exploitation of African men as slaves in the world appeared, and because of the strategic location of Cape Verde deep in the Atlantic, they decided to turn the archipelago into a storehouse for slaves. Folk taken from Africa, namely from Guiné, were placed in Cape Verde as slaves. But little by little, as the numbers grew and laws in the world were changed, they had to give up the slave trade. They then turned to exerting on these folk a pressure similar to the pressure they exerted in Guiné, that is a colonial force. There was constant resistance to this force. If the colonial force was acting in one direction, there was always our force which acted in the opposite direction. This opposite force took many different forms: passive resistance, lies, doffing one's cap, 'Yes, Sir', to use all possible and imaginable stratagems to fool the Portuguese. As we could not challenge them face to face, we had to fool them, but with our energies wasted beneath this force: misery, suffering, death, disease, calamity, in addition to other consequences of a social nature, such as backwardness in comparison with other peoples in the world. Our struggle today is the following: with the creation of our Party, a new force has arisen which opposes the colonialist force. The question is knowing, in practice, if this united force of our people can overcome the colonialist force: this is what our struggle is about.

Now, taken together, unity and struggle mean that for struggle unity is necessary, but to have unity it is also necessary to struggle. And this means that even among ourselves, we are struggling; perhaps you have not understood this properly. The significance of our struggle is not only in respect of colonialism, it is also in respect of ourselves. Unity and struggle. Unity for us to struggle against the colonialists and struggle for us to achieve our unity, for us to construct our land as it should be.

The rest is the application of this basic principle of ours. Anyone who does not understand it, must understand, because if not he has understood nothing of our struggle. And we must carry out this principle in three fundamental contexts: in Guiné, in Cape Verde, and in Guiné and Cape Verde. Anyone who has studied the Party programme knows that this is the case.

From this talk you will already have understood what the contradiction is that we had and have permanently to overcome so that we can ensure the unity necessary for the struggle in Guiné. From the examples I gave you also, you have understood more or less what the contradictions were and are that we have to overcome in Cape Verde so that we can ensure the unity necessary to carry out the struggle in Cape Verde. You know that the Portuguese badly divided us, and we divided ourselves, as a consequence of the evolution of our life.

Take Guiné, for example. On one side at least there are folk of the city, on the other, folk of the bush. What is there in the city? In the city there are whites and blacks. Among the Africans there are senior staff and middle staff who have the assurance that at the end of the month their pay is certain. They have that notion of buying their own little car, as I for example, have my own car. They have a refrigerator, a fine figure of a wife, children who will certainly go to secondary school and who even, if they study hard, will go to Lisbon. Then there are those petty employees who enjoy Saturdays with their red wine and their piece of cod, who can buy a transistor radio, small possessions. Then there are the dock workers, car repairers, and we can include drivers and others who live a little better. Salaried workers in general. And then there are the folk who have nothing to do, who live by their wits each day, here and there, who do not even know what to do to arrange a life style. Or folk with an easy life, like prostitutes, or beggars, tricksters, thieves, etc., folk who have nothing to do. This is what makes up society in the cities.

But if you consider carefully, you can see that those descendants of Guineans and Cape Verdians who are well off in life have a single common interest: they all cling to the Portuguese, pretend as hard as they can to be Portuguese, even forbidding their children to speak any other language at home except Portuguese, as you well know. And if we look at another group, their interest is also more or less the same. The Zé Marias, the João Vas, and others as well obviously, who were domestics. There are some of you, for example, who were domestics but who are nationalists, isn't that so? But their interests were more or less the same; they always live in the same sphere, the same social group.

Likewise with the dock workers, boat workers, stevedores, who are already part of another group. You might meet them, to chat, but you know that you will not sit down with them at the table to eat. Just like in the Portuguese group, for example, in the families of the governor, of the director of the bank, of the director of finances, etc., we never see there the wife of a Portuguese labourer or of anyone who is a panel-beater. Only if he should have a very beautiful daughter, whom everyone admires, she might now and then go to a dance with the upper crust. But her mother who cannot read and write does not go. She accompanies her daughter to the door and leaves. You remember such instances in Bissau.

Society in Cape Verde is similar: the same kind of city society. Only in Cape Verde this group of Africans of some means was long since much bigger than in Guiné; both as civil servants and as proprietors, owners of land. Although the land is in the bush, they live in the city. And in the city, the situation is more or less like this: civil servants or staff of some standing, petty officials and employees, workers who can be dismissed at any moment and those who have nothing to do. This is the city society, both in Guiné and in Cape Verde. In Guiné or Cape Verde, the number of whites was always low. In Guiné it never went above three thousand, and in Cape Verde it seems that it never even reached a thousand. I mean civilian whites, leading a normal life as officials, technicians, businessmen, employees, etc.

Obviously for us to achieve unity, we must see this city society in relation to the struggle. For against the Portuguese colonialists, we accept even persons from this group of whites in the struggle on our side, it they so wish. Because among the whites there may be some who are in favour of colonialism and others who are anticolonialists. If the latter join us, that is fine, it is an additional force against the colonialists. Moreover, you know that we make good use of this. If Comrade Luiz Cabral, for example, succeeded in escaping it was because whites took him out of Bissau, to reach Ensalma and go on to the frontier. Two whites, you all know. One person who had an effect on our Party work in Bissau was a Portuguese woman. Only someone outside the Party would not know this. The first person who taught Osvaldo things about the struggle was she, not I. I did not know Osvaldo.

This means: for the struggle against the colonialist enemy, let all the forces we can bring together come. But not blindly; we must know what is the position of each one in relation to the colonialists. So in the cities we see the following: very few whites took any action against the colonialists. First, because they are the *colonial class,* those most representative of colonialism in our land. Second, because some have no interest in this, as they have their own life, want to go away when they have made their pile, are not looking for trouble. Third, because the whites, the Portuguese who live in our land, do not generally have sufficient political training to take a clear, specific position against any regime, wherever they might be.

And what about us as Africans? Among the groups we might term petty bourgeoisie, those with an assured living, whether descendant from Guineans or Cape Verdians, there always appear three categories of persons. A minute but powerful group who are in favour of the colonialists, who do not even want to hear about this, about struggle against the Portuguese. Some of these persons went to my house in Pessubé, high ranking, with good positions, eating and drinking well, who went on holidays, etc. They sat down and said: 'Well, we want to talk to you. You, the son of so-and-so, we know you well. You are mixing yourself up in matters, you are spoiling your career as an engineer. We want to give you some advice. We have nothing against the Portuguese, we are all Portuguese.' For such as those there is no cure. The vast majority of the petty bourgeoisie are undecided, were undecided and certainly are still undecided today, because they think: 'Cabral comes along with his schemes with his followers, and in fact it would be good if we could chase out the Portuguese, but...' Those who must suffer from the Portuguese are these city folk, with the Portuguese constantly on top of them, chivvying them in the cities, that is Mansoa, Bissau, Bissorã, Praia, S. Vicente. Whites who arrive, even if they are worthless, climb and become great figures while they themselves remain stuck as cadets or clerks. If there are competitive appointments, the whites soon go to the fore. Take, for example, Cruz Pinto's father – so many persons who passed ahead of him, but he stayed put like the fathers of others who are here. It is such folk who suffer directly from colonialism every day. While, for example, the man who lives in the bush, deep in Oio, or in Foréa, may well die without ever having seen a white man. I remember, for example, that when a Portuguese agronomist went with me to visit certain areas in Oio, the children came up to him and rubbed his arm to see why he was white like that. Some even asked him: 'But why are you like this?' They had never seen a white man. While anyone who lives in the city sees whites every day. To resume, this is a group of persons, a large group of petty bourgeoisie, who have their pay packet at the end of the month. Their wish in fact is that the Portuguese would go away, but they are afraid, because they do not know if we can really win. 'Cabral comes along with his followers, with his schemes, but what if we lose? We lose our refrigerator, our pay at the end of the month, our radio, our dream of going to Portugal for holidays.' Those holidays in Portugal are so that they can come back afterwards to boast about them (to brag). All this keeps them undecided, on the fence. But there is a smaller group who from the start rose with the idea of struggling against Portuguese colonialism, and ready to die if necessary. And it is from this group that persons came who adhered to the Party. For if you consider carefully, the majority of those who created the Party, neither paid poll tax, nor received beatings, nor suffered from lack of employment, but on the contrary had a reasonable life. This is the position of our petty bourgeoisie towards the struggle, whether in Guiné or in Cape Verde.

And what about our salaried workers? The majority are sympathetic to the struggle, at least at the beginning. The majority – carpenters, masons, above all sailors, mechanics, even drivers – felt exploitation cruelly and earned miserable wages. And when a man who works as a mason earns ten escudos, and a white man earns eighty, if not 800, the former feels greatly exploited in his living conditions. But in this group also there are some who do not want to struggle, who are sympathetic to colonialism.

And in the group who have nothing to do, who do not have jobs, we have not usually found elements for the struggle. Generally many of them serve as agents of PIDE, while others are moderate.

In the case of Guiné, specifically, it should be noted that there is a group who come between the petty bourgeoisie and the salaried workers, and I do not really know what name to give them. Many lads without steady work, who can read and write, who work here and there, and who often live at the expense of an uncle in the city – and we have much of this in our land – but who are in permanent contact with the colonialist. Footballers, a little dazzled by the Portuguese, but also a little humiliated, because despite being good players they cannot go to the dances at the Bissau International Sports Union...These folk came to the struggle very readily. And they have played an important role in this struggle, because on the one hand they are of the city and on the other they are closely tied to the bush. They had nothing to lose except their football playing or some measly job (tailor, carpenter). But they scarcely even wanted that job because they well knew that it was not worth much in allowing them to live (to strut) alongside the Portuguese. They want to strut alongside the Portuguese, but they want Africa as well. These are folk who have learned in the city how agreeable it is to have fine possessions, but who, because of the humiliation they suffer, feel that the Portuguese are superfluous. And the Party helped them to deepen their consciousness of this situation.

And what about the bush? In the bush it all depends: if it is our Balanta society, there is no difficulty. The Balanta have what is called a horizontal society, meaning that they do not have classes one above the other. The Balanta do not have great chiefs; it was the Portuguese who made chiefs for them. Each family, each compound is autonomous and if there is any difficulty, it is a council of elders which settles it. There is no State, no authority which rules everybody. If there has been in our times, you are young; it was imposed by the Portuguese. There are Mandinga imposed as chiefs of the Balanta, or former African policemen turned into chiefs. The Balanta cannot resist, and they accept, but they are only play-acting towards the chief. Each one rules in his own house and there is understanding among them. They join together to work in the fields, etc., and there is not much talk. And it can even happen in the Balanta group that there are two family compounds close to each other and they do not get on with each other because of a land dispute or some other quarrel from the past. They do not want anything to do with each other. But these are ancient customs whose origin one would need to explain, if we had time. Old stories, of blood, of marriage, of beliefs, etc. Balanta society is like this: the more land you work, the richer you are, but the wealth is not to be hoarded, it is to be spent, for one individual cannot be much more than another. That is the principle of Balanta society, as of other societies in our land. Whereas the Fula and Manjaco have chiefs, but they were not imposed by the Portuguese; it is part of the evolution of their history. Obviously we must tell you that in Guiné the Fula and Mandinga at least are folk who came from abroad. The majority of Fula and Mandinga in our land were original inhabitants who became Fula and Mandinga. It is good to know this well so as to understand certain aspects. Because if we compare the life style of Fula in our land with that of the true Fula in other regions of Africa, there is a slight difference; even in the Futa-Djalon there is a difference. In our land many became Fula: former Mandinga became Fula. Even the Mandinga, who came and conquered as far as the Mansoa region 'Mandingized' persons and changed them into Mandinga. The Balanta refused and many people say that the very word 'balanta' means those who refuse. The Balanta is someone who is not convinced, who denies. But they did not refuse so much, because we find the Balanta-Mané, the Mansoaner. There were always some who accepted, and who were gradually growing in number, as they accepted becoming Moslems.

Balanta, Pepel, Mancanha, etc., were all folk from the interior of Africa whom the Mandinga drove towards the sea. The Sussu of the Republic of Guinea, for example, come from Futa-Djalon, from where the Mandinga and the Fula drove them, The Mandinga drove them and later came the Fula who in turn drove the Mandinga. As we have said, the Fula society, for example, or the Manjaco society are societies which have classes from the bottom to the top. With the Balanta it is not like that: anyone who holds his head very high is not respected any more, already wants to become a white man, etc. For example, if someone has grown a great deal of rice, he must hold a great feast, to use it up. Whereas the Fula and Manjaco have other rules, with some higher then others. This means that the Manjaco and Fula have what are called vertical societies. At the top there is the chief, then follow the religious leaders, the important religious figures, who with the chiefs form a class. Then come others of various professions (cobblers, blacksmiths, goldsmiths) who, in any society, do not have equal rights with those at the top. By tradition, anyone who was a goldsmith was even ashamed of it – all the more if he were a 'griot' (minstrel). So we have a series of professions in a hierarchy, in a ladder, one below the other. The blacksmith is not the same as the cobbler, the cobbler is not the same as the goldsmith, etc.; each one has his distinct profession. Then come the great mass of folk who till the ground. They till to eat and live, they till the ground for the chiefs, according to custom. This is Fula and Manjaco society, with all the theories this implies such as that a given chief is linked to God. Among the Manjaco, for example, if someone is a tiller, he cannot till the ground without the chief's order, for the chief carries the word of God to him. Everyone is free to believe what he wishes. But why is the whole cycle created? So that those who are on top can maintain the certainty that those who are below will not rise up against them. But in our land it has sometimes occurred, among the Fula, for example, that those who were below rose up and struggled against those at the top. There have sometimes been major peasants' revolts. We have, for example, the case of Mussa Molo who overthrew the king and took his place. But as soon as he had taken the place, he adopted the same ancient law, because that was what suited him. Everything remained the same, because like that he was well off. And he soon forgot his origin. That, unhappily, is what many folk want.

In this bush society, a great number of Balanta adhered to the struggle, and this is not by accident, nor is it because Balanta are better than others. It is because of their type of society, a horizontal (level) society, but of free men, who want to be free, who do not have oppression at the top, except the oppression of the Portuguese. The Balanta is his own man and the Portuguese is over him, because he knows that the chief there, Mamadu, is in no way his chief, but is a creature of the Portuguese. So he is the more interested in putting an end to this so as to remain totally free. And that is also why, when some Party element makes a mistake with the Balanta, they do not like it and become angered quickly, more quickly than any other group.

Among the Fula and Manjaco it is not like this. The broad mass who suffer in fact are at the bottom, tillers of the soil (peasants). But there are many folk between them and the Portuguese. They are used to suffering, to suffering at the hands of their own folk, from the behaviour of their own folk. Someone who tills the soil has to work for all the chiefs, who are numerous, and for the district officers. So we have found the following: once they had really understood, a large proportion of the peasants adhered to the struggle, except one or other group with whom we had not worked well. Among those above them (the professionals), some adhered and others not. But among the self-interested, those who work largely on their own account (artisans) and among the religious leaders and the chiefs, very few adhered to the Party, because they are afraid of losing their privileges in favour of the struggle. In these class societies, there is one group which plays a special role: those who transport merchandise from one point to another, for sale or barter (within or outside the country). They barter merchandise, lend money to the chiefs, etc. They are the Dyulas. It is a very special group in the framework of our society.

These are societies divided into classes: a ruling class, an artisan class, a peasant class. It was essential for us to achieve the greatest possible unity of the forces of the different classes, of the different elements of the society, so as to wage the struggle in our land. It is not necessary to unite everybody, as I have already said, but it is necessary to have a certain degree of unity. But this is looking at society only from the viewpoint of its *social structure,* in the broad sense. For in our society there are various ethnic groups, that is groups with differing culture and customs, who in their own belief came from various groups of differing origin: Fula, Mandinga, Pepel, Balanta, Manjaco, Mancanha, etc., not forgetting descendants in Guiné of Cape Verdians.

In Cape Verde in the countryside, in the bush, it is complicated. There are landowners (large and small), tenant farmers (usually linked to the large landowners), and sharecroppers, who till land that does not belong to them and later share with the owner the product of the harvest. Tenants till the land but must pay rent to the owner of the land. And there are some agricultural labourers, but few; they are not enough to form a class. They work on the properties of others. Happily in one respect but unhappily in another, as there was great calamity, the large landowners lost much of their land in the crises in Cape Verde, through drought, but mainly through Portuguese maladministration. They had to mortgage, that is deliver the title to the Bank for the Bank to lend them money, but then they could not pay back and lost their land. So the Bank and the Savings Bank are today the largest landowners in our land. There are still some small landowners. The tenants, however, rent land from the Bank or the Savings Bank, or from one or other of the remaining landowners. This means that this group is a group of folk who do not have land. Whereas in Guiné we cannot say to anyone, 'let us struggle to have land', in Cape Verde we can already tell these folk: 'let us struggle because anyone who struggles can have his own plot of land to cultivate'. This is the basic difference between the bush in Guiné and the bush in Cape Verde. All the latter group will, if we do our work properly, support the struggle. The large landowners certainly will be against the struggle. Of the small landowners, some will be for and some against, for they are comparable to the petty bourgeoisie: some for, others against and others undecided. Some are against because they think that we want to take the land and will abolish private property, and that group is against because it is still hoping. Some are for because they think that we shall take the land and there will be liberty, and they can turn their tiny plot into a large holding. Others are in doubt because they do not know what we want; they might gain something, they might lose, they are still more or less well off under the Portuguese, and they are hesitant.

But there are other contradictions: for example, in Guiné, there are ethnic groups, the so-called tribes, whom we call *races* in créole. We know how great the contradictions were between them in the past, and sometimes a not-so-distant past. In the thirties in Bissau, in the Bissalanca area, in Chão-dos-Manjacos. And we know that, for example, in Oio in 1954 (I was there myself) there was serious contradiction between Balanta and Oinca. All this because of old ideas, which persist in the heads of persons, but because of specific practical interests; either because they had stolen cattle, or had carried off young women, or were tilling land which did not belong to them, etc. And the Portuguese can and do exploit this to provoke conflicts between our folk. These are some of the contradictions we wanted to explain to you.

In Guiné and in Cape Verde our aim was to eliminate the contradictions in the best way possible, to raise everybody to unite around a common objective: to chase out the Portuguese colonialists.

And what about the context of Guiné and Cape Verde taken together? Is there any contradiction? Each one can think carefully and see. The contradiction there, or the seeming contradiction, was as follows: many colonial civil servants and staff in Guiné, and some district officers in Guiné, are Cape Verdians. Given that in Cape Verde education was more developed, there is more potential for Cape Verdians to gain posts than for the Guineans themselves. This might suggest that they (the Cape Verdians) are taking into their hands the interests of the people of Guiné. They are the ones who are benefiting. But if we look carefully, there are also Guineans in the same situation as Cape Verdians and there has never been any contradiction between these folk in the cities and our folk in the bush. It is in the city that we find contradiction. Contradiction between whom? Among Guinean descendants who would like to lead the life that the Cape Verdians had (as district officers, who are agents of the colonialists) against our people. Whereas in Cape Verde, the people are also exploited just as they are exploited in Guiné. And in some respects more harshly exploited in Cape Verde, with starvation and with the export of men as contract workers for S. Tomé and for Angola, almost like animals. So the contradiction which might exist between Guineans and Cape Verdians is a contradiction in the hunt for jobs, for good positions. For example, an individual who has primary school certificate or third year of secondary school in Guiné, sees a

Cape Verdian come along and take up a district officer's appointment; the latter eats chicken and goat, people doff their cap to him, etc., and the former has not yet risen so high. A certain resentment is born in him. But if we study the question closely, we see that the general tendency of this Guinean petty bourgeoisie is to coexist easily with the Cape Verdian petty bourgeoisie. The general tendency is for them to understand each other, alongside the Portuguese. And we have never seen in the bush, for example, any contradiction between Cape Verdians and Guineans. Nothing which can at all match the profound contradiction we have seen between certain ethnic groups from Guiné itself. Almost all of you can see this clearly.

So we, PAIGC, have not found such difficulties from the analytical point of view in the objective of our struggle for unity of Guiné and Cape Verde, as we have in the case of unity in Guiné and unity in Cape Verde. If we just take Guiné we see many internal contradictions. In Cape Verde, taking this case on its own, there are many contradictions. But taking them together, the contradictions are lessened. The contradiction is limited to that among the petty bourgeoisie, that is where there are some contradictions. And it is from this petty bourgeoisie that the opportunist groups arise who have fought PAIGC. Groups of opportunists who, in the first movement they launched, were already ministers of this and that, with a sense of careerism, appointments, nothing more.

Obviously for us the question of unity of Guiné and Cape Verde is not raised merely as our caprice. It is not because Cabral is the son of a Cape Verdian, but born in Bafata, that he has great love for the people of Guiné, but also great love for the people of Cape Verde. It has nothing to do with this, although it is true. I saw folk die of hunger in Cape Verde and I saw folk die from flogging in Guiné (with beatings, kicks, forced labour), you understand? This is the entire reason for my revolt. But the fundamental reason for the struggle for unity of Guiné and Cape Verde stems from the very nature of Guiné and Cape Verde. It is the interests themselves of Guiné and Cape Verde which lead us to this. Anyone who is not ignorant and who gives serious study to these questions, who has a deep knowledge of history, as much in regard to the ethnic groups in our land, in Guiné and Cape Verde, as to colonial history, such a person, if he is really interested in the advance of our people, must be in favour of the unity of Guiné and Cape Verde. But there is a further point in the potential for practical struggle for our land of Guiné and Cape Verde. Anyone who wants to struggle seriously, as PAIGC has struggled and is struggling, can understand one thing through analysis and through studying the question in depth. It is the following: struggle in Guiné would be impossible, if it were not jointly, united – in PAIGC; struggle in Cape Verde would be impossible, if it were not jointly, united – in PAIGC. Do you know what is the practical proof of this? For example, there is not movement which said, 'For us, the sons of Guiné alone', and which advanced. Do you know of one? There is no movement in Cape Verde for the sons of Cape Verde alone which advanced; there is none. This shows that our analysis was right and just, above all if we bear in mind the prospects as a viable political and economic entity in Africa, able in fact to achieve a new life. Obviously all those who struggle for African unity understand that we are a unique example of effective struggle for African unity (with Tanzania, which resulted from union of Tanganyika with Zanzibar). But there is no real difficulty in struggling for the unity of Guiné and Cape Verde, because by nature, by history, by geography, by economic tendency, by everything, even blood, Guiné and Cape Verde are one. Only an ignorant man does not know this.

The Portuguese knew this very well. Carreira, with all his abuses as a colonialist in Guiné, knew it well. But they pretend not to know so as to divide us. Their hope was that if Cape Verde took up the struggle, they would mobilize the Guineans to fight the worthless Cape Verdians who were in Guiné as district officers. If the Guineans took up the struggle, they would mobilize the Cape Verdians, in Guiné and in Cape Verde, for a hard fight against the sons of Guiné, to prevent them rising, to prevent them being free. Now our Party has given them a great shock, a tripping up. The greatest shock of their life for the Portuguese was this: in the first batch of folk who went to prison there were Guineans and Cape Verdians together. The Portuguese were stunned. And if you consider carefully, look at this: there are many folk in Bissau who could speak on the radio. Doesn't this strike you as odd? They could speak on the radio, to slang us, etc., they could produce good talks on the Portuguese radio, but no one does this. On the radio there are only Alfa Umaru, Malam Ndjai and I don't know who else, or perhaps some scoundrel who fled from the Republic of Guinea or from Senegal and went to speak in French in Bissau. Have you already seen the point? How is it that not one of our countrymen, whether from Guiné or from Cape Verde, who went to school and who knows enough to speak on the radio, would do this in our Guiné? There is no one because the Party long ago scored its blow. The Portuguese have lost confidence in these folk once and for all, and these folk too have lost confidence and do not become mixed up with the Portuguese, because they do not know what might happen. But the Portuguese not so long ago, a little after the beginning of armed struggle, were already declaring in Portuguese and even in créole: 'Sons of Guiné and Cape Verde, you are one, under the flag of Portugal'. Did you never hear that? But at the same time they were saying, in Mandinga, that the Cape Verdians were worthless. To see if they could still maintain a certain division. Today they are slowly giving this up. But from time to time they put an individual up to say: 'I am one hundred per cent Guinean, not the child of a foreigner like some who were born here.' To see if they can maintain a certain idea of division.

Similarly at the start of the struggle, they would say: 'Fula, it is with your help that we are going to win this war, because you are the best sons of

Guiné.' When they speak in Manjaco, they say something similar. They say that the Pepel are harming the Fula, that the Fula are harming the Pepel, to divide. But they have now seen that this serves no purpose. In our Party no one is divided, but on the contrary we are more united every day. Here there is neither Pepel, nor Fula, nor Mandinga, nor sons of the Cape Verdians, nothing like that. What we have is PAIGC and we are going forward. The Portuguese are desperate. So it is they themselves, for example, who in their reviews today, like the one called *Ultramar,* have long articles studying the question of Guiné and Cape Verde.[1] They write: 'Guiné and the Cape Verde Islands – their historical and demographic unity'. And do you know who wrote that article? Carreira. Because in fact he does know about many questions of history. And in this article he collected all the documents in the Portuguese archives and studied where the sons of Guiné went when they were sent to Cape Verde. To Santiago? – Balanta, Mandinga, Beafada, etc. To S. Vincente? – went Fula, etc. With reports, on their arrival, etc. At the beginning the Portuguese were opposed to this, but they know that we are the same folk, in Guiné and in Cape Verde.

This means the same from the viewpoint of historical knowledge, of the reality of our life in the past, of understanding of the interests of our people and of Africa, and from the viewpoint of the strategy of stuggle. Anyone who takes the struggle seriously knows this. There is no independence for Guiné without the independence of Cape Verde. Nor is there independence for the Republic of Guinea, for Senegal or for Mauritania, if they want to be treated seriously as countries, without Cape Verde being independent. There is none. Only someone who understands nothing about strategy can think that this part of Africa can be independent with Cape Verde occupied by colonialists. It is impossible. The converse is true. Cape Verde cannot have real independence without the independence of Guiné and without the real independence of Africa. Anyone who places the interests of his people above his personal interests – the serious analysis of questions above any whims or ambitions – can reach only one conclusion. It is the following: the finest thing PAIGC did, that the group who formed PAIGC did, was to establish as the fundamental basis – unity and struggle: unity in Guiné, unity in Cape Verde and unity of Guiné and Cape Verde.

Anyone who has not yet seen this will see it later. But many Africans have already begun to understand. Many of the forces friendly to us have begun to see it, but our enemies as well. The concern of the imperialists today is the following: 'Will Cabral accept or not the independence of Guiné without Cape Verde?' That is their great concern. Will PAIGC accept or not the independence of Guiné without Cape Verde? That is what the imperialists want to know and they even asked me. I replied to one of them: 'Tell the

[1]António Carreira, 'A Guiné e as Ilhas de Cabo Verde: A sua unidade histórica e populacional', *Ultramar,* 23, 1968

Portuguese to ask, you are not Portuguese.' For they know very well the significance of our entirety. One day an African leader said to us: 'You are bright.' We asked him how and he said: 'I know your folk in Guiné and your folk in Cape Verde. If you should really succeed in doing what you are doing, despite being a mini-state, you will be a powerful country within Africa.' Let us see, we replied.

So let us go forward, strengthened by the certainty that we are right. The creation of PAIGC, on the basis which I have just outlined, has been the greatest achievement of our people towards the conquest of freedom and the building of their progress and happiness in Guiné and Cape Verde.

5. To start out from the reality of our land – to be realists

The reality

Another question we can proceed to discuss is the following principle of our Party:*we advance towards the struggle secure in the reality of our land (with our feet planted on the ground).* This means, as we see it, that it is impossible to wage a struggle under our conditions, it is impossible to struggle effectively for the independence of a people, it is impossible to establish effective armed struggle such as we have to establish in our land, unless we really know our reality and unless we really start out from that reality to wage the struggle.

What is our reality?

Our reality, like all other realities, has positive aspects and negative aspects, has strengths and weaknesses.

Wherever our head might be, our feet are planted on the ground in our land of Guiné and Cape Verde, in the specific reality of our land. This is the key factor that can guide the work of our Party.

There are those in the world who take the view that reality depends on the way in which man interprets it. For such, reality – things seen, touched, felt, the world around each human being – are the consequence of what man has in his head. There are others who take the view that reality exists and that man forms part of reality. It is not what he has in his head that defines reality, but reality itself that defines man. Man is part of reality, man is within reality and it is not what he has in his head that defines reality. On the contrary, reality itself under which the man lives is what defines the things man has in his head.

You may ask: what is our position in PAIGC in respect to these two views? Our view is the following: man is part of reality, reality exists independently of man's will. To the extent to which he acquires consciousness of reality, to the extent in which reality influences his consciousness, or creates his consciousness, man can acquire the potential to transform reality, little by little. This is our view, let us say the principle of our Party on relations between man and reality.

A very important aspect of a national liberation struggle is that those who lead the struggle must never confuse what they have in their head with reality. On the contrary, anyone who leads a national liberation struggle must have many things in his head, and more each day (from the starting point of the particular reality of his land, and of the reality of other lands), but he must weigh up and make plans which respect reality and not what he has in his head. This is very important. Failure to respect it has created many difficulties in the peoples' liberation struggle, mainly in Africa.

I may have my own opinion on various matters, on the way to organize the struggle, to organize a Party – an opinion I formed, for example, in Europe, in Asia, or even perhaps in other African countries, from books and documents I have read, or because of someone who influenced me. But I cannot presume to organize a Party, to organize a struggle, in accordance with what I have in my head. It must be in accordance with the specific reality of the land.

We can give many examples. Obviously we cannot presume, for example, to organize our Party on the lines of parties in France or any other country in Europe, or even in Asia, using the same form of Party. We began a little like that but gradually we had to change to adapt to the specific reality of our land. A further example: at the start of our struggle, we were convinced that if we were to mobilize the workers in Bissau, Bolama and Bafata to go on strike, to demonstrate in the streets, to challenge the administration, the Portuguese would change and would grant us independence. But it is not true. In the first place, the workers in our land do not have the same strength as in other lands. Their strength is not so great from the economic point of view, because the great economic strength in our land lies basically in the countryside. But it was almost impossible to have strikes in the countryside, given the conditions of our people's political situation, political awareness, and even their immediate interests. It was impossible to ask our people to halt cultivation of those items the colonialists were exploiting. Moreover, the Portuguese, our colonialist enemy, are not like us who show a measure of respect for certain things. The Portuguese responded to strikes and demonstrations by falling upon us to kill everyone, to finish everything off.

So we had to adapt our struggle to different conditions, to our land, and could not do as was done in other lands.

And many other things show clearly that it is essential to bear in mind the *specific reality* of the land in waging the struggle. Even in the question of mobilization and training, etc., we had to look at the problem one way in Guiné and another way in Cape Verde, Because in the case of Guiné, we can be temporarily in the Republic of Guinea or in Senegal, coming and going. For Cape Verde it is already more difficult, because it lies in the middle of sea. We had to devise another procedure to give better security to the struggle, so that there should not be the need for much to-ing and fro-ing. And in the evolution of the struggle, later on, when we shall begin armed struggle in Cape Verde, it has to be armed struggle waged a little differently from that in Guiné. Because we cannot face the difficulty as, for example, in 1962 in our land. Our comrades were in great danger in the bush – we did not yet have weapons – and we gave orders for all the cadres to leave. And more than two hundred cadres went out to avoid serious calamity. Later we went in again and we advanced with the struggle. In Cape Verde we cannot do this, cannot pull many folk out rapidly.

We have to consider in each specific case the specific reality. Even in Guiné, for example, we made a serious mistake in our analysis before the struggle. We had given a fair amount of attention to the living conditions of the Balanta people, the Fula, the Mandinga, the Pepel. . . and their attitude to the struggle. We had given attention to the petty bourgeoisie, salaried workers, shop staff, port workers and their attitude to the struggle, descendents of Cape Verdians and their attitude to the struggle. We had given attention to all this, but we made a serious mistake. Namely that we did not really take into consideration the position of the traditional chiefs, of the notables (Fula, Manjaco), above all those two. We did not really take them into consideration, because we started out from the following principle: they (their forbears) had earlier struggled against the Portuguese, and were defeated, so they must have the will to struggle once again. It was an error; we were mistaken.

We must consider that we were learning how to wage struggle in step as we were advancing (on the path). The struggle on the coastline of our land is one thing: among the Manjaco it is another; in Oio it has to be different again. There are many differences. Take for example the Mandinga elders, we have to understand the way to deal with them, not the same way as we treat the Balanta elders. But in Gabu we had to wage the struggle in a completely different way. If we compare the struggle in Gabu with the struggle in the South of our land, they are two struggles as if it were a matter of two different lands.

Realism is essential, to consider the specific reality. Even in respect of certain things which are gradually advancing. At the start, the men did not want meetings with women. We did not force the pace, while in some areas women soon came to the meetings without difficulties. We must be aware of reality, not only of the general reality of our land, but also of the particular realities of every thing, so as to be able to guide the struggle correctly. It is only the responsible officials or leaders who take this sense of reality into consideration (who do not think that truth is what they have in their head, but that truth is what is outside their head), who can properly guide their work as militants, as responsible officials, in a struggle like ours. Unhappily, we must acknowledge that many comrades have taken on responsibilities in this struggle without considering this factor, although we have always spoken about it.

But reality never exists in isolation. For example, our comrade Manuel Nandingna is a reality, is a real fact. But he cannot exist alone, he alone is nothing; a reality is never isolated from other realities. No matter what reality we consider in the world or in life, however great or small, it always forms part of another reality, is integrated in another reality, is affected by other realities, which in turn have an effect in or on other realities. So our land of Guiné and Cape Verde, and our struggle, form part of a greater reality that is affected by and affects other realities in the world. For example, if we consider the reality of Guiné and the reality of Cape Verde, immediately there is a greater reality, Guiné and Cape Verde. But the latter reality is within the reality of West Africa, with our two closest neighbouring countries. We can look a little wider, with our two neighbouring countries first, then with West Africa, and with the reality of the whole of Africa, and with the reality of the world, although there might be other realities between these.

This means that our own reality is at the centre of a complex reality, but it is the former that most concerns us. For others it would not be the same, it would be at some other focus, and theirs would be the central reality. But even if we think of ours at the centre, our reality is not isolated, is not on its own. In many of the things we have to do, we have first to realize that we are integrated with other realities. This is very important for us not to make mistakes.

Let us imagine the position of a unit of our army at some point. It can never operate as if it were an isolated reality, but has always to operate as integrated in a PAIGC army, integrated in the struggle of the people of Guiné and Cape Verde. If it operates like this, it is operating correctly; if it does not operate like this, it is operating badly. A political commissar in Quinara, for example, or somewhere else, S. João, for example, has always to operate as integrated in Quinara, but not only in Quinara, in the South, in the whole of the South, and not only there, in the whole of Guiné, and not only there, in Guiné and Cape Verde together. We must at all times see the part and the whole. Only in this way can we operate correctly. Unhappily the tendency of many comrades is to treat their reality as the only reality there is, forgetting the rest. To such an extent that we can find, for example, comrades in a given area who know that the comrades in another area do not have any ammunition and the former are not able to mobilize their folk to deliver ammunition. This shows our failure of awareness in seeing our own reality, and how we are integrated in a greater reality, that we ourselves have created but have not yet fully absorbed into our awareness.

Furthermore we must bear in mind the reality of others. Within our land the work of a political commissar may be very good, in Sara let us imagine. But if the political work is not good in Oio, in Biambi, or in the Bafata area, the work in Sara does not take us very far. A unit of our army, in Canchungo, or the Nhacra area, let us imagine, can be struggling quite well, attacking the Portuguese every day. But if in other areas other units of our army are not struggling quite well, the sacrifice and the victories of Nhacra or Canchungo do not have their due value. But we are faced with still more: if the struggle in Guiné were to go well forward, but the struggle in Cape Verde did not go forward at all, sooner or later we should seriously prejudice the struggle in Guiné. It suffices to mention the following from the strategic point of view: there can be no peace in Guiné if the Portuguese have air bases in Cape Verde; it is impossible. If we were to liberate Guiné totally, for example, the Portuguese could bombard us with air bases installed in Cape Verde. They could procure many more aircraft, and South Africa, which has interests in Cape Verde, could supply them on a grand scale. We have to study the potential for taking the two realities forward simultaneously as a joint reality, a single reality.

But if we in Guiné and Cape Verde were to struggle hard, and the peoples of Angola and Mozambique did not struggle at all, and if perhaps the Portuguese could withdraw all their troops from Angola and Mozambique and send them to our land, I do not know when we would win our independence, as the Portuguese would stay on in all our villages. They would be so numerous that they could occupy all the villages and cultivate the rice. We are seeing, therefore, that the reality of our struggle forms part of the struggle of the Portuguese colonies, whether we like it or not. It is not a question of wishing. It was not I who decided this, nor the Political Bureau of the Party, nor any of you who decided it. Whether we like it or not, it is so. This is the strength of reality. To sum up: we must be aware of this, must work so that we can follow the path together, as it should be. It is the only explanation of the policy of our Party, the commitment of our Party to CONCP, that is the group of movements in the Portuguese colonies, in their entirety. Because we know what the reality is. We even had a strong influence on the creation of FRELIMO, the Mozambican movement, because it was essential and urgent to struggle in Mozambique.

But we might struggle in all the Portuguese colonies even to the point of winning our independence, and if racism were to continue in South Africa, with the colonialists still ruling, directly or indirectly, in many African lands, we could not have confidence in real independence in Africa. Sooner or later calamity would strike again. So we form part of a specific reality, namely Africa struggling against imperialism, against racism and against colonialism. If we do not bear this in mind, we could make many mistakes.

It is the same thing for our land facing the Republic of Guinea and Senegal, with Cape Verde before them in the middle of the sea, and in turn Cape Verde facing Mauritania, Senegal and Guiné. We constitute a whole whose parts are interdependent. For example, our struggle depends heavily on the Republic of Guinea and on Senegal. From the start we realized how important the Republic of Guinea and Senegal were for us. We guided our whole struggle in the direction of going forward with them, in creating favourable conditions to take advantage of the consequences of this reality. But we must be aware of the following: both the Republic of Guinea and Senegal are aware that our reality is also important for their reality, and on this awareness depends whether they may give more or less aid. For each of them must think: who will rule that land tomorrow? Is this to our advantage or against our interest? It is all one question. But the Portuguese too have a clear conception of this. Just a few days ago I went to Mauritania. All the radio stations of the world reported that I had talks with President Ould Daddah, and that I was very cordially received, etc. Immediately the Portuguese unleashed a campaign on their radio station, and South Africa for its part also unleashed a campaign, to the effect that I went to Mauritania to establish a base for an attack on Cape Verde. And they have been saying for a long time that our aim is to damage the Atlantic treaty. So you see how all the realities are related. But all of us, in Africa, form part of one reality — in the world — which has all the difficulties with which you are familiar. Whether we like it or not, we are involved in these difficulties.

Today man walks on the moon, collecting pieces of the moon's soil to bring back to earth. It might seem that this has nothing to do with us, the sons of Guiné and Cape Verde. We still have our feet in the mud to drive the Portuguese from our land. But the moon-walk is of great importance for our cause tomorrow, and if we were not in this difficult struggle, we ought to hold a great celebration of the fact that man has reached the moon. This is of great significance for the future of mankind, of our land, of this planet where we live.

The reality of others therefore concerns us; the experiences of others too. If I knew that one of you went out along a given path, was tripped on all sides and bruised and arrived badly hurt, and then I had to go along the same path, I should have to be careful; someone already knows the reality of this path and I know of his experience.

If there were another, better path, I would try to follow it, but if there were not, then I would have to feel my way with all the care possible, crawling on the ground if need be. The experience of others is highly significant for someone undergoing any experience. The reality of others is highly significant for each one's reality. Many folk do not understand this, and grasp their reality with the passion that they are going to invent everything: 'I do not want to do the same as others have done, nothing that others have done.' This is a sign of great ignorance. If we want to do something in reality, we must see who has already done the same, who has done something similar, and who has done something opposite, so that we can learn something from their experience. It is not to copy completely, because every reality has its own questions and its own answers for these questions. But there are many things which belong to many realities jointly. It is essential that the experience of others benefits us. We must be able to derive from everyone's experience what we can adapt to our conditions, to avoid unnecessary efforts and sacrifices. This is very important. Obviously it is the same thing with our struggle. A good political commissar is working, for example, and another political commissar is by his side, but the latter does not take an interest in the work of the former, does not try to learn from his experience, does not try to understand why the other is working well. He turns his back and goes off alone to do his work. A commander is in an area, other commanders, even of lower rank than his, are in the same area, but the latter are not able to exchange views with the former, not able to ask him how to solve certain difficulties, on the basis of his greater experience, his longer service in the struggle. They do not want to know. These men are destroying the struggle. Obviously in a struggle like ours, it is essential to link reality with the development of the struggle. Yesterday we spoke a fair amount about certain contradictions on the social plane of our land, both in Guiné and in Cape Verde.

For us to develop our struggle we must examine the geographical reality of our land, its historical reality, its ethnic reality, that is of *races* and cultures, and the cultural, social and economic reality. And all this is incorporated in the greater reality of our land in struggle, which is the political reality, namely: we are under Portuguese colonial domination in Guiné and in Cape Verde.

Geographical reality

You know in broad terms the geographical reality of our land. We are a tiny territory of about 40 000 square kilometres, counting Guiné and Cape Verde, with Guiné nine times the size of Cape Verde – ten islands – on the west coast of Africa, as an enclave between two African countries (the Republic of Guinea and Senegal) and Cape Verde, about 400 miles off shore. So our reality is that we have one part on the mainland and one part insular, or islands, comprising the Bijagos islets and the Cape Verde islands, making in all more than a hundred islands and islets.

Even today many folk have not perhaps taken in the significance this has, but it is highly significant in all aspects of our land – from the defence of our land to the economy, wealth and strength of our land. Our geographical reality is further that Guiné in almost its entirety has no mountain, no high point (there are merely some hills in the environs of Boé, with a maximum height of 300 metres) and that Cape Verde is made up of volcanic and mountainous islands. Even in this aspect we see that the one complements the other. One land has no mountains and the other is all mountains. This is also of great significance not only for the economy but also for the social and cultural life, etc., that we find in our people's circumstances.

In Guiné the land is cut by tongues of the sea that we call rivers, but which at bottom are not rivers. Farim is only a river near Candjambari. Geba is only a river from Bambadinca onwards, and even near Bambadinca the water is sometimes salt. Mansoa is only a river after Mansoa town, towards Sara, near Caroala. Buba is in no sense a river because until we reach dry land there is only salt water. Cumbidja and Tombali are entirely tongues of the sea, except for the upper reach with a little bit of fresh water in the rainy season, particularly the Bedanda river which draws fresh water from the Balana. The only genuine river in our land is the Corubal. This is a highly significant reality for us because if on the one hand we have many ports though which to enter our land in boats, we can on the other hand see the danger which this presents for us. If our land were entirely closed off, with all the twists and turns entailed by this struggle, the Portuguese would already have become desperate because their barracks would be without food. But as they have boats and our militants do not attack the boats sufficiently, they can use the tongues of the sea to take food and equipment to their barracks in the interior.

But from the economic point of view, for example, it is good and useful to have navigable rivers or tongues of the sea. That is from the point of view of the future of our land. For the struggle itself we can see how important it is for us to bear all these things in mind to develop our struggle. At the start of the struggle it was very helpful that there were many rivers in our land, many tongues of the sea, many streams, etc., for we isolated ourselves, could always defend ourselves from the Portuguese, cause them difficulties on swampy ground, make them cross rivers, etc. Today the difficulty is rather more on our side. If Bissau were on the mainland, if there were no island of Bissau, if it were not for the Corubal, if the river Mansoa were not on the other side, we should already have been inside Bissau. We could fire on Bissau every day as we did at Mansoa, for example. But in this respect geography favours the Portuguese, as the river Buba favours the Portuguese who make good use of it for their boats. On the Farim it is the same. You see therefore the significance attached to this simple aspect of geographical reality.

Anyone who has read books about guerrilla warfare will certainly remember the assertion that the major physical feature conducive to guerrilla warfare in a terrain is the mountains. But in Guiné there are no mountains. If we did not attach importance to our own reality, to put it under analysis and draw conclusions on how to operate, we should have said that it is impossible to wage guerrilla warfare in Guiné because there are no mountains. Cape Verde has mountains, this is significant, but what kind of mountains? It is essential to take this into account, and furthermore that mountains alone do not suffice. It is not the mountains which open fire; the people must be mobilized. In Guiné we have, for example, the Bijagos islands. Why is it that we did not start the struggle in the Bijagos islands but began on the other side, on dry land? Because of another reality, the economic reality.

In Cape Verde we face a serious difficulty. If Cape Verde were a single island, like Cyprus, or like Cuba, it would be easier, but there are ten islands. So we have to consider in which of the islands are we going to start armed struggle, if it is going to be effective? The same goes for mobilization: in which island or islands should we begin mobilizing? All this was and is highly relevant. We had the difficulties of communications from where we are to the islands, between the islands, etc. All this is a consequence of the geographical reality of our land.

Economic reality

Another reality we have to consider is economic reality. Our principal economic reality is that we are Portuguese colonies, because when all is said and done the political situation is a consequence of the economic situation.

We, in Guiné and Cape Verde, are a people exploited by Portuguese colonialists, our labour is exploited by Portuguese colonialists. This is what is significant. This is the economic reality.

But are we a developed country? No. We are economically backward, with scarcely any development, in Guiné or Cape Verde. There is no real industry, agriculture is backward, our agriculture belongs to the age of our grandparents. The wealth of our land was drained off, above all man's labour. But the Portuguese did nothing to develop any resource in our land, absolutely nothing. Our ports are worthless, both in Bissau and in S. Vicente. They could have made good ports, but they merely made some mooring quays which are worthless. When we look at Dakar's port, or Conakry's port, which are good ports, or better still those of Abidjan, and of Lagos, in Nigeria, we can see how the French and the British built big ports, where twenty or so ships can moor. And then we see how much time the Portuguese wasted in teasing us, tinkering and playing with us. They did nothing for our land.

So that is our economic reality and, for peace or war, we in Guiné and Cape Verde are an economically backward people, whose principal means of livelihood is agriculture. Tilling the soil for subsistence food, and not always reaching subsistence level, as in Cape Verde, for example. Even in Guiné in some areas, if there is not much rain, there are always shortages at least until the *fundo* is ripe. The Portuguese have been here for so many years and the situation has remained static, economically backward. We have no real industry to speak of, either in Guiné or Cape Verde. In Guiné we have a so-called mini-plant for pressing oil from rice shelling. This is not a factory, it is no more than a great 'pestle'. We have a mini-plant for treating rubber (tappings), and a small fishmeal factory in Bijagos. In Cape Verde, there are three fish-packing stations, where the Portuguese work for as long as they feel like it, fill their pockets with money, close down the factory and go away to relax. And just to give you some idea of the shamelessness of the Portuguese, I recall, for example, how when I was at secondary school, my mother went to Cape Verde and took a job at the fish-packing station, because she made nothing from sewing. And do you know how much she earned per hour? Fifty cents an hour. If there were a lot of fish, she might work eight hours a day, earning four pesos (escudos). But if fish were scarce (and she had to walk a long way to reach the factory), she would work for one hour and earn fifty cents.

So, a backward economy; this has a strong bearing on the war. You see: we are a people who do not have factories, we cannot capture factories from the Portuguese to start manufacturing something. Today we have vast liberated areas; if there were factories there, it would be useful. Perhaps we could make cloth, perhaps we could make soap on a proper scale, instead of comrade Vasco's tiny soap bars. We could manufacture other things if we had mines. Then there would be many more folk wanting to help us, more than those who now help us. Friends and enemies would try to help us if we had mines in operation, with the promise of a lot of bauxite, a lot of petrol. Many of them would come rushing. And if the petrol in our land had already begun to be exported, perhaps even Standard Oil would be sympathetic to us against the Portuguese. Perhaps the American government would be sympathetic to us against the Portuguese. Perhaps it would even have the courage to say to the Portuguese: 'Either you stop and give independence to Guiné now, or we shall withdraw all our aid to you, and attack you in the United Nations.' And why? Out of their own interests. But as our land has nothing developed, they think of us as a corridor between the Republics of Guinea and Senegal, a simple passageway.

But as I have said, the backwardness of our economy has a bearing on the war situation, and so does our unfamiliarity with our resources. For example, it would be a lot different if our people already had enough experience in iron casting to manufacture weapons. There are peoples who are struggling and while some fight at the front others are making weapons in the rearguard. We cannot do this; we can only make muskets, but muskets are ineffective. If it is only with muskets that we are going to win the war against the Portuguese, or against any colonialist, our struggle will be very long indeed.

But if we had a developed economy, this would mean that our people would also be culturally stronger in the modern perspective, would have more schools, more secondary schools, and would be able to handle mortars, artillery and even aircraft. The commanders would be more capable of understanding all the questions of strategy and tactics and would all know how to read maps. We see, therefore, the significance of having to struggle in an economically backward country.

Social reality

All of you know what the social reality of our land is, the disastrous consequence of colonialist exploitation. But let us not put all the blame on the colonialists. There is also exploitation of our folk by our own folk. You saw this yesterday when I spoke to you about the social structure of our land. We are in fact exploited by colonialists in our land of Guiné and Cape Verde. In trade in Cape Verde and in Guiné it is always the colonialists who profit most to the last, because in Cape Verde, for example, there is no commercial enterprise which is not tied to an enterprise in Portugal. Likewise in Guiné, the monopoly on all our trade (not ours, their trade) belonged to *Gouveia* and *Ultramarina*, tied to the banks, all Portuguese. But we must tell the truth. Many of the Cape Verdian people suffered because of exploitation by landowners, themselves Cape Verdians. Similarly in Guiné, part of the great suffering of our people was at the hands of our own folk. We must not at all forget this, so that we shall know what to do in the future.

This therefore is the specific reality. In Cape Verde our population endure wretchedness. In years of heavy rains there is abundance, one eats well, fills the belly and can even stretch out and relax a little; but for most of the time when there are insufficient rains, there is famine. During the last fifty years more people have died from starvation in Cape Verde than the population today. Others were contracted for S. Tomé and transported like animals in the holds (those who died were thrown into the sea), some were sent to Angola. In Guiné, as you know, the whole range of colonialist exploitation existed: forced labour on the roads, all kinds of outrages, abuses humiliations. And Portuguese doctors who studied the situation in Cape Verde said that they came away with one certainty, the certainty in their scientific opinion, that the whole population showed symptoms of malnutrition. If it was not a question of total starvation, it was a case of specific starvation, meaning a lack of certain elements which are essential to the well-being of the human body. This specific starvation also exists in Guiné. In Guiné nearly everyone has malaria; if we were now to make tests on all the comrades present here, we would find that nearly all have intestinal worms. There is widespread leprosy, diseases of all kinds.

Social disaster for our people, which makes us a weak people from the scientific and sanitary point of view. A man who lives almost exclusively on rice cannot have the same resistance as a man who eats rice, meat, milk, eggs etc. It is true that when a foreigner comes to our land and goes marching with our comrades in the bush he lags behind. That is something else. But from the point of view of fitness, we know that a person in our land who is aged thirty has already begun to age. In our land it is unusual to come across old men with a beard and white hair. The average life-span in our land of Guiné and Cape Verde is thirty years. Our life expectancy is thirty years: anyone who lives beyond the thirties is lucky. Now life expectancy in other lands where one eats well, drinks well (I do not mean getting drunk) as one should, is sixty and sixty-seven years and each year grows higher. On any count it is more agreeable. If someone is born with the certainty that he is going to live for seventy years, he has time to make something of it. But what can one do in thirty years? The difference is due to inadequate diet, hygiene and health care and to wretched living conditions. That is the social condition of our land: abuses by the Portuguese, abuses by some sons of our land who misuse others, wretchedness, diseases, famine, and on top of all that a short life-span. A difficult situation, very difficult.

Cultural reality

From the cultural point of view, it is true that conditions in Cape Verde are a shade better than in Guiné. Given the conditions under which the population developed, the question of being or not being an *indigenous inhabitant* never arose, so in theory any Cape Verdian child can go to school (the official school). It is no less true that overall there are far fewer schools than in Guiné.

There are some things that you do not know and which might mislead you. It is true that in Cape Verde more folk learned to read and write than in Guiné under the colonial system. But the level of illiteracy in Cape Verde, contrary to the boast of any Cape Verdian who thinks he knows it all, is 85 per cent. The Portuguese liked to boast that in Cape Verde there were no illiterates. This is a lie! When I went there for holidays in 1949, I made some tests of those who could read. There were folk who had gained primary school certificates (some four or five years before) in the bush, in Godim or in Santa Catarina, for example, to whom I would give the newspaper to read, but they did not know what they were reading. There are also illiterates who can pick out the letters. There are many such folk in the world, even some doctors. But we must shed many illusions.

In Guiné 99 per cent of the population could not go to school. Schooling was exclusively for the assimilated, the children of the assimilated – you know the whole story, I am not going to tell it again. But it was a disaster that the Portuguese caused in our land, by not allowing our children to advance, to learn, to understand the reality of our life, our land, our society, to understand the reality of Africa and the modern world. This is a great obstacle, an enormous difficulty for the development of our struggle. Only today I told you that the Fula people migrated across Africa, as did the Mandinga people, as it happens, though many of you did not know, nor do many comrades. A Beafada who is called Malam something or other, for example, does not know that in ancient times Malam, Braima and suchlike were not Beafada names. And what happened with the Beafada happens to many folk of our land. Take for example, Vasco Salvador Correia. Formerly his folk would not be called Vasco, nor Salvador, still less Correia. It means that the Mandinga in dominating the peoples of our land practised assimilation (the Portuguese were not the first to want to *assimilate* in our land) and so those dominated began to adopt Mandinga names. Likewise the Mandinga of today did not have the same names in that epoch. The ancient names of the Fula were not Mamadu or anything of the sort. All this is borrowed from Arabic. Mamadu means Mohamed, Iussufe means Joseph, Mariama is Mary, semitic names.

The cultural reality of our land in Cape Verde (raising now the question of the colonialists who did not allow us much advance) is the consequence of the fact that the colonialists allowed Cape Verdians to study, to the extent that they needed to train folk as agents of colonialism, as they had used Indians. Just as the British used Indians in colonization and the French used Dahomeyans, so the Portuguese too used Cape Verdians, by teaching a certain proportion. But at a certain stage they closed the path once and for all; no more than a certain number of primary schools, no more than one secondary school; one secondary school which moreover Vieira Machado, the then Minister for 'Overseas', wanted to change into a training centre for fishermen and carpenters, just when I was about to begin secondary school. I waited three months without going to classes at secondary school, because they had closed it. For them what they had done was enough, no more was needed. From then on only training centres for fishermen and carpenters. The population rose and protested, and the secondary school began operating once more.

But now the reality of our own cultural situation in Cape Verde is the following: it is the transfer of African cultural reality to the islands. Then came contact between this African culture with other cultures from outside, from Portugal and elsewhere. Many folk think of Cape Verde as Praia or S. Vincente. But anyone who knows the bush in Cape Verde feels in Cape Verde an African reality as palpable as any other fragment of Africa. The culture of the Cape Verde people is quintessentially African: in beliefs it is identical – in Santiago there is the *polon* which some still regard as a sacred tree. The *polon* is not common because of the many droughts. But those which still exist are sacrosanct. There is moreover *morundade* sorcery. 'Spirits' which walk at night, flying creatures, who make up an interpretation on life's reality which almost totally matches that in Africa – not to speak of the casting of spells.

Cape Verde was a melting pot of various ethnic groups and there was a fusion of their cultures; but until the 1940s, for example, some distinct groups retained some of their own characteristics. For instance groups who were settled around Praia in Santiago retained the word *tabanca* for the village and their festivals were of a given kind, while elsewhere, in Achada Santo Antonio, for example the village was of another type, and different again for the folk of Santa Catarina, Picos, etc.

In Guiné, the culture of our people is the product of many African cultures: each ethnic group has its own culture, but they all share a common base, in their world view and their relations in society. And we know that although there are Moslem populations, at bottom they are also animists, like the Balanta and others. They believe in Allah, but also believe in the *iram* spirit and in sorcerers. They have the Koran but an amulet on their arm and other things. And the success of Islam in our land, as in Africa in general, is that Islam is able to understand this, to tolerate the culture of others, whereas the Catholics want to put a quick finish to all this and have only belief in the Virgin Mary, Our Lady of Fatima and in God and Our Lord Jesus Christ.

This is the cultural reality of our land. But we must consider our culture carefully; it is dictated by our economic condition, by our situation of economic underdevelopment. We must enjoy our African culture, we must cherish it, our dances, our songs, our style of making statues, canoes, our cloths. All this is magnificent, but if we rely only on our cloths to clothe all our folk, we are wrong. We have to be realists. Our land is very beautiful, but if we do not struggle to change our land, we are wrong.

There are many folk who think that being African is being able to sit on the ground and eat with one's hand. Yes, this is certainly African, but all the peoples of the world have gone through the stage of sitting on the ground and eating with one's hand. There are many folk who think that it is only Africans who eat with their hands. No, all the Arabs in North Africa do it. But even before they were Africans, before they came to Africa (they came from the East to Africa), they used to eat with their hands and seated on the ground. We must be aware of our things, we must respect those things of value, which are useful for the future of our land, for the advancement of our people.

No one should think that he is more African than another, even than some white man who defends the interests of Africa, merely because he is today more adept at eating with his hand, rolling rice into a ball and putting it into his mouth. The Portuguese, when they were still Visigoths, or the Swedish, who give us aid today, when they were still Vikings, could also eat with their hands.

If you see a film about the Vikings of olden days, you can see them with great horns on their heads and amulets on their arms, setting off for war. And they would not set off for war without their great horns on the head. No one should think that to be African one must wear horns on one's chest and an amulet round one's waist. Such persons are individuals who have not yet properly understood the relationship between man and nature. The Portuguese did the same, the French did it when they were Franks, Normans, etc. The English did it when they were Angles and Saxons, voyaging across the sea in canoes, great canoes like those of the Bijagos.

We must have the courage to state this clearly. No one should think that the culture of Africa, what is really African and so must be preserved for all time, for us to be Africans, is our weakness in the face of nature. Any people in the world, of whatever status, has gone through the stage of these weaknesses, or has to go through them. There are folk who have not reached it: they spend their lives climbing trees, eating and sleeping, nothing more yet. And then what myths they still believe! We should not persuade ourselves that to be African is believing that lightning is the fury of the deity (God is feeling angry). We cannot believe that to be African is to think that man has no mastery over the flooding of rivers. Anyone who leads a struggle like ours, who bears responsibility in a struggle like ours, has to understand gradually what concrete reality is.

Our struggle is based on our culture, because culture is the fruit of history and it is a strength. But our culture is filled with weakness in the face of nature. It is essential to know this. And we could point out further, for example, that certain of our dances represent relationships of man to the forest: folk appear clothed in straw, in the shape of birds, and others like great birds, with a huge beak, and folk run in fear. We can do many such dances, but we have to go beyond this, we cannot merely stop there. We can preserve the memory of all these things, to develop our art and our culture which we display to others. But as we have already gone beyond this, we know that it is we who rule in the forest, in the bush, we, human beings, and not any animal or spirit lurking there. This is very important. But this is the cultural reality of our land. Various comrades who are sitting here have an amulet at their waist, in the belief that this will allow them to escape Portuguese bullets. But not one of you can say to me that not one of the comrades who have already died in our struggle had an amulet at his waist. They all had them! It is just that in our struggle we have to respect this, we have to respect this because we start out from reality. We cannot in the least order the comrades to tear off the amulet, or we would be treating our comrades as the Germans would. Many years ago, the Germans would not go to war without an amulet. Even today there are some who carry an ikon of Our Lady of Fatima inside a small book; it is their amulet. The Bible is their amulet and before beginning battles they cross themselves. The Portuguese come along with a great cross on their chest and at the moment of beginning the battle, they kiss it; it is their amulet. And there are still some who believe in our amulets.

This is a question of our cultural level in relation to the specific reality of war. We accept it, but no one should think that the leadership of the struggle believes that if we wear an amulet at the waist we shall not die. We shall not die in the war if we do not wage the war, or if we do not attack from a position of weakness. If we make mistakes, if we are in a position of weakness, we shall die for sure, there is no getting away from it. You can tell me a whole series of tales you have in your head: 'Cabral doesn't know. We have seen occasions when it was the amulet which spared the comrades from death, the bullets were coming and turned back in ricochet.' You can tell me this, but I live in hopes that the children of our children, when they hear of this, will be happy that PAIGC was able to wage the struggle in accordance with the reality of their land. But they will have to say: 'Our fathers fought hard, but they had some funny ideas.' This discussion may be premature, I am talking about the future, but I feel sure that the majority understand what I am saying and that I am right.

The amulet is characteristic of Africa. Even lawyers I know in other African countries go about decked with their amulet at the waist and, when they are going to plead cases at court, put on a big amulet: 'Never know when I might win with this.' Even some comrades from another Portuguese colony, because our struggle was making good progress, sent to ask us if there was some lucky charm which we could send them too.

I merely call the comrades' attention to the fact that they should see this as a strength and as a weakness. It is a strength, because a comrade who puts on his amulet believes in something other than the words of the Party and we cannot overlook that he feels more courageous. It is a weakness because in his trustfulness he could make many mistakes.

There were cases of our comrades dying in the following way. An aircraft arrives, everyone dives for the ground, the aircraft bombards but nothing happens. Suddenly a comrade remembers that he does not have his amulet with him; he stands up, runs to his hut and grabs the amulet; on his return he is machine-gunned and dies with the amulet in his hand. Perhaps some of you know of similar cases. But how many of you can think this: what foolishness this is, how can it be?

The fact of the matter is that our struggle has its strong face and its weak face. Many of us believed that we should not install ourselves in certain bush areas because they belonged to the *iram* spirit. But today, thanks to many *iram* spirits of our land, our folk understood, and even the *iram* understood, that the bush belongs to man and no one is afraid of the bush any more. We are even well established in the Cobiana bush, the more so because that *iram* spirit is a nationalist. It 'said' openly that the Portuguese had to go away, had no right to be in our land.

But you must understand that all this is also an obstacle to the struggle. At one time many comrades who had taken up this life and were solid – my comrades whom I hold in high regard and who had spent a long time with me – if they were told by me: 'Go into the interior, stick tight to the work of mobilizing the people', and Secuna Baio or some other soothsayer told them: 'Do not go, I have cast your fortune and see great harm for you if you go into the interior', perhaps they would kill themselves because they were ashamed of facing Cabral, but they would not go. There were comrades who did not make ambushes just because a 'soothsayer' told them they should not make ambushes as one of them was going to die. And the comrades used to be so accustomed to the elders giving them orders, making decisions for them about the war, that later it was the elders who came to complain: 'Cabral, what is happening, the youngsters don't obey us any more, they go into attack without consulting us?' I answered: 'Elder, look at it this way. If once upon a time the youngsters would not attack without consulting you, I never said anything to them about it. So today I am not saying anything to them. But I never appointed you as commander, they are the commanders. If in the past they consulted you, that is their business. Now they don't want to any more? That's none of my business.' The elder was a little angry, but he is not stupid, he is cunning. When all is said and done, the elders were the intellectuals of our society, of our genuine, real society. They were the ones who saw things clearly, who understood everything (our strengths and our weaknesses) and they soon shifted their ground, adapted themselves to the new situation.

On the cultural plane, our Party has tried to derive the best possible result, the best possible benefit from our cultural reality. It does so by not banning what it is possible not to ban without prejudicing the struggle, or by creating new ideas in the comrades' spirit, new ways of seeing reality. And further by making the best possible use of those who already have a little more education, both to lead the struggle itself and to be sent to study how to train cadres for the future. All this might seem very simple, but it is difficult, it is very complex to find the right answer for this.

Political reality

The political reality of our land is that greater reality that we all know well, it is the fact that we were a Portuguese colony. Our people could rule themselves neither in Guiné nor in Cape Verde. The Portuguese ruled even if they might appoint a black administrator – as only Honorio Barreto had the honour or disgrace of being – and the truth was that the Portuguese ruled in our land, Portuguese colonialism. And it was this greater reality that created the conflict between us and the Portuguese, exploitation of our people, under cover of Portugal's policy. This basically is what generated our struggle.

Our struggle grew so much that we must take advantage of it to transform even geographical reality, to the extent that we can. It would seem improbable, but it is the truth. For when we build dams, bridges, etc., we shall change the geographical landscape of our land, we are going to make a new human geography that we are creating in our land. When we completely transform the islets of Bijagos, when we make Cape Verde into a magnificent centre for world tourism, for example, this will already be a new geographical reality that we are creating. The ships which now pass by far out to sea will begin to stop there. But we must through this struggle transform the economic reality of our land. Let us put an end to exploitation by the

Portuguese, but let us put an end to exploitation of our people by our own folk. And we must develop our land, make it progress as much as possible. This is what our struggle means: social reality, cultural reality, everything is going to change. And already a new political reality has arisen in our land and it is the following: we are ruling ourselves.

Obviously our reality has strengths and weaknesses, as I have already shown you. For example, the fact that we do not have great economic development is a serious weakness. But it is also a strength, for if our land had important mines, important factories, etc., the imperialists would have come into the war more quickly and in greater strength. Perhaps we should have had to fight not only against the Portuguese, but against other imperialists as well. As it is, at least we have a quieter life, just bush and desert.

But we cannot let ourselves sleep. Obviously the social reality of our land – where, for example, there are no grand bourgeois, no great capitalists – is helpful for our struggle, because we do not have the difficulty of having to fight those who have super-exploited our folk. But it is also a weakness, because in some lands some local capitalists adhered strongly to the struggle, with all their resources, with all their money, etc., and gave significant help. As in Cuba, in China and in other countries where many local capitalists took the revolution seriously. And some leaders are the sons of great capitalists.

Another advantage is that our land does not have great class differences, very wide differences, and that the better-off classes, who have most resources, are small in number, very few persons. This avoids many difficulties of division on social grounds for us. But in the social reality of our land, and we talked about this yesterday, there is the question of ethnic groups and it is a great weakness. For in this very room there may still be folk capable of thinking: I am Pepel. I am Mancanha and the Mancanha does not fail his companion. I am Mandinga. This is a great weakness of our struggle. And it would be very damaging if in fact we let it go on, if in fact we were not able to eliminate all this on the path of struggle.

I want to call your attention to the factor, which you should consider carefully to see what is happening in Africa, of questions of tribes, the so-called tribalism, wars between ethnic groups, etc. It is not the people who invent all this, the people do not heed it, because the people pursue reality with great realism, defend their own interests. The truth is the following: the era of tribes in Africa has already passed. There was an era in which the tribes struggled against each other because of land, to take land to graze their cattle, etc., to find better soils, or because of their children, their wives, to test their own strength, but this is over and done with.

As soon as our African peoples succeeded in forming States, even States of the military type, as soon as the African peoples succeeded in bringing together folk from different tribes for one task, to serve one class, the tribes had begun to disappear. When the Portuguese and other colonialists came they did away with it once and for all, except that they tried to preserve the superstructure, meaning those who were ruling the tribes, or the groups, so that these would serve as intermediaries to help the colonialists to rule. Our people today, Oinca or Balanta, or some other, may retain ancient memories – 'We and the Mandinga did not get on very well in fact' – but if there were no one to incite them, they would no longer go this way. The same happens with Ibo and Yoruba in Nigeria, or Bakongo and other groups in Congo. It takes someone to incite them, someone who says: 'Let's start something. They've got big ideas, but the Mandinga will show them.'

Some folk even despise their tribes, folk who no longer even want to know about this. They have studied in universities, in Lisbon, or Oxford, or even in the capital city of their own land. Today, because Africa has acceded to independence, they want to rule, they want to be President of the Republic, they want to be Minister, so that they can exploit their own people. So when for some reason this is denied them, they remember their tribe: 'I am Lunda, born of Lunda, descendant of the Lunda king. Lunda people, rise because the Bakongo want to eat us.' But it has nothing to do with Lunda or Bakongo; it is wanting to be president, to have all the diamonds, all the gold, all those fine things in one's hand, to do as one pleases, to live well, to have all the women one wants in Africa or in Europe. It is for the sake of touring Europe, being received as presidents, wearing expensive clothes – a morning coat or even great bubus to pretend that they are Africans. All lies, they are not Africans at all. They are lackeys or lapdogs of the whites.

What happens in Nigeria also happens among us, at least shows among us, namely some folk want to serve only their own political ambition. It means that we must recognize that only ambition can defend divisiveness whatever the ground of division might be. The Portuguese, for example, have done much harm to us but we cannot lump all whites together as 'Portuguese'. Only some overly ambitious fellow would be able to say: we cannot accept the help of so and so, in Bissau, who is white, or of so and so, in Catio, who is white. How? This is no good. If we want to serve our land, our Party, our people, we must accept everyone's help. But as a friend, as a companion in struggle. Someone who is looking after his own belly, a good job for himself, might think: 'Whether he is clever or stupid, perhaps we could accept him, but to walk over him. Otherwise, it is best for him to clear off, or he might take my place from me.' That is not correct.

This is why we need to know the reality of our land, reality in all aspects, of all kinds, so that we shall be able to guide the struggle, in general and in particular. We have to recognize that in the specific circumstances of reality in our land of Guiné and Cape Verde, much courage is required to answer with confidence this question: 'Can we in fact wage a war like this?' Obviously we can say yes, because we are doing it. But at the start it was difficult. There was the man who asked: 'But how are we going to struggle against the Portuguese, if we do not even have clothing, if we cannot read or write? The Portuguese warfare is made by commanders, majors, etc., trained at university or senior academies; how are we going to struggle against them? We don't have anything. Where are we going to find material for struggle? How can this be?'

We have to do some straight thinking so as to answer yes, we can. We have to place our reality in the reality of the modern world. We can say: we were all divided, each group isolated; but in the reality of the modern world, many folk can bring our people to the understanding that we can be united, Balanta, Pepel, Mandinga, descendants of Cape Verdians, etc. We can go forward together without panicking. And we have shown that this is really possible. In the reality of the modern world, a new Africa has risen to independence, to progress, and we must count on it. There is a socialist camp which has grown from the October Revolution, which placed the following assertion before everything: self-determination for all peoples, each people must choose their destiny, take it into their own hands. There are moreover international laws established in the United Nations.

We must bear all this in mind, the reality of the whole world, the world wars there were, with all the difficulties they brought, so that we should have the courage to prosecute the struggle in our land. For if we were to limit ourselves to an isolated reality, within our village, it would be impossible to imagine how we should go and struggle against colonialism.

You see therefore the importance of knowing our reality and of knowing also all the realities. It is for us to know where ours is among the others, for us to know our total strength and our total weakness. Only in this way can we see the actual situation. We could struggle, we could wage our own struggle, could make many sacrifices, but it would not be enough to wage the struggle from our own resources. It could not be enough. What was essential was that our Party should be able to take advantage of other favourable conditions in the world and in Africa for us to take our struggle forward. And we did take advantage and we are constantly taking more advantage. So we were able to have weapons, ammunition, clothing, medicines, hospitals, etc., that we could not have in our land. We asked of ourselves the sacrifice and the effort that we could give, but we counted also on the reality of the modern world, on strengths which might come from outside. This is the significance that aid from other countries has for our struggle. Aid for us has only one condition: that it is unconditional. We guarantee that all the aid we receive is put to the service of our Party and our people.

We might say that no liberation movement in the world has made better use of aid given to it than our Party. We all are familiar with the admiration we arouse in all those who see our achievements, outside and inside our land, and who see that we have in fact put everything we received to the service of our struggle, to the service of our people. We have tried to use in the Party's service the skills of all the comrades. If some do not give everything they can it is because they are unwilling. There is no lack of example, or lack of encouragement. We have tried constantly to raise standards, making direct use of the help we receive in training cadres. So we have the need to use our own experience, our own strength, our own sacrifice and effort to transform our reality. But we need as well to know the experience of others, and to have the help of others and to use this help correctly.

Through the marrying of our strengths with the strengths that might come from outside, we can effectively transform the reality of our land. We have already changed a great deal, because today, in our land, in the greater part of our land, the Portuguese do not rule. In Guiné the Portuguese are squeezed in a colonial war they know is lost. In Cape Verde, where matters are already on the boil, they are harrassed to the point of calling on their friends to come to the rescue. The loss of Cape Verde for them means the end of Portuguese domination in Africa. We know therefore that we are able to transform this reality. The mere fact of holding this meeting is further clear evidence of a new reality of our land. In the land we used to know - in the reality Cruz Pinto left when he went to study in Portugal, or Bobo left when he went to study politics – a meeting of comrades like this one was not possible, whether inside or outside our land. Once upon a time in Bissau, I called the closest friends of my household, and said to them: 'Comrades, you are close friends of my mother, you are my friends too. You come to my house, we eat, we joke, but the time for joking has ended. Let us start a little discussion.' They replied: 'Yes, surely.' We discussed, we arranged a meeting. But only one or two came. The others did not come because they thought that this was madness. If we compare that moment with the moment today, we can see in fact that the creation of PAIGC was the point of departure for creating a new reality in our land of Guiné and Cape Verde. We must go on creating and developing it more and more each day so that we can serve not only and principally the interest of our people, but also the interest of Africa and the progress of mankind.

6. Our Party and the struggle must be led by the best sons and daughters of our people

Our struggle is not mere words but action, and we must really struggle. You will recall that in the early 1960s, many folk persuaded themselves that struggle meant speaking on the radio. Famous victories were scored on the airwaves of Dakar or of Conakry, even against PAIGC, but not against Portuguese colonialism, because the opportunists never did anything against the colonialists. Those were olden days when persons rushed to see who could be the first to speak on the radio. As if that were the struggle.

In our Party we have always considered as basic and correct the following: the struggle is not a debate nor verbiage, whether written or spoken. Struggle is daily action against ourselves and against the enemy, action which changes and grows each day so as to take all the necessary forms to chase the Portuguese colonialists out of our land.

And we must wage this struggle wherever it might be necessary. First, inside our land, because rice is cooked inside the pot and not outside. But we must never forget that a struggle like ours must also be waged outside our frontiers, against our enemies and at the side of our friends, to obtain the necessary means for our struggle and to build the potential for supplying the struggle inside our land.

The fact that PAIGC had established the principle that the struggle must be waged seriously and that everyone, no matter who, must struggle, drove many folk away from the Party. For some persons approached PAIGC, or even managed to join PAIGC, with the idea that they would have to struggle on the radio and that tomorrow they would take up an appointment as Minister. When they discovered that to be in PAIGC's struggle, one had to be inside or outside the country, as the leadership decided, some went away and went so far as to rejoin the Portuguese to have a little enjoyment of the crumbs of colonialism. This is one of the main reasons why the opportunists in Dakar, for example, combat our Party! Some of them would dearly love to join our Party, but they do not have the courage. They know that the Party could tell them: 'Stick tight, let's go inside.' But what they want is to leave Dakar to go straight to Bissau and sit down on a departmental director's chair.

Everyone must struggle – that is another certainty in the context of our Party. And gradually in our Party we have reached the stage when in theory and in practice there is no distinction between the interior and the exterior in our struggle. At the start of the struggle there were some who preened themselves because they were inside the land. They thought that those outside were afraid and did not do much, as they were outside. Anyone who in a struggle like ours hangs on to this idea or other complexes of vanity and fear, because he is inside or is outside, has not understood our struggle.

But anyone who has never left the bush and has withstood seven years of struggle but has failed to understand the significance for the struggle inside the land of the work of those who are working outside the land, has not understood anything either. And someone who is outside, seated in an office or somewhere, and has failed to understand the value of those who are inside the land and who are opening fire, or preparing the political ground and suchlike, and the value of the latter, has also not understood anything. Our Party, without much talk, without great debate, has reached this position: we all know today that there is no interior or exterior, because all are as likely to be inside as outside the land. Obviously we are not going to confuse other people's lands – the Republic of Guinea or Senegal – with our land of Guiné and Cape Verde. Rice is cooked inside the pot, but we know how important firewood and many other things necessary for cooking rice are. Some Party comrades had the idea that by virtue of going into the bush for the struggle, they were kings and could walk over anyone around. They were mistaken. Now we know that it is not true, it is not like that. The Congress at Cassaca made it known that this was not true. If anyone goes into the bush to command guerrilla warfare and to struggle, but does not strictly follow the Party watchwords, then he should watch out, for we are going to forget the Portuguese a while to go and deal with him first. But some in their work outside pick up bad habits, thinking that they cannot dirty their feet in the mud, that they cannot be bitten by mosquitoes, that they cannot go through what our combatants, our leaders, our responsible workers are going through in our land. They are badly mistaken! They are folk who in fact are not really committed to the struggle. Perhaps we made the mistake in making them leaders of the Party, but sooner or later they will find out that it is not like this.

Our Party has the situation that no one is 'inside' or 'outside', everyone is inside or outside according to the needs of the Party. Leaders of the struggle and the Party must always be abreast of everything happening outside or inside our land which touches the type of work they are doing in the Party. For several years now we have been able to say the following: not one of our leaders, not one of our responsible workers has not carried out missions outside the land, and not one of our leaders has not also worked inside the land.

Obviously there are some militants or responsible workers even who have spent more time outside than inside, and who spend their time pleading to go inside. It is pleasant to hear this, but one must ask if their duties and their training require them to be inside the land or outside. This is the crucial point, because tourism we can leave for later. There are also folk in the interior who plead to go to Europe. Later on, if they do not manage to go now, if they are not given a mission there, when we have retaken our land, if they work hard, they will fill their pockets with money and can take a trip to Europe and return. But the movement of our workers, whether outside or inside, is determined by the needs of our struggle. This is basic for us. In my case as a leader, I must respond personally to the needs of our struggle in conferences, in meetings with Heads of State or with leaders of other Parties in the world. This represents for me, as for other comrades who work with me, a decisive task in our struggle. But it is a great strength to me to have the certainty that there is no important operation in our war, no important political project of which I am not personally aware, which I do not study. There is no change or real development on the political plane or in the armed struggle which does not go through my hands. The trouble is that we have human limitations. Unhappily I cannot be everywhere at the same time but I have spent as much time as possible at the side of our combatants and militants.

Another principle linked to what I have just mentioned is that we must struggle without rushing, struggle in stages, develop the struggle progressively, without making great leaps.

If you consider carefully, you see that many struggles began by forming a Political Bureau, a General Staff, etc., but we did not begin with this. Many struggles began by forming early on a national liberation army; we did not begin with this. We began our struggle as one plants a seed in the ground, to yield. One plants a seed, a seedling is born, which grows and grows until it produces flowers and fruit: that is the path of our struggle, stage by stage, step by step, progressively without great leaps. Moreover, each stage means at the same time greater demands on our work, on our dedication, on our energy. This is basic; it is like a growing child who at the start is satisfied with a feeding bottle of milk, or mother's breast milk, but when he is aged three complains if he is given a feeding bottle of milk or the breast, because this is no longer enough for him.

The same happens in our struggle, in our Party which co-ordinates our struggle. In step as we grow, as we develop, as the struggle goes on to new stages, it is fundamental that each of us gives more and more and more. More in moral behaviour, in political behaviour, in political awareness, in work each day and each moment, more in the influence that each brings to bear on other comrades to put them on the right course. Unhappily we must admit that this has not been true for everybody, and the opposite even has happened with some comrades. In step as the Party advances, grows, has greater strength, in step as our struggle advances, as our responsibilities grow, these comrades have neglected their work. They have sought comfort, to flee from responsibilities, an easier life, to begin enjoying themselves, thinking that they already have independence in their grasp. This is one of the greatest weaknesses of our Party, one of the biggest factors which has held back the work of our Party. For these comrades, including some leaders, were not able to progress at the same rate as the struggle. Instead of advancing, by studying more, learning more, studying the lessons of each day, they lagged behind, through idleness, softness, even vices. This is happening to various comrades. We have done our best to help them, not to let them follow this course, for our struggle makes constantly greater demands, and the demands are that much greater when the responsibilities of a militant are greater.

These comrades have not matched the greater demands of the struggle. They seek comfort, pretend to be working and are not working at all. In their own conscience, they know it. Other comrades begin to work with enthusiasm, and fervour, making a reasonable contribution, and suddenly it is as if they have been put out by a shower of cold water. Why? Because they were not able to follow the struggle, to understand profoundly the meaning of the work they were doing. This is very damaging; it brings great harm to our struggle. If we are not able to combat this vigorously, if each of you is not able to keep this clearly in mind, particularly you, the youth, who are taking on responsibilities in the Party, if we cannot keep our older comrades firmly on course, we are going to face great difficulties. Neither heroism in the armed struggle, nor the support of our people, nor the skill of the Party leadership, nothing can save us, if we, as men and women, cannot follow the demands of the struggle, to give more, constantly more, in all aspects of our life.

Some comrades, even among those seated in this room, have a tendency to seek comfort in step as their responsibilities grow. It seems that some comrades spend several years waiting for responsibilities in order to make the mistakes which others have made in the position. We must combat this courageously, for the struggle is demanding, and our Party is constantly more demanding. And we must throw out those who do not understand, however much it hurts us. We cannot allow it, while the struggle advances, our people sacrifice themselves in the cause of our struggle, some comrades die and others are wounded or disabled, while we grow old in the struggle, giving our whole life to the struggle with so many folk putting their hope in us, inside and outside our land. We cannot allow some militants or responsible workers to lead a soft life and commit acts which go against our responsibility to ourselves, to our people, to Africa and to the world.

Many folk think that this is Cabral's backyard, that he is the one who has to spot what has gone wrong or who has gone wrong. They are wrong. Each of us has to notice, to stand firm in correction, for if not, nothing can save us, whatever victories we might have won. So our struggle is like the basket which separates clean rice from the husk, like the sieve which sieves pounded flour, to separate the fine flour from the coarse grain and other things. The struggle unites, but it also sorts out persons, the struggle shows who is to be valued and who is worthless. Every comrade must be vigilant about himself, for the struggle is a selective process; the struggle shows us to everyone, and shows who we are. This is one of the great advantages for our people in waging a struggle, above all armed struggle, to liberate themselves.

There was one elder, who by the way is still in the struggle, who said to me three years ago: 'Cabral, I pray every day for Salazar not to die.' 'Why, my elder?' 'So that the struggle continues a while longer, so that Salazar continues obdurate, so that we should continue, so that we should know each other better.' This is a sound truth; today we know each other well, today we know who is worthy and who is not.

We are making an effort for the unworthy to improve, but we know who is worthy and who is not worthy; we even know who may tell a lie. There are some that we do not yet know well. You know me too. You know other leaders of the Party whom we respect highly, for they will be steadfast to the end, and you know this well, There are others of whom some are afraid, because they know that their only merit is the power they wield. Some of you here have seen Party leaders make serious mistakes but you go on obeying them because you are afraid of them. Today we know ourselves well. Some of you have seen responsible workers in the Party treat other persons badly and knew in your conscience that this was not just, but you kept silent, covered it up. But you then were certain that such were not good leaders, were not good responsible workers, as they maltreated, acted against the Party line, and did this with the certainty that the Party leadership collectively would not find out.

Each of you here, who has been close to a responsible worker or a leader, has a clear idea about that man or woman. The struggle has allowed us to know each other very well and this is highly important. Some have been able to improve each day, others have sunk further each day, despite all the help we tried to give, to bring each person on, with head held high in the service of the Party, to serve our people correctly.

Whether we like it or not, the struggle operates a selection. Little by little, some pass through the sieve, others remain, for our firm resolve as long as we are here as leaders of this Party is the following: only those will go forward who really want to struggle, those who in fact understand that the struggle goes in stages. We can advance only those who truly understand that the struggle constantly makes more demands and gives more responsibilities and who are therefore ready to give everything and demand nothing, except respect, dignity, and the opportunity to serve our people correctly.

I should like to remind you, in respect of struggle by stages for example, that many of our comrades thought that the struggle would advance more quickly, that we should soon enter Bissau. It is not like that; it must be by stages and we must be prepared for a long struggle. At the point we have reached, our independence could come tomorrow or the day after or in six months' time, because the Portuguese are driven to desperation in our land and if we stand firm they will be increasingly desperate. But we must have our morale adjusted to a long struggle, we must prepare new militants to carry it on, if need be.

And you, the youth here, must take your responsibilities on your shoulders. You must fully understand the following: if the struggle were to end tomorrow, you should be ready, as youth, to ensure the work of our people, to build the progress our Party wants. But if it were to last ten more years, you, the youth here, have the duty of taking the place of the older men who can no longer carry on, and have the duty of preparing other young men, so that they are trained in time to take up the struggle. The Vietnamese say that they will win the war for certain, because if the Americans are ready to fight for ten years, they are ready to struggle for ten and a half years; if the Americans are ready to fight for twenty years, they are ready to struggle for twenty and a half years. This is the consciousness of a people who know their national rights, that their land is theirs, and whose youth and adults are ready really to serve their people.

It is clear that a struggle like ours, a Party like ours, require secure leadership, united leadership, enlightened leadership, and it is our own reality which shapes awareness. We need to be aware, for to the measure that man is aware of reality, he acquires the strength to change that reality, to transform it into a better reality. In the framework of a struggle like ours, of a Party like ours, the leadership must go to the most aware men and women, whatever their origin, and wherever they come from: that is, to those who have the clearest concept of our reality and of the reality that our Party wants to create. We are not going to look to see where they come from, who they are and who their parents are. We are looking only at the following: do they know who we are, do they know what our land is, do they know what our Party wants to do in our land? Do they really want to do this, under the banner of our Party? So they should come to the fore and lead. Whoever is most aware of this should lead. We might be deceived today, or deceived tomorrow, but the proof of the pudding is in the eating, it is practical experience which shows who is worthy and who is not.

So that is our principle: the best sons and daughters of our land must lead our Party, our people. But does this mean that we have in fact always appointed the best? Some are worthless, but we are still going through an experimental phase. The truth is that we have always given persons the opportunity to improve, we have given all workers in the Party the opportunity to advance, to show their leadership capacity. There are comrades sitting here who three years ago were raw recruits in our military training camps. Today they are members of our Inter-regional Committees or leaders of our armed forces. This shows to what extent our Party has been able to open a broad path for our comrades to progress, for those who are most aware and most worthy to lead.

Our struggle demands enlightened leadership and we have said that the best sons and daughters of our land must lead. It is hard to know soon after they have come in who is the best. Following the principle we talked about at the start – trusting wins trust – and as some reveal their ability, we shall bring them forward. Then we shall see if they are in fact the best or not, if they improve or degenerate.

The truth is that no one can say that in this Party the opportunity to command is not given to everybody. Everybody has this, the way is wide open for everybody. Our hope has always been the following: the more who are able to command the better, for we can choose the best of the best to command. We have done our utmost to improve the training of comrades, to think more about the difficulties, to show more initiative, more enthusiam, more dedication, to make progress. And we have done our best to be fair, to bring forward those who really deserve it because of their own efforts, and not for their pretty faces or because they can be someone's stooge.

In the Party we have rigorously avoided anything which smacked of some persons being subject to others, or some being stooges of others. From the very start, I said the following: we do not want servants, we do not want stooges, we do not want errand boys. We want men, comrades who know what they are doing, our comrades, who can look us straight in the face, who can engage in debate with due respect on both sides. We want men and women who understand and who hold their heads up. We have struggled firmly against a tendency for leaders and responsible workers to form a retinue of 'laddies', or to treat responsible workers under their orders as if they were their messenger boys. But we have also fought in the morale of comrades the attitude of letting others take their responsibilities.

Obviously there has been some resistance to this. A particular instance was the occasional stubborn, silent resistance to the presence of women among the leadership. Some comrades do their utmost to prevent women taking charge, even when there are women who have more ability to lead than they do. Unhappily some of our women comrades have not been able to maintain the respect and the necessary dignity to protect their position as persons in authority. They were not able to escape certain temptations, or at least to shoulder certain responsibilities without complexes. But the men comrades, some, do not want to understand that liberty for our people means women's liberation as well, sovereignty for our people means that women as well must play a part, and that the strength of our Party is worth more if women join in as well to lead with the men. Many folk say that Cabral has an obsession about giving women leadership positions as well. They say: 'Let him do it, but we shall sabotage it afterwards.' That comes from folk who have not yet understood anything. They can sabotage today, sabotage tomorrow, but one day it will catch up with them.

Another resistance which persisted for a while in the Party was the following: we were the few leaders, and no one else could be a leader. Various comrades of ours, good combatants, able men, were overlooked, held in their tracks, because some of the leadership never gave them the chance to come forward. This is killing the Party, as if one suffocated it. For while we older ones have breathing space, we are getting on, but when our breath is failing, there is no one to take our place. The strength of our Party is only effective if we, the leaders, are able to open the way for the youth to progress, youth like you, other youth who are still behind, in their hundreds, in their thousands, to take over and to bring the best forward to lead.

We in the Party leadership, and I in particular, have done our utmost to back all those who show willingness to work. My greatest joy is to see a comrade, man or woman, carrying out duties conscientiously and willingly without being pushed, as it is so often necessary to push some to do what they have to. This is a great encouragement for us, and gives us the certainty that we can overcome, do what our Party wants. Everyone in the Party knows what friendship, what regard, what respect, what warmth we have for those who can carry out their duty. Everyone we see working with complete enthusiasm is like a part of ourselves, a new part which is a guarantee of the future of our Party and victory for our people. That is why our work is to encourage and to seek to develop in everyone, the youngsters, men and women, the will to stand firm, to understand the Party's aims, and to go forward. This should be the task of every leader, of every responsible worker in our Party.

But some comrades show the following tendency. A political commissar, for example, spots a young lad as a good militant. Instead of taking an interest in him to help him to understand more, to make progress, instead of stimulating him, no, he turns him into a messenger boy. For the latter is wide awake, knowledgeable, quick moving. If you give him something to look after, he looks after it well. So the commissar gives him his kitbag to look after, instead of making him an asset for our land. Or it might be a case of a bright and fairly attractive girl. Instead of helping her, giving her a hand to make progress in becoming a nurse or a teacher, in going to study, or become a good militia fighter or something of the sort, no, he makes her his mistress. For the latter is very beautiful and he has the right to take charge of her. We must put an end to this.

We do not want to ban servants, girlfriends, or children, it is not that. What we must do is to stop spoiling the future of our Party. Anyone who wants a servant must wait till the morrow of our independence. Let him work and if he has the means, let him find his servant, if there are folk who want to be servants. He cannot use the authority of the Party, which the Party has put in his hands, to find his servant. Anyone who wants a girlfriend, today or tomorrow, can find her, woo her, marry her, but he must not use the authority of the Party to have all the women he wants. As long as this goes on we are making mistakes and justifying the Portuguese and all the enemies of our people.

We must be aware of this. And you, the youth, as militants or responsible workers in our Party, must be aware of this. Your task is not to have children today, it is to serve the Party, to raise the Party banner high. Your task is to help the men and boys, women and girls of our land to rise in revolt, and not to be running after terylene trousers from Senegal or quick deals here and there. That is not it. If you do that, you will roundly fail in your historic mission which is to be at the age of twenty or so a responsible worker in this Party.

Some of you who have travelled out of our land have seen the respect our Party inspires, the consideration our Party receives, and how much hope our Party has given to other folk in the world, and in Africa. But comrades often forget this, deep in the bush they forget completely their responsibility as leaders. Some have tried to make the utmost use of the authority the Party gave them so as to satisfy their own stomachs, their vices, their convenience. This must stop. And it is you who must stop this at all levels.

This is also why we must be vigilant against opportunists. Opportunists are not only those who are in Senegal trying to make their fringe movements. There are also opportunists among us, who knowing that our leadership requires the best sons and daughters of our land to lead may pretend to be the best. Or they may try their hardest to please their responsible workers, so that the latter will propose them as leaders or as responsible workers. We must be careful of this, we must unmask them and combat them. You must understand that the only good leader, the only good responsible worker is one who face to face car report the mistakes others make. Many comrades in responsible positions at various levels have made the serious mistake of hiding the mistakes of others: 'I shall keep mum. If Cabral finds out, all right, if he does not find out, forebearance.' That is destroying the work and the sacrifice the individual is himself giving, for he is compromising himself and spoiling the other.

We must be careful to unmask all opportunists among us, all the liars, all the cowards, all those who do not respect the Party line. We must have the courage to shoulder our responsibilities; that goes for all of us, young responsible workers or leaders of our Party. We must have the courage to look each other straight in the eye, because our Party can only be led by men and women who do not have to lower their eyes before anyone.

Another important aspect we have to defend in the Party leadership, which is already stated clearly in the published watchwords, is that our Party is led collectively, it is not led by one person. At any level, in political action or in the armed forces, in security or in education, anywhere and at the different levels there is always collective leadership. But the tendency of some comrades is to monopolize leadership just for themselves. They decide everything, they do not consult the views of anyone at their side. This cannot go on, for two heads are always worth more than one, even if one is clever and the other stupid.

On this point you must read carefully the lecture we had on collective leadership (leading in a group). But I remind you that collective leadership (leading in a group) does not mean that everyone must command, and that there is no longer any authority. Some think: 'If we must command, then let's command even if we have no idea how to command, just to give the appearance that everyone commands.' This is a nonsense. Long ago I said that even if it is not necessary to be a doctor to command in our Party, we must not forget that there are some tasks which cannot be done by someone who cannot read or write. Otherwise we are fooling ourselves and we must never fool ourselves. There are some tasks which can or cannot be done according to educational level. We must also remember that the Party has a hierarchy, that is a ladder of persons in command, and this must be respected, really respected, and it has not always been respected as it should be.

In the specific conditions of our national struggle, before the historic needs of our people, our Party must at this moment have clearly defined chiefs so that everyone should know who is who and so that there should be no confusion. Whatever their level of command, in the Political Bureau or whatever, they should aim at this attitude: here is a chief who does not have to remind anyone that he is chief, who mixes with everyone, who does not have the least pretentiousness, and so is the one to be our chief. He is not puffed up by showing to everyone that he is in command, but he never forgets at any moment that he has to be a chief, and he does remind anyone who forgets it.

The leadership of our Party is the strength of our people, and is responsible for everything done by our militants, responsible workers, combatants, etc. Our leadership must be one and united. We cannot allow any division among us. When we speak of the higher leadership of the Party, we are speaking of leadership at any echelon, whether at the Inter-regional Committee or at the Party Zone Committee; no one can turn his back on his companion in struggle. Anyone who does not understand this is a wrecker.

Take, for example, the armed forces leadership. Various instances have occurred when the political commissars did not get on well with the commanders. It is criminal to have these misunderstandings when they have the Portuguese before them to fight. We have had occasion to transfer comrades because they were ambitious and jockeying with other companions in struggle. We can no longer tolerate this. The time has come to reduce the grades of all those who do not get on with each other. There will be no more transfers. They will come down in grade, to become ordinary private soldiers or ordinary militants. We have passed the stage of teaching comrades that we must understand each other. Our enemy is the colonialist Portuguese and not some other enemy.

In this very room there are comrades who worked together and were not able to get on with each other. They should be ashamed. And why? Because they were thinking of their belly, their ambitions, instead of serving the interests of the Party? This is the mentality of petty ambition, of caprice. Instead of devoting their attention to the struggle, to Party work, they look to see who has more, who has less, petty squabbles, shabby intrigues... And at bottom it is a lack of courage, cowardice when all is said and done.

This cannot go on; the time has come to stop this. In the bush or out of the bush, the time has come for each one to bear the weight of his consciousness, to put aside caprices, to take a firm grip on work, so as to make no mistake on the path. And we must remind the comrades from the zones, above all them, of the importance local leadership has for retaining the people's enthusiasm. We cannot tolerate that a comrade should be Political Commissar of any area for one, two or three years and should come to the end without having any authority, so that everyone does what he pleases and takes no notice of his leadership. This is a total failure for a comrade. And we must observe that some local leaderships, which were working very well at the start, only began to do badly and to make mistakes when the leaders began to think of their belly, treating their area as if it were already independent and beginning to think of their own life.

There is a film I never forget because it taught me a great lesson. There was once a young lad who was educated in some priests' college and who believed strongly in miracles. He knew nothing about life, because he had spent his life in the college and left as a man of twenty-one. All the injustices he discovered were one evil; he did not understand that on one side was misery and human suffering and on the other the rich. But he managed to find a dove which wrought miracles. And so, as his thoughts were on the sufferings of others, he resolved to do everything to help others, so that there should be no hunger or cold, so that everyone should have houses in which to live, so that each one should achieve his desires. He did not think about himself but asked the dove to do miracles for others. So the dove appeared to him and perched on his hand. He said: 'Give houses to the poor' – and the houses appeared, with all their furnishings. 'Give food to the starving' – and food appeared, good food. He would even call persons to ask them what they wanted, and he would grant it. Until the day when he found a girl with whom he fell in love. His beloved would ask him for something and he would grant it. Other folk said that they too had wants, but he had no more time, now he had time only for his beloved. Suddenly the dove took wing and flew away. The miracles ended and everything he had done as a miracle began to disappear; while the dove was still in his hand, the miracles ended. He could no longer do anything for others, because he was thinking only of his girlfriend, of his belly.

There is a great moral in this. So far as we are able to think of our common problem, the problems of our people, of our own folk, putting in their right place our personal problems, and, if necessary, sacrificing our personal interests, we can achieve miracles. That is how all the leaders, responsible workers and militants of our great Party must be – in the service of the liberty and progress of our people.

7. Struggle of the people, by the people, for the people

A basic principle for our struggle is that it is the struggle of our people, and that it is our people who must wage it, and its result is for our people.

You have already clearly understood what the people are. The question we now pose is the following: against whom are our people struggling?

Obviously a people's struggle is effectively theirs if the reason for that struggle is based on the aspirations, the dreams, the desire for justice and progress of the people themselves and not on the aspirations, dreams or ambitions of half a dozen persons, or of a group of persons who are in contradiction with the actual interests of their people.

Against whom must our people struggle? We answered this clearly right from the start. We, as colonies of Portugal in Guiné and Cape Verde, are dominated by a foreigner, but it is not all foreigners who dominate us and within Portugal it is not all the Portuguese who dominate us.

The force and oppression which is exerted on us comes from the ruling class in Portugal, from the Portuguese capitalist bourgeoisie, which exploits the people of Portugal as much as it exploits us. And as we know well, the ruling class in Portugal, the colonialist class in Portugal, is tied to world domination by other classes in other countries, who together make up imperialist domination. It is tied to the ensemble of capitalist forces in the world which as well as dominating their own countries have a vital need to dominate other peoples, other countries, both to have raw materials for their industry and to have markets for their manufactures. In short we are dominated by the Portuguese colonialist capitalist class, tied to world imperialism.

Our people are therefore struggling against the Portuguese capitalist colonialist class, and struggling against that means necessarily to struggle against imperialism, because the Portuguese class is a piece, albeit minute and rotting, of imperialism. So we know against whom we are struggling.

But we face the question not only of liberation but also of progress for our people. And on this basis we quickly see that our struggle cannot only be against foreigners, but must also be against their internal enemies. Who? All the social strata of our land, of *classes* of our land, who do not want progress for our people, but merely want progress for themselves, their family, their own. And so we say that our people's struggle is not only against anything that might be contrary to their liberty and independence, but also against anything that might be contrary to their progress and happiness.

The struggle in our land must be made by our people. We cannot for a moment think of liberating our land, of building peace and progress in our land, by bringing in foreigners from outside to come and struggle for us. In Guiné and Cape Verde we are the ones who must struggle, we are the ones who must buckle down to all the means of struggling. And in fact this is what has happened.

It is now quite common to hear this exchange in our Party; someone asks: 'Are you of the people?', and the other replies: 'No, I'm army'. 'Are you of the people?', 'No, I'm militia'. 'Are you of the people?', 'No, I am a responsible worker.' That is how we commonly talk, but all those folk are people. It is enough to see where our combatants, our responsible workers, our leaders come from to understand that they are all people from our land. Naturally enough in the armed struggle in Guiné, the majority are from Guiné itself. Likewise in the struggle in Cape Verde, the majority are from Cape Verde itself. Guiné and Cape Verde are separated by sea and it is not easy to transfer large forces from one point to the other.

But there can be no doubt that it is our people who wage our struggle, through their children as militants, leaders, combatants, militia, etc. The fundamental strength is our people, themselves. Our population, or rather the population linked to the work of our Party, mobilized and organized by our Party, has from the beginning fed our struggle, borne sacrifices for our struggle, and so has been the principal strength of our struggle. It would have been impossible for us to wage the struggle, in the era of clandestinity, were it not that our people kept us alive among them like a fish in water.

The enemy know that it is our own people who share in the struggle, and so they make efforts to separate the part of our people who are Party and the part of our people who are population, to draw from us this principal strength in the liberation struggle, namely the support of the mass of the people. We might say that our struggle has the more potential for victory, the more we can keep on our side the support of the mass of the people in our land. The Portuguese know this too, and so they are making every effort to take this support from us.

Our struggle is for our people, because its objective, its purpose, is to satisfy the aspirations, dreams and desires of our people: to lead a decent and worthy life, as all the peoples in the world want, to have peace in order to build progress in their land, to build happiness for their children. We want everything we win in this struggle to belong to our people and we have to do our utmost to form an organization such that even if some want to divert the conquests of the struggle to their own advantage, our people will not let them. This is very important.

Our people now do really feel that the struggle is theirs. Not only because it is their children who have the weapons in their hands. Not only because it is their children who study and are trained as cadres, nurses, doctors, engineers, technicians, etc. Not only because it is their children who lead. But also because even in the villages, the militiamen or civilian population take up what principally symbolizes our struggle: weapons. It is not by chance, or for any other reason, that our Party leadership has given weapons, and constantly gives more, to our population. It is precisely so that no one should take it into his head that only those who take up arms in the people's army or in the guerrilla force are effectively struggling for results in this struggle. The more weapons there are for our supporters, the more certainty our population and our people will feel that the struggle is really theirs, and the fewer illusions there will be in the heads of our combatants and leaders that the struggle is their exclusive concern.

We are struggling for the progress of our land. We must make all the sacrifices to succeed with progress for our land of Guiné and Cape Verde. We must put an end to all injustices, miseries and suffering. We must guarantee for the children born in our land today and tomorrow a certainty that no barrier or wall should be put in their way. They must go forward, according to their capacities, to give their utmost. They must constantly improve the lot of our people and our land, serving not only our interests but also those of Africa and of all mankind. That is why from the start our Party set out on the best course for this, namely organization based on mobilizing our people, mobilizing the population of our land for the struggle against Portuguese colonialism.

Our Party has trained the children of our land to mobilize the people of our land. This work was no laughing matter. Many of you here, young lads who are today responsible workers in the Party, cannot imagine how difficult this work was. Morover we have organized within the framework of our Party a large proportion of the population of our land. This was the principal political strength of our struggle, which provided the potential for our struggle to advance as well as it has advanced. We must train our people, we must train ourselves - leaders and militants of our Party, our combatants who are making the sacrifice today - to defend at all costs the conquests our people are making through their struggle.

Today the people born in the bush, who yesterday could express no views on their lives and on their destiny, can express their views, can make decisions. They can decide issues in the Party committees and in the people's courts, where the descendants of our land have shown the ability to try the errors, crimes and other wrongdoings committed by other descendants of our land. This is further clear evidence that this struggle is of our people, by our people and for our people.

But various Party comrades, with high or low responsibilities, and even ordinary combatants have not understood this very well. They have tried to turn the struggle a little to their advantage, after all they are the people, it would seem. The struggle of our people, by our people, but for them. This is one of the most serious mistakes that can be made in a struggle like ours. We cannot in the least allow our armed forces, our militants or our responsible workers to forget for a single instant that the greatest consideration, respect and dedication is owed to the the people of our land, to our population, above all in the liberated areas of our land. Anyone who is ready to die from some bullet in this war but is able to show lack of respect for our people, the village folk, the population, will die without knowing why he is dying, or dies under a delusion.

The more we can do in our land to raise the morale of our people, to give them greater courage and greater enthusiam for the Party, the more it helps the present and future of our people, helps our Party. Anything that is done to destroy the population's confidence in us, to bully the population, to show lack of consideration for them, to steal their goods, to abuse their sons and daughters, is the worst crime that a combatant comrade or a responsible worker could commit. It damages our Party, and damages the future and present of our land.

It is better that we should be few in number but incapable of doing any injury to the population of our land than that we should be numerous but include folk capable of causing harm. For anyone among us who turns the population against our Party, to mistrust the Party, to lose confidence in the Party, is the best ally the Portuguese could have. You know – and what I am saying is not in my imagination – that there are comrades who behaved badly towards our population. Fortunately the situation has become much better because the Party has been vigilant in this matter.

So at each moment of this great struggle we are waging, we must focus on two phases: one, against the colonialist capitalist ruling classes in Portugal and imperialism which want to dominate our land economically and politically; the other, against all the internal forces, whether material or spiritual (meaning ideas from the mind), which might arise against our people's progress on the path of liberty, independence and justice. These demand courageous struggle against imperialist agents. But in addition permanent and determined struggle against those who, even if they are militants, responsible workers or leaders of the Party, do anything which could prejudice our people's march to total conquest of their dignity, their liberty and their progress.

8. Independence of thought and action

Another important principle in our Party line is the following: independence in our thought and in our action.

We are struggling for the independence of our land, for the independence of our people. The first condition for this is that our Party and its leadership should be independent in its way of tackling questions and of answering them, and in its action inside or outside our land. This has been our Party line.

All decisions we take in the framework of our Party, about our work inside or outside our land, on the African or the international plane, are taken with absolute independence in our way of thinking and acting. This is one of our sacrosanct principles, which we must defend at all costs.

But we must understand that independence is always relative. In many things we have to decide, for example, we have to gauge them in the light of the interests of our neighbouring countries as well for us to go forward. In many decisions we take on the African or international plane, we are guided by the interests of Angola and Mozambique as well, Some positions we may take, or even some decisions on war material, for example, or our action, are not solely dependent on us but are also dependent on our friends who give us aid. But this does not destroy the truth of the principle.

The PAIGC leadership has always acted on the basis of independence of thought and action. We have been capable, and must constantly be more so of thinking deeply about our problems so as to be able to act correctly, to act strongly so as to be able to think more correctly. Many comrades have not done this in keeping with their responsibilities. Some have limited themselves to acting without thinking, and others have lots of ideas without doing anything in practice. We must be able to bring these two basic elements together: thought and action, and action and thought. This independence in our thought and action is relative. It is relative because in our thought we are also influenced by the thought of others. We are not the first to wage an armed struggle for national liberation, or a revolution. Others have done this, there are other experiences. We did not invent guerrilla warfare – we invented it in our land. But in the framework of this relative independence, we must be aware that no struggle can be waged without an alliance, without allies. In all struggles we must make a choice, that is we have to choose one path or another. We cannot wage a struggle without knowing what path we must follow. So we must first know one thing: who are our allies in Africa and in the world.

We talk a lot about Africa, but we in our Party must remember that before being Africans we are men, human beings, who belong to the whole world. We cannot therefore allow any interest of our people to be restricted or thwarted because of our condition as Africans. We must put the interests of our people higher, in the context of the interests of mankind in general, and then we can put them in the context of the interests of Africa in general.

In Africa our allies are those governments, parties or states, individuals or organizations who really want effective independence for Africa, who really want their people's independence, economic independence so as to hold their history in their hands, for their people to hold the wealth in their hands, so as to advance, so as to build a better life. But our specific and immediate ally is anyone openly opposed to Portuguese colonialism in Africa. You know that there are Africans who are not in the least opposed to Portuguese colonialism. But our closest ally, our real ally is anyone who not merely offers words but also aid against Portuguese colonialism. It is not enough to say 'I am African' for us to say that person is our ally; these are mere phrases. We must ask him frankly: 'Do you in fact want the independence of your people? Do you want to work for them? Do you really want our independence? Are you really opposed to Portuguese colonialism? Do you help us? If the answers are yes, then you are our ally.'

We are also part of the world. Who are our allies in the world? It is not difficult to know today. All our people know. Why? Because we have practical proof. Who gives us aid? They are our allies, those who give us aid. Who gives us aid?

First in the world, the socialist countries. But there are some socialist countries who betrayed their role in providing aid for our struggle, in being our allies, when they put the interests of their states, their concerns, their ideas, above the interests of our struggle. They went so far sometimes as to try in an underhand way to divide us, so as to defend their ideas rather than the interests of our struggle. So even in the socialist environment, one must ask specifically: 'Do you in fact help us? Do you do nothing against us? Are you giving us the aid you can, the aid that you owe as part of the world vanguard? If you are, you are fulfilling your duty as our ally, if not, then you are not in fact our ally.'

There are other men and women in the world who are our allies. In capitalist countries there are persons who are opposed to Portuguese colonialism: they are our allies. We have one criterion to distinguish our friends from the friends of the Portuguese. Anyone who is opposed to Portuguese colonialism is our friend, is our ally. Anyone who supports Portuguese colonialism is our enemy, is the ally of the Portuguese.

But in the world, as part of mankind and of Africa, we have taken a clear stand in the anti-imperialist struggle.

We are not the only ones, there are other peoples. We must be consistent. If we demand solidarity with us from other peoples, we must show solidarity with them as well. We must show solidarity with all the African peoples who struggle for the genuine independence of their land, for the liberty, progress and happiness of their people, and above all with those who struggle against the colonialist-racism of the whites in southern Africa. In pride of place, our comrades in Angola and Mozambique, our companions in struggle. We have to be able to show them the greatest possible solidarity, because their struggle is our own struggle.

We must show solidarity with the Asian people who struggle against imperialism, especially with the peoples of Vietnam, of Laos and of Korea, in their struggle against American imperialism. We must show solidarity with the Latin American peoples in the struggle against imperialism, especially with the people of Cuba who were able to overcome reaction and imperialism in their land, to establish a just system which is encircled and threatened by imperialists. We must show the utmost solidarity with them and with all the Latin American liberation movements.

In North America, we must show solidarity, real solidarity, with the descendants of African slaves who are today part of the North American population and are Americans. We have to give courageous support to their struggle, without pretending that we are going to wage the struggle for them.

Our duty is to wage our struggle in our land. Neither in Africa, nor anywhere else are we going to wage the struggle for others. We are going to struggle in our land. This is difficult enough, let alone struggling for others.

We must be able all the time to show solidarity with the socialist countries. There are many folk who think that it is the duty of the socialists to give everything, but they should receive nothing in return, not even at least a word of thanks. This is wrong. If the German Democratic Republic gives us aid, if the Soviet Union gives us more aid than anyone, if other countries give us aid, this does not fall from the sky. It comes from the labour of their countrymen, the labour of the workers, and the sweat of each one's brow. There nothing falls from the sky except rain and snow and here we have only rain. We have to be aware of this and have the courage to thank them. When something is being done against them, we should close in solidarity with them, stand at their side, because they are our companions in struggle; they help us.

Many comrades went to study in socialist countries and instead of showing solidarity with them, their friends, they live there and come back enraged against them. Because such comrades do not have awareness, but only obsessions, only complexes. Many Africans behave like this, many comrades know what sacrifices are made to help us, but they are not able to develop friendship and dedication towards those who give us aid. That is not the Party's line. Our Party must be appreciative, must show solidarity with those who give us aid. Happily, many comrades have understood this properly and have behaved extremely well in this regard.

In the list of our allies we must put very high the name of the Republic of Guinea, as our first ally, our most cherished brothers, those who have given us most help. Generally speaking, it is the country which helps us most, through all kinds of facilities it gives us. It has also accepted the sacrifice of its own people through the shelling of its villages. We must put high up the name of Senegal, although not as high as that of Guinea, even though we know there have been difficulties for us. Unhappily, Senegal even today is making many difficulties for us. For example, our supporters are not now allowed to go about in Senegal in uniform. Why? This is good for the Portuguese, but it is not good for us. It is a long time since they did not want us to enter Senegal armed, now they do not want us to enter in uniform. Why are they making this trouble? But even so, we must say that Senegal helps us a little. We must be aware that this also has a certain value for our struggle, although, as I say again, there may be many difficulties and we are already beginning to be tired of them.

In connexion with Guinea we must put very high the name of the PDG (Democratic Party of Guinea). It is our people's good fortune that Guinea should have a Party like the PDG led by a man like Sékou Touré and by really patriotic folk, really concerned for Africa. Because if on each border of our land we had folk like those who are making such difficulties for us in Senegal, we should be in a bad way. We must be aware of this. There was no shortage of folk in Guinea who also wanted to make difficulties for us, and there are still some today, but the leaders, the Party, always supported the liberation of our people. For a while they watched who was really struggling for this, and when they saw that it was PAIGC they supported us to the hilt.

In the context of the general anti-imperialist struggle, we also have as allies the working class movements in various countries in Europe, or in

America, or in Asia – in the capitalist countries of Asia – but above all in Europe and America. They are also our allies as they struggle against imperialism, against the forces which dominate our land. We must be aware of this and develop our ties of friendship and solidarity with these movements.

9. Not everyone is of the Party

Work of leadership

Let us look at another principle of our Party which is the following: our struggle is based fundamentally on the work of our Party, the PAIGC.

You know what struggle is. You have understood already that struggle is a normal condition of all realities in motion. In everything that moves, that exists, if you like (for everything that exists is in motion), there is always a struggle. There are contrary forces which act on each other. For every force operating in one direction there is another force operating in the opposite direction.

Take a tree, for example. It is an enormous struggle for a tree to grow, live, bear fruit, seed or another tree. First for its root to pierce the soil and find sustenance in the ground. There is an enormous struggle between the root and the resistance of the ground. Moreover a certain capacity is needed, a certain strength to extract from the dampened soil the sustenance which enters the plant's root. When the sustenance has been extracted it must be carried to other parts of the plant. There is always a resistance against a resistance. In addition there is resistance to rain and to storms. And the plant has one great disadvantage: the plant cannot move from its position.

Plants, like animals (and even a piece of wood or iron) contain a struggle within, and there may be thousands of such struggles. But the fundamental struggle is between the capacity for preservation and the destruction which time brings to things. Iron rusts, wood crumbles to dust, the passage of time is written on things, from man to the most trifling thing. All this is expressed in struggle. But the struggle is more visible, evident, when an object exerts a force on another object, when it takes place between two distinct objects.

Our struggle is the consequence of the pressure (or oppression) which the

Portuguese colonialists exert on our society. Anyone who acquires a certain awareness, or who was witness to some event, or who has some interest in regard to Portuguese colonialism, faces the following choice: to wage his own struggle or not to wage any struggle. Many folk were struggling in our land, in Guiné and in Cape Verde, and sometimes wrote poems or some other thing as a call to struggle. Closing the windows and doors to one's room and insulting the Portuguese (who cannot hear) is a form of struggling. In Canhabaque a Bijago woman comes with water to sell. The Portuguese district officer tells her: 'One escudo? No. Five cents', and gives her the five cents. But she pours the water out on the ground – it is a form of struggling. Often subservience (the act of accepting humiliations) is also a form of struggling. But other forms of struggle are revolts. One case, for example, with which I was familiar and which I never forget, occurred in Angola on the plantations. I used to think that the contract workers were poor devils who never revolted. But they revolted, one by one, and though it was not often possible to sense the revolt, each of them was trying to express revolt. Some would pass themselves off as madmen, would go out with cutlasses and chop down all the young palm trees planted by the colonialists. It is a form of struggling. But when one, two, three or four join together, pool their interests, they can make a revolt. How many silent revolts, which perhaps no one saw, were there in Guiné, how many revolts were there in Cape Verde, at S. Vincente, S. Antão, Santiago; a struggle against Portuguese colonialism.

But for a struggle really to go forward, it must be organized and it can only really be organized by a vanguard leadership. Starting out from scratch, as we did, to wage the struggle to liberate a people can be compared with the struggle man has waged over distance, for example. In olden days one of man's biggest difficulties was the following: man was dominated by distance, by the rivers, by the seas. He wanted to travel but it was difficult, he did not have the means for this. One day, perhaps, a man sitting on a river bank saw a tree trunk floating by and for the first time came the idea that perhaps man could go on the tree trunk along the river. If this happened, this was the moment when the first boat appeared, as the legend recounts. But for man to conquer distance, to cross rivers and seas and even to travel through the air, to overcome and to control distance, he had to develop the means. The means were small and weak at the beginning. Little by little they were developed. He used all possible means, water currents, winds, sea currents, and then he began to use forms of energy he had himself discovered: steam power, electrical power and today atomic energy. You see how man's struggle over distance was extraordinary. So much so that man who at quite an advanced stage took years to go round the world can now circle the globe by satellite in eighty minutes, or even less if he wants. In Jules Verne's book the journey took eighty days, and he was a visionary for the future, he foretold the future.

Party

For the struggle against colonialism means are also required. In the first place one must create an instrument of struggle. Our Party is that instrument. You might say that the Party is a base instrument, the mother instrument. Or if we like, the principal means which creates other means linked to it. It is the root and the trunk which produce other branches for the development of our struggle.

The first question we can pose is the following: why have we formed a Party, and others formed movements? Movements, fronts, etc., were formed...but if you consider carefully, we are the only ones who formed a Party, an organization with the title of Party. It might have had other titles, but we are a Party, although there had never been a Party in our land before. This is not by chance, it is not because we like the title Party. It has a clear meaning for today and tomorrow. It is because we take the view that a Party is a much more defined, much clearer organization. A Party represents all those who share a given idea, a given aim, on a given path. A movement is something very vague. Perhaps today our Party is still really a movement, but our task must be to transform it increasingly into a Party. And we gave it the title of Party right from the start because everyone understood that we had very clear ideas on the path we were following, on what we wanted, in the service of our people in Guiné and Cape Verde, in the service of Africa and mankind, in so far as we could make some contribution.

We called it Party, because we understood that to lead a people to liberation and progress, the fundamental need was a vanguard, folk who show in fact that they are the best and can prove it in practice. During the liberation struggle, many folk try deception but little by little they must show their position clearly as belonging to that vanguard, the entirety of those who are the best sons of our people in Guiné and Cape Verde.

We know that our Party was formed in clandestinity. I am not going to tell you the whole history; it is recorded in many books. You can read it if our comrades in the Ideological Commission do their work properly. But if was formed in clandestinity (in hiding). At the start it was truly a Party, with very few followers, a minuscule Party, but the supporters were of like mind and trusted profoundly in the line we drew, like anyone who has had in his life the opportunity to follow this path. Little by little it grew and grew until it was transformed into a broad national liberation movement. Not a movement in name, but in the hard fact of struggle, as an entirety of folk in movement against Portuguese colonialism.

Objective

But we are, as I say again, a Party. Our case can be explained in this way. Those of us who struggle in Guiné and Cape Verde against Portuguese colonialism are all in the national liberation movement; everyone is for the 'Party'. But admission in fact to the Party is only open to someone who genuinely has a single idea, thinks only towards one target, and who has to have a given kind of behaviour in his private life and his social life. What idea, what target, what behaviour?

Our Party comprises only those who in fact want the Party programme. We are PAIGC – Guiné and Cape Verde. There is no racism, there is no tribalism; we are not struggling merely so that we may have a flag, an anthem and ministers – we may not even have ministers in our land. We are not going to install ourselves in the Governor's palace, that is not our objective, to take over the palace to place Cabral and others there. We are struggling to liberate our people not only from colonialism but also from any kind of exploitation.

We want no one to exploit our people any more, neither whites nor blacks, because it is not only whites who practise exploitation, there are blacks who are more ready to exploit than the whites. We want our people to rise and to advance. If we want our people to rise, it is not only the men, because the women too are our people. The members of our Party and those who must rule in our land are those who have understood that a woman has the right to advance, to be taught, to go to school like any other human being, to do any work of which she is capable. They are those who have really understood that so long as a man has three or four wives he will never be a true man and that no people can advance while men have four wives. They are those who have really understood that a female child is not to be sold, and that the mother likewise cannot be sold, that there are no slave women. They are those who have understood that children are the only beings to whom we must accord privileges, that they are the flowers of our life and it is for them that we make all the sacrifices so that they should live happily. They are those who carry out well the tasks allocated by the Party in the service of our people.

I do not command because I am an engineer or a doctor, but because I really work, and no one who has completed his studies is higher than those who have not. No position is higher than another. Only someone who works more, who produces more is higher. Anyone who has understood our Party programme correctly, whether he is from Guiné or Cape Verde, can be admitted to our Party. But he should be ready at any moment to give his life in the cause for which we are struggling.

But while some are admitted to the Party, others perhaps may leave, without much ado, but they will leave. Why? Because they fail to do some of these things, or because they show that they do not understand them or do not want to understand. For example, there are still some in our Party who do not agree with this unity of Guiné and Cape Verde, but who are waiting to see. Some from Cape Verde and others from Guiné who do not agree much, but who are still hesitant, wanting to see what will emerge. They are mistaken. Perhaps they will form another Party, but ours they will leave, they will leave for sure.

Members

I will state the question of our task clearly to you. There should only be honest and serious persons in the Party. Anyone who is dishonest should leave, as should all those who take advantage of the Party to serve their personal interests. Today they may deceive us, but tomorrow they will leave for sure. Anyone who lies should leave, as should anyone who is only chasing his own idea, to have terylene trousers and pretty shirts, to abuse our girls, or anyone who goes about misusing the people of our land. All those who fail to respect the people of our land, hiding this in front of the leadership, but behind their backs in their own area treating the people as if they were colonialist district officers or administrators, should leave. All those who have the idea that they are struggling and making sacrifices in this struggle so that they can misuse their authority like district officers, should leave. The time has come for frank speaking about this. There are some comrades who are making great sacrifices but with the idea that tomorrow they will reap the benefit with a fine motor-car, servants, several wives, etc. They are making a mistake. They are not of our Party and they are going to find this out for sure.

Our Party is open to the best sons of our land. Today we are all for the 'Party', but little by little the nucleus who are the Party is being defined. Anyone who is in fact of the Party is in or will join that nucleus; anyone who is not of the Party will leave. We can only genuinely achieve what we want in our land if we form a group of men and women who are strong, able not to cheat their comrades and not to lie, able to look their comrades straight in the eye, and able to accept that the youth will be the masters tomorrow in our land of Guiné and Cape Verde.

We must, therefore, do our duty as well as possible, to provide all the potential for progress. Anyone who has ambitions for chieftaincy in our Party will sooner or later leave. Anyone who has not learned to respect his companion in struggle as a human being, man or woman, correctly will sooner or later leave. Anyone who thinks that tomorrow our policy will be at the bidding of one or other foreign nation will leave, because we are not going to stand this. We are struggling for independence.

So as you can see it is going to be increasingly difficult to be a member of our Party. And this vanguard we are creating, this instrument we have forged to build the independence of our land, as a man builds a house, must be constantly more honed, more sharpened, more perfect, and *our people must constantly embellish it.*

It is essential for all comrades to study the Party programme, above all the younger ones, to understand it properly and prepare themselves to be of the

Party in fact. And more still to make an early commitment to the Party, because we are going to demand increasingly of each responsible worker a total commitment to the Party. Not commitment to his own idea, not commitment to Amilcar Cabral, or to João, or N'Bana or Bacar, or to any other person who is his chief. Commitment to the Party, to the ideas of the Party, to the Party's ideas which are its lifeblood. He has to show evidence that he has absorbed the Party's ideas, the ideas which the Party has put forward as obligatory for everyone. Anyone who does not do this is in error. Furthermore, later on before anyone can be a Party member, he will have first to be a candidate for the Party. He will have to show evidence that he deserves in fact to be admitted to our Party, and then he will be admitted. It has to be like this, because we want to serve the people of our land effectively. We cannot afford mistakes.

It is easy to bundle everyone into a Party. As soon as a child is born his name is put down for the Party. But what use is this? What is the Party then? In a football club one must pay a subscription, go to the field to applaud and cheer. Are we going to allow everyone into the Party, children, men, women? No. In a liberation struggle it is all right, and necessary: everyone, let us march onward. But in the midst of all this we shall constantly know better who is in fact of the Party. We must be able to come into a room like this and say: that one yes, that one is of the Party, and that one and the other, but that one over there is not yet of the Party.

It must be like this. This is the only way we can serve our people. If we mix everyone up, we will go wrong. The test of a true element of the Party is the wish for constant improvement, for anyone who stays put, dies. Many comrades have not yet understood this, some comrades take advantage of the Party. For them, being in the Party, being a Party leader, means leading a good life, reaping benefits. They want to take their advantages quickly because they do not believe in the Party, do not believe in the future. They want the benefits now and quickly: fine clothes, money in their pocket, the abuse of power, turning comrades into their servants, and other malpractices. This is candidacy for expulsion from the Party and there are many who, if they do not leave today, will leave tomorrow, however much work they have done, however much help they have given. Either they will break with the Party, or they will be expelled.

But the best way is for them to correct themselves, correct themselves quickly, put themselves on the correct line. We have made every effort to set the comrades on the line so that they will not have to leave the Party tomorrow.

Some have already been lost by the wayside because it was impossible for them to correct themselves. As our situation is vulnerable, if someone does not mend his ways, he will turn against us, will turn traitor. We have to fight this at every step, with all the care necessary, so that we give each person the best possible chance to be of the Party, but we cannot allow them to cheat us, to pretend to be of the Party, when they are not of the Party at all.

Any comrade who has in his head the idea that his 'tribe' is the one which should rule in our land, should watch out because there will be war against him. But there are still comrades in the Party who are unable entirely to kill this idea of 'tribe' that they have in their head. Because they are ambitious, merely because they are ambitious they want to be the highest authority in everything. Folk like that are not of the Party. In our Party someone rules if he is worthy of it; more authority is given to someone who has given practical proof that he knows how to use authority and we have only one objective: to serve the people.

Today our Party means all those in our land who are ready to put an end to Portuguese colonialism and ready to follow the Party's watchwords and to respect and carry out the orders of our Party leadership. They are of the Party. But tomorrow the Party will mean only those who have exemplary moral conduct, as men and women worthy of our land. It will mean those who work and have work, for there can be no place for idlers in our Party. It will mean those who dedicate themselves body and soul to the programme of our Party in our land, ready to fight any enemy. What programme of our Party? The one you know but which you will know better all the time. These will form our Party tomorrow and, among them, the effective leaders of the Party are those who will be able to transform the Party constantly into a better organization which is still at the service of our people.

But what are the people?

Many comrades say: oh my people! Many comrades who make mistakes or are in a muddle over Party matters quickly begin to talk about the people. This will soon come to an end but we must understand clearly what the people means.

The definition of *people* depends on the historical moment which the land is experiencing.

Population means everyone, but the people have to be seen in the light of their own history. It must be clearly defined who are the people at every moment of the life of a population. In Guiné and Cape Verde today the people of Guiné or the people of Cape Verde mean for us those who want to chase the Portuguese colonialists out of our land. They are the people, the rest are not of our land even if they were born there. They are not the people of our land; they are the population, but not the people. This is what defines the people today. The people of our land are all those born in the land, in Guiné or Cape Verde, who want what corresponds to the fundamental necessity of the history of our land. It is the following: to put an end to foreign domination in our land. Those who are ready to work hard for this, to stand firm, are those in our Party. The majority of our people, therefore, are of our Party. The leadership of our Party most represents the people. No one should think that merely because he was born in Pico da Antonio or in the heart of Oio, he is more representative of the people than the leadership of our Party. The genuine and true cornerstone of the people of our land is the leadership of our Party, which defends the interests of our people and was able to create the whole of this movement for the defence of our people's interests.

I shall try to throw more light on this question. All those of the population of our land who at this moment want the Portuguese colonialists to leave our land, so that we should gain our freedom and independence, are our people. But among them are some who take a real grip on work, who struggle with weapons in their hands, in the political work or in education or in some other branch and under the leadership of our Party: they form our Party. If you like, the vanguard of our people is our Party and the principal element of our people at this time is the leadership of our Party. So those who have love of our people, have love of the leadership of our Party: anyone who has not yet understood this, has not understood anything.

This is true of this phase, this moment. But in a while, when we have gained our independence, anyone who then wants our land to be independent, for example, but does not want women to be liberated, but wants to go on exploiting women in our land, though he is of the people today, he will not be so tomorrow. If we want all children in our land to be respected and someone among us does not want this, he will be part of the population, he will not be part of the people.

Our objective is to ensure progress and happiness for our people, but we cannot achieve this against our people. If some persons in our land do not want this, we face an alternative. Either they are not the people and then we can do anything against them, even imprison them. Or they are numerous and represent the people, and at that point we give up. We can do nothing more because one cannot ensure happiness and progress for anyone against his will.

We have to understand clearly, therefore, that in each phase of a nation's history, of a land, of a population, of a society, the people are defined in terms of the main stream of the history of that society, in terms of the highest interests of the majority of that society.

The term democracy was coined in Greece, in Athens (from demo+cracy ▪ people's rule). But who coined it? In Athens there were nobles, gentlemen (landowners) and then slaves, who worked for all the others. Democracy for them was only for those on top; they were the people, the others were slaves. Even today it it the same in many places. Anyone who has strength in his hand, power, makes a democracy for himself. We in our land want power to be in the hands of the majority. But we want power to be in the hands of our people.

Anyone who follows the correct path, wants increasingly greater progress and happiness in our land, progress not only for Fula, not only for Mandinga, not only for descendants of Cape Verdians, not only for Balanta but progress for all in Guiné and Cape Verde – such a person is part of our people.

Parties and movements

If I go on talking about the instrument our people forged to develop the action of some of their sons and daughters for the struggle for liberation and progress in our land, I want to stress the fact that right from the start of our work we always had the feeling and certainty that it was not necessary to create several movements to liberate our land. On the contrary, it was essential to make a great effort to have a single organization for struggle which would take action in Guiné and in Cape Verde. This was the line we drew on the basis of analysing our specific situation, our reality, and the line we defended strongly during several years, although at some moments we found it necessary to retreat to be certain if we were right or not.

Yesterday we talked about contradictions in our society. We saw that in social terms properly speaking, that is strata of society, or classes, if you like, the contradictions are not very great, above all in Guiné. They are a little more pronounced in Cape Verde, where there were some folk with land, with property, and some owners of businesses and small industries. But I drew your attention to the fact that this was insignificant, did not constitute a class properly speaking, from the quantitative point of view, that is in number. But we noted clearly that because of the influence of the past, and as a result of division the enemy caused among us, there were contradictions between ethnic groups, between what we call 'tribes' in Guiné. Obviously in Cape Verde the main contradiction is between the landless peasants and those who have secure means of livelihood, including landowners.

The greatest nonsense that could have occurred in our land would have been to create parties or movements in Guiné on the basis of ethnic groups. This would have been an excellent means for the enemy not only to divide us further during the struggle but also to ensure his victory; the destruction of our independence after the struggle, as you have seen in some African countries. In Cape Verde it would have been absurd to think of creating one Party of those who own something and one Party of those who own nothing to struggle against Portuguese colonialism.

In anticolonial struggle, it is fundamental, important and decisive to bring together all those who want independence, who want to struggle against colonialism. Precisely for this reason, when some tiny groups of nationalists arose in Bissau in 1959 who were not controlled by us, our comrades, particularly Comrades Aristides Pereira, Fortes, Luiz and others, did their utmost to bring those tiny groups into our Party to avoid dispersing our strength.

You all know that the Party was founded in 1956 and the time I am talking of was 1959. Later on some persons from our land began to talk about a front, even the Party went so far as to talk about a front. Some of you might ask why we did not form a front in our land. Precisely because a front means a union of various organizations. We did not know of any other organization in our land. When our Party began making contacts outside the country, from 1960 onwards, it was discovered that there were folk outside, whether from Guiné or Cape Verde, who had created the so-called movements outside the land. Our Party had to make a concession. It had to make a step backward from its idea of having only a Party and not a front to see if it could bring in those folk, to struggle for the independence of Guiné and Cape Verde. It was for this reason that we formed a so-called Front with the Liberation Movement for Guiné and Cape Verde which was in Conakry but had been formed by comrades of ours who had become linked to PAIGC, and with the Liberation Movement for Guiné and Cape Verde which was in Ziguinchor.

Later on I could tell you the history of what was going on in Conakry, but the essence is that because of the great fuss, the difficulties raised by our brothers from Guiné and Cape Verde in Senegal, we decided to launch an appeal for unity of all the Liberation Movements for Guiné and Cape Verde. We organized a conference in Dakar with the then Liberation Movement for Guiné and Cape Verde, which was based in Dakar and which included Guineans and Cape Verdians. There were certain people there known to you but it is not worth giving them undue importance by quoting their names here. This conference was also attended by the Ziguinchor movement and the Liberation Movement for Guiné and Cape Verde which was based in Conakry and by PAIGC, represented by some of its members. All this was basically a concession on our part, a tactic, to see what those folk really wanted, what their intentions were, just how far they were committed to real struggle and if they in fact wanted to struggle or were merely interested in finding positions. In practice we organized the entire conference. We took well prepared documents, and they, who had been entrusted with preparing the conference, had not even drawn up the programme yet. The conference was held in fact with the help of the Senegalese authorities, with the help of Comrade Marcelino dos Santos, representing the CONCP, and of other bodies.

The point of view of our Party was vigorously defended by its representatives, and supported by the Guiné and Cape Verde liberation movements from Conakry and Ziguinchor. Obviously the objective of those from Dakar was not to create unity, but to put an end to PAIGC. This was their idea and when they saw that it was impossible they accepted all the resolutions proposed in conference. But soon afterwards they began sabotage. Obviously they were later unmasked as folk who did not want unity, and who did not want unity because they did not want to struggle. They made a pretence of talking about unity, but all they wanted was a foothold from which to manoeuvre to gain jobs and to liquidate our Party.

So you see that the Party, although it had established as its vital principle a single organization, a single banner and no confusion in the establishment of this liberation movement, was able to make concessions. It was able to retreat to give to everyone the chance to demonstrate if they did or did not want really to struggle for our independence. When the Party came to the conclusion that after all those folk were only telling lies, only sought dishonesty and only went looking for jobs, were only trying to create confusion, and so were serving the Portuguese colonialists, the Party made the following resolution: we no longer want unity with anyone; anyone who wants unity with PAIGC should come inside the land to make unity with PAIGC. This was the position we took and we resisted all the pressures brought to bear on us, because we were certain that we were on the certain and sure path.

Rejection of opportunism

Another point we should like to make clear about our Party, our organization, is the following: right from the start (we have already spoken to you about this among our principles) *we rejected opportunism.* We could have tried to bring into our Party, for example, certain highly influential men in Guiné, invite them into the Party so that we could use their influence, such as some personalities in Bissau, or some chiefs – I recall that several chiefs were Party members – but we never told them that they could come and rule.

There were chiefs in Manjaco territory, or Mancanha territory, who went to call others to come under the Party banner. There were chiefs in the Mansoa area and other areas who were arrested for support of the Party banner, but we never said to them that as they were chiefs of our population, they were also chiefs of the Party. We rejected this once and for all, because we did not want to deceive anyone. In a new organization, founded to liberate our land, the leaders are and will be those who are equipped for this task, and not because they were chiefs yesterday. It has been shown and is still being shown in various regions of Africa that it mortgages the future, stores up difficulties for tomorrow, to practise the opportunism of putting traditional chiefs into the leadership of a national liberation organization.

10. Revolutionary democracy

In the context of the principle of *revolutionary democracy,* to which we have already referred several times, each responsible worker must bear his responsibility bravely, must demand respect from others for his activities and must show respect for the activities of others.

However we must not hide anything from our people, we must not deceive our people. Deceiving our people is to build a foundation for calamity for our Party. We must combat this in some comrades vigorously. We cannot allow the population to come to the frontier to fetch merchandise for the people's stores, for example, and once they have arrived find themselves obliged to load up with war material. Doing this is behaving worse than the colonialists, it is abusing our authority, abusing the good faith and good will of our people. It is preferable to say frankly to elements of the population that they should prepare themselves to go and fetch war material, because the war is for our land, and that if they do not want to go, they will be arrested and taken by force. If necessary they can be arrested, but they must know where they are going. This is better than lying, cheating and looking small in the people's eyes, for they, however wretched and suffering, are like any people, and they know the difference between the truth and a lie, justice and injustice, good and evil, and they are wise enough to lose respect for anyone who has lied to them.

We must put an end to lying, we must be able not to deceive anyone about the difficulties of struggle, about the mistakes we make, the defeats we may suffer, and we cannot believe that victory is easy. Nor can we believe in evasions like 'it seems that' or 'I thought that'. This is one of the great defects of some comrades. 'Comrade, how did this happen?' - 'It seems that...' This is no use for those who are making a revolution, who seek the progress and happiness of their people through a liberation struggle. We must be aware of this.

There are comrades who are not able to make a clear report on what is happening in the area where they are. Happily there are others who are capable. I am focusing on the negative aspects, but you all know that there are many positive aspects. That is exactly why we are seated here and it would be disastrous for us if there were only negative aspects. But my duty is to point out what is not going well, so that we can improve and go forward. We trust appearances, our imagination; we have a tendency to trust our imagination.

Revolutionary democracy demands that we combat all opportunism, as I have already told you, and that we combat as well the attitude comrades have of being too hasty in forgiving mistakes. I am a responsible worker, you make a mistake, and I forgive you with the following intention: that now you know you are in my hands. This is not acceptable. No one has a right to forgive mistakes without first discussing the mistakes in front of everyone. Because the Party is ours, for all of us, not for each of us but for all of us. We find it too easy to excuse comrades. We find excuses very quickly, and we must fight this. The time has come to stop finding excuses. There is work to be done; it should be done and done well without excuses.

We can find all kinds of excuses. There are responsible workers whose work consists in finding excuses for their group for doing nothing, in trying to explain to the Party leadership why nothing has been done – difficulties in the terrain, poor conditions, the enemy advance, there is heavy bombardment, etc, etc. They do this instead of making an effort and working to overcome all the difficulties. Struggle is the following: permanent victory over difficulties. If there were no difficulties, it would not be a struggle, it would be a cakewalk, a picnic.

We must combat the whole tendency to friendships and comradeships which do not serve the Party, but to scratch one another's backs, which are not in the interest of the Party and our people. We know that this goes on in our Party. There are comrades who fall to pieces when their companion in struggle is changed, they can no longer live without their companion in struggle. We must combat this forcefully in our own mind and in the mind of others. There is no 'matiness' here unless it is to serve the Party, to serve the people in our land. There is no 'matiness', camaraderie or friendship, for us to sit drinking cane spirit or palm wine, or to hide from other comrades what someone does with the young girls of our land, or to hide mistakes in connexion with the armed struggle, for example, or for us to remain silent when a responsible worker does not fight as he should. This is a betrayal of our Party and our people, and serves the Portuguese; it is friendship on the side of the Portuguese. We have it among us, and we must combat it forcefully and bravely. You all know that it exists and unhappily some of you are guilty of it.

Our criterion for friendship, 'matiness' or camaraderie, should be the following: you are worthy, respect the watchwords of the Party correctly, you are my comrade, you are my friend. If you do not do this, you had better go and join the opportunists or join the lackeys of the Portuguese. But our passion for friendship is so strong that comrades of ours who know that someone is an agent of the Portuguese are able to spend their time in his house, to frequent his house, to eat in his house, to drink in his house. Tell me if this is right. But comrades say: 'I have known that person for a long time', or 'He is a relative of my mother'. This shows a lack of political awareness, or even a lack of awareness of the sacrifices that our people are making for the struggle. But even Party leaders do this. Happily, it looks as if it is coming to an end.

Then we have this example: everyone knows that a given comrade has made a serious mistake in the Party, inside or outside the land, and was sent for. We are waiting for him. He arrives and all the comrades stand up with hugs, kisses and so on as if he were the best comrade in the world. What is this lack of awareness? What is this lack of sense of responsibility? If someone is unworthy, we must show him that he is unworthy. There is no friendship, there is no consideration for him. He must be cast aside.

The time has come for us to be friends with those who are worthy, but those who are worthless cannot be our comrades, our friends. Anyone who betrays the Party, who tries to divide us, who makes plans to sabotage the Party, who serves the enemy, who consorts with the enemies of our Party can no longer sit with us, cannot eat with us from the same bowl, cannot drink from the same glass or mug, cannot sleep in the same bed. Either we are able to distinguish the worthy from the unworthy or it is not worth our while going on with our struggle as we are doing, because sooner or later we shall drown in a sea of great confusion of our own making.

Irreplaceables

We must avoid the obsession of some comrades that everything is spoiled, everything is over if they should leave the posting where they are. Nobody is indispensable in this struggle; we are all needed but nobody is indispensable. If someone has to go and goes away and then the struggle is paralysed, it is because the struggle was worthless. The only pride we have today, that I myself have, is the certainty that, after the work we have already done, if I were to go away, to be stopped, to die or disappear, there are those here in the Party who can carry on the Party's task. If this were not so, then what a disaster; we would have achieved nothing. For a man who has an achievement that only he can carry on has not yet done anything. An achievement is worth while to the extent that it is an achievement of many, and if there are many who can take it up and carry it on, even if one pair of hands is taken away.

But there are comrades who have obsessions that if they should leave their place, everything will be ruined. This is an obsession that we must combat, that we must put a stop to. This is without mentioning cases of other comrades who think, when they are transferred, that they are going to die, because they have already established all the conditions for working in one spot and are called upon to go to another. What blindness! As if our land were just their little corner! This shows a lack of awareness of the real reason, the aim and the characteristics of our struggle.

We must be able to stand by the truth, to tell the truth before everyone, without fear, even if the truth entails some difficulties. We must speak the exact truth face to face.

Militants must not be afraid of any responsible worker in the framework of our Party. Anyone who is afraid has not yet understood or is a coward by nature. Our Party has given everyone the same strength not to be afraid of anyone. We have said that we are struggling to put an end to fear among our people in Guiné and Cape Verde. We must not be afraid of anyone. The lowliest militant must not be afraid of anyone, not of the Secretary-general, nor of anyone. He must show correct respect, for this is a matter of self-respect.

Responsible workers should not fear the militants. There are responsible workers of whom militants and combatants are afraid. The former are barbarian chiefs of olden days, they are not leaders or responsible workers of PAIGC. But they sometimes fear the militants. If they hear militants chatting they want to know what it is about, because they fear that the militants are going to make difficulties for them with the Party leadership. We must put an end to this.

Revolutionary democracy demands in effect that responsible workers and leaders should live among the people, before the people, behind the people. They must work for the Party in the certainty that they are working for the people in our land. And we must struggle so that at all costs the people feel that it is they who have the power in our land in their hands. Up till now they have not felt this very much. In the liberated areas some comrades have usurped this power of our people. We must deliver it into the hands of our people. We are still at war and it is still a little difficult. But in step as we advance we have to deliver power to our people so that they have the certainty that power is in fact theirs.

No one in the Party should be afraid of losing power. Many countries have come to ruin because the rulers were afraid of losing the lead. We must not be afraid of anything. We must tell the truth frankly to our people, to our militants, to our comrades. If they are not happy and they can, they will chase us out, throw us out. But none of us must be afraid of anything, we must not hide the truth to preserve our position. This would be a betrayal of the interest of our people, our land and all those who put their trust in us.

We must not deceive the people with fine words, with false promises. We must tell them frankly the difficulties. At a meeting in Boé, for example, the population told me: 'Send us this, that. We want this, that, etc. in the shop.' I answered the population: 'No. We cannot do this and that. What we are sending is already a great sacrifice. If you are not satisfied, do what you will, even leave the Party, but we are not sending. You must remember that you are not the only ones with needs. Other persons in our land also have needs.' I took this opportunity of being with our supporters to teach them, to make them aware, not to tell them lies, or deceive them with false promises. They all understood.

As I have said, we must constantly go forward to put power into the hands of our people, to make a profound change in the life of our people, even to put all the means for defence into the hands of our people, so that it is our people who defend our revolution. This is what revolutionary democracy will be in fact tomorrow in our land. Anyone who rules his people but fears the people is in a bad way. We must never fear the people.

In the framework of revolutionary democracy, as I have already said, we must bring to the fore the best sons and daughters of our land. The worst and the worthless must be left behind. Our task is to prepare our hoe, our plough, our hammer, with which we are going to construct the future of our people in freedom, progress and happiness. Let us constantly improve our Party, for the better our Party is, the more certainty we have of achieving what we want for our people. For this reason we must, as we have already said, act so that our Party belongs more each day to those who are able to make it constantly better.

11. Fidelity to Party principles

Another principle of our Party that we adopt as a rule in life is: *being faithful to principles.*

Many have principles but when the moment comes to apply them they forget themselves, they are not faithful to principles. We must be faithful to our principles, we must apply them every day, we must not compromise our principles, whether on the internal plane, in our internal life, or on the external plane, in our relations in the external field.

Our leaders and responsible workers have the courage to struggle constantly against all temptation to practise opportunism, to take the easiest path. The path of struggle is never an easy path, but there are many among us who have a tendency for the easy way out. The consequence is that at every step they forget our Party principles; the consequence is that they lie at every step. And when one begins to lie, one lies so much that one ends by being caught out.

We must respect our principles. We have established our strategy, that is the broad line of our struggle, in accordance with our principles, and on this score we make no concessions, we do not retreat for anyone; we do not accept this. But on minor matters, on matters which do not affect our principles, we have to know how to make concessions. We have to be able to give way. We have to be able to use the tactics needed on the political and the military level, above all on the political level.

The skill of a leadership, of a leader, lies in knowing where he may give way and where he must not give way. This means that faced with a given problem we must ask the following question: what is essential and what is secondary? Is it in fact an essential problem or a secondary problem? Is it a problem just for today or for always, permanent or temporary? We must distinguish the essential from the secondary. We must know how to make concessions, to give way, to give Party liaison deeper roots, to open the way for the Party to advance.

In relations with militants, with combatants, we can make certain concessions, we can give way on certain points, but without giving way on our principles. In the armed forces, for example, we cannot make any concession on discipline, but we can give way a little to comrades on matters which do not spoil our work, which do not prejudice our principles as the fundamental rules for our work.

There, put very briefly, are some of the fundamental principles on which our Party work is based. We have based ourselves on them and continue to base ourselves on them: today, in the struggle against Portuguese colonialism; tomorrow in the struggle against misery, suffering and disaster in our land, against all injustices, for the progress and happiness of our people in Guiné and Cape Verde.

12. For the improvement of our political work

Let us say something about what we should do at this moment to hasten the victory of our people on the various resistance fronts.

What should we do?

We must improve our political work. We must better organize our armed forces and make them operate more and more intensively. We must strengthen and increasingly consolidate our liberated areas. We should give better guidance to our supporters in all fields of activity, and guide correctly our students and our cadres under training. We should operate with increasing efficiency, with more awareness and for better results on the external plane, in our relations with Africa and with the world in general.

We must constantly improve our thinking and behaviour to give better service to our great Party in the service of our people in Guiné and Cape Verde.

One can never say too strongly that the political work is a fundamental task of our struggle, so fundamental that, as I told you a while ago, every shot fired is also a political act. It is fundamental that in our Party the leaders in the armed struggle are political leaders. Comrade Nino is at this moment deploying his efforts to carry out a plan which I drew up point by point after discussion with all concerned to develop a new kind of operational action in our struggle. He is commander-in-chief of this operation and he is a member of the Political Bureau of our Party. Any leader of our armed struggle, like Tchutchu or Bobo, who are sitting here, or Lucio or Nandingna, or others here, are also Party leaders, in its political leadership, and some of them have already been members of Party Committees at various stages, heads of Party Committees or ordinary members of a Regional Committee. We feel therefore that we do not draw a distinction between politics and other tasks, for to give health treatment, education, to supply cloth and other goods to raise living standards is also political. To fire shots, to work at the international level is also political. But given that our life is complex with various functions to fulfil, there are persons who have the specific task of devoting themselves to political work. Under the guidance of the higher leadership of the Party, in the various echelons of Party leadership our political commissars have duties of political work, at Inter-regional or Zone level, aided by political brigades. But Party Committees and village committees must also carry out political work. The latter are also basically political bodies.

Political work by our political commissars, like that of all those who work in politics, aided by all the other responsible workers of the Party at any level, is a decisive task for our struggle. We can defeat the Portuguese at Buba or at Bula, we can enter and take Bissau, but if our population has not been well trained politically, is not fully wedded to the struggle, we shall lose the war, not win it. So it is fundamental that our political commissars should clearly understand this, understand the significance of their work, but also that all the Inter-regional and Zone Committees should understand the significance of their work, for the latter are the political instruments of the Party working at grass roots level. Whether they be a member of the security service, a political commissar, a responsible worker for health, for education, for supply, they are the political force in operation each day to improve our work.

Clearly the victories of our armed forces must strengthen the political work. Some of our comrades are, for example, trying to win over the Fula population in the areas between Quirafo and Bangacia, but when the latter hear that the Portuguese have pulled out of Madina Xaquili it is easier to make them believe in us. So we see how the two aspects always link up to help the political work.

What is essential is that we, as members of the Inter-regional or Zone Committee, should be capable and devoted to our Party. We must identify totally with the interests of our Party. The first condition for improving our political work is to improve our political workers. It is fundamental that our political commissars, our responsible workers for the militia, security, health, education, should be profoundly conscious of their task. They should be such as most cherish our Party, have most love for our people and are most determined to put into practice the watchwords of the Party. They must be persons who can raise high the name of the Party, the leadership of the Party, and who must have confidence in the Party leadership. They must be such as reflect their conscious willingness to die for our Party by working from morning to night every day for our Party, dedicating their lives, which is much easier than dying. They must be such as are vigilant, whether or not in the security services, vigilant against any attempt to destroy our Party, to betray our Party. They must be such as to keep as friends only the friends of our Party, and to be implacable enemies of all our Party's enemies. They must be such as will not tolerate any act against the interests of our Party. When they have to speak about Party questions in front of the people, in front of the leaders, in all circumstances they will shout loudest, will raise highest the banner of our Party, the name of our Party. They must draw the masses behind them. They must be behind the masses, among the masses, in front of the masses, to mobilize them and always the first to set the example of our Party's banner. We cannot yet say that we have only had the best Party militants in our committees. Some are by no means the best, others are even afraid really to speak up about the Party. From now on, you must all work to the end that we can put at the head of our Party Committees those who really are of the Party. If we look into their hearts, we shall find only the banner of the Party. If we look into their heads, we shall find only the ideas of the Party. If we give them the floor, they will shout loud, really loud, the name of the Party, to encourage everyone to struggle for our Party. And night and day, at any hour when work is needed, they buckle down to the work of our Party. This is the first condition for us to improve our political work; to improve the work of our cadres we must improve our cadres who are tied exclusively and directly to the civil and political work of the Party.

We must improve the work among our people, we must hold meetings with our people as much as possible. The zone political commissars must be in permanent contact with the villages within their zone, in permanent contact, holding village meetings, discussing people's difficulties, trying to find out what is going on so as to help solve difficulties. The security should be with them also doing this work. And health and education representatives, controlling, helping and solving difficulties. That is how it should be. We must be permanently mobilizing, organizing our people, helping our village committees to hold their meetings to discuss their difficulties, helping our people to govern themselves, to solve their own difficulties. Only in this way can we match up to the demands of our struggle today. And this work has to be carried out with vigilance in regard to all enemy actions, whether it is enemy infiltration among us – security has to watch out for this – enemy propaganda on their radio or by any other means; we have to neutralize it immediately. We have to explain to our masses, to our population, their difficulties, the deceptions the Portuguese want to plant in their mind. Political work has to be a permanent task among our people. We all know well what we must do.

We have constantly to improve political work among the armed forces as well. All our cadres tied to political work, including our armed forces commanders and political commissars, must work to raise the political level of our armed forces. There cannot be any separation between the political commissar in the zone or the Inter-region and the armed forces. No. The political commissar for the Inter-region, the security member for the Inter-region, the People's Militia in the Inter-region or Zone, are all part of the armed forces, as our orders that they should all carry weapons show. They are armed forces detached on political duty. Those in the armed forces are detached on duty in the armed struggle. So we must not have any separation; they must always be in harmony, living hand in hand, working together politically. And the zone political commissars must from time to time hold meetings with the armed forces in that zone, in liaison with the armed forces political commissar. They must talk about relations with the population and discuss questions about the population, and about the armed forces. They must discuss whether they are operating well or badly, to praise those who are operating well, to agree on ways of reinforcing aid to the population and ways for the population to aid the armed forces, to co-ordinate their work between the armed forces and the population, and to make it a single body. It is no use the political commissar and the committee being one thing, and the command political commissar being another, or each working on his own and turning his back on the other. It should not be like this. We must admit frankly that in our armed forces today some political commissars are not political commissars at all. They have never known how to hold a political meeting, never hold political meetings with Party comrades who are in the armed forces. Generally speaking in other countries the armed forces have some Party members and some non-Party. We accept all the comrades in the armed forces into the Party, and we must work with them, explain to them. There are comrades who die on the battle-fronts without knowing what the Party is. Why? Because sometimes our political commissars do not know what the Party is. We must put an end to this. There are some who understand, sometimes even without being taught they understand. There are some who really do political work, but a large proportion do no political work among the armed forces. Sometimes the commander himself does not allow the political commissar to do anything, because he as commander controls everything. He forgets that he himself is the first political commissar. He is a political commissar and commander, the other is a political commissar. They must work together, do the political work together. The more politicized our armed forces are, the greater certainty we have of security in our land a victory in our struggle. We have also clear watchwords about political work in our armed forces, and I do not need to go over it all again here. I will merely remind you of some fundamental aspects.

We must be constantly more selective about our leaders, our responsible workers, our militants. As I have told you, up till now to belong to our Party it has been enough to want to chase the Portuguese, the Portuguese colonialists, out of our land and to support the PAIGC. There was even an oath to PAIGC. We had this for quite a while, but then we dropped it. At the start when it was difficult, when one joined the Party one had to take an oath and anyone who believed in kola nut, had to eat kola. We stopped this as the struggle grew very much and there were a lot of people to eat kola. I can even remember how comrade Tiago, who supervised the taking of oaths to the Party, began to suffer a little as he ate too much kola. We soon stopped this, but at bottom, in the conscience of each one when he joins PAIGC, he takes an oath even if he does not speak, even if he does not sign any document. But very soon it will be necessary to give specific evidence to become a militant of our Party. Today it is not yet required. Tomorrow to become a de facto militant of our Party it will be necessary to give specific evidence that one satisfies certain requirements. One must thoroughly know the Party programme, one must know what the Party seeks, so that it is a conscious act, that one does not come to join and then not know why after all. And we must be constantly more strict about our responsible workers and our leaders; the example must come from the top.

Authority must be based on real work, on the accomplishment of duty and on conduct or behaviour which is an example to everyone. We must constantly demand more from our responsible workers. Some fairly reasonable responsible workers were trained through the difficult struggle we have had, but we must admit that we did not have time or opportunity to deal more strictly with some other responsible workers. I am not going to repeat here all the praises that are due to some responsible workers in our Party, political commissars, members of security, armed forces chiefs, who have worked bravely enough, skilfully enough, albeit making the occasional mistake. Likewise I am not going to repeat the mistakes that our responsible workers have made (I have already given this in my talk). Our criticism of this is still valid. We stated it in that document we called 'On reorganization of the armed forces'. Our comrades must read it, because it is all written out there frankly and openly, even explaining why the majority of our responsible workers who make the most mistakes are those who came from the towns.

In this seminar today I call your attention to everything we have already criticized in other talks. I call your attention to the fact that the time has come for us to put a stop to mistakes by responsible workers. The time has come for us to put a stop to responsible workers who receive the Party watchwords and put them aside; they keep them so that they are not lost but they do not read them. The time has come for us to put a stop to responsible workers or leaders who never present a report on the situation of their work.

The time has come for us to put a stop to responsible workers at any level, even Party leaders, who prefer feasting to a serious life of work and study. The time has come for us to put a stop to responsible workers and leaders who have more than one wife and who in the struggle have provided more children than work.

The time has come for us to put a stop to responsible workers and leaders who are unable to study to increase their knowledge, even in the depths of the bush, so that they should be more responsible workers, more really leaders. The time has come for us to put a stop to responsible workers or leaders who, when they are asked something about their work, tell lies. The time has come for us to put a stop to responsible workers and leaders who are able to do harm to others to prevent their advance, for fear that the latter will take their place. The time has come for us to put a stop to responsible workers and leaders who, when they are transferred to another spot, think that they are going to die, because they have lost their corner, because where they were they had already built up their chieftaincy.

The time has come for us to put a stop to responsible workers or leaders who are unable to get on with their comrades in a Front or in an Inter-regional Committee. The time has some for us to put a stop to responsible workers or leaders who do not want our women to advance as well to become responsible workers or leaders. The time has come for us to put a stop to responsible workers and leaders who can show disrespect to leaders or responsible workers who are over them. The time has come for us to put a stop to responsible workers and leaders who fail to show in their every act love for our Party, respect for the leadership of our Party, bearing in mind that the most important thing in their life is the Party's work. But it is all of us who must put a stop to this. The time has come for us to put a complete stop to being afraid of responsible workers or leaders of the Party. There is no need to be afraid of authority. And anyone who abuses his authority is committing a more serious crime than those of the Portuguese colonialists.

The time has come too for us to raise really high the name of those militants, responsible workers and leaders who were able to accomplish the Party's task, setting an example for others, showing the right path that we must follow in our work. Every responsible worker, every leader must always keep well in mind that we are an organization and so we must be organized. Some comrades prefer things disorganized so that they can escape control. Some of our comrades think that when we send someone to see what they are doing he is going to spy. The time has come for us to establish an entire control service so that each person, if he is a leader or a responsible worker, should clearly understand that control and inspection are to serve him, to help him to take a better course. The time has come for us to regard as genuine Party Committees those who can in fact meet periodically, as the Party orders, study difficulties, as the Party orders, make reports, as the Party orders. Anyone who cannot do this is not a leader, nor a responsible worker of the Party, nor any part of a committee. It is an imposture: he deceives himself and is deceiving us. The time has come for us to insist that our village committees really meet periodically to discuss their difficulties, to give satisfaction to and also receive satisfaction from the leaders in zone or Inter-regional Committees, to keep in touch and to take the pulse, to know what is really happening in our land, to solve difficulties before they become worse. In this context, we must do everything to bring on the young comrades who have shown the capacity to become responsible workers capable of leadership.

And in the context of this necessity, there is a great necessity incumbent on us today to strengthen our security service. We can work hard, die in struggle, tire ourselves out, worry, age, sicken, etc., but if we allow the 'termite' to gnaw our timbers from within, one day we shall lean on the timbers and they will fall because they are rotten inside. The 'termite' may as well be agents of the Portuguese among us as ourselves, any one of us.

A responsible worker or leader who gets drunk, for example, is more dangerous for us than an agent of the Portuguese. The former not only fails in his duty and sets a bad example, but he is also killing himself with the bottle. Now it is just what the Portuguese want that he should die, that he should not work well. A responsible worker or Party leader whose concern wherever he is is to find the prettiest girls to woo is acting worse than an agent of the Portuguese. First, he is cutting off our possibility of giving dignity and status to the women of our land. Second, he is setting a bad example for everyone, for other responsible workers and for militants and combatants and is moreover demobilizing our people. Third, he is ruining himself as a leader or a responsible worker. A good Party worker, a good leader, who fulfils his duty correctly and is aware of our struggle, must be able to choose his company carefully to set a good example. It is normal that a man needs a woman and that a woman needs a man, that we have company. In the present circumstances of our land, anyone who governs can in general have as many women as he wants. That is still the Africa of today. Look at ministers in Africa in general: how many women do they have? But they are not making progress in their land. We have to cut this out completely in our land. Each one of our responsible workers or leaders has to set an example, a good example, which everyone will follow, so as to have the authority to rebuke others when the occasion arises for rebuke.

But we must see all this in the context of our security, we must be vigilant in this regard. Security does not merely mean catching agents of the Portuguese, preventing our people from going to sell rice to the Portuguese. Selling rice is a delicate question, for example. If we were working well, had things under control, we could even send our supporters to go and sell rice to the Portuguese, with the aim of collecting information, carrying out espionage and even to obtain certain things we have not yet been able to have. Unhappily, we believe that it is a bit difficult in our circumstances. But security also means the follwing: 'I am on your side, you are a leader, you behave wrongly, I tell you so frankly: I complain about you.'

It is not forbidden to drink, for example. Anyone may drink – unless he be a Moslem – but in moderation. But moderation is the hard part, because everyone has his appetite. We must avoid drinking to excess. A security agent must always be ready to act openly against this, whether it be a commander, a Party leader, even the Secretary-general, with all the respect he has for them. If one of them is drunk, arrest him. This is what security means. 'Stop, for you are wrecking our work' – that is real security. Not the security when in order to please the responsible worker you find him drink and even go on the spree with him. This is not security. This is to be an accomplice in the destruction of our struggle.

But we must also strengthen security in our struggle in regard to the enemy. The enemy is very active. We must strengthen our security on the basis of our security services, to which we must give more serious development. The Party has trained many cadres in the security branch. Unhappily, some have not shown that they have really learned this work, because they have displayed much lack of initiative.

We must base our security on the work of our people's militia, which is an instrument for security in our liberated areas. We have made some effort to organize our people's militia, some responsible workers have made efforts either individually or in the framework of our people's militia committees in liaison with the Inter-regional Committee. But we have to do much more. We have to organize the people's militia, but not on the lines of the bigroup[1], as some have had a tendency to do, going so far as to organize people's militia bases. No. The people's militia must be among the people in the villages or among the people in the bush. The best sons of our land who are in the villages and have not yet joined the army are the ones who must form our people's militia – good militants, who have proved themselves , the youth, according to our definition, between the ages of fifteen and thirty. They will fulfil a specific role, which is to strengthen our security and self-defence as much against the robbers sent by the enemy as against invasions on the part of the enemy. The vanguard of our village population in the liberated areas must form our people's militia in liaison with the Inter-regional Committee and the Party political commissar. We must form groups of people's militia in the villages within each area, and we can also form groups of people's militia between various villages. The people's militia are folk who work at home, in the fields, etc., but when they are needed, they should muster immediately, when they are needed for a job, they should come. We must train our people's militia in the arts of warfare, in vigilance, to carry out patrols, etc.

We must put into effect the watchword of the Party, which has already been stated, to arm our people's militia. It has already begun but it is not yet completed. Some weapons have rusted, others are at the frontier waiting to be delivered to the people's militia. Other weapons arrived in the people's militia areas and were not distributed as they should be; quite recently the Portuguese came and captured them in the Fifioli area in sector 2 of the Eastern Front. There are weapons for the people's militia such as *Ricos,*

[1]The usual tactical unit of the PAIGC army – a 'double group' of 30-50 men.

which we provide for the people's militia, and carbines of various types for the people's militia, which we still have not distributed as we should. We must strengthen our armed and civil defence, setting to work elements of the population with weapons in their hands. We gave the watchword to arm the population. We ourselves began to arm the population in the Quitafine area; we ourselves carried out the first distribution of weapons. But this work has not been carried on as it should. So we should make an effort to do better, for this is improving our political work.

Another important task for us is to strengthen our organization, our liaison with the urban centres where the enemy still is, to improve the clandestine organization of the Party in the urban centres. But anyone who is in the bush as a political commissar, in an Inter-regional Committee, in a Zone Committee, must in his area maintain close liaison with our comrades and our brothers within the towns who really want to struggle for our Party. We must be able to send agents into the towns to prepare supporters, to work with our supporters. Unhappily, it is rare that any responsible worker of the Party has done this to any serious extent. It has been forgotten that our land is also its towns – Bissau, Bafata, Bambadinca, Mansoa, Bissorã, Catio, etc. It is true that there are some, in security and in political affairs, who have developed their work effectively. But what we have done so far is not enough, we must do much more. We must strengthen the clandestine organization of our Party within the urban centres; this is mainly a task for our security, but also for all our politicals, workers in the political field. Where there is nobody in an urban centre, we must send one or two on detachment there, in disguise, so that they can organize it as it should be. This is fundamental. It is no use our training dozens and dozens of cadres for the security services, who are taught clandestine work, espionage, clandestine organization, handling of explosives, etc., counter-espionage, reconnaissance, etc., for them then to reach our land, sit down and do nothing. So-and-so is not in security because he can catch someone who is going to sell rice to the Portuguese. That is not enough. The time has come for us to put these cadres from security to work right in the urban centres, to establish new organizations, and to strengthen our Party's presence in these places. This is fundamental.

To improve our work, we must strengthen and constantly consolidate our liberated areas. Our struggle has made great strides, rapid strides, and perhaps even at the beginning too rapid strides. In a short space of time we found ourselves faced with the great responsibility of having liberated areas. This is very good, because the liberated areas are the base, the rearguard for the advance of our armed forces in the struggle. Moreover they allow us to acquire experience in governing our people. But it also creates much toil. We have to lead the people; we have to meet the wishes of the population. We have to improve the population's living conditions and organize their life better. We have to work much harder. But there is not the slightest doubt that we have made a little headway, to the point that the Portuguese recognize that in the majority of the liberated areas it would be impossible now for our people to return to accepting colonialist domination.

Some good work has been done but we must do still more and better work. We must put a stop completely to the drain of our folk from liberated areas. We must persuade our folk to return to liberated areas in our land, among those who went to the cities and among those who went outside our land. We must do still more to consolidate Party organization in the liberated areas. We must further develop our educational work, although we have reduced the number of schools to give a better return. We must work well in our hospitals, in our health centres, few though they are, to show that they are useful. Our people's stores should function correctly. Our militants who work in the people's stores should not pilfer. This is very important. We must do everything to give the people in the liberated areas the opportunity to control our people's stores.

The first condition for construction in our liberated areas is the one we have already mentioned: improving our political work. This requires that Party leaders, in the zone or Inter-regional Committee, live in fact among the population, with the population. Unhappily, the tendency is to set up central bases. The Inter-regional Committee has its base, the Zone Committee is in its base, while the population are in their compounds or their villages and the leader is far away, creating a chasm between him and the population he leads. A long time ago we issued the watchword: leaders of the Zone and Inter-regional Committees must be with the people. There are to be no special compounds, special bases. If he is in the Zone, his base must be every compound of the people, every village of the people. One day he is in one, the next day in another, always on the move, because as leader of the Zone he must never be stuck in one spot. This not only increases the return on his work, makes him carry out his duty better, but also increases his own security. In the Zone, the political commissars, security, the education heads, health heads, supply heads, must never be still, must always be in liaison with the people, following all the difficulties of the people, trying to solve their problems with the people. In the Inter-region, the political commissar, security, the responsible worker for education, for health, for supply, for the militia must always be on the move through the Zones and even, if they can be, also in the compounds and the villages, always living with the population. At every place they reach, they should meet with the local Zone Committees, giving instructions, taking the pulse to find out the situation, holding meetings with the population, explaining and helping to solve the difficulties which the Zone Committees cannot solve, in close liaison with the Zone leaders and through them, and directly as well with the mass of our people in the liberated areas. This is how we must work hard to lead and to increase the consolidation of our liberated areas.

But our armed forces commanders, principal commanders or army corps commanders, must also be in liaison with the combatants everywhere, not shut up at their commands while the forces are in operation. In the north and the south they shut themselves up at their commands and are not in touch with their forces. We must have forces everywhere. If there are big groups at the Buba junction, the commander must go there to see them. If they are near Nhala, he must go there to see them. Or at Gangenia, or Madina de Baixo, or in the Jabada area, infiltrated between the Portuguese, or in the surroundings of Gantongo, at Sambuia, N'Goré, or at any other base in the north, in the Mansaba area, or in the Maqué area. A commander or a political commissar must always be with the armed forces, always on the move, finding a place or several places to hold meetings with other responsible workers, but always on the move.

In addition, as our commandants, our principal responsible workers in the armed forces are usually political leaders as well, they have the duty of meeting the Inter-regional Committee to discuss difficulties. They must co-ordinate the work of Zone Committees, and even co-ordinate work with the population, to help political commissars, security, etc., in their work. This is the best method of consolidating our position in the liberated areas, in our struggle as a whole.

We must accept that the place of Party leaders is among the population, not settled at any base. The place of armed forces leaders is among the combatants and not settled at any command. He may have a command, or a really safe position, where there are, for example, a radio, one or two trustworthy persons, a guard, where he can go from time to time, but he must be always on the move, even for his own security. There were responsible workers in our armed forces who were killed because they spent too long sitting in the bases.

To consolidate our liberated areas we have to work more closely with our population, to raise production. We must be able to make our people cultivate more land, grow more rice, even prepare our people for new crops. For sooner or later we must begin to grow groundnuts in our liberated areas for sale abroad, and other crops still. We must promote as a Party watchword in the liberated areas: diversification. This means varying the agricultural crops so that our people can eat better, so that our combatants too can eat better. In liberated areas where there are combatants we must make the combatants work as well, as we have already said.

We have to develop our agriculture step by step, patiently. We have to develop our craft-work, help our population make cloth, mats and baskets, pots and pitchers. Above all we should encourage them to make works of art, sculptures. This could be of great value for our Party and demonstrate our skills outside. We must work hard to bring constant improvement to our system of supply to the liberated areas of essential items. One essential item, for example, is soap; our people have to wash their clothes, their bodies, etc. We have already begun to manufacture soap in our liberated areas, but up till now we have not been able to manufacture soap well, although this is easy and we have plenty of palm oil. Our responsible workers in production who were given this task have had some results, but they fall far short of the results they could have reached. There are other items we could manufacture in our liberated areas. We must make an effort to help our people obtain iron to make agricultural implements, tools for the fields, and materials for our smiths to work with.

Our people's stores must be able to distribute properly the goods our Party supplies, must be able to store and distribute properly the goods bought from the people in exchange for essential items, like cloth and other things. So far we have had some success but our people's stores are still not functioning well. Obviously there is the big difficulty that sometimes we have nothing to send them, but I am talking of when there is something. The Party in its external work is making greater efforts to achieve a continual rise in the quantity of merchandise. Happily we have good prospects for this year. If our struggle is well maintained, if we manage to pin the enemy on the ground as we should, so that they can do nothing against us, we should give our people many essential goods this year. But to do this we must distribute properly, at set times, without any funny tricks, without trying to deceive the people. On the other hand we must strictly collect from the people the things they must deliver: rice, kola, coconut, wax, animal hides, etc. And our responsible workers in production must store these correctly, preserve them correctly, to be used or sold as appropriate.

We have to have control over production. We cannot tolerate lack of control. We cannot compromise. As happened, for example, when we put one comrade in control of our administration and the comrades did not appreciate this. They were angry with him because he would not let them sell cows belonging to the Party. So then began a series of intrigues against the comrade. There were manoeuvres so that even the combatants would be annoyed on the grounds that he was not letting anyone eat beef. But this was not the motive; the motive was to make them turn against him so that he would be dismissed, because he was the one who prevented certain responsible workers from selling the cows. We must put a stop to this. We must accept control and inspection. It is not a question of distrust, it is a question of security.

We have constantly to improve our education, our boarding schools, our Pilot School. This too is consolidating our liberated areas; although our Pilot School is abroad[1], it forms part of our liberated areas because it takes the best students from our schools in the liberated areas, and is integrated in our educational system for the liberated areas. It is abroad because there we have better conditions to do the work we want to do in the school at this phase of our struggle. Improving our education means increasing the number of

[1]It was in Conakry.

schools. But increasing the number of our schools is not enough to improve our education, and may even harm it sometimes. If we make the number of schools too high, then we shall not have enough materials to give to the students and we shall not have good teachers to make the students learn effectively. It is preferable to have a set number of schools, even a few, guaranteeing a good education for the students at all necessary levels. Then little by little, as the Party has the resources, we can increase the number of schools, above all when we have the human resources, meaning good teachers. For it is not worth anything to have teachers to teach nothing, just to waste time. We have to make our schools fulfil the duty the Party has laid down for them – education and work. Work to maintain the school correctly, work for agricultural production to feed the students and our combatants, for physical exercise for our students, and so that no one thinks that going to school means no more tilling the soil. One of the disasters of modern Africa is the following: anyone who has a primary school certificate no longer wants to take the plough or the hoe to till the soil. In our land even if we take our people as far as the final year of secondary school we will have to take the plough or hoe today and tractors tomorrow to till our soil as we should.

It is fairly important to have boarding schools in our liberated areas, but before we establish boarding schools we have to see if we can really maintain them, if there is sufficient security for the students not to run the risk of being killed in the boarding school, if we have sufficient means to provide food for the boarding school. We cannot found a boarding school with the idea that the Party is going to send food from abroad. The Party can make an effort to send clothes, shoes, shorts and sports clothes in general for the boarding school, books, exercise books, pencils, chalk, ink, pens, etc., but the boarding school must at least supply its own food. This is our instruction: a boarding school which cannot supply its own food should close. The circumstances of our struggle in our land do not allow us to try to send food for boarding schools from outside our land. This is impossible. The boarding school must be sustained either by our people inside our land who give food for their children or by the boading school itself which cultivates rice and other crops to supply its own food, to store and eat properly.

Our Pilot School, which is one of the essential elements in our educational system, is opening the way to train cadres to serve tomorrow, the future of our struggle. The cadres may be military or political, electricians or industrial workers in any branch, doctors or engineers, nurses or radio operators or any speciality (no one should think that going to the Pilot School means becoming a doctor or engineer, for he would be mistaken). The Pilot School must be constantly more exacting in regard to the students it takes. We must send to the Pilot School the best pupils from our land, who receive the highest assessments, within certain age limits. We cannot admit to the Pilot School over-age students who have other work to do. But in the Pilot School we must be constantly more exacting. Last year, for example, we only allowed into the Pilot School those who had been graded at least 'fair'. This year we shall only allow in those who have been graded 'good', because the Pilot School is for the elite of our students, meaning the best of all our students. Why? Because our land has many young people, boys and girls, who want to go to the Pilot School to learn. We cannot allow that there should be boys and girls in the Pilot School who do not learn anything, who fail some years, having to repeat them, and so taking the place from others in our land who have willingness and ability. We cannot allow this. We have made and must make only one exception, which is as follows: we demand from girls a little less than from boys for admission to the Pilot School, above all on the question of age and on the question of academic level. Boys must have a primary school certificate. But for girls, mainly because when a girl reaches primary school leaving she is regarded as trained and her father usually looks for some way of marrying her off, we have to do what we can if she is intelligent to take her and put her in the Pilot School quickly. So we admit girls with third-year primary education and even if they are fifteen or sixteen years old we must take them. We want the emancipation and advancement of our women. The best advancement, one of the principal means of advancement, is to teach them to read and write well. This is the reason why we discriminate between boys and girls on the question of admission to the Pilot School.

We must constantly improve health care in our liberated areas. In the north and the south of our land, comrades have for some time worked hard to advance our health services and have made fairly good progress and have established sound foundations for our health services. Hospitals and health centres have been built as far as possible, and health brigades have been formed. In addition to care for our combatants, which is the main objective of our health care as we are at war, we began to provide care for our population. This came as a great surprise to many of our comrades, who were saying that our people did not want doctors. They did not want 'white man's amulet', they only wanted 'native amulet', only wanted 'healers' or marabouts. Our people showed that this was false, our people accepted the doctors, took an interest in the doctors and the nurses. They showed such interest, friendship and regard for the doctors that our people began to give their children the names of the doctors, the names of the foreign doctors who had come to help us. This was a real eye-opener for those of our comrades who were thinking that our people wanted to remain backward instead of progressing. No. Our people want to advance like all and any people in the world. This does not mean that there are not folk in our land who want their own 'healers', and who when they are given medical treatment in one place go off to find their traditional treatment in another. Even some responsible workers in the Party, who have a big hospital at Boké[1] where they can be

---

[1] In the Republic of Guinea, next to Guinea-Bissau.

treated by good nurses and doctors sometimes say to me: 'Cabral, I want to go for a traditional remedy'. We are still in this situation: let us put up with it. But the truth is that more and more our people are coming to understand that the doctors and nurses have a great importance for their lives and have saved the lives of many of our children, even when they were not combatants. But we have to improve our work in health, we have to make our men and women nurses work more, we have to set an example, whether in the hospital at Boké, or in the hospitals in the interior, everywhere. Our nurses and doctors must work harder than the foreign doctors who help us.

We must improve the distribution of medicaments, we have to be sparing of medicaments and must show tenderness to our sick and our wounded. This must be supervised, controlled by our Zone Committees, by our Interregional Committees. We must exercise permanent control over the work of the health services and the education services.

For the genuine improvement of our liberated areas, we must from now on be able to establish a principle and practice which stimulate our people very much. It is the following: let us see who is able to work best, in friendship, in esteem and in collaboration. This means we must establish among us what is called constructive emulation, meaning competition but for well-being, not for our stomach, for us to serve our Party, our People. You and I work in some branch of activity which we share. I help you, you help me, but each of us is trying to do the most he can. And we must give high praise to the one who does more, but without jealousy, without jockeying, without elbowing the other. Our political commissars, for example, must say the following: 'Comrades, whoever among the population of this area, this locality, produces the most rice this year will receive a prize or a medal from the Party. In addition the Party is going to invite him to go abroad to learn about other lands.' That is just an example. The same goes for whoever produces most potatoes, the same goes for the most manioc. This is what is called constructive emulation. But in the framework of our work day by day, we should always be thinking like this: What the devil, if João or Bakar are working hard, why shouldn't I work hard as well? I am going to make an effort to do even more than Bakar, more than João. But then Bakar sees me and sees that I am advancing and so he decides to do even more. I am content that he has advanced, for our work has improved, but I shall go on doing still more.

In the field of our armed struggle, we should spur on our combatants, push them into doing better all the time. The leadership of our Party must make an assessment of the action of our commanders, the political commissars, and give them high praise as the best exponents of our work. They are to the fore in the emulation that we are establishing as a practice. We must therefore institute constructive emulation, positive competition, in the service of our Party and our people in all activities.

13. Homage to Kwame Nkrumah[1]

After the speeches we have heard today and, most of all, after the statement, as militant as it was moving, by our elder brother and companion in struggle, President Ahmed Sékou Touré, what more is there to say? But we must speak, for at this moment if we did not speak, our heart might break.

Here, beside the mortal remains of President Kwame Nkrumah – one of the greatest men mankind has seen this century – we are living an epoch-making moment in the history of the struggle for liberation and progress in Africa; we might say simply, in history.

We must, therefore, meditate deeply on this moment, and draw all the lessons from events; as President Kwame Nkrumah would say, the positive lessons and the negative lessons.

Before saying a very little of what I have in my heart and my head, I should like to greet all the delegates here and, on behalf of the African liberation movements, to recall that the fact that we should all be here together, beside the mortal remains of President Kwame Nkrumah, is not only evidence of respect and consideration for his person and his achievement, but likewise a pledge to the total liberation of Africa and the progress of African peoples.

On behalf of the combatants of our Party, who are the legitimate representatives of our people in Guiné and Cape Verde, we should like to offer our fraternal condolences to his widow, Madame Nkrumah, to the whole Nkrumah family, to the President and our companion in struggle Ahmed Sékou Touré, who was always a faithful comrade of President Nkrumah, to the Ghanaian people and to the whole of Africa!

However, our tears should not drown the truth. We, as freedom fighters, are not weeping for the death of a man, even of a man who was a companion in struggle and an exemplary revolutionary. For, as President Ahmed Sékou Touré often says: 'What is man before the infinite and transcendent becoming of peoples and mankind? Nor are we weeping for the Ghanaian people, whose finest accomplishments, whose most legitimate aspirations are smothered. Nor are we weeping for Africa's betrayal. But we are weeping with hatred for those who were capable of betraying Nkrumah in the ignoble service of imperialism!

But treason, like fidelity, is characteristic of man. Treason to Ghana, as to the Congo and elsewhere in Africa, has a positive aspect: it shows the true

[1]Speech given at the symposium organized by the Democratic Party of Guinea, at the People's Palace in Conakry, on the occasion of the day dedicated to Kwame Nkrumah, 13 May 1972.

human dimension of African man. And, in this specific case, it allows one better to grasp the true stature of Nkrumah as a political giant, and contributes to immortalizing him further.

We have heard talk of rehabilitation for Nkrumah. We understand this expression only in the sphere of the language of diplomacy, or of tactics, because for us, as freedom fighters, those who must truly be rehabilitated are those who in betraying the Ghanaian people and Africa betrayed Nkrumah.

Africa, by demanding through the voice of the people of the Republic of Guinea, interpreted faithfully, as always, by President Ahmed Sekou Touré, that Nkrumah be restored to his rightful place – on the highest peak of the Kilimanjaro of the African revolution – Africa is rehabilitated before itself and before history.

We have heard much said today about the action and gigantic achievement accomplished by Nkrumah in a relatively short time.

President Nkrumah, to whom we pay homage, is primarily the strategist of genius in the struggle against classic colonialism. He is the man who created what we might call 'African positivism', to which he himself gave the name *positive action.* Positive action has been the best, the most appropriate solution found for the struggle, in the context of British colonial domination.

We pay homage to the pioneer of Panafricanism, to the tireless, constantly inspired combatant for African unity. We pay homage to the avowed enemy of neocolonialism in Africa and elsewhere, to the strategist of the economic development of his country.

As far as neocolonialism is concerned, everyone now knows that Nkrumah's book *Neocolonialism: the Last Stage of Imperialism* is a profound, materialist analysis of reality, the terrible reality which neocolonialism is in Africa. As far as his country's development is concerned, we reject the slanderous criticisms by Africa's enemies – and some of the Western press – even some cesspits which pass themselves off as being the African press – criticisms which purport to show Nkrumah's economic bankruptcy. Everyone knows very well that from 1970, on the basis of all the economic measures taken by Nkrumah and his government, Ghana was to become a fully developing country which would show the world that Africa was not only able to win political independence but also to build its economic independence.

We hail in Nkrumah the freedom fighter for the African peoples, who was always able to grant unconditional support to the national liberation movements. And we wish to say to you here that for us in Guiné and Cape Verde, while it is true that the primordial external factor in the development of our struggle was the independence of the Republic of Guinea – the heroic *'No'* of the Guinean people on 28 September 1958 – it is also true that we embarked on the struggle with the strong encouragement of the practical support of Ghana, and particularly of President Nkrumah.

We hail finally Nkrumah, the philosopher and thinker. As President

Sekou Touré said. philosopher and thinker because he could apply himself
to the consequent practice.

We hail likewise and pay homage to the personal friend. to the comrade
who could always encourage us in the difficult but exciting struggle we are
waging against the most retrograde of all colonialisms. Portuguese colonialism.

We must remember at this moment that every coin has two sides. All of
life's realities have two aspects: positive and negative. Positive action
always opposes and is opposed by a negative action and vice versa. If
President Nkrumah lives on in the history of Africa and the world. it is
because the balance of his *positive action* is not only positive. but also shows
an epoch-making achievement. fruitful creative activity in the service of the
African people and of mankind.

We must however draw the lesson from all events. Even at this moment of
grief. we must ask ourselves some questions the better to understand the
past. live the present and prepare for the future.

For example. what economic and political factors made the success of the
betrayal of Ghana possible. despite Nkrumah's personality. courage and
positive action?

True. imperialism is cruel and unscrupulous. but we must not lay all the
blame on its broad back. For. as the African people say: 'Rice only cooks
inside the pot'.

Just how far would the success of the betrayal of Ghana have been linked
or not to the questions of class struggle. contradictions in the social
structure. the role of the Party and other institutions. including the armed
forces. in the framework of a newly independent state? Just how far. we
wonder. would the success of the betrayal of Ghana have been linked or not
linked to the question of a correct definition of that historical entity. that
craftsman of history. the people. and to their daily action in defence of their
own conquests in independence? Or then. just how far might not the success
of the betrayal be linked to the key question of choice of men in the
revolution?

Pondering on these questions might perhaps enable us to understand
better the greatness of Nkrumah's achievement. likewise the complexity of
the problems that he had to face. so often alone. Such problems will surely
bring us to the conclusion that. so long as imperialism is in existence. an
independent African state must be a liberation movement in power. or it will
not be independent.

President Nkrumah understood this truth very well and never tired of
pointing it out to us during the long. friendly conversations that we had
whether in Accra or here in Conakry. It is enough to read his works again to
see that they are studded with preoccupations over these questions.

There are truths that we must utter to each other at this moment. but we
must above all tell those who would like to shed crocodile tears over the

mortal remains of Kwame Nkrumah.

The African peoples and particularly the freedom fighters cannot be fooled. Let no one come and tell us that Nkrumah died from cancer of the throat or any other sickness. No, Nkrumah was killed by the cancer of betrayal, which we must tear out by the roots in Africa, if we really want to liquidate imperialist domination definitively on this continent.

But we, Africans, strongly believe that the dead remain living at our side. We are societies of the living and the dead. Nkrumah will rise again each dawn in the heart and determination of freedom fighters, in the action of all true African patriots. Nkrumah's immortal spirit presides and will preside at the judgement of history on this decisive phase in our peoples' lives, in lifelong struggle against imperialist domination and for the genuine progress of our continent.

We, the liberation movements, will not forgive those who betrayed Nkrumah. The Ghanaian people will not forgive. Progressive mankind will not forgive. Let those who are due for rehabilitation make haste to rehabilitate themselves. It is not yet too late.

As an African proverb says: 'Those who spit at the sky will soil their face'. Those who have tried to soil the brilliant personality of Kwame Nkrumah should now understand very well that the African people are right. Another African proverb says: 'A hand, however big, can never cover the sky'. There it is: those who have tried to disparage the magnificent achievement of Kwame Nkrumah must today admit that this African proverb is right as well.

Before closing - although we know that we should not do this - allow me, on behalf of all the African freedom fighters, to offer fraternal and militant thanks to the people of the Republic of Guinea, to the Democratic Party of Guinea, and to their beloved leader, President Ahmed Sekou Touré, for this further evidence of unlimited courage they have shown us. First, in welcoming Kwame Nkrumah, and giving him his due position as Co-president of this Republic. Then, in insisting and by fighting for the national funeral to be held here in Guinea, African soil and symbol of African liberation and dignity.

If at this moment of grief in our life, a new understanding could be born between Guinea and Ghana, we should all be deeply content and it would be another significant achievement of Kwame Nkrumah.

For us, as Africans, the best homage we can pay to Kwame Nkrumah and his immortal memory, is reinforced vigilance in all fields of the struggle, more strongly developed and intensified struggle, the total liberation of Africa, success in development and economic, social and cultural progress for our peoples, and in the building of African unity. That was the fundamental aim of Kwame Nkrumah's action and thought. This is the oath we should all take before history in respect of the African continent.

For us, freedom fighters, the finest flowers with which we can garland

Kwame Nkrumah's memory, are the bullets, the shells, the missiles of every kind that we fire against the colonialist and racist forces in Africa.

We are certain, absolutely certain that framed by the eternal green of the African forests, flowers of crimson like the blood of martyrs and of gold like the harvests of plenty will bloom over the grave of Kwame Nkrumah; for Africa will triumph.

THE WEAPON OF THEORY

14. Presuppositions and objectives of national liberation in relation to social structure[1]

The peoples and nationalist organizations of Angola, Cape Verde, Guiné, Mozambique and São Tomé and Principe sent their delegations to this Conference for two main purposes: first, because we wish to attend and take active part in this epoch-making event in the history of mankind; second, because it was our political and moral duty to bring the Cuban people clear evidence of our fraternal combatant solidarity at this doubly historic moment – the seventh anniversary of the revolution and the first Tricontinental Conference.

Allow me, therefore, on behalf of our struggling peoples and on behalf of the militants of each of our national organizations, to offer warmest congratulations and fraternal greetings to the people of this tropical island on the seventh anniversary of the triumph of their revolution, on the holding of this Conference in their beautiful and hospitable capital and on the successes they have been able to attain on the path to building a new life. This last has the essential aim of achieving in full the aspirations for freedom, peace, progress and social justice felt by all Cubans. I hail in particular the Central Committee of the Cuban Communist Party, the Revolutionary Government and its exemplary leader – Commandant Fidel Castro – to whom I express our wishes for continued success and long life in the service of his country Cuba, and the progress and happiness of its people, and in the service of mankind.

If any of us, when we reached Cuba, brought any doubt about the deep-rootedness, strength, maturity and vitality of the Cuban Revolution, such doubt was swept away by what we have had the chance to see. Unshakable confidence warms our hearts and encourages us in the hard but glorious struggle against the common enemy.

No power in the world will be able to destroy the Cuban Revolution, which is creating in the countryside and the cities not only a new life but also – what is more important – a new Man, fully conscious of his national, continental and international rights and duties. In all fields of activity, the Cuban people have made significant progress in the past seven years,

[1] Speech delivered on behalf of the peoples and nationalist organizations of the Portuguese colonies to the First Solidarity Conference of the Peoples of Africa, Asia and Latin America (Havana, 3–12 January 1966) in the plenary session on 6 January.

especially in the last year – Agriculture Year. This progress is demonstrated in material and daily reality and in the Cuban men and women, in their calm confidence as they face a world in effervescence, where contradictions and threats, but hopes and certainties as well, have reached an unprecedented pitch.

From what we have seen and are learning in Cuba, we should like to mention here a particular lesson which we think contains one of the secrets, if not the secret, of what many would not hesitate to call 'the Cuban miracle': the communion, identification, harmony, mutual confidence and loyalty between the mass of the people and their leaders. Anyone who was present at the mass rallies of the past few days and, in particular, heard Commandant Fidel Castro's speech during the seventh anniversary commemoration, we have measured, as we did, in all its grandeur the specific – perhaps decisive – character of this primordial factor in the success of the Cuban Revolution. The vanguard of the Cuban Revolution has mobilized, organized and politically educated the people, kept them permanently informed about national and international questions which affect their life and made them take active part in answering these questions. The vanguard, which soon understood that the dynamic existence of a strong and united Party was indispensable, has been able not only to interpret correctly the objective conditions and specific demands of the environment, but also to forge the most powerful of weapons for defence, security and guarantee of continuity for the Revolution:*revolutionary consciousness of the mass of the people.* The latter, as we know, is not and never was spontaneous in any part of the world. We believe that this teaches us all a lesson, but especially a lesson for the national liberation movements, and specifically for those who aim that their national revolution should be a Revolution.

Some will not fail to note that certain Cubans, albeit an insignificant minority, have not shared the joys and hopes of the celebrations for the seventh anniversary, because they are against the Revolution. We realize that it is possible that some others will not attend the commemorations of the next anniversary, but we want to state that we regard the policy of 'an open door for the departure of enemies of the Revolution' as a lesson in courage, determination, humanity and confidence in the people, and as a further political and moral victory over the enemy. To those who in a friendly way are concerned about the dangers this departure could represent, we guarantee that we, the peoples of the African countries still partly or wholly dominated by Portuguese colonialism, are ready to send to Cuba as many men and women as may be needed to compensate for the departure of those who, for reasons of class or inadaptability, have interests and attitudes incompatible with the interests of the Cuban people.

Retracing the once sad and tragic path of our forefathers (notably from Guiné and Angola), who were shipped to Cuba as slaves, we would come now as free men, as willing workers and as Cuban patriots, to fulfil a productive role in this new, just and multiracial society, to help defend with our own blood the conquests by the Cuban people. But we would come also as much to strengthen the bonds of history, blood and culture that unite our peoples to the Cuban people, as to enjoy the magical relaxation, the gut rejoicing and the infectious rhythm which make the building of socialism in Cuba a new phenomenon for the world, a unique and for many, unfamiliar event.

We are not going to use this platform to vilify imperialism. There is an African proverb very common in our country – where fire is still an important tool and a treacherous friend – this shows the state of under-development in which colonialism is going to leave us – this proverb goes: 'When your hut is burning, it is no use beating the tom-tom'. In a Tricontinental dimension, this means that we are not going to succeed in eliminating imperialism by shouting or by slinging insults, spoken or written, at it. For us, the worst or best we can say about imperialism, whatever its form, is to take up arms and struggle. That is what we are doing and will go on doing until foreign domination has been totally eliminated from our African countries.

We came here determined to provide this Conference with as detailed information as possible on the specific situation of the national liberation struggle in each of our countries and particularly in those where there is armed struggle. We shall do this before the appropriate committee and through documents, films, photographs, bilateral contacts and the Cuban information media in the course of the Conference.

We ask your indulgence to use this occasion in the way that we think most useful. It is true that we came to this Conference convinced that it provided a rare opportunity for a broad exchange of views between combatants in the same cause, for study and solution of problems central to our common struggle, with the aim not only of strengthening our unity and solidarity, but also of improving the thought and action of each of us in the daily practice of struggle. That is why, as we want to avoid anything which might be a waste of time, we are quite determined not to allow any extraneous factors, or factors not directly connected with the questions which should concern us here, to disturb the chances for success of this Conference. We are justified in saying that this is the position taken by all the other national liberation movements represented at this Conference.

Our agenda includes topics whose importance and acuteness are beyond doubt and in which one concern is predominant: *The Struggle*. We note, however, that one type of struggle we regard as fundamental is not explicitly mentioned in this agenda, although we are sure that it was present in the minds of those who drew it up. We are referring to *the struggle against our own weaknesses*. We admit that other cases may differ from ours. Our experience in the broad framework of the daily struggle we wage has shown us that, whatever difficulties the enemy may create, the aforenamed is the most difficult struggle for the present and the future of our peoples. This struggle is the expression of the internal contradictions in the economic, social and cultural (therefore historical) reality of each of our countries. We are convinced that any national or social revolution which is not founded on adequate knowledge of this reality runs grave risks of poor results or of being doomed to failure.

Absence of ideology

When the African people say, in their plain language, that 'no matter how hot the water from the well, it will not cook your rice', they express with staggering simplicity a basic principle not only of physics but also of political science. We know in fact that the unfolding behaviour (development) of a phenomenon-in-motion, whatever its external conditioning, depends mainly on its internal characteristics. We also know that on the political level – however fine and attractive the reality of others may be – we can only truly transform our own reality, on the basis of detailed knowledge of it and our own efforts and sacrifices.

It is worth recalling in this Tricontinental gathering, so rich in experiences and examples, that however great the similarity between our cases and however identical our enemies, unfortunately or fortunately, national liberation and social revolution are not exportable commodities. They are (and increasingly so every day) a local, national, product – more or less influenced by (favourable and unfavourable) external factors, but essentially determined and conditioned by the historical reality of each people. Victory is only achieved by the adequate resolution of the various internal contradictions characterizing this reality. The success of the Cuban Revolution, taking place only ninety miles from the biggest imperialist and anti-socialist power of all time, seems to us, in the form and content of its evolution, a practical and conclusive illustration of validity of this stated principle.

We must however recognize that we ourselves and the other liberation movements in general (we are referring here above all to the African experience) have not been able to pay sufficient attention to this significant question of our common struggle.

The ideological deficiency, not to say the total lack of ideology, on the part of the national liberation movements – which is basically explained by ignorance of the historical reality which these movements aspire to transform – constitutes one of the greatest weaknesses, if not the greatest weakness, of our struggle against imperialism. We nevertheless believe that a sufficient number of varied experiences have already been accumulated to enable us to define a general line of thought and action in order to eliminate this deficiency. A full discussion of this matter could therefore be useful, and would enable this Conference to make a valuable contribution towards improving the present and future action of the national liberation movements. This would be a practical way of helping these movements and, in our opinion, no less important than political support and assistance with money, weapons and other material.

It is with the intention of contributing, although modestly, to this discussion, that we present here our view on *presuppositions and objectives of national liberation in relation to social structure.* This view is shaped by our own experience of struggle and by a critical appreciation of the experiences of others. To those who see this view as being theoretical, we would recall that every practice gives birth to a theory. If it is true that a revolution can fail, even though it be nurtured on perfectly conceived theories, nobody has yet successfully practised Revolution without a revolutionary theory.

The class struggle

Those who assert – and in our view rightly – that the motive force of history is the class struggle, would certainly agree to re-examining this assertion to make it more precise and give it even wider application, if they had a deeper knowledge of the essential characteristics of some of the colonized peoples (dominated by imperialism). In fact, in the general evolution of mankind and of each of the peoples in the human groups of which it is composed, classes appear neither as a generalized and simultaneous phenomenon throughout all these groups, nor as a finished, perfect, uniform and spontaneous whole. The formation of classes within one or more human groups is basically the result of progressive development of the productive forces and the way in which the wealth produced by this group – or usurped by other groups – is distributed. This means: the socio-economic phenomenon *class* arises and develops as a function of at least two essential and interdependent variables: the level of productive forces and the system of ownership of the means of production. This development takes place slowly, unevenly and gradually, by generally imperceptible quantitative increases in the essential variables. Once a certain point has been reached in the process of accumulation, it then leads to qualitative changes which are shown by the appearance of class, classes and class conflict.

Factors external to a given dynamic socio-economic whole can have a more or less significant bearing on the process of development of classes, speeding it up, slowing it down or even causing regressions in it. When, for whatever reason, the influence of these factors ceases, the process recovers its independence, and its rhythm is then determined not only by the specific internal characteristics of the whole, but also by the resultants of the temporary action of the external factors. On a strictly internal level, the rhythm of the process may vary, but it remains continuous and progressive. Abrupt advances are only possible as a function of abrupt rises or alterations – mutations – in the level of productive forces or in the system of ownership. These abrupt transformations carried out within the process of development of classes, as a result of mutations in the level of productive forces or in the system of ownership, are, in the convention of economic and political language, called *revolutions*.

Clearly, however, the possibilities for external factors, especially the interaction of human groups, to have a significant bearing on this process was considerably increased by the advance in means of transport and communications. This advance has made one world and mankind, by eliminating the isolation of human groups within one area, of areas within one continent and of continents. The advance, characteristic of a long historical period which began with the invention of the first means of transport, was already more evident with the voyages of the Carthaginians and Greek colonization, and was accentuated by maritime discoveries, the invention of the steam engine and the discovery of electricity. In our own times with the progressive harnessing of atomic energy, it is possible to promise, if not to sow man across the stars, at least to humanize the universe.

What has been said enables us to pose the following question: does history begin only from the *moment* of the launching of the phenomenon of class and, consequently, of class struggle? To reply in the affirmative would be to place outside history the whole period of life of human groups from the discovery of hunting, and later of nomadic and sedentary agriculture, to cattle raising and to the private appropriation of land. It would also be to consider – and this we refuse to accept – that various human groups in Africa, Asia and Latin America were living without history or outside history at the moment when they were subjected to the yoke of imperialism. It would be to consider that the populations of our countries, such as the Balanta of Guiné, the Cuanhama of Angola and the Makonde of Mozambique, are still living today – if we abstract the very slight influence of colonialism to which they have been subjected – outside history, or that they have no history.

Our refusal, based as it is on detailed knowledge of the socio-economic reality of our countries and on analysis of the process of development of the phenomenon of class as we saw earlier, leads us to conclude that if class struggle is the motive force of history, it is so in a specific historical period. This means that *before* the class struggle (and, necessarily, *after* the class struggle, since in this world there is no before without an after) some factor (or several factors) was and will be the motive force of history. We have no hesitation in saying that this factor in the history of each human group is the *mode of production* (the level of productive forces and the system of ownership) characteristic of that group. But, as we have seen, the definition of class and class struggle are themselves the result of the development of productive forces in conjunction with the system of ownership of the means of production. It therefore seems permissible to conclude that the level of productive forces, the essential determinant of the content and form of class struggle, is the true and permanent motive force of history.

If we accept this conclusion, then the doubts in our minds are cleared away. Because if on the one hand we can see that the existence of history before the class struggle is safeguarded, and we thus avoid for some human groups in our countries (and perhaps in our continents) the sad position of being peoples without history, then on the other hand we can see that history has continuity even after the disappearance of class struggle or of classes. And as it was not we who, on scientific bases, postulated the disappearance of classes as a historical inevitability, we can feel content with this conclusion. To a certain extent it re-establishes coherence and at the same time gives to those peoples who, like the people of Cuba, are building socialism the agreeable certainty that they will not cease to have a history when they complete the process of elimination of the phenomenon of class and class struggle within their socio-economic whole. Eternity is not of this world, but man will outlive classes and will continue to produce and to make history, since he can never free himself from the burden of his needs, of hand and brain, which are the basis of the development of productive forces.

On the mode of production

The foregoing and contemporary reality enable us to state that the history of a human group or of mankind goes through at least three stages. In the first, corresponding to a low level of productive forces — of man's mastery over nature — the mode of production is of rudimentary character: private appropriation of the means of production does not yet exist, there are no classes, nor, consequently, is there class struggle. In the second, when the raising of the level of productive forces leads to private appropriation of the means of production, the mode of production is progressively more complicated: conflicts of interest are provoked within the dynamic socio-economic whole, the eruption of the phenomenon of class and hence of class struggle is possible, as the social expression of the contradiction in the economic field between the mode of production and the private appropriation of the means of production. In the third stage, once a given level of productive forces is reached, the elimination of private appropriation as the means of production is made possible and is carried out; the phenomenon of class, and hence of class struggle, is removed and new and unknown forces in the historical process of the socio-economic whole are unleashed.

In politico-economic language, the first stage would correspond to the communal agricultural and cattle raising society. in which the social structure is horizontal, without a State. The second stage would correspond to agrarian societies (feudal or assimilated and agro-industrial bourgeois societies), in which the social structure develops vertically, with a State. The third stage would correspond to socialist and communist societies. in which the economy is mainly. if not exclusively, industrial (since agriculture itself becomes an industry). and in which the State tends progressively to disappear or actually disappears: the social structure returns to developing horizontally, at a higher level of productive forces. social relations and appreciation of human values.

At the level of mankind or of parts of mankind (human groups within one area or of one or more continents). these three stages (or two of them) can be concomitant. as is shown as much by the current reality as by the past. This is the result of the uneven development of human societies. whether caused by internal reasons or by one or more external factors speeding up or slowing down their evolution. On the other hand. in the historical process of a given socio-economic whole. each of the stages mentioned contains. once a certain level of transformation is reached. the seeds of the following stage.

We should also note that, in the present stage of the life of mankind and for a given socio-economic whole. the sequence in time of the three distinct stages is not indispensable. Whatever its present level of productive forces and characteristic social structure. a society can progress rapidly. through defined steps appropriate to the specific local (historical and human) realities. to a higher stage of existence. Such progress depends on the specific possibilities for the development of the society's productive forces and is mainly conditional on the nature of the political power ruling that society. that is on the type of State or. if we like. on the nature of the dominant class or classes within the society.

A more detailed analysis would show that the possibility of such a *leap* in the historical process is basically a result. in the economic field. of the power of the means available nowadays to man for the mastery of nature. and. in the political field. of the new event that has radically changed the face of the world and the march of history – *the creation of socialist states.*

We see. therefore. that our peoples have their own history. whatever the stages of their economic development. When they underwent imperialist domination. the historical process of each of our peoples (or of the human groups of which each is composed) was subjected to the violent action of an external factor. This action – the impact of imperialism in our societies – could not fail to influence the process of development of the productive forces of our countries and the social structures of our peoples. as well as the content and form of our national liberation struggles.

But we also see that. in the historical context in which these struggles develop. our people have the specific possibility of going from their present situation of exploitation and underdevelopment to a new stage of their historical process. which can lead them to a higher form of economic. social and cultural existence.

Imperialism

The political report drawn up by the International Preparatory Committee of this Conference. for which we reaffirm our complete support. placed imperialism. clearly and by succinct analysis. in its economic context and historical position. We will not repeat here what has already been said before this assembly. We shall merely say that imperialism may be defined as the worldwide expression of the profit motive and the ever-increasing accumulation of *surplus values* by monopoly financial capital. in two regions of the world: first in Europe and. later. in North America. And if we wish to place the fact of imperialism within the general direction of the evolution of the epoch-making factor that has changed the face of the world -- capital and the process of its accumulation -- we might say that imperialism is piracy transplanted from the seas to dry land. piracy reorganised. consolidated and adapted to the aim of plundering the natural and human resources of our peoples. But if we can calmly analyse the phenomenon of imperialism. we shall not shock anybody if we have to admit that imperialism. which everything goes to show is really the last stage in the evolution of capitalism was a historical necessity, a consequence of the development of productive forces and the transformations of the mode of production, in the general context of mankind, considered as a dynamic whole. This is a necessity like those today of the national liberation of peoples. the destruction of capitalism and the advent of socialism.

The important thing for our peoples is to know whether imperialism. in its role as capital in action. has or has not fulfilled in our countries its historical mission: the speeding up of the process of development of the productive forces and transformation in the direction of increasing complexity of the characteristics of the mode of production: sharpening class differentiation with the development of the bourgeoisie and intensification of class struggle: and appreciably raising average standard levels in the economic. social and cultural life of the populations. It is also worth examining the influences or effects of imperialist action on the social structures and historical processes of our peoples.

We shall neither condemn nor excuse imperialism here. but merely say that. whether on the economic level. or on the social and cultural levels. imperialist capital has been a long way from fulfilling in our countries the historical mission carried out by capital in the countries of accumulation. This means that on the one hand. imperialist capital has had in the great majority of the dominated countries the simple function of multiplying surplus values. It can be seen on the other hand that the historical capacity of capital (as the indestructible accelerator of the process of development of the productive forces) is strictly dependent on its freedom. that is to say on the degree of independence with which it is utilized. We must, however, recognize that in some cases imperialist capital or moribund capitalism has had sufficient interest, strength and time to raise the level of productive forces (as well as building cities) and to allow a minority of the local population a better or even privileged standard of living, thus contributing, by a process which some would call dialectical, to sharpening the contradictions within the societies in question. In other, rarer cases, there has been the possibility of accumulation of capital, giving rise to the development of a local bourgeoisie.

On the question of the effects of imperialist domination on the social structure and the historical process of our peoples, we should first of all examine the general forms of imperialist domination. There are at least two forms:

1. Direct domination – by means of a political power made up of agents foreign to the dominated people (armed forces, police, administrative agents and settlers – which is conventionally called *classical colonialism* or *colonialism*.
2. Indirect domination – by means of a political power made up mainly or completely of native agents – which is conventionally called *neo-colonialism*.

   In the first case, the social structure of the dominated people, at whatever stage they are, can suffer the following experiences:

a Total destruction, generally accompanied by immediate or gradual elimination of the aboriginal population and consequent replacement by an exotic population.
b Partial destruction, generally accompanied by more or less intensive settlement by an exotic population.
c Ostensible preservation, brought about by confining the aboriginal society to areas or special reserves generally offering no means of living and accompanied by massive implantation of an exotic population.

The two latter cases, which are those we must consider in the context of the problematic of national liberation, are widely present in Africa. One can say that in either case the main effect produced by the impact of imperialism on the historical process of the dominated people is paralysis, stagnation (even in some cases, regression) in that process. However, this paralysis is not complete. In one sector or another of the socio-economic whole in question, noticeable transformations may occur, caused by the continuing action of some internal (local) factors, or as a result of the action of new factors introduced by the colonial domination, such as the introduction of money and the development of urban conglomerations. Among these transformations, we should particularly note, in certain cases, the gradual loss of prestige of the native ruling classes or strata, the forced or voluntary exodus of part of the peasant population to the urban centres, with the consequent development of new social strata: salaried workers, employees of the State and in commerce and the liberal professions, and an unstable stratum of workless. In the countryside, there grows up with very varied intensity, and always with ties to the urban milieu, a stratum made up of petty farm-owners. In the case of so-called neocolonialism, whether the majority of the colonized population is aboriginal or of exotic origin, imperialist action takes the form of creating a local bourgeoisie or pseudo-bourgeoisie, in fee to the ruling class of the dominating country.

The transformations in the social structure are not so marked in the lower strata, above all in the countryside, where the structure largely retains the characteristics of the colonial phase, but the creation of a native pseudo-bourgeoisie, which generally develops out of a petty bourgeoisie of bureaucrats and intermediaries in the trading system (compradores), accentuates the differentiation between the social strata. By strengthening the economic activity of native elements, this opens up new perspectives in the social dynamic, notably by the gradual development of an urbanized working class and the introduction of private agricultural property, which slowly gives rise to the appearance of an agricultural proletariat. These more or less noticeable transformations of the social structure, determined by a significant rise in the level of productive forces, have a direct influence on the historical process of the socio-economic whole in question. While in classical colonialism this process is paralysed, neocolonialist domination, by allowing the social dynamic to be awakened – conflicts of interest between the native social strata or class struggle – creates the illusion that the historical process is returning to its normal evolution. This illusion is reinforced by the existence of a political power (national State), composed of native elements. It is only an illusion, since in reality the subjection of the native 'ruling' class to the ruling class of the dominating country limits or holds back the full development of the national productive forces. But in the specific conditions of the present-day world economy, this subjection is an inevitability, and thus the native pseudo-bourgeoisie, however strongly nationalist, cannot effectively fulfil the historical function that would fall to this class: it cannot *freely* guide the development of productive forces, in short cannot be a *national bourgeoisie.* For, as we have seen, the productive forces are the motive force of history, and total freedom of the process of their development is an indispensable condition for their full functioning.

We see, therefore, that both in colonialism and in neocolonialism the essential characteristic of imperialist domination remains the same – denial of the historical process of the dominated people, by means of violent usurpation of the freedom of the process of development of the national productive forces. This observation. which identifies the essence of the two apparent forms of imperialist domination, seems to us to be of primordial importance for the thought and action of national liberation movements. both in the course of the struggle and after the winning of independence.

On the basis of the foregoing. we can state that national liberation is the phenomenon in which a socio-economic whole rejects the denial of its historical process. In other words. the national liberation of a people is the regaining of the historical personality of that people. it is their return to history through the destruction of the imperialist domination to which they were subjected.

Now we have seen that the principal and permanent characteristic of imperialist domination, whatever its form, is the usurpation by violence of the freedom of the process of development of the dominated socio-economic whole. We have also seen that this freedom. and it alone. can guarantee the normal course of the historical process of a people. We can therefore conclude that national liberation exists when. and only when. the national productive forces have been completely freed from all and any kind of foreign domination.

It is often said that national liberation is based on the right of all peoples to decide their destiny freely and that the aim of this liberation is to gain national independence. Although we might agree with this vague and subjective way of expressing a complex reality. we prefer to be objective. For us the basis of national liberation. whatever the formulas adopted in international law. is the inalienable right of every people to have their own history; and the aim of national liberation is to regain this right usurped by imperialism. that is to free the process of development of the national productive forces.

For this reason, in our view any national liberation movement that does not take into consideration this basis and this aim may struggle against imperialism. but will certainly not be struggling for national liberation.

This means that. bearing in mind the essential characteristics of the present-day world economy, as well as experiences already gained in the field of anti-imperialist struggle. the principal aspect of national liberation struggle is the struggle against what is conventionally called neocolonialism. Furthermore. if we accept that national liberation demands a profound mutation in the process of development of the productive forces. we see that the phenomenon of national liberation necessarily corresponds to a revolution. The important thing is to be aware of the objective and subjective conditions in which this revolution may occur, and to know the types or type of struggle most appropriate for its accomplishment.

We will not repeat here that these conditions are openly favourable in the present state of the history of mankind. We shall merely recall that unfavourable factors also exist, just as much on the international level as on the internal level of each nation struggling for its liberation.

On the international level, it seems to us that the following factors at least are unfavourable to the national liberation movement: the neocolonial situation of a great number of states which, having won political independence, are tending to join up with others already in that situation; the progress made by neocapitalism, notably in Europe, where imperialism is resorting to preferential investments to encourage the development of a privileged proletariat with a consequent lowering of the revolutionary level of the working classes; the open or concealed neocolonial situation of some European states which, like Portugal, still have colonies; the policy of so-called 'aid' to underdeveloped countries, practised by imperialism with the aim of creating or reinforcing native pseudo-bourgeoisies necessarily subjected to the international bourgeoisie, and thus obstructing the path to revolution; the claustrophobia and timidity about revolution which leads some recently independent states, whose internal economic and political conditions are favourable to revolution, to accept compromises with the enemy or with their agents; the growing contradictions between anti-imperialist states; and, finally, the threats to world peace, posed by the prospect of atomic war on the part of imperialism. All these factors combine to strengthen the action of imperialism against the national liberation movement.

If the repeated interventions and growing aggressiveness of imperialism against the peoples can be interpreted as a sign of desperation before the extent of the national liberation movement, they are to some extent explained by the weaknesses within the general front of anti-imperialist struggle created by these unfavourable factors.

On the internal level, it seems to us that the most significant weakness or unfavourable factors are inherent in the socio-economic structure and in the trends of its evolution under imperialist pressure or, better still, in the little or no attention paid to the characteristics of this structure and these trends by the national liberation movements in drawing up their strategy for struggle.

By saying this we do not wish to minimize the significance of other internal factors which are unfavourable to national liberation, such as economic underdevelopment and the consequent social and cultural backwardness of the mass of the people, tribalism and some other minor contradictions. It should, however, be noted that the existence of tribes is only manifested as a significant contradiction as a function of opportunist attitudes (generally on the part of detribalized individuals or groups) within the national liberation movement. Contradictions between classes, even when the latter are embryonic, are of far greater importance than the contradictions between tribes.

★

Although the colonial and neocolonial situations are identical in essence, and the main aspect of the struggle against imperialism might be the neocolonialist aspect, we feel it is vital to distinguish between these two situations in practice. In fact the horizontal structure of the native society, whether more or less differentiated, and the absence of a political power composed of national elements in the colonial situation, make possible the creation of a broad front of unity and struggle that is vital for the success of the national liberation movement. But this possibility does not remove the need for a rigorous analysis of the indigenous social structure and the trends of its evolution, and for the adoption in practice of appropriate measures for ensuring a genuine national liberation. While we admit that everyone knows best what to do in his own house, we feel that among these measures it is vital to create a firmly united vanguard, conscious of the true meaning and objective of the national liberation struggle which it must lead. This necessity is al the more acute because it is certain that, with rare exceptions, the colonial situation neither allows nor invites the meaningful existence of vanguard classes (an industrial working class and rural proletariat) which could ensure the vigilance of the mass of the people over the evolution of the liberation movement. On the contrary, the generally embryonic character of the working classes and the economic, social and cultural situation of the major physical force in a national liberation struggle – the peasants – do not allow these two principal forces of that struggle to distinguish on their own genuine national independence from fictitious political independence. Only a revolutionary vanguard, generally an active minority, can have consciousness *ab initio* of this distinction and through the struggle bring it to the awareness of the mass of the people. This explains the fundamentally political nature of the national liberation struggle and to some extent provides the significance of the form of struggle in the final outcome of the phenomenon of national liberation.

In the neocolonial situation, the more or less accentuated structuring of the native society as a vertical one and the existence of a political power composed of native elements – national State – aggravate the contradictions within that society and make difficult, if not impossible, the creation of as broad a united front as in the colonial case. On the one hand, the material effects (mainly the nationalization of cadres and the rise in native economic initiative, particularly at the commercial level) and the psychological effects (pride in believing oneself ruled by one's fellow-countrymen, exploitation of religious or tribal solidarity between some leaders and a fraction of the mass of the people) serve to demobilize a considerable part of the nationalist forces.

But on the other hand, the necessarily repressive nature of the neocolonial State against the national liberation forces, the aggravation of class contradictions, the objective continuance of agents and signs of foreign domination (settlers who retain their privileges, armed forces, racial discrimination), the growing impoverishment of the peasantry and the more or less flagrant influence of external factors contribute towards keeping the flame of nationalism alight. They serve gradually to awaken the consciousness of broad popular strata and, precisely on the basis of awareness of neocolonialist frustration, to reunite the majority of the population around the ideal of national liberation.

In addition, while the native ruling class becomes increasingly 'bourgeois' the development of a class of workers composed of urbanized industrial workers and agricultural proletarians – all exploited by the indirect domination of imperialism – opens renewed prospects for the evolution of national liberation. This class of workers, whatever the degree of development of its political consciousness (beyond a certain minimum that is *consciousness of its needs*), seems to constitute the true popular vanguard of the national liberation struggle in the neocolonial case. However, it will not be able completely to carry out its mission in the framework of this struggle (which does not end with the gaining of independence) unless it allies itself firmly with the other exploited strata: the peasants in general (farm labourers, tenants, sharecroppers, petty farm-owners) and the nationalist petty bourgeoisie. The achievement of this alliance demands the mobilization and organization of the nationalist forces within the framework (or by the action) of a strong and well-structured political organization.

Another important distinction to draw between the colonial and neocolonial situations lies in the prospects for struggle. The colonial case (in which the *nation class* fights the repressive forces of the bourgeoisie of the colonizing country) may lead, ostensibly at least, to a nationalist situation (national revolution): the nation gains its independence and theoretically adopts the economic structure it finds most attractive. The neocolonial case (in which the class of workers and its allies fight simultaneously the imperialist bourgeoisie and the native ruling class) is not resolved by a nationalist solution; it demands the destruction of the the capitalist structure implanted in the national soil by imperialism and correctly postulates a socialist solution.

This distinction arises mainly from the different levels of the productive forces in the two cases and the consequent sharpening of the class struggle. It would not be difficult to show that in time this distinction becomes scarcely apparent. It is sufficient to recall that in the present historical circumstances – alienation of imperialism which lays its hands on every possible means to perpetuate its domination over our peoples, and consolidation of socialism over a considerable part of the globe – there are only two possible paths for an independent nation: to return to imperialist domination (neocolonialism, capitalism, State capitalism) or to take the socialist road. This option, on which depends the compensation for the efforts and sacrifices by the mass of the people during the struggle, is considerably influenced by the form of struggle and the degree of revolutionary consciousness of those who lead it.

The role of violence

The facts make it unnecessary for us to waste words proving that the essential instrument of imperialist domination is violence. If we accept the principle that *the national liberation struggle is a revolution,* and that it is not over at the moment when the flag is hoisted and the national anthem is played, we shall find that there is and there can be no national liberation without the use of liberating violence, on the part of the nationalist forces, in answer to the criminal violence of the agents of imperialism. Nobody can doubt that imperialist domination, whatever its local characteristics, implies a state of permanent violence against the nationalist forces. There is no people in the world which, after being subjected to the imperialist yoke (colonialist or neocolonialist), has gained independence (nominal or effective) without victims. The important thing is to decide what forms of violence have to be used by the national liberation forces, in order not only to answer the violence of imperialism but also to ensure, through the struggle, the final victory of their cause, that is true national independence.

The past and recent experience of various peoples; the present situation of national liberation struggle in the world (especially the cases of Vietnam, Congo and Zimbabwe); as well as the very situation of permanent violence, or at least of contradictions and upheavals, in certain countries which have gained independence by the so-called peaceful way show us not only that compromises with imperialism are counter-productive, but also that the normal road of national liberation, imposed on peoples by imperialist repression, is *armed struggle.*

We do not think we shall shock this assembly by stating that the only effective way of completely and definitively fulfilling the aspirations of peoples for national liberation is by armed struggle. This is the great lesson that the contemporary history of liberation teaches all those who are truly committed to the national liberation of their peoples.

On the petty bourgeoisie

It is obvious that both the effectiveness of this road and the stability of the situation to which it leads after liberation depend not only on the characteristics of organization of the struggle but also on the political and moral awareness of those who, for historical reasons, are in a position to be the immediate heirs of the colonial or neocolonial State. For events have shown that the only social stratum capable both of having consciousness in the first place of the reality of imperialist domination and of handling the State apparatus inherited from that domination is the native petty bourgeoisie. If we bear in mind the unpredictable characteristics and complexity of the trends naturally inherent in the economic situation of this social stratum or class, we find that this specific inevitability in our situation is yet another weakness of the national liberation movement.

The colonial situation, which does not admit the development of a native pseudo-bourgeoisie and in which the mass of the people do not generally reach the necessary degree of political consciousness before the launching of the phenomenon of national liberation, offers the petty bourgeoisie the historical opportunity of leading the struggle against foreign domination. By virtue of its objective and subjective position (higher standard of living than that of the masses, more frequent humiliation, higher grade of education and political culture, etc.) it is the stratum that soonest becomes aware of the need to rid itself of foreign domination. This historical responsibility is assumed by the sector of the petty bourgeoisie that, in the colonial context, one might call *revolutionary*, while the other sectors retain the characteristic hesitation of this class or ally themselves to the colonialist so as to defend, albeit illusorily their social position.

The neocolonial situation, which postulates the elimination of the native pseudo-bourgeoisie so that national liberation is achieved, also offers the petty bourgeoisie the opportunity of playing a prominent – and even decisive – role in the struggle for the elimination of foreign domination. But in this case, by virtue of the relative advances made in the social structure, the function of leading the struggle is shared, to a greater or lesser extent, with the most enlightened sectors of the classes of workers and even with some elements of the national pseudo-bourgeoisie inspired by patriotic sentiment. The role of the sector of the petty bourgeoisie that takes part in leading the struggle is all the more important as it is clear that, in the neocolonial situation too, it is the most ready to assume these functions, both because of the economic and cultural limitations of the mass of workers, and because of the complexes and limitations of an ideological nature that characterize the sector of the national pseudo-bourgeoisie which joins the struggle. In this case still, it is important to stress that the mission with which it is entrusted demands from this sector of the petty bourgeoisie a greater revolutionary consciousness, and the capacity for faithfully expressing the aspirations of the masses in each phase of the struggle and for identifying with them more and more.

But, no matter the degree of revolutionary consciousness of the sector of the petty bourgeoisie called on to undertake this historical function, it cannot free itself from an objective reality: the petty bourgeoisie, as a service class (that is not directly involved in the process of production) does not have at its disposal the economic bases to guarantee the taking over of power for it. In fact history shows that whatever the role (often important) played by individuals coming from the petty bourgeoisie in the process of a revolution, this class has never possessed political power. And it never could, since political power (the State) has its foundations in the economic capacity of the ruling class. In the circumstances of colonial and neocolonial society, this capacity is retained in the hands of two entities: imperialist capital and the native classes of workers.

To maintain the power that national liberation puts in its hands, the petty bourgeoisie has only one road: to give free rein to its natural tendenc'es to become 'bourgeois' to allow the development of a bourgeoisie of bureaucrats and intermediaries in the trading system, to transform itself into a national pseudo-bourgeoisie, that is to deny the revolution and necessarily subject itself to imperialist capital. Now this corresponds to the neocolonial situation, that is to say, to betrayal of the objectives of national liberation.

In order not to betray these objectives, the petty bourgeoisie has only one road: to strengthen its revolutionary consciousness, to repudiate the temptations to become 'bourgeois' and the natural pretensions of its class mentality; to identify with the classes of workers, not to oppose the normal development of the process of revolution. This means that in order to play completely the part that falls to it in the national liberation struggle, the revolutionary petty bourgeoisie must be capable of committing *suicide* as a class, to be restored to life in the condition of a revolutionary worker completely identified with the deepest aspirations of the people to which he belongs.

This alternative – to betray the revolution or to commit suicide as a class – constitutes the dilemma of the petty bourgeoisie in the general framework of the national liberation struggle. The positive solution, in favour of the revolution, depends on what Fidel Castro recently fittingly called *development of revolutionary consciousness*. This dependence necessarily draws our attention to the capacity of the leaders of the national liberation struggle to remain faithful to the principles and the fundamental cause of this struggle. This shows us, to a certain extent, that if national liberation is essentially a political question, the conditions for its development stamp on it certain characteristics that belong to the sphere of morals.

This is the modest contribution which, on behalf of the nationalist organizations of African countries still partly or wholly dominated by Portuguese colonialism, we thought we should bring to the general debate of this assembly. As we are firmly united within our many-nation organization – CONCP – we are determined to remain faithful to the interests and just aspirations of our peoples, whatever our origins in the societies to which we belong. Vigilance in regard to this fidelity is one of the main objectives of our organization, in the interest of our peoples, of Africa and of mankind struggling against imperialism. For this reason we are already fighting, with weapons in hand, against the Portuguese colonialist forces, in Angola, Guiné and Mozambique, and we are preparing to do the same in Cape Verde and São Tomé and Principe. For this reason we devote the closest attention to political work among our peoples, improving and constantly strengthening our national organizations, in whose leadership all the sectors of our society are represented. For this reason we remain vigilant against ourselves and, on the basis of specific knowledge of our strengths and weaknesses, we try to reinforce the former and to transform the latter into strengths, for the constant development of our revolutionary consciousness. For this reason we are in Cuba, attending this Conference.

We shall not shout 'vivas' or here proclaim our solidarity with this or that people in struggle. Our presence is in itself a cry of condemnation of imperialism and a proof of solidarity with all peoples who want to sweep the imperialist yoke from their country, and in particular with the heroic people of Vietnam. But we firmly believe that the best proof we can give of our anti-imperialist stand and our active solidarity with our companions in this common struggle is to return to our countries, to develop the struggle further and to remain faithful to the principles and objectives of national liberation.

Our wish is that every national liberation movement represented here may, with weapons in hand, be able to echo in its own country, in unison with its people, the already legendary cry of the people of Cuba: *'Patria o muerte, Venceremos!'* ('Country or death, we shall triumph!')
Death to the forces of imperialism!
A free, prosperous and joyful country for each of our peoples!
We shall triumph!

15. National liberation and culture[1]

It is a great honour to take part in this ceremony held in homage to our companion in struggle and worthy son of Africa, the late lamented Dr. Eduardo Mondlane, former President of FRELIMO, who in a cowardly way was assassinated on 3 February 1969, in Dar-es-Salaam by the Portuguese colonialists and their allies.

We should like to thank Syracuse University and particularly the Programme of Eastern African Studies, directed by the scholar and teacher Marshall Segall, for this initiative. It is evidence not only of the respect and admiration you feel for the unforgettable personality of Dr Eduardo Mondlane, but also of your solidarity with the heroic struggle of the Mozambican people and of all the peoples of Africa for national liberation and progress.

In accepting your invitation – which we regard as addressed to our people and our combatants – we wanted once more to demonstrate our militant friendship and our solidarity with the people of Mozambique and their beloved leader, Dr Eduardo Mondlane, to whom we were linked by fraternal ties in the common struggle against the most retrograde of all colonialisms, Portuguese colonialism. Our friendship and solidarity are most sincere, even though we did not always agree with our comrade Eduardo Mondlane, whose death was moreover a loss for our people too.

Other speakers have already had the chance to draw a portrait and to give a well-deserved eulogy of Dr Eduardo Mondlane. We should merely like to reaffirm our admiration for the figure of the African patriot and eminent man of culture that he was. Similarly we should like to say that Eduardo Mondlane's great merit was not his decision to struggle for his people's liberation. His greater merit was being able to integrate himself in his country's reality, to identify with his people and to acculturate himself by the struggle he led with courage, wisdom and determination.

Eduardo Chivambo Mondlane, an African man who came from a rural background, a son of peasants and of a tribal chief, a child educated by missionaries, a black pupil in white schools of colonial Mozambique, a university student in racist South Africa, helped in

[1]The Eduardo Mondlane Memorial Lecture, delivered at Syracuse University, New York (Programme of Eastern African Studies), 20 February 1970.

youth by an American foundation, scholarship student of a United States university, with a doctorate from Northwestern University, a senior official of the United Nations, a professor at Syracuse University, president of the Mozambique Liberation Front, fallen as a combatant for the freedom of his people.

The life of Eduardo Mondlane is, in fact, singularly rich in experience. If we consider the brief period during which he worked as an apprentice-labourer on an agricultural holding, we find that his life-cycle encompasses practically all the categories of colonial African society: from the peasantry to the assimilated 'petty bourgeoisie', and on the cultural level from the village universe to a universal culture opened towards the world, its problems, contradictions and prospects for evolution.

The important thing is that, after this long course, Eduardo Mondlane was able to achieve the return to the village, in the personality of a fighter for the liberation and progress of his people, enriched by the often overwhelming experiences of today's world. In this way he has given a fruitful example: facing up to all the difficulties, fleeing the temptations, freeing himself from the compromises or engagements of cultural (hence political) alienation, he was able to rediscover his own roots, identify with his people and dedicate himself to the cause of national and social liberation. This is what the imperialists have not forgiven him.

Instead of limiting ourselves to the more or less significant questions of the common struggle against the Portuguese colonialists, let us focus our lecture on an essential question: dependent and reciprocal relations between the national liberation struggle and culture.

If we manage to persuade the African freedom fighters and all those concerned for freedom and progress of the African peoples of the conclusive importance of this question in the process of struggle, we shall have paid significant homage to Eduardo Mondlane.

A cruel dilemma for colonialism: elimination or assimilation?

When Goebbels, the brain behind Nazi propaganda, heard the word 'culture', he reached for his pistol. This shows that the Nazis – who were and are the most tragic expression of imperialism and of its thirst for domination – even if they were all degenerates like Hitler, had a clear idea of the value of culture as a factor of resistance to foreign domination.

History teaches us that, in certain circumstances, it is very easy for the foreigner to impose his domination on a people. But it likewise teaches us that, whatever the material aspects of this domination, it can be maintained only by the permanent and organized repression of the cultural life of the people concerned. Implantation of domination can be ensured definitively only by physical elimination of a significant part of the dominated population.

In fact, to take up arms to dominate a people is, above all, to take up arms to destroy, or at least to neutralize and to paralyse their cultural life. For as long as part of that people can have a cultural life, foreign domination cannot be sure of its perpetuation. At a given moment, depending on internal and external factors determining the evolution of the society in question, cultural resistance (indestructible) may take on new (political, economic and armed) forms, in order fully to contest foreign domination.

The ideal for foreign domination, whether imperialist or not, lies in this alternative: either to eliminate practically all the population of the dominated country, thereby excluding the possibilities of a cultural resistance; or to succeed in imposing itself without damage to the culture of the dominated people, that is, to harmonize economic and political domination of these people with their cultural personality.

The first hypothesis implies genocide of the indigenous population and creates a void which empties foreign domination of its content and its object: the dominated people. The second hypothesis has not, until now, been confirmed by history. The broad experience of mankind enables us to postulate that it has no practical viability: it is not possible to harmonize the economic and political domination of a people, whatever the degree of their social development, with the preservation of their cultural personality.

In order to escape this alternative – which might be called the *dilemma of cultural resistance* – imperialist colonial domination has tried to create theories which, in fact, are only crude formulations of racism, and which, in practice, are translated into a permanent state of siege for the aboriginal populations, on the basis of racist dictatorship (or democracy).

This, for example, is the case with the supposed theory of progressive *assimilation* of native populations, which is no more than a more or less violent attempt to deny the culture of the people in question. The unmistakable failure of this 'theory', put into practice by several colonial powers, including Portugal, is the most evident proof of its non-viability, if not of its inhuman character. It reaches the highest degree of absurdity in the Portuguese case, where Salazar asserts that *Africa does not exist.*

This is likewise the case with the supposed theory of *apartheid,* created, applied and developed on the basis of the economic and political domination of the people of southern Africa by a racist minority, with all the crimes against humanity that this entails. The practice of *apartheid* takes the form of unrestrained exploitation of the labour force of the African masses, incarcerated and cynically repressed in the largest concentration camp mankind has ever known.

National liberation, an act of culture

These examples give a measure of the drama of foreign domination in the face of the cultural reality of the dominated people. They also show the close, dependent and reciprocal connexion existing between the *cultural factor* and the *economic* (and political) *factor* in the behaviour of human societies. In fact, at every moment of the life of a society (open or closed), culture is the result, with more or less awakened consciousness, of economic and political activities, the more or less dynamic expression of the type of relations prevailing within that society, on the one hand between man (considered individually or collectively) and nature, and, on the other hand, among individuals, groups of individuals, social strata or classes.

The value of culture as an element of resistance to foreign domination lies in the fact that culture is the vigorous manifestation, on the ideological or idealist level, of the material and historical reality of the society that is dominated or to be dominated. Culture is simultaneously the fruit of a people's history and a determinant of history, by the positive or negative influence it exerts on the evolution of relations between man and his environment and among men or human groups within a society, as well as between different societies. Ignorance of this fact might explain the failure of several attempts at foreign domination as well as the failure of some national liberation movements.

Let us examine what *national liberation* is. We shall consider this phenomenon of history in its contemporary context, that is national liberation in the face of imperialist domination. The latter is, as we know, distinct both in form and content from preceding types of foreign domination (tribal, military-aristocratic, feudal and capitalist domination in the age of free competition).

The principal characteristic, common to every kind of imperialist domination, is the denial of the historical process of the dominated people by means of violent usurpation of the freedom of the process of development of the productive forces. Now, in a given society, the level of development of the productive forces and the system of social utilization of these forces (system of ownership) determine the *mode of production*. In our view, the mode of production, whose contradictions are manifested with more or less intensity through class struggle, is the principal factor in the history of any human whole, and the level of productive forces is the true and permanent motive force of history.

For every society, for every human group considered as a dynamic whole, the level of the productive forces indicates the status reached by the society and each of its components in the face of nature, its capacity to act or react consciously in relation to nature. It indicates and conditions the type of material relations (expressed objectively or subjectively) existing between man and his environment.

The mode of production, which at every stage of history represents the result of the ceaseless search for a dynamic equilibrium between the level of productive forces and the system of social utilization of these forces, indicates the status reached by a given society and each of its components before itself and before history. In addition, it indicates and conditions the type of material relations (expressed objectively or subjectively) existing between the various elements or groups which constitute the society in question: relations and types of relations between man and nature, between man and his environment; relations and types of relations between the individual or collective components of a society. To speak about this is to speak of history but it is likewise to speak of culture.

Culture, whatever the ideological or idealist characteristics of its expression, is thus an essential element of the history of a people. Culture is, perhaps, the resultant of this history just as the flower is the resultant of a plant. Like history, or because it is history, culture has as its material base the level of the productive forces and the mode of production. Culture plunges its roots into the humus of the material reality of the environment in which it develops, and it reflects the organic nature of the society, which may be more or less influenced by external factors. History enables us to know the nature and extent of the imbalances and the conflicts (economic, political and social) that characterize the evolution of a society. Culture enables us to know what dynamic syntheses have been formed and set by social awareness in order to resolve these conflicts at each stage of evolution of that society, in the search for survival and progress.

Just as occurs with the flower in a plant, the capacity (or responsibility) for forming and fertilizing the germ which ensures the continuity of history lies in culture, and the germ simultaneously ensures the prospects for evolution and progress of the society in question. Thus it is understood that imperialist domination, denying to the dominated people their own historical process, necessarily denies their cultural process. It is further understood why the exercise of imperialist domination, like all other foreign domination, for its own security requires cultural oppression and the attempt at direct or indirect destruction of the essential elements of the culture of the dominated people.

Study of the history of liberation struggles shows that they have generally been preceded by an upsurge of cultural manifestations, which progressively harden into an attempt, successful or not, to assert the cultural personality of the dominated people by an act of denial of the culture of the oppressor. Whatever the conditions of subjection of a people to foreign domination and the influence of economic, political and social factors in the exercise of this domination, it is generally within the cultural factor that we find the germ of challenge which leads to the structuring and development of the liberation movement.

In our view, the foundation of national liberation lies in the inalienable right of every people to have their own history, whatever the formulations adopted in international law. The aim of national liberation is therefore to regain this right, usurped by imperialist domination, namely: the liberation of the process of development of the national productive forces. So national liberation exists when, and only when, the national productive forces have been completely freed from all kinds of foreign domination. The liberation of productive forces and consequently of the ability freely to determine the mode of production most appropriate to the evolution of the liberated people, necessarily opens up new prospects for the cultural process of the society in question, by returning to it all its capacity to create progress.

A people who free themselves from foreign domination will not be culturally free unless, without underestimating the importance of positive contributions from the oppressor's culture and other cultures, they return to the upwards paths of their own culture. The latter is nourished by the living reality of the environment and rejects harmful influences as much as any kind of subjection to foreign cultures. We see therefore that, if imperialist domination has the vital need to practise cultural oppression, national liberation is necessarily an *act of culture*.

The class character of culture

On the basis of what has just been said, we may regard the liberation movement as the organized political expression of the struggling people's culture. Thus the leadership of that movement must have a clear notion of the value of culture in the framework of struggle and a profound knowledge of the culture of their people, whatever the level of economic development.

Nowadays, it has become a commonplace to assert that every people has its culture. The time is past when, in an attempt to perpetuate the domination of peoples, culture was regarded as an attribute of privileged peoples or nations and when, out of ignorance of bad faith, culture was confused with technical skill, if not with the colour of one's skin or the shape of one's eyes. The liberation movement, as representative and defender of the culture of the people, must be conscious of the fact that, whatever the material conditions of the society it represents, the society is the bearer and the creator of culture. The liberation movement must in addition understand the mass character, the popular character of culture, which is not and could not be an attribute of one sector or of some sectors of society.

In the thorough analysis of social structure which every liberation movement must be able to make, by virtue of the imperatives of struggle, the cultural characteristics of each social category have a place of prime importance. For, while culture has a mass character, it is not uniform, it is not evenly developed in all sectors of society. The attitude of each social category towards the struggle is dictated by its economic interests, but is also profoundly influenced by its culture. We may even admit that the differences in cultural levels explain the differing behaviour towards the liberation movement of individuals within the same socio-economic category. It is at this point that culture reaches its full significance for each individual: understanding and integration in his environment, identification with the fundamental problems and aspirations of society, acceptance of the possibility of change in the direction of progress.

In the specific conditions of our country – and we should say of Africa – the horizontal and vertical distribution of levels of culture is somewhat complex. In fact, from the villages to the towns, from one ethnic group to another, from the peasant to the artisan or to the more or less assimilated indigenous intellectual, from one social class to another, and even, as we have said, from individual to individual within the same social category, there are significant variations in the quantitative and qualitative level of culture. It is a question of prime importance for the liberation movement to take these facts into consideration.

In the societies with a horizontal structure, like the Balanta society, for example, the distribution of cultural levels is more or less uniform, variations being linked solely to individual characteristics and to age groups. In the societies with a vertical structure, like that of the Fula for example, there are important variations from the top to the bottom of the social pyramid. This shows once more the close connexion between the cultural factor and the economic factor, and also explains the differences in the overall or sectoral behaviour of these two ethnic groups towards the liberation movement.

It is true that the multiplicity of social and ethnic categories somewhat complicates the determining of the role of culture in the liberation movement. But it is vital not to lose sight of the decisive significance of the *class character* of culture in development of the liberation struggle, even in the case when a category is or appears to be still embryonic.

The experience of colonial domination shows that, in an attempt to perpetuate exploitation, the colonizer not only creates a whole system of repression of the cultural life of the colonized people, but also provokes and develops the cultural alienation of a part of the population, either by supposed assimilation of indigenous persons, or by the creation of a social gulf between the aboriginal elites and the mass of the people. As a result of this process of division or of deepening the divisions within the society, it follows that a considerable part of the population notably the urban or peasant 'petty bourgeoisie', assimilates the colonizer's mentality, and regards itself as culturally superior to the people to which it belongs and whose cultural values it ignores or despises. This situation, characteristic of the majority of colonized intellectuals, is crystallized to the extent that the social privileges of the assimilated or alienated group are increased with direct implications for the behaviour towards the liberation movement by individuals in this group. A spiritual reconversion – of mentalities – is thus seen to be vital for their true integration in the liberation movement. Such reconversion – *re-Africanization* in our case – may take place before the struggle, but is completed only during the course of the struggle, through daily contact with the mass of the people and the communion of sacrifices which the struggle demands.

We must, however, take into consideration the fact that, faced with the prospect of political independence, the ambition and opportunism from which the liberation movement generally suffers may draw into the struggle individuals who have not been reconverted. The latter, on the basis of their level of education, their scientific or technical knowledge, and without losing any of their class cultural prejudices, may attain the highest positions in the liberation movement. On the cultural as well as the political level vigilance is therefore vital. For in the specific and highly complex circumstances of the process of the phenomenon of the liberation movements, all that glitters is not necessarily gold: political leaders – even the most famous – may be culturally alienated.

But the class character of culture is still more noticeable in the behaviour of privileged groups in the rural environment, notably where ethnic groups with a vertical social structure are concerned, where nevertheless the influences of assimilation or cultural alienation are nil or virtually nil. This is the case of the Fula ruling class, for example. Under colonial domination, the political authority of this class (traditional chiefs, noble families, religious leaders) is purely nominal, and the mass of the people are aware of the fact that the real authority lies with and is wielded by the colonial administrators. However, the ruling class retains in essence its cultural authority over the mass of the people in the group, with very important political implications.

Knowing this reality, colonialism, which represses or inhibits significant cultural expression at the grass roots on the part of the mass of the people, supports and protects the prestige and cultural influence of the ruling class at the summit. It installs chiefs whom it trusts and who are more or less accepted by the population, gives them various material privileges including education for their eldest children, creates chiefdoms where they did not exist, establishes and develops cordial relations with religious leaders, builds mosques, organizes journeys to Mecca, etc. Above all, by means of the repressive organs of colonial administration, it ensures the economic and social privileges of the ruling class in relation to the mass of the people. All this does not remove the possibility that, among these ruling classes, there may be individuals or groups of individuals who join the liberation movement, although less frequently than in the case of the assimilated 'petty bourgeoisie'. Several traditional and religious leaders join the struggle from the start or in the course of its unfolding, making an enthusiastic contribution to the cause of liberation. But there again vigilance is vital: holding strongly onto their class cultural prejudices, individuals in this category generally see in the liberation movement the only valid means for using the sacrifices of the mass of the people to eliminate colonial oppression of their own class and hence to re-establish their complete cultural and political domination over the people.

In the general framework of challenge to imperialist colonial domination and in the specific circumstances to which we are referring, it can be seen that among the oppressor's most faithful allies are found some senior civil servants and assimilated intellectuals from the liberal professions, and a significant number of representatives of the ruling class in the rural areas. This fact gives some measure (negative or positive) of the influence of culture and of cultural prejudices on the question of the political option towards the liberation movement. It likewise shows the limits of this influence and the supremacy of the class factor in behaviour of the various social categories. The senior civil servant or the assimilated intellectual, characterized by total cultural alienation, identifies in the political option with the traditional or religious leader, who has experienced no significant foreign cultural influence. For these two categories set above all factors or demands of a cultural nature – and against the aspirations of the people – their own economic and social privileges, their *class interests*. That is a truth which the liberation movement cannot ignore, on pain of betraying the economic, political, social and cultural aims of the struggle.

Towards a definition of national culture

As on the political level and without minimizing the positive contribution which privileged classes or strata may make to the struggle, the liberation movement must, on the cultural level, base its action on popular culture, whatever the diversity of cultural levels in the country. The cultural challenge to colonial domination – the primary phase of the liberation movement – can be effectively envisaged only on the basis of the culture of the mass of workers in the countryside and the towns, including the (revolutionary) nationalist 'petty bourgeoisie', which has been re-Africanized or is disposed towards a cultural reconversion. Whatever the complexity of this cultural panorama at the base, the liberation movement must be capable of distinguishing within it the essential from the secondary, the positive from the negative, the progressive from the reactionary in order to characterize the key line of progressive definition of *national culture*.

For culture to play the important role which falls to it in the framework of development of the liberation movement, the movement must be able to conserve the positive cultural values of every well-defined social group, of every category, and to achieve the *confluence* of these values into the stream of struggle, giving them a new dimension – the *national dimension*. Faced with such a necessity, the liberation struggle is, above all, a struggle as much for the conservation and survival of the cultural values of the people as for the harmonizing and development of these values within a national framework.

The political and moral unity of the liberation movement and of the people it represents and leads implies the achievement of the cultural unity of the decisive social categories for the struggle. This unity take the form on the one hand of total indentification of the movement with the environmental reality and with the problems and fundamental aspirations of the people and on the other hand of progressive cultural identification of the various social categories which take part in the struggle. The latter process must harmonize divergent interests, resolve contradictions and define common aims in the search for liberty and progress. If broad strata of the population become aware of these aims and this is shown in determination in the face of all the difficulties and all the sacrifices, it is a great political and moral victory. The same result is likewise a decisive cultural achievement for the further development and success of the liberation movement.

Cultural bankruptcy of colonialism

The greater the differences between the culture of the dominated people and that of the oppressor the more possible such a victory becomes. History shows that it is much less difficult to dominate and preserve domination over a people whose culture is similar or analogous to that of the conqueror. It could perhaps be asserted that Napoleon's failure, whatever the economic and political motives of his wars of conquest, lay in his not having had the wisdom (or ability) to limit his ambitions to the domination of peoples whose culture was more or less similar to that of France. The same could be said of other ancient, modern or contemporary empires.

One of the most serious mistakes, if not the most serious mistake, made by the colonial powers in Africa, may have been to ignore or underestimate the cultural strength of African peoples. This attitude is particularly clear in the case of Portuguese colonial domination, which was not content with denying absolutely the existence of cultural values of the African and his condition as a social being, but has persisted in forbidding him any kind of political activity. The people of Portugal, who have not even enjoyed the wealth usurped from African peoples, but the majority of whom have assimilated the imperial mentality of the country's ruling classes, are paying today a high price in three colonial wars for the mistake of underestimating our cultural reality.

The political and armed resistance of the peoples of the Portuguese colonies, as of other countries or regions of Africa, was crushed by the technical superiority of the imperialist conqueror, with the complicity of or betrayal by some indigenous ruling classes. The elites who were faithful to the history and to the culture of the people were destroyed. Entire populations were massacred. The colonial kingdom was installed with all the crimes and exploitation that characterize it. But cultural resistance of the African people was not destroyed. African culture, though repressed, persecuted and betrayed by some social categories who compromised with colonialism, survived all the storms, by taking refuge in the villages, in the forests and in the spirit of generations of victims of colonialism.

Like the seed which long awaits conditions favourable for germination, in order to conserve survival of the species and its evolution, the culture of African peoples flourishes again today across the continent in the struggles for national liberation. Whatever the forms of these struggles, their successes and failures and the length of their development, they mark the beginning of a new phase in the continent's history and are in form and content the most significant cultural factor in the life of African peoples. As the fruit and the proof of cultural vigour, the liberation struggle of African peoples opens up new prospects for the development of culture, in the service of progress.

Cultural wealth of Africa

The time is past when it was necessary to seek arguments to prove the cultural maturity of African peoples. The irrationality of the racist 'theories' of a Gobineau or a Lévy-Bruhl neither interests nor persuades anyone but racists. In spite of colonial domination (and perhaps because of this domination) Africa has been able to impose respect for her cultural values. She has even been shown to be one of the richest of continents in cultural values. From Carthage or Giza to Zimbabwe, from Meroë to Benin and Ife, from the Sahara or Timbuctoo to Kilwa, across the immensity and the diversity of the continent's natural conditions, the culture of African peoples is an undeniable fact: in works of art as in oral and written traditions, in cosmogony as in music and dances, in religions and creeds as in dynamic equilibrium of economic, political and social structures that African man has been able to create.

If the universal value of African culture is now an incontestable fact, it should not, however, be forgotten that African man, whose hands, as the poet said, 'have laid the foundation stones of the world', has developed his culture in often, if not always, hostile conditions: from deserts to equatorial forests, from coastal marshes to the banks of great rivers subject to frequent flooding, through and against all the difficulties, including scourges which destroy not only plants and animals but man as well. In agreement with Basil Davidson and other researchers of African societies and cultures, we can say that the accomplishments of the African genius on the economic, political and cultural levels, in the light of the inhospitable character of the environment, are an achievement to be ranked with the major historical examples of the greatness of man.

The dynamic of culture

Obviously, this reality constitutes a motive for pride and stimulus for those who struggle for the freedom and progress of African peoples. But it is important not to lose sight of the fact that no culture is a perfect, finished whole. Culture, like history, is necessarily an expanding and developing phenomenon. Even more important, we must bear in mind that the fundamental characteristic of culture is its close, dependent and reciprocal connexion with the economic and social reality of the environment, with the level of productive forces and the mode of production of the society which created it.

Culture, as the fruit of history, reflects at all times the material and spiritual reality of the society, of man-the-individual and man-the-social-being, faced with conflicts which set them against nature and the imperatives of life in common. It follows from this that any culture contains essential and secondary elements, strengths and weaknesses, virtues, defects, positive and negative aspects, factors for progress and stagnation or for regression. It follows likewise that culture – a creation of the society and a synthesis of the checks and balances society devises to resolve the conflicts that characterize it at each stage of history – is a social reality independent of men's will, the colour of their skin or the shape of their eyes.

A profound analysis of cultural reality removes the supposition that there can be continental or racial cultures. This is because, as with history, culture develops in an uneven process, at the level of a continent, a 'race' or even a society. The co-ordinates of culture, like those of any developing phenomenon, vary in space and time, whether they be material (physical) or human (biological and social). The fact of recognizing the existence of common and special traits in the cultures of African peoples, independently of the colour of their skin, does not necessarily imply that one and only one culture exists on the continent. In the same way that from the economic and political point of view one can note the existence of various Africas, so there are also various African cultures.

Without any doubt, underestimation of the cultural values of African peoples, based upon racist feelings and the intention of perpetuating exploitation by the foreigner, has done much harm to Africa. But in the face of the vital need for progress, the following factors or behaviour would be no less harmful to her: unselective praise; systematic exaltation of virtues without condemning defects; blind acceptance of the values of the culture without considering what is actually or potentially negative, reactionary or regressive; confusion between what is the expression of an objective and historical material reality and what appears to be a spiritual creation or the result of a special nature; absurd connexion of artistic creations, whether valid or not, to supposed racial characteristics; and finally non-scientific or ascientific critical appreciation of the cultural phenomenon.

The important thing is not to waste time in more or less hair-splitting debates on the specificity or non-specificity of African cultural values, but to look upon these values as a conquest by a part of mankind for the common heritage of all mankind, achieved in one or several phases of its evolution. The important thing is to proceed to critical analysis of African cultures in the light of the liberation movement and the demands of progress – in the light of this new stage in the history of Africa. We may be aware of its value in the framework of universal civilization, but to compare its value with that of other cultures, not in order to decide its superiority or its inferiority, but to determine, within the general framework of the struggle for progress, what contribution African culture has made and must make and contributions it can or must receive.

The liberation movement must, as we have said, base its action on thorough knowledge of the culture of the people and be able to assess the elements of this culture at their true worth, as well as the different levels it reaches in each social category. It must likewise be able to distinguish within the totality of the people's cultural values the essential and secondary, the positive and negative, the progressive and reactionary, the strengths and weaknesses. This is necessary by virtue of the demands of the struggle and in order to be able to centre its action on the essential without forgetting the secondary, to instigate development of positive and progressive elements and to fight, with subtlety but strictness, negative and reactionary elements; finally so that it can make effective use of strengths and remove weaknesses, or transform them into strengths.

National culture, a condition for development of the struggle

The more one becomes aware that the major goal of the liberation movement goes beyond the conquest of political independence to put itself on the superior plane of total liberation of productive forces and the building of the people's economic, social and cultural progress, the more evident becomes the need to proceed to a selective analysis of the values of the culture within the framework of the struggle. The negative values of the culture are generally an obstacle to the development of the struggle and to the building of that progress. The need for analysis becomes more acute in the cases where, in order to face up to colonialist violence, the liberation movement must mobilize and organize the people, under the leadership of a strong and disciplined political organization, with the aim of resorting to liberating violence – *the armed struggle for national liberation.*

In this perspective, the liberation movement must be able, beyond the analysis mentioned above, to achieve, step by step but surely, as its political action develops, the *confluence of the cultural levels* of the various social categories available for the struggle. The movement must be able to transform them into the national cultural force which serves as a basis for development of the armed struggle and is a condition for it. It should be noted that the analysis of cultural reality already gives a measure of the strengths and weaknesses of the people, faced with the demands of the struggle, and therefore represents a valuable acquisition for the strategy and tactics to be followed both on the political and military level. But only in the cause of struggle, launched from a satisfactory base of political and moral unity, is the complexity of cultural questions raised in its full range. This frequently requires successive adaptations of strategy and tactics to the realities which only the struggle can reveal. Experience of the struggle shows how utopian and absurd it is to seek to apply schemes developed by other peoples in the course of their liberation struggle and solutions which they found to the questions with which they were or are confronted, without considering local reality (and especially cultural reality).

It might be said that at the start of the struggle, whatever the degree of preparation, both the leadership of the liberation movement and the mass of militants and of the people are not clearly aware of the weight of influence of cultural values in the development of the struggle. They do not know what possibilities it creates, the limits it imposes and principally, how and how much culture is for the people an inexhaustible source of courage, of material and moral support, of physical and psychic energy, which enables them to accept sacrifices and even to do 'miracles'. But likewise, in some respects they do not know how much it is a source of obstacles and difficulties, of erroneous conceptions of reality, of deviations in the fulfilment of duty and of limitation on the rhythm and efficiency of the struggle in the face of the political, technical and scientific demands of a war.

Armed struggle, an instrument for unification and cultural progress

The armed struggle for liberation, launched in response to aggression by the colonialist oppressor, turns out to be a painful but effective instrument for developing the cultural level both for the leadership strata of the liberation movement and for the various social categories who take part in the struggle.

The leaders of the liberation movement, drawn from the 'petty bourgeoisie' (intellectuals, employees) or from the background of workers in the towns (labourers, drivers, salaried workers in general), having to live day by day with the various peasant strata, among the rural populations, come to know the people better. They discover at its source the wealth of their cultural values, (philosophical, political, artistic, social and moral) acquire a clearer awareness of the economic realities of the country; of the difficulties, sufferings and aspirations of the mass of the people. The leaders realize, not without a certain astonishment, the wealth of spirit, the capacity for reasoning and clear statement of ideas, the facility for comprehension and assimilation of concepts on the part of populations who only yesterday were forgotten if not despised and regarded by the colonizer, and even by some nationals, as incompetent beings. The leaders thus enrich their culture – they cultivate the mind and free themselves from complexes, strengthening their capacity, to serve the movement in the service of the people.

On their side, the mass of workers and, in particular, the peasants, who are generally illiterate and have never moved beyond the confines of the village or region, in the contact with other categories shed the complexes which constrained them in their relations with other ethnic and social groups. They understand their situation as determining elements of the struggle; they break the fetters of the village universe to integrate gradually into the country and the world; they acquire an infinite amount of new knowledge, of use to their immediate and future activity within the framework of the struggle; and they strengthen their political awareness, by absorbing the principles of national and social revolution postulated by the struggle. They thus become fitter to play the decisive role as the principal force of the liberation movement.

As we know, the armed liberation struggle demands the mobilization and organization of a significant majority of the population, the political and moral unity of the various social categories, the efficient use of modern weapons and other means of warfare, the gradual elimination of the remnants of tribal mentality, and the rejection of social and religious rules and taboos contrary to development of the struggle (gerontocracy, nepotism, social inferiority of women, rites and practices which are incompatible with the rational and national character of the struggle, etc.). The struggle brings about many other profound changes in the life of the populations. The armed liberation struggle implies, therefore, a veritable forced march along the road to cultural progress.

We should add to these inherent features of an armed liberation struggle: the practice of democracy, of criticism and self-criticism, the growing responsibility of populations for the management of their life, literacy teaching, the creation of schools and health care, the training of cadres from peasant and labourer backgrounds – and other achievements. We should thus find that the armed liberation struggle is not only a product of culture but also a *factor of culture*. This is without doubt for the people the prime recompense for the efforts and sacrifices which are the price of war. In the light of this perspective, it behoves the liberation movement to define clearly the aims of cultural resistance, as an integral and determining part of the struggle.

The aims of cultural resistance

From all that we have just said, it can be concluded that in the framework of the conquest of national independence and in the perspective of building the economic and social progress of the people, these aims must be at least the following:

Development of a *people's culture* and of all aboriginal positive cultural values

Development of a *national culture* on the basis of history and the conquests of the struggle itself

Constant raising of the *political and moral awareness* of the people (of all social categories) and of *patriotism*, spirit of sacrifice and devotion to the cause of independence, justice and progress

Development of the technical and technological *scientific culture*, compatible with the demands of progress

Development, on the basis of a critical assimilation of mankind's conquests in the domains of art, science, literature, etc., of a *universal culture*, aiming at perfect integration in the contemporary world and its prospects for evolution

Constant and generalized raising of feelings of humanism, solidarity, respect and disinterested devotion to the human being.

The achievement of these aims is indeed possible for, under the specific conditions of life of the African peoples, facing the imperialist challenge, the armed liberation struggle is an act of making history bear fruit, the highest expression of our culture and of our African-ness. At the moment of victory, it must be translated into a significant leap forward of the culture of the people who are liberating themselves.

If this does not happen, then the efforts and sacrifices made during the struggle will have been in vain. The struggle will have failed in its aims, and the people will have missed an opportunity for progress in the general framework of history.

When we celebrate the memory of Dr Eduardo Mondlane at this ceremony, we are paying homage to the political man, to the freedom fighter and particularly to the man of culture. It was a culture that was not only acquired during his personal life and on university benches, but principally in the midst of his people, in the framework of his people's liberation struggle.

One might say that Eduardo Mondlane was *savagely* assassinated because he was capable of identifying with the culture of his people, with their deepest aspirations, through and against all attempts or temptations for the alienation of his personality as an African and a Mozambican. Because he had forged a new culture in the struggle, he fell as a combatant. It is easy enough to accuse the Portuguese colonialists and the agents of imperialism, their allies, of the abominable crime committed against the person of Eduardo Mondlane, against the people of Mozambique and against Africa. It was they who cravenly assassinated him. But it is necessary for all men of culture, all freedom fighters, all spirits eager for peace and progress – all the enemies of colonialism and racism – to have the courage to bear on their shoulders part of the responsibility as behoves them for this tragic death. For, if Portuguese colonialism and imperialist agents can still with impunity murder a man like Dr Eduardo Mondlane, it is because something putrid continues to decay in the heart of mankind: *imperialist domination.* It is because men of good will, defenders of the culture of peoples, have not yet accomplished their duty over our planet.

In our view, that gives a measure of the responsibilities of our audience in this temple of culture in regard to the liberation movement of the oppressed peoples.

PART 2
Revolutionary Practice

THE STRATEGY FOR POLITICAL MOBILIZATION

16. Message to Guinean and Cape Verdian civil servants and employees in commerce

Brothers!
There is and can be no power in the world able to prevent the total elimination of Portuguese colonialism from our African lands. As has happened in almost all the countries of Africa, the peoples of Guiné and Cape Verde are going to put an end to the odious colonial domination. We are going to chase the Portuguese colonialists from our lands. Our peoples are struggling and will struggle by all means possible, in order to be free, in order to be able, in peace, to build a life of progress and happiness for all their children.

Obviously, the position which our peoples, when they have freed themselves from the barbarous Portuguese colonial domination, will have to take in regard to all inhabitants will depend on the position each of the latter has taken in regard to our national liberation struggle. The suffering to which our peoples have been subject for centuries, the sacrifices they are making and will make to free themselves, the sacred objective of our struggle – all this demands the application of stern justice in judging the action of every Guinean and Cape Verdian in regard to the interests of our peoples. By force of the circumstances prevailing in our countries, you, as civil servants and employees in commerce, are the servitors of Portuguese colonialism. Through this service you seek to ensure a home, bread, health, education and the welfare of your families, things which as you know are denied to our peoples because of the hated Portuguese colonial domination. In the light of the development of our liberation struggle which is going to eliminate Portuguese colonialism, it is natural that many of you should be hesitant and apprehensive. In your minds there must be doubts like these: 'What will become of us? What should we do?'

The answers to these doubts and to all the others which naturally worry you depend on one thing only: the attitude you take towards our liberation struggle. Each of you has to have the courage to shoulder the responsibility of being an African at this decisive moment in the history of our peoples. Many with awareness of this necessity have bravely put themselves on the side of our peoples and are our companions in struggle.

You are our brothers. Whatever your employment – education, health, customs, finance, post office, technical services, civil administration, banking or commerce – there is one thing you cannot escape: you are

Africans, descendants of our lands and of our peoples. Because of this, many of you, although more able than your Portuguese colleagues, have never succeeded in overcoming the stumbling-block of subordinate positions; you were passed over or discriminated against in competitions, to the advantage of the Portuguese; have suffered and suffer increasingly strongly the hypocritical racial discrimination practised by the Portuguese colonialists. Even the few who, at a sacrifice of personal worth and hard struggle, have succeeded in 'making their way' – even these cannot and should not forget the injustices they have suffered as a reflex of the injustices which have weighed on our peoples for centuries.

Brothers!

Your destiny must be the destiny of our peoples. The fact that as civil servants or employees in commerce you are serving Portuguese colonialism does not strip from you your characteristic of being Africans and patriots. But at this decisive moment what counts, what determines your character as Africans and patriots, is the attitude you are able to take and what you are able to do in support of our liberation struggle. Our peoples hope and pray that you will be their true sons, that you will not stay outside our struggle, and that you will line up on their side and prepare to act at the right moment in order to give your best in serving the liberation of our lands.

Like all those who live under Portuguese colonial domination and in spite of the fierce repression to which we are subject, you can choose between being patriots or being traitors. This depends on you alone. You can choose the path of life, put yourselves on the side of our peoples, share in our liberation struggle and regain your dignity as men and Africans. Or drawn on by selfishness and blind ambition, you can put yourself on the side of the Portuguese colonialists, serve our peoples' enemies and, along with our oppressors and exploiters, face inevitable destruction by our struggle. This is the choice that each of you must make, in the certainty of this inescapable truth: *the future of our lands belongs to our peoples, who are going to eliminate completely Portuguese colonialism*

You surely know what you should do. Organize clandestinely in all places of work, contact our organizations for the struggle, enrol in them or give them your collaboration, prepare to give your best to serve our liberation. You should turn each post you hold, in the civil service or in commerce, into a fortress of combat for the immediate destruction of Portuguese colonialism. Bravely, intelligently, without useless sacrifices, with strong conspiratorial sense and within the framework of our organizations, you should be ready to heed the directives of our struggle.

You are Guineans and Cape Verdians, like those whom the circumstances of life have put at the head of our liberation struggle. You are one of the greatest treasures of our peoples, since you are in the vanguard of our human values. We are confident that you will not commit the crime of putting this treasure and this value at the service of those who dominate and exploit our peoples. On the contrary, you will be able to put yourselves at the service of our liberation struggle, so that tomorrow, in our free, democratic and progressive country, without barriers of any kind, you may fulfil the honourable duties which will fall to you in the construction of progress and happiness for our peoples. For, whatever the strength of the Portuguese colonialists and the collaboration they have, our peoples are going to chase them out so that, free of foreign domination and of all traitors, they may build a life in which they will never be exploited.

This is the message we address to you at this grave and decisive moment. Now is your time, for word and action – the definitive choice – in the face of the struggle our peoples are waging for the reconquest of their freedom and dignity.

Guinean and Cape Verdian civil servants and employees in commerce!
Mobilize and organize to serve our struggle!

Do not seek to tie your destiny to the destiny of Portuguese colonialism, whose days are numbered!

Every employment should be a combat post for the immediate elimination of Portuguese colonialism!

Forward with our peoples' liberation struggle!
Down with Portuguese colonialism!

> Bissau, October 1960
> For the Political Bureau of PAI
> Amilcar Cabral (Abel Djassi)
> (Five more signatures of leaders in
> clandestinity follow)

17. Message to the Portuguese settlers in Guiné and Cape Verde

The deepest spirit of human understanding and brotherhood brings us to address this message to you. The moment is grave and every man or woman should have the necessary courage to grapple with the reponsibility of his conscious attitude towards the aspirations and the struggle of the African peoples.

Your colonialist forebears conquered Guiné by force of arms. They enslaved, sold, massacred, dominated and savagely exploited the Guineans during five centuries. Today, in order to defend the interests of certain Portuguese and non-Portuguese companies, the colonialists persecute, imprison, torture and massacre the Guineans and Cape Verdians who are struggling to reconquer the freedom and dignity of the Guinean people.

With slaves wrested from Africa, above all from Guiné, the Portuguese slavers and colonialists created an entrepôt for the slave trade in Cape Verde. When they had been freed from slavery, the Africans in Cape Verde and their descendants, through their labour, won the right to dispose of themselves and all the resources of the archipelago which is today their native country. But the Portuguese colonialists do not recognize the right of Cape Verdians to build for themselves, in freedom and national independence, a life of progress in which they will never again be the victims of the exploitation, misery and hunger that Portuguese colonialism has imposed on them.

The peoples of Guiné and Cape Verde, who are linked by indestructible ties of blood and history, are determined to put an end to Portuguese colonial domination. They want to build in peace, in dignity and in the African context, a free, democratic and progressive country, in which any man, of any origin, will have the opportunity for free development of personality and to contribute effectively for the progress of all. But the colonialists stubbornly maintain their odious domination over our peoples. To do this, they persecute, imprison, torture and massacre; they foment hunger, misery, and ignorance; they constantly strengthen their armed forces and cynically prepare to go on drowning in blood all attempts at liberation on the part of our peoples. You know all this, because you are either authors or witnesses of all that happens in our land. You were authors or witnesses of the massacre in the Pidjiguiti Docks (Bissau, 3 August 1959). You were present at the death of more than 30,000 Cape Verdians, decimated by starvation between 1942 and 1947.

But there are things that you must be told so that tomorrow none of you can claim the excuse that you *did not know.*

Our people are going to put an end to Portuguese colonialism – and they are going to put an end to it very soon. Our peoples are not struggling for vengeance against those who carried out the crimes of Portuguese colonialism: they are struggling to reconquer their freedom and dignity – basic elements of their human condition. For this very reason, since our human nature is the central foundation of our struggle, we are looking carefully at your situation at this grave and decisive moment. We hope that you, men just as we are, will not fail to understand our aspirations, our rights, our struggle.

We draw a distinction between *Portuguese colonialism* and *Portuguese settlers* just as we draw a distinction between a cart and its wheels. A cart cannot run without wheels. Colonialism cannot function without settlers. You are the wheels of the old and detested cart of Portuguese colonialism which tries to continue running against all the realities of history, at the cost of exploitation and destruction of our peoples. But the Portuguese colonialists are mistaken. And you should not be mere cogs in an anachronistic machine that is doomed to extinction: *you should be men.*

In our lands and under the cover of colonial violence, you have been and go on being the masters. You have grown accustomed to proposing and disposing of our lives and our goods, with a degree of inhumanity only rarely alleviated by the solidarity or good will of precious few. Many of you will never succeed in ridding your conscience of the crimes you have committed against our peoples whether in private life or as agents of colonialism. Others, who in your country were understanding and progressive men, arrived in our lands and forgot the fine feelings and reason and adapted yourselves to the demands and crimes of the colonialists. The colour of your skin has been and goes on being sufficient reason to ensure your supremacy in our lands, in contempt of the feelings, rights, culture, civilization and just aspirations of our peoples. Today you face with anxiety and anguish the prospect of a radical change in all these things.

But, whatever the cost, things are going to change. *Our peoples are going to become masters of their own destiny.* You would have no reason for anxiety and anguish if you wanted and were able to act as conscientious men and not as unconscious cogs in a machine of dominion and exploitation. Everything depends on the attitude in regard to our liberation struggle that you adopt at this moment. We, who are not hypocrites like the Portuguese colonialists, already guarantee that, after our liberation, the just interests of all foreigners who live and work in our lands will be respected. We want to co-operate with all the peoples on earth, we want the friendship and co-operation of all men who always respect the sacred rights of our peoples.

Portuguese Settlers in Guiné and Cape Verde!

The days of Portuguese colonialism are numbered and you know this very well. As conscientious men, you must not accept the absurdity of tying your destiny to the destiny of Portuguese colonialism! You should not go on being the mercenaries of a lost cause, you should not go on allowing the Portuguese colonialist companies, with the inglorious sacrifices of your persons and families, to use you in order to defend their vile interests! If you do not have the courage to support our struggle, preserve your human dignity by refusing to serve the colonialists and maintaining *neutrality* towards our liberation struggle!

You can be sure of this: *no power in the world can prevent the complete elimination of Portuguese colonialism from our lands, that is to say, the destruction of all forces which support it and which have, knowingly or unknowingly, opposed the liberation of our peoples.*

So it is for you to decide your destiny in a free, democratic and progressive country that our peoples are going to build after the total and imminent elimination of the detested Portuguese colonial domination. In the certainty that our peoples will not fail to exercise the sternest justice with regard to each of you and from this moment.

Long live friendship, equality and peaceful co-operation between all peoples!
Long live the liberation struggle of all oppressed peoples!
Down with Portuguese colonialism!
Long live the African Independence Party!

October, 1960
For the Political Bureau of PAI
Amilcar Cabral (Abel Djassi)
(Six signatures of leaders in clandestinity follow)

18. Message to the soldiers, officers and NCOs of the Portuguese colonial army

The moment of truth has come, the time has come for you to have the real proof of all that our Party has announced to you with the humane intention of helping you to protect your lives against the criminal lies and orders of your colonialist bosses.

At this difficult time, as filled with hopes and certainties for our people as it is filled with despair and doubts for you, we want to repeat what we have already told you.

Our people who will fight until victory for the independence of our land are not the enemy of the Portuguese people. You are the sons of the Portuguese people, but you are being used by the colonialists as tools to kill our people, in order to try to prevent us being free and masters of our own land.

We want peace, freedom and co-operation between men and between all peoples. But for this very reason and cause, we must put an end to Portuguese colonialism in our land, we must remove all obstacles to our national independence, we are fighting and are going to eliminate all those who, with weapons in hand, seek but certainly in vain to prevent the liberation of our people.

Portuguese soldiers, NCOs and officers!

You know, and everyone knows – and the Portuguese Government itself before anyone – that the cause of the colonialists is an unjust and a lost cause. You know as well that no power in the world will be able to prevent the liberation of our people from the colonial yoke.

We are aware of this truth, we fight bravely against you and we shall fight until victory. Experience has already shown you that all the descendants of our land – young and old, men and women, children even – are ready to give their life for the freedom, progress and happiness of our people.

And you – Portuguese soldiers, officers and NCOs, the youth of Portugal, the hope of your people – why and for what are you dying in our land?

From the dozens of your countrymen who have already died in our land – soon they will be hundreds and may become thousands – look at the cases of the soldiers No.834/59, Verissimo Godinho Ramos and No.224/60, Fernando Cristiano Pereira, Lance-Corporal Francisco Moreira and Corporal Abilio Monteiro de Brito. Many of you will certainly remember these four youngsters, the hopes of their families who moreover in Portugal live a life of suffering and hardship.

Like you, they were pressganged, tricked and forced to come to our land to wage a war of colonial domination against us. Heedless of our advice, they went on with impunity for a long time to commit the most heinous crimes against our people. They tortured, killed, massacred, burned. At will they used against our defenceless populations the most modern heavy weapons in the certainty that there would be no reply.

But today our people, under the leadership of our great Party and guided by their best sons, have modern heavy weapons too – and will have more each day – in order to defend themselves from the crimes of the colonialists and in order to develop our struggle and to win freedom.

Why did your comrades we mentioned and so many others die? Why is there mourning and misfortune for so many homes, above all for so many poor homes? Why?

Because your colonialist bosses have tricked you and go on tricking you. Because your Government and your military chiefs act against the interests of your people and force you to take up arms to fight against our desire for freedom and to destroy our people, who like all peoples want to be owners of their own land and masters of their destiny. Because – the whole truth must be told – you have accepted and go on accepting the shameful and unworthy role as unconscious tools in the service of colonial oppression and repression instead of being with bravery conscious beings in the service of the true interests of your people.

For what did your compatriots die, for what do you go on running the constant risk of dying in our land? For what?

To serve the criminal and exploitative interests of CUF, of the Overseas Commercial Society, of the Overseas National Bank – of the Portuguese colonialists and their imperialist bosses. In order to serve, in point of fact, the interests of some rich families in Portugal, which have nothing to do with the true interests of your families and of your people.

Portuguese soldiers, NCOs and officers!

You know that your people, who must struggle for freedom and democracy in their own land, need your help. Your families, who mostly belong to the poor classes in Portugal, are longing for your return in order to ensure their future – the future of your fathers, mothers, sisters, brides, sons and daughters. It is essential to act.

As young men, you have a sacred duty to fulfil in your country, namely to struggle to be able to build a worthy future for your people, who are still living in misery, ignorance and suffering.

As conscious beings, you have the right to unmask the colonialist lie, to disobey the impositions of an unjust and lost cause, in order to help mankind to build a world of freedom, peace and well-being.

As Portuguese and patriots, you have the duty to do everything to keep safe the potential for friendly co-operation between the African peoples and the people of Portugal, between our people and yours, on the basis of equality of rights, duties and advantages.

Soldiers, officers and NCOs or the Portuguese colonial army!
The moment of truth has come, the moment for great decisions.

You still have time to take a just, conscious and brave decision in your own interest and in the interest of your people.

For this reason – and because we are firmly determined to carry out our duties as conscious beings, as African patriots – we are sending you this further message of brotherhood, understanding, encouragement and wishes for a long life in your country, in the service of your people.

Give up serving as tools of colonialism, refuse to take up arms against the freedom and independence of a peaceful people!

Bravely refuse to fight against our people!

Do not seek to serve as watchdogs of the unjust interests of CUF and other colonial companies, which are not your interests nor those of your people!

Do not seek the wretched fate of your countrymen who fell ingloriously in the service of an unjust and irreparably lost cause!

Rise in revolt against your Fascist and colonialist chiefs who are sending you to death!

Show that you are conscious beings determined to serve the true interests of your people!

Follow the example of your brave companions who refuse to fight in our land, who rose in revolt against the criminal orders of your chiefs, who have co-operated with our Party or who have deserted the colonial army and found in our midst the finest welcome and fraternal assistance!

Demand your immediate return to be with your families in Portugal!

Long live peace, friendship and co-operation between all peoples!

Long live the struggle for national and social liberation of all oppressed peoples!

Long live the African Independence Party!

Down with Portuguese colonialism and its lackeys!

22 January 1963
Amilcar Cabral

19. Memorandum from the African Party for the Independence of Guiné and Cape Verde (PAIGC) to the Portuguese Government

The African Independence Party (PAIGC), which is struggling for the total and immediate independence of the Guinean and Cape Verdian peoples in the framework of African unity, has followed closely all the steps taken by the Portuguese Government in order to try to maintain its colonial dominion over the peoples of Guiné and Cape Verde. Our Party, forced by colonial oppression and police repression to operate in clandestinity, has mobilized and organized the mass of the people for the struggle for urgent elimination of Portuguese colonial domination from Guiné and Cape Verde.

Although they know too well the attitude adopted by the Portuguese Government in regard to the characteristic phenomenon in our century of *decolonization,* the peoples of Guiné and Cape Verde and our Party have been 'hoping for the best without failing to be prepared for the worst'. We have waited patiently for the current leaders in Portugal to make up their minds to analyse specifically the situation of our countries and the Portuguese interests themselves – and to come to a decision to recognize for our peoples the right to self-determination, enshrined in the United Nations Charter and respected by the overwhelming majority of colonial powers.

Instead of deciding to take a courageous attitude in the sense of fulfilling its obligations towards our peoples – and extricating itself from an unbearable situation manifestly contrary to the international laws and spirit of our age, the Portuguese Government has had recourse to all the methods it can lay hold of to strengthen and to try to maintain its dominion over our peoples. It is with deep disgust that we record this reality, because it has come so far as to destroy the potential for the Portuguese people and our peoples, after the winning of national independence for Guiné and Cape Verde, to achieve a fruitful co-operation in peace and equality of rights and duties. Even if it is not for us to judge the Portuguese Government in what concerns defence of the interests of the people of Portugal themselves, we are forced to recognize that these interests are being greatly harmed by the attitude that Government persists in maintaining in regard to the fundamental rights of our peoples and our liberation struggle.

After the *Pidjiguiti Docks massacre* (Bissau, 3 August 1959), in which Portuguese soldiers and civilians shot to death dozens of Guinean workers on strike, a wave of repression and terror, planned and commanded by PIDE, brought a hardening of the life and struggle of the people in Guiné. Along with this, the colonial administration, by increasing rice exports, succeded in creating another weapon of oppression – starvation – which currently afflicts a high proportion of the Guinean people. Not content with these steps, whose clear aim is to try to break the firm decision of the Guinean people to free themselves from colonial domination, the Portuguese Government has begun to make feverish preparations, by means of resorting to the armed forces, to drown in blood any attempt at insurrection on the part of the people of Guiné.

In Cape Verde, besides all the repressive steps adopted by the colonial administration and by PIDE, the Portuguese Government returned to letting thousands of people die last year of starvation. The Cape Verdian population, which in a six-year period (1942 to 1947), for example, suffered a drop of 30 000 persons decimated by starvation, goes on being at the mercy of so-called *agricultural crises* and, hence, subject to a periodic drain of thousands of its sons, as *contract* workers, for the Portuguese plantations in other colonies.

More recently, along with police and armed repression, the colonial administration has had recourse to non-violent tactics – largesse, bribery, trips for traditional 'chiefs' to Portugal, granting of scholarships, special radio broadcasts for the 'natives' and the stirring up of discord and quarrels between the various ethnic groups – in order to try at the same time to win over part of the population and to 'divide and rule'. Shaken by the firm decision of the Guinean people to put an end to Portuguese domination, the colonial administration now plans the elimination of various traditional chiefdoms, after experiencing resounding failure in some duly prepared meetings held in October of this year in order to sound out public opinion on the Portuguese presence in Guiné. With the elimination of the chiefdoms (cantons) the colonial administration seeks to exert direct action and greater control over the mass of the people and further to ensure the latter's submission by means of granting special authority to some African traitors to the cause of the liberation of the people of Guiné, such as the Manjaco Joachim Baticã and the Pajadinca Seni Sane.

On the other hand, with the aim of strengthening the military support on which it counts from certain powers, the Portuguese Government has been making generous concessions to non-Portuguese capital (mainly American, West German and Dutch) for the exploitation of natural resources (petrol, bauxite, etc.) and the human assets of Guiné. Moreover, with the intent of ensuring greater strength for military repression against our peoples, the Portuguese Government is very keen to transform Guiné and Cape Verde into military bases for NATO and to become a power in that organization.

Still convinced that an increase in the European population could put the brake on the development of the liberation struggle of our peoples, the Portuguese Government has been studying the drafting of a plan for the urgent despatch of thousands of families of Portuguese settlers to Guiné and Cape Verde.

While all this is happening in our lands, the Portuguese Government, certainly in vain, is trying to persuade world public opinion that 'nothing is going on in its overseas provinces' and that the peoples it dominates 'live in blissful unconcern at what is going on in other African countries'. With this attitude the Portuguese Government has achieved only one result: to fool itself and stir up misunderstanding between the Portuguese people and our peoples.

In fact, as a result of the activity of our Party both inside our countries and in the international field, everyone now knows the truth about the situation of the peoples in Guiné and Cape Verde – and the position of the Portuguese Government is increasingly untenable and absurd.

In our lands, the work of our Party and the very escalation of repression are from day to day raising the political awareness of the masses who are prepared and increasingly preparing to eliminate Portuguese domination.

In the international field, we have today the unconditional support of the overwhelming majority of the peoples of the world and we can count on the effective aid of various friendly countries, in the framework of the principles enunciated at Bandung, at the Conference of African Peoples and at the Afro-Asian Peoples' Solidarity Conferences.

At the United Nations the resolution taken by the Trusteeship Council on November 12 put a full stop to the false argument that the Portuguese delegates had been able to sustain for some years over the juridical nature of the territories occupied by Portugal and about the obligations of the Portuguese Government towards the peoples of those territories. The thesis we had always sustained has just won complete victory over the Portuguese position – and the myth of the 'overseas provinces' is definitively buried. Guiné and Cape Verde are, therefore, non-selfgoverning territories and *a fortiori* colonies. Even the Spanish Government had to break with its now traditional solidarity towards the Portuguese Government, and the latter now finds itself totally isolated, since in United Nations votes it has no one except one undesirable partner – the most racist and most colonialist of all governments.[1]

For the peoples of Guiné and Cape Verde and for our Party, the resolution of the Trusteeship Council, which will very probably be ratified by the United Nations General Assembly, is only a moral victory over Portuguese colonialism and in no way changes the character of the latter. But this resolution shows a reality which must not be overlooked: the overwhelming majority of the states represented in the United Nations is determined to intervene effectively in the solution of the conflict prevailing between the peoples of the Portuguese colonies and the Portuguese Government. The now generally accepted principle of 'solution of conflicts by means of negotiation'; the need to defend peace and international security, threatened

[1] South Africa.

so long as there are colonies; the evident need for freedom and progress for colonial peoples; and further the active solidarity of Afro-Asian peoples – all these fully justify the position adopted by states which are determined to *find a solution* for the case of the Portuguese colonies. The Portuguese Government is certainly aware that neither demonstrations by a certain sector of the Portuguese population against the United Nations, nor those held by the settlers in territories occupied by Portugal, will succeed in changing this position. Such demonstrations do no more than increase the isolation of the Portuguese Government and deepen the misunderstanding between the Portuguese people and the peoples of the Portuguese colonies.

There is, however, one undeniable truth: Portuguese colonialism, like all the other colonialisms, is going to be completely eliminated, and will be so very soon.

In regard to Guiné and Cape Verde, this truth mainly follows from the fact that the Guinean and Cape Verdian peoples and their vanguard organization – our Party – are determined urgently to eliminate Portuguese colonial domination, whatever methods are needed to do it.

Bearing in mind their basic interests as well as the need to defend world peace and security and further the desire to keep safe the potential for fruitful co-operation with the Portuguese people – the peoples of Guiné and Cape Verde and the PAIGC look forward with pleasure to a negotiated solution of the conflict which sets them against the Portuguese Government. Such a solution seems to us a possibility, with or without the intervention of entities who are not directly connected with this conflict.

But for our peoples and our Party all solutions which lead to the total elimination of Portuguese colonial domination are fine. With the certainty, however, that our peoples and our Party are watchful and will not accept any solution which, without their consent and effective participation, aims at changing the external aspects of colonial domination, whether on the basis of an 'Africanization of cadres', or by means of the imposition of 'African leaders' who have nothing in common with the sacred interests of our peoples and who for this reason would only serve the designs of colonial domination.

The route which leads to the total elimination of Portuguese colonialism from Guiné and Cape Verde depends exclusively on the Portuguese Government. Meanwhile our peoples and our Party, who are prepared and are increasingly prepared to face up to the worst, deem it their duty to remind the Portuguese Government that it is not yet too late to proceed to peaceful elimination of Portuguese colonial domination from our lands. Unless the Portuguese Government would like to drag the people of Portugal towards the disaster of a colonial war in Guiné and Cape Verde.

We believe in the advantage and the real possibility of a peaceful solution to the conflict that sets our people against the Portuguese Government and we are aware of the justice of our position and the invincibility of our forces in this conflict. We further believe that out of a simple matter of good sense that Government will surely not make the mistake of pushing the people of Portugal into the inglorious and vain sacrifice of a colonial war in Guiné and Cape Verde.

For this reason, the African Independence Party, faithfully expressing the most just aspirations of the Guinean and Cape Verdian peoples, takes the initiative of proposing to the Portuguese Government the urgent taking of the following steps for the peaceful elimination of colonial domination from our lands:

1. Solemn and immediate recognition of the right of the Guinean and Cape Verdian peoples to self-determination.
2. Immediate withdrawal of the Portuguese armed forces and political police (PIDE) from the territories of Guiné and Cape Verde.
3. Total and unconditional amnesty and immediate release of all political prisoners.
4. Freedom of thought, political freedom, freedom of assembly, of association, of formation of political parties and of trade unions, freedom of the press, and guarantees for the exercise of these freedoms without distinction as to race, cultural level, sex, age and property.
5. Voting rights for all Guineans and for all Cape Verdians without distinction as to race, type of culture and civilization, cultural level, sex and property. One person – one vote.
6. Constitution of a Chamber of Representatives of the people of Guiné, on the basis of one representative for every thirty thousand inhabitants.
7. Constitution of a Chamber of Representatives of the people of Cape Verde, on the basis of one representative for every ten thousand inhabitants.
8. Both in Guiné and in Cape Verde, the Chamber of Representatives must be elected by universal suffrage, direct and secret, in free general elections supervised by a United Nations Special Commission. This Commission should be composed of representatives of African countries.
9. Immediately following their constitution, the holding of a joint meeting of the two Chambers of Representatives in order to study and decide on the possibilities, bases and form of achieving, in the framework of African unity, the organic union of the peoples of Guiné and Cape Verde, on the foundation of the blood ties and the historic ties which link these peoples.
10. In the event of a decision in favour of union:
    a Constitution of a Parliament, with Guinean and Cape Verdian

deputies, chosen from the members previously elected to the Chambers of Representatives and in accordance with the bases established in the joint meeting of the two Chambers of Representatives. The Parliament thus constituted will be the supreme organ of legislative power in Guiné and Cape Verde.

b Nomination by the constituted Parliament of the Government of Guiné and Cape Verde, in accordance with the bases established in the joint meeting of the two Chambers of Representatives. The Government thus nominated will be the supreme organ of executive power in Guiné and Cape Verde.

c Execution of any other decision which may be taken by the joint meeting of the two Chambers of Representatives.

11.   In the event of a decision against union:

a Transformation of the Chambers of Representatives into National Parliaments. The Guinean Parliament and the Cape Verdian Parliament will be the supreme organs of legislative power in Guiné and in Cape Verde respectively.

b Nomination of the Government of Guiné by the Guinean Parliament and of the Government of Cape Verde by the Cape Verdian Parliament. These Governments will be the supreme organs of executive power in Guiné and in Cape Verde respectively.

12.   All matters affecting the life of the Guinean and Cape Verdian peoples must be settled and controlled by those peoples, through their legitimate representatives. This condition is the indispensable basis for the peoples of Guiné and Cape Verde to be able at any moment and in complete freedom to decide their own destiny.

These are the specific and constructive proposals which, on behalf of the peoples of Guiné and Cape Verde, the African Independence Party deems it essential to present to the Portuguese Government at this grave and decisive moment.

The Portuguese Government will surely understand that, in order to enable world opinion to make an immediate assessment of the responsibilities incumbent on that Government in the evolution of the conflict in question and further in regard to the events which will follow in Guiné and Cape Verde, our peoples and the African Independence Party cannot neglect giving this Memorandum the widest publicity.

The Political Bureau of the African Independence Party.

For security reasons the following who are responsible for the African Independence Party sign with their pseudonyms of the struggle. They state here and now that they are ready to reveal their identity as soon as the Portuguese Government puts into effect the first four proposals in this Memorandum.

PAIGC headquarters, Guiné, 15 November 1960.
(Followed by eight signatures)
Conakry, 1 December 1960.
Secretary-general of PAIGC
Amilcar Cabral (Abel Djassi)

The PAIGC Delegation in Dakar and the Liberation Movement for Guiné and Cape Verde, with headquarters in Conakry, likewise gave their complete agreement to the proposals contained in the memorandum, on 28 November and 2 December 1960 respectively.

20. An open note to the Portuguese Government

The Portuguese Government has announced that it is going to put some reforms into effect in its African colonies. According to these reforms, the entire population of Guiné will be regarded as *civilized.* This means that about 99.7 per cent of the African population of our country will in future in principle enjoy the rights of citizenship which were always denied them by the Portuguese Government.

It is clear that, for world opinion as for us, this change of attitude on the part of the Portuguese Government is a specific result – a conquest – of the heroic struggle by our people for national independence. On the other hand, everyone recognizes that the Portuguese Government in taking that decision to grant us Portuguese citizenship without considering our views has once more spurned the rights of our people to self-determination. In these circumstances, the reform in question must be interpreted as an attempt to put the brake on the development of our liberation struggle. The Portuguese Government knows very well that the peoples of Guiné and Cape Verde are not struggling to be Portuguese: we are struggling to win national independence.

In order to achieve this sacred objective, our peoples are firmly decided to have recourse to all possible means. This is proved by the direct action already launched in Guiné and by the great unrest which reigns in Cape Verde, as a response to the police and armed repression practised in silence by the Portuguese colonialist forces. Our people possess and will increasingly possess the means needed to bring about the total destruction of the bases of Portuguese colonial exploitation in our countries.

However, the African Independence Party, expressing the just aspirations of our peoples to national independence, peace, progress and peaceful co-operation with all peoples, including that of Portugal, again takes the initiative of proposing to the Portuguese Government that it resolves by peaceful means the conflict which sets our peoples against it, thus following the example of what was done by the governments of other colonial powers in Africa.

Therefore, the African Independence Party proposes to the Portuguese Government:

1.   Immediate carrying out of the steps proposed in the memorandum addressed to the Portuguese Government in December 1960; or
2.   Immediate acceptance, before world opinion and the United Nations, of the principle of self-determination for our peoples and the holding by the end of this year of a conference between representatives of the Portuguese Government and representatives of the nationalists of Guiné and Cape Verde, with the following agenda:
      a Self-determination and national independence for the peoples of Guiné and Cape Verde.
      b Co-operation between the Portuguese people and the peoples of Guiné and Cape Verde.

Conscious of its duties towards the interests of our peoples, peace and security in the world, as well as the safeguarding of the potential for fruitful co-operation between the Portuguese people and our peoples, the African Independence Party makes this last bid with the Portuguese Government towards the peaceful elimination of colonial domination from our African countries.

Clearly if the Portuguese Government insists on not reconsidering its position – which spurns the interests of our peoples and is against the interests themselves of the Portuguese people – no power will be able to prevent our Party fulfilling its historic task: developing our national liberation struggle, answering with violence the violence of the Portuguese colonialist forces and, by all the means possible, completely eliminating colonial domination from Guiné and Cape Verde.

Secretary-general of PAIGC, Conakry, 13 October 1961
For the Political Bureau of PAIGC
Secretary-general
Amilcar Cabral

21. Proclamation of direct action

On 3 August 1959, in Bissau the Portuguese colonialists massacred fifty African workers on strike. In an epoch of decolonialization, it was the first brutal repression practised by the Portuguese colonialists against the patriots of our countries.

On 3 August 1960, a day of solidarity towards the patriots of the Portuguese colonies was celebrated by all peace and freedom-loving peoples. It was unanimous condemnation of Portuguese colonialism and evidence of solidarity towards our struggling peoples.

On 3 August 1961, in the face of the fiercely negative attitude of the Portuguese Government which refuses to adopt a peaceful solution for the elimination of colonial domination from our countries:

in consideration of the firm will of our peoples to free themselves from the colonial yoke, whatever the means needed;

in consideration that this liberation must be achieved urgently, and that our peoples are ready to achieve it;

in consideration of the peculiarly difficult circumstances that our peoples face in the struggle against Portuguese colonialism;

in consideration of the necessity to prevent new colonial wars in Africa and to maintain world peace;

THE AFRICAN INDEPENDENCE PARTY

proclaims 3 August 1961, as the date of the passage of our national revolution from the phase of political struggle to that of national insurrection, to direct action against the colonial forces;

declares that all its militants and cadres are mobilised for direct action in the national liberation struggle;

invites all the nationalist organizations of our countries to improve their organization, to strengthen their preparation for the struggle of liberation of Guiné and Cape Verde and to co-ordinate their action in the United Front for the Liberation of 'Portuguese' Guiné and Cape Verde (FUL);

reaffirms the active solidarity of our peoples towards the struggling people of Angola;

reaffirms the will of our peoples at any moment, by way of negotiation, to seek a peaceful solution to the conflict which sets them against the Portuguese Government, in accordance with their inalienable right to

self-determination and national independence;
appeals to all peace- and freedom-loving peoples, particularly African and Asian peoples, to give practical and immediate aid to our peoples struggling against foreign domination.
Forward with our liberation struggle!
Down with Portuguese colonialism!

Conakry, 3 August 1961
Secretary-general of PAIGC

22. The battle of Como and the Congress of Cassaca[1]

Two main events characterize and sum up in their content and consequences the development of our national liberation struggle – of activity in our combatant organization – in 1964: the *battle of Como* and the *First Party Congress*, held in the month of February in one of the liberated areas in the south of the country.

The coincidence in time and the geographical proximity of these two events (we held the Party Congress from 13 to 17 February 1964, at the very moment when the battle of Como was reaching its climax no more than fiteen kilometres from this coastal island) constitute striking evidence of the dynamic interdependence of two fundamental aspects of our struggle: armed action and political action. It shows likewise the success and progress already achieved by our fight for liberty at the start of 1964, that is one year after the launching of armed struggle.

The battle of Como

As our communiqués at the time reported, even down to details, the facts concerning the battle of Como, we will limit ourselves in this account to the

[1] Report on the development of the national liberation struggle in Guiné and Cape Verde in 1964 (extracts).

essential aspects of this now historic event for our people. To recapture the island of Como – the first stretch of national territory liberated by our forces – had from the start of 1964 become a fundamental – even vital – need in the context of the military and political plans of the Portuguese authorities. And this primarily because this island was the essential launching pad for the reconquest and effective control of the liberated South. Moreover, because of the effects that such a reconquest would have at the political level – above all among our people – given that the population of this island, like that of the Mores zone, was known throughout the country for its fierce commitment to the struggle and indefatigable zeal for the cause of our Party.

When they had had recourse to all the means available – air force, navy, infantry (with a total of 3000 well equipped men, including about 2000 elite soldiers and officers transferred from Angola) – the Portuguese colonialists launched the reconquest of the island in January 1964. The Portuguese General Staff travelled from Lisbon to Bissau to follow the operations close at hand.

After 75 days of fighting in the course of which our forces did not stint acts of heroism and sacrifices, we succeeded in driving the enemy forces towards the sea, inflicting on them the most crushing defeat in Portuguese colonial history and causing them heavy losses in human lives. We estimated these losses at 650 men; but Portuguese deserters, including soldiers who had taken part in the battle, stated that at least a total of 900 of their colleagues had been killed or have died of wounds suffered at Como.

Much more than for the Portuguese colonialists, the battle of Como was a test for ourselves. In fact, it has enabled us to become aware of our own strength, of the capacity for resistance of our combatants and of our people in the face of the most difficult conditions for struggle, of the moral – hence military – weakness of the enemy, of political maturity and of fierce determination of the civilian population (men, women and children) in the liberated areas – from now on *definitively liberated* – not to fall again under Portuguese domination.

But the victory at Como at the same time as it showed the solidarity of our positions and of our capacity for military recovery in these areas – even the justness of our strategy and our tactics for struggle – stamped a new content on the activity of our combatants, bolstering their courage, tenacity, spirit of initiative and daring. It was thus that our combatants, stimulated by the news of this victory, countered all attempts to reconquer the liberated areas in the north of the country, notably in the Oio region, which had been attacked repeatedly by the enemy forces.

Moreover, as it was won at the height of the dry season, the victory at Como once more confirmed the thesis of our Party which argues that the rainy season is not necessarily the best time for intensifying our struggle in the specific conditions of our country. This confirmation enabled us to spare and make better use of our energies during the course of the recent rainy season (June – November) and a considerable proportion of our combatants devoted themselves to agricultural work, thus contributing to the increase in production. When we had taken advantage of the rainy season to improve our political and military organization and to strengthen our methods of struggle, we were able at the start of the dry season (November – December) to launch a series of attacks and operations against the enemy, upsetting and neutralizing the plans they had prepared for this season.

However, the battle of Como brought us new political and military problems, unexpectedly showing up weaknesses and mistakes, some of which could become dangerous for our Party and for our struggle.

By enabling us to become aware of these mistakes and weaknesses – which were immediately discussed in depth in the course of our Congress – the battle of Como made an effective contribution to the improvement of various aspects of our life and our struggle.

It goes without saying that the crushing defeat suffered by the colonialist forces at Como provoked widespread demoralization among those forces, sharpened the contradictions and conflicts already present and increased the confusion of the civil and military colonial authorities. These demoralizations, contradictions and confusions were clearly shown through risings in the barracks, and more conspicuously still by the dismissal of the whole civil and military administration in our country.

In overcoming the colonialist forces at Como, we won a great military victory which to some extent was the basis for other victories won by our forces in the course of 1964. It should, however, be noted that even if the Portuguese forces had succeeded in reoccupying Como, it would have been difficult – or even impossible – for them to reconquer the south of the country. This shows that the sacrifices made by our combatants at Como had a political aim, that of the liberation of our country. Our armed actions are not acts of war: they are the only means the colonialists have left us of reclaiming the fundamental rights of our people.

The Party Congress

By holding, in the course of the battle of Como and a few kilometres from the theatre of operations, a great assembly of cadres and delegates, including some sixty of the main political and military leaders of our organization, we succeeded not only in bringing our combatants and our people decisive encouragement in the struggle, but also in providing striking evidence of the irreversible successes of our combat.

For seven days (including the preliminary meetings), almost all the leading cadres of the Party and the delegates from all regions of the country were able to meet, despite the Portuguese artillery and aircraft, to discuss basic questions of our life and our struggle. The nature of these questions and the scope of the decisions taken there at the political, military, economic and social levels gave this Congress a historic character and stamped a new spirit of vitality and confidence on the activity of our Party. The enthusiasm with which the mass of the people welcomed this Congress and all the initiatives which accompanied or followed it was additional evidence of the political awareness of our people.

The implementation of the resolutions and decisions of our Congress enabled us to make noteworthy progress in the course of 1964, which significantly transformed the situation in our country. Moreover, by putting the deficiencies and errors made within the Party under severe criticism and sincere self-criticism, our Congress decided on the steps needed to eliminate these faults. Our organization thus became stronger than ever in the course of 1964.

Among the main achievements accomplished in 1964, we cite:

1. At the political and administrative level

Reorganization of the Party both at the base and at the level of leadership bodies. Effective establishment of section committees and other local bodies of Party leadership, and transformation of departments of the Central Committee, in such a way as to adapt them to the new demands of our life and our struggle. In the liberated areas, the transfer of power into the hands of local bodies and the creation of special administrative committees (registries, justice, education, health, etc.).

Strengthening of political work among the mass of the people with the aim of constantly raising the level of political awareness, notably in the regions not yet liberated.

Decisive progress in mobilizing and organizing the mass of the people in Cape Verde, where, we can state, almost all the young workers, pupils and students are now ready to follow the watchwords of the Party and fight for independence. This fact enables us to envisage for the near future a profound transformation of the struggle in this part of our national territory: the passage to armed action.

Elimination of enemy manoeuvres aimed at dividing and demobilizing our people by the creation of puppet movements.

2. At the military level

Reorganization of the armed struggle, notably by the restructuring and redistribution of our armed forces and by the creation of inter-regional commands and a central body to direct the armed struggle (the War Council).

Creation of the People's Revolutionary Armed Forces (FARP), encompassing the guerrilla force, the militia and the people's army. Making operational several units of our *people's army,* a factor which, allied to intensification of action by the guerrilla force, completely upset the enemy's plans for the dry season.

Broadening and stepping up the battle fronts which have touched all the regions not yet liberated, causing a profound transformation in the physiognomy of the war – from now on the enemy have to fight throughout the country — so opening up new prospects for development of our fight for liberty.

Intensification and increase of the frequency of our attacks on the Portuguese barracks, as our combatants now possess more effective means to destroy the enemy forces.

Training of special military cadres (in heavy arms, anti-aircraft weapons, etc.) and cadres destined for armed struggle in the Cape Verde Islands.

Significant victories won by our combatants, notably in the Gabu region (the fiefdom of certain traditional chiefs hitherto sympathetic to the Portuguese colonialists), Boé (the principal zone of bauxite deposits in the southeast of the country and now almost entirely controlled by our forces), Cachungo (in the east of the country where the Manjaco population, recruited by the Party, had long been waiting for the launching of armed struggle), S. Domingos and adjacent regions along the northern frontier. Our combatants, who have destroyed various Portuguese barracks in the liberated areas and elsewhere, have moreover increased the number of enemy losses in operations, in some cases capturing significant quantities of material.

Consolidation of our positions in the liberated areas, reinforced by the acquisition of more effective means of defence. The various attempts made by the enemy to reoccupy stretches of these regions met total failure. Elsewhere, we intensified the isolation of the enemy barracks remaining within liberated areas.

The success of our fighting in 1964 radically changed the military situation in our country. With the opening of a new phase in our struggle, these successes are the more significant as the intensification of our armed action did not bring any appreciable increase in our losses.

23. The eighth year of armed struggle for national liberation[1]

The year 1970 – the eighth year of our fight for liberty – was very rich in events of great significance for our struggle, even for the general struggle of African peoples against imperialist domination.

At the internal level, the most important factor is the very continuity and vigorous development of our action, in the diverse and increasingly complex aspects of our life and our struggle. And this all the more as while we continue to confront difficulties of all kinds, because of the precarious material living conditions of our people, the colonialist enemy, continually and effectively aided by their powerful allies, have had recourse to all available means to destroy our fight for liberty.

While it is true that our determination is only equalled by the strength of the historical and moral reason on our side, it is no less true that we face a conflict – a veritable war – in which material, financial and economic means play a primordial role.

One need not minimize either the exciting magnificence of the sacrifices offered by our people or the decisive character of the aid which our allies and friends throughout the world grant us, to observe that there is no common measure between the human and material resources enjoyed by the colonialist enemy and those available to us so far. The more so as, in step as our combat advances, the colonialists not only use more powerful and manifold methods of warfare to try and destroy the basis of the struggle (population, crops, cattle, etc.) but also cunningly exploit the weaknesses of our economic and financial situation by stepping up concessions to the populations they still dominate and by developing their 'psycho-social campaign' with the aim of demobilizing our people and undermining our struggle.

The disparity of means available to the oppressor and the oppressed is a normal characteristic of confrontations between peoples and imperialist domination, a general trait of colonial wars or national liberation struggles. This fact, which is another common factor in the general struggle of peoples against imperialist domination does not, however, obviate either the serious difficulties we face at the material and financial level or the specific circumstances of our struggle.

That is why the continuity of our fight and the constant strengthening of our action are already an important victory for our Party and our people in the

[1]Report on the situation of the struggle, January 1971.

face of the Portuguese colonialists who, despite the mounting aid from their allies in all domains and despite the fact that they can make free use of the resources of a state, are obliged to admit that only 'a miracle' can reverse the situation they face in our country.[1]

At the external level, the past year will remain in the history of our struggle as a period of strengthening of international solidarity in regard to our people and to those of the other African countries still under Portuguese occupation. But the most important fact at this level remains the crushing defeat inflicted on the Portuguese colonialists by the brother people of the Republic of Guinea on the occasion of the odious imperialist and Portuguese joint agression against Conakry and in the region of Kundara.

The sinister General Spinola,[2] who replaced General Arnaldo Schultz,[3] transferred after four years of vain criminal efforts to halt the march of our struggle, arrived among us with the boast that he would put an end to our struggle during the year 1969. But our combat did no less than develop and intensify on all fronts, as the growing experience of our combatants and the improvement in certain material resources enabled us to deal still harder blows against the enemy and cause them heavier losses in 1970.

After being obliged to see the bitter failure of his plans for all out war and apparently following instructions from the new head of the Portuguese Government, Marcello Caetano, the new military governor initiated a policy of 'smiling and bloodshed', of concessions and abominable crimes, of manoeuvres of every kind with the aim of feeding the war on war and demobilizing the population and the combatants, in order to destroy the principal bases of our movement.

But this policy did not yield the results counted on. And this, owing to the vigilance of our Party, to the high level of political awareness attained generally by the populations, including those of the remaining occupied zones, and to the intensification of our armed action, notably the attacks on urban centres.

Moreover the elimination of three Staff commanders and the death – following a heart attack – of the military commander, Brigadier Castro Nascimento, deprived the Governor of his main colleagues who were the specialists in the new policy of attempted subversion of the bases of our struggle, and masterminds of the psycho-social war. One can well understand the difficult situation in which the present chief of the colonialists finds himself in our country, and, according to information from Lisbon, he continues to occupy his post only because the Government of Marcello

[1]Speech by the head of the Portuguese Government, during a lightning visit to our country in April 1969.

[2]Former Commander of the Republican National Guard, the main instrument of Fascist armed repression in Portugal, former commander of the mounted cavalry in Angola.

[3]Salazar's former Minister of the Interior, former operations commander in Angola.

Caetano has no further room for choice in the matter.

In Guiné, our fight for independence and progress is developing successfully. Our combatants, who in 1969 put out of action about 1500 enemy solders, killed and wounded, strengthened their operations on all fronts during the course of last year. We inflicted more significant losses on the colonialists both quantitatively and qualitatively, as we eliminated not only some of the main cadres of the filthy war which the colonialists are waging against our people but also some of the main African collaborators who serve them in their policy of lies and slander aimed at destroying our struggle.

Bravely confronting the criminal acts of the colonialists, who stepped up their napalm bombardments and terrorists raids on the populations, we consolidated our state and administration in the liberated areas, strengthened our activity at the political level and at that of national reconstruction.

After managing to produce food (notably rice) in sufficient quantity to maintain a constant rise in the rate of struggle, the populations had the benefit of a greater quantity of essential items. New textbooks and other teaching material in greater quantity than before were provided for thousands of pupils in our schools. Supply to hospitals and health centres was improved. Moreover, the return to the country of some dozens of middle level and professional university cadres, who had finished their studies abroad, had the effect of improving the capacity for Party work, in the domain of politico-military struggle and in that of national reconstruction.

In the context of warfare, we have begun to use certain heavier weapons, which have aggravated the already difficult conditions the enemy had in the fortified camps and in the urban centres. In addition several hundred young combatants have been trained in our politico-military school.

In Cape Verde, where the Portuguese colonialists had to admit to the existence of our Party organization, the growth of repression only had the effect of strengthening the resolve of patriots and militants on the path of development of struggle. The progress achieved last year in clandestine work by our Party is increasingly reflected in the contradicitions and conflicts between the population (notably workers) and the colonial authorities.

The colonialists, who know better than anyone the strategic importance the archipelago has for their colonial wars, have seen the failure so far of their absurd efforts to persuade their allies to include the islands and Guiné in the geographical framework of the North Atlantic Treaty.

The growing interests taken by the Cape Verdian diaspora in our Party and struggle is also highly significant. In 1970 it showed increasing evidence of political awareness and patriotism that will certainly be translated into an appreciable strength for the development of struggle in the archipelago.

In Portugal, the people – notably the workers, students and anticolonialists and anti-Fascist intellectuals – strengthened their action against the colonial war. In 1970, the number of desertions within the colonial army rose considerably.

These desertions culminated during recent months in the collective rejection of the colonial war by a significant number of officers. The latter, after they had gone abroad, publicly manifested their disgust at the colonial war while in Portugal itself demonstrations by workers and students have shown to the world that the Portuguese people have already understood that this war is a crime not only against the African peoples but also against them.

In addition, sabotage carried out in some troop transport ships, like other practical actions by Portuguese patriots against the colonial war machine, show that a new phase of the brave struggle for freedom by the Portuguese people has begun.

The countries adjacent to ours continue to grant us the facilities we need for the growing development of the struggle. The abominable aggression against the Republic of Guinea, which was turned into a shameful defeat for the Portuguese colonialists, only had the effect of tightening the fraternal links in combat between our Party and the Guinean State.

Several African states which had not earlier given direct attention to our struggle, during the course of last year showed the desire to help us, and those who were already granting us their moral, political and material support gave practical proof of their decision to reinforce their solidarity in all fields.

On the other hand, the African tendency that we might call 'Malawism' or 'Banda-ism', whose principal mission lies in betraying Africa, betraying the liberation movements for a repugnant alliance with the racists and colonialists, was unmasked and severely isolated. This took from the Portuguese colonialists the vain hope of seeing the African liberation movements, and particularly our Party, abandoned by the Africans themselves.

We consolidated and developed our relations with the socialist countries who have always supported us and we opened up new prospects for co-operation with other anti-colonialist forces in the world.

The Rome Conference and the audience with Pope Paul VI marked a new step in our struggle on the international level, which provoked a confusion in the colonialist enemy they were unable or powerless to hide. Several support committees for our struggle were formed in Europe; we managed to awaken and develop solidarity towards our people even in the countries which are the first allies of Portuguese colonialism.

Sweden, which like other Scandinavian countries, is ready to grant us very useful humanitarian aid, increased by 75 per cent the aid which it had granted us for 1970. In all continents, interest and solidarity towards our struggle, towards our Party, are growing every day.

In accordance wtih the specific reality of our country, attested to by dozens of visitors of various nationalities, world opinion now knows that in our country our Party is the true wielder of power over almost the whole of national territory. Everyone now knows that our situation is comparable to that of an independent state which has part of its national territory, mainly the urban centres, occupied by foreign armed forces. This, despite all the manoeuvres and lies of the Portuguese colonialists, is a further significant victory for our Party, for our people. We must take all the advantages from it.

However strong our certainty of victory, it should not lead us to harbour illusions about the criminal obstinacy of the Portuguese colonialists to pursue their colonial war against our people and against Africa. Marcello Caetano in his speech of 27 September 1970 reaffirmed the determination 'to hold on at all costs', an attitude which the supposed reforms of the Constitution have in no way changed. New financial and material resources are put at the disposal of the Portuguese Government by its NATO allies, notably the United States, Federal German Republic and France.

German weapons and munitions, German and French launches and gunboats, French and Dutch helicopters, American, German and Italian aircraft, the most modern logistical resources have reached our home. A new 100 kilowatt broadcasting station was installed for the needs of colonial propaganda.

Moreover, mercenaries of various nationalities continue to train near Bissau citizens of the Republic of Guinea for acts of sabotage and aggression against that country. Frequent attacks were also made against the frontier villages of Senegal and Guinea. The Government of Portugal frequently renews its offer for NATO to establish bases in our country. An admiral was chosen for the post of commander-in-chief of the colonial troops in the Cape Verde Islands, which gives a measure of the importance the colonialists attach to the political advances made by our struggle in the archipelago.

For the successes already won and the favourable prospects for struggle to be translated into new and decisive victories, we must develop and intensify military action, strengthen the political work and internal information and improve our work at the African and international level with the aim of strengthening practical solidarity in regard to our liberating struggle, which has already been for some years a veritable war.

To achieve these main aims we must be in a position to satisfy the *basic needs* for supply of essential items to the populations in liberated areas, to pursue the task of economic, social and cultural construction begun in these areas, to strengthen and improve war material and logistical resources and to meet the growing costs of the struggle in all fields. We have, therefore, greater need of essential items, teaching and health equipment and medicaments, weapons and munitions and cash, for a war is very costly, even if it is waged by a poor people who have had to take up arms to free themselves from foreign domination.

The international character of the Portuguese colonial war is not merely a juridical fact, but above all political and material. For, as we know only too well, Portugal would already have been defeated in our country if it did not have effective political and material support from its NATO allies, from the racists in southern Africa and others.

Our armed struggle for national liberation, founded on the inalienable rights of our people and on the international ethics and legality of our times, belongs to the whole of Africa, to all states, nations, national and international organizations and persons desirous of freedom, justice and progress. That is why we are encouraged by the hope and certainty that all our allies throughout the world – notably the African states, the socialist countries and the anticolonialist forces generally – will not spare any efforts to strengthen the practical aid they grant to our fight. Hope and certainty that were strengthened by the undeniable success of the Rome Conference, whose encouraging resolutions will certainly not remain mere pious wishes.

In the face of the difficult material living conditions of our people, to be aware of the realities of our struggle is also to understand how much it relies on the practical solidarity of our allies, to whom we will never be able to show enough of our fraternal and combatant gratitude. It is likewise to remind them of their growing responsibilities in the light of the development of our fight, which demands constantly more effective, appropriate, regular and multiform aid.

The Portuguese colonialists are aware of this. They know that if the necessary and appropriate aid is not failing, they can be chased out of our country within a short while. They are making desperate efforts – both at international level and in the interior of our country – to prevent this, since a possible defeat against us would sound the deathknell of Portuguese domination in Africa. But the situation they face and the successes we have won in 1970 cannot allow them to sustain many illusions.

1. The political manoeuvres of the Portuguese colonialists; the psycho-social war

After they had been forced to admit, in the voices of their main chiefs, that they cannot stop our struggle nor win their filthy colonial war against our people and against Africa, the criminal Portuguese colonialists adopted new tactics to try to destroy our Party. They began to employ the most despicable and most vile methods in the framework of a policy that reveals more clearly every day that the Portuguese colonialists are real gangsters or bandits without the least scruple, able to commit the most savage crimes and to use the most shameless lies.

Having failed in the attempt to sow confusion in our struggle, by selling conditional freedom at the price of treason to a certain number of our detained countrymen, the Portuguese colonialists have had recourse to other means. They invented lies about divisions within the Party; they wrote letters to some leaders, promising them a fortune, a fine life and honours; tried to exploit opportunism, ambition and base feelings, convinced that the militants and leaders of our Party are like those who serve them. But they were mistaken. Their attempts met no other response than contempt and disgust on the part of our comrades. And the criminal action of the enemy contributed to strengthening unity and vigilance within our Party and its national leadership.

Seeing that it was impossible to divide the leadership of our Party or to seduce any of its leaders into betrayal, the Portuguese colonialists decided to mobilize the opportunists living abroad so that the latter should try to draw some responsible workers in our armed struggle into treason. They promised a lot of money, but they failed once more. Showing evidence once more of their high political awareness as true militants of our Party, the responsible workers who were contacted arrested the opportunists and the traitors who were justly tried and convicted.

Then on the Canchungo front (in the west centre of the country), the Portuguese colonialists put into operation some of their main military specialists in psychological warfare to try to buy some of those responsible workers on this front. After making some contacts, writing ridiculous letters, giving presents and promises of all kinds, the colonialists suffered a shameful defeat. Our comrades wiped out the commanders and other officers and soldiers who thought they could buy us. This is further evidence that we know exactly what we want and that we are patriots: we are not for sale.

In despair at these defeats and at the strengthening of our organization and struggle, the Portuguese colonialists made detailed plans to perpetrate the physical elimination of our leaders, notably the Secretary-general of the Party. It was in this criminal perspective that the Portuguese colonialists invented the lie, as barefaced as it was rediculous, of the supposed 'Conakry message' through which, according to their invention, combatants of our Party had sought guarantees for their return to the country. Convinced that they would succeed in killing the Party Secretary-general in Dakar, they sought, with this lie, to strike a decisive blow at the morale of our combatants and militants, to prevent any possibility of pursuit of the struggle after this assassination.

Once more the criminal plans of the Portuguese colonialists failed. The Party leaders remain firm at their posts, and the lie of the 'Conakry message' has made even clearer the brazenness and despair of the Portuguese colonialists and their military chiefs in our country.

The Portuguese colonialists know very well that, for our combatants as for our leaders, the question of returning to the country does not arise, precisely because they are at home. It is for them, for the colonialists, that the question arises more acutely all the time: they have to leave our country and return to theirs. They may go away after suffering a shameful defeat or leave with an understanding with us, with our Party, but they will be forced to leave, for we are going to complete the liberation of our country.

In a vain bid to destroy our Party and put a stop to the struggle, the Portuguese colonialists carried out their criminal aggression against the Republic of Guinea, made intrigues and gave fallacious promises to the Government of Senegal. But in vain.

The Republic of Guinea constantly reinforces its unconditional and total support to our Party and struggle. The Republic of Senegal, after overcoming certain hesitations, is determined to grant all the support possible to our Party and to our people's struggle. Once more, the criminal action of the enemy, intended to destroy our organization and the struggle, has resulted in a defeat for the colonialists and a significant victory for our Party.

When all their plans to suborn the leaders, responsible workers and militants of our Party had failed, the Portuguese colonialists tried and are trying to demobilize the populations of our liberated areas. Some African enemy agents infiltrated into these areas, with the aim of spreading confusion and demobilizing the people.

A high proportion of these agents, like Cuor Sano and others, have already been arrested and justly convicted. Others will be, as we are strengthening vigilance and the security services and constantly operate with more efficiency, with the aim of detecting, arresting, trying and convicting enemy agents. The latter must be severly punished, as happened recently to one of the most wretched lackeys of the Portuguese colonialists, Ioro Bamba, who was wiped out by our brave combatants.

To deceive Portuguese public opinion, the colonialists invented 'visits' by Portuguese delegations to our country. After the propaganda made on the subject of the 'visit' by the Minister for the Colonies, who practically only travelled by helicopter, we wiped out the three staff commanders, thus showing that if we did not eliminate the minister, it was only because we had no interest in doing so.

More recently, out of eight parliamentarians who had come to 'visit' what still remains of the colony our country once was, four lost their lives in a helicopter brought down by our combatants. Among them was the well known African traitor, Jaime Pinto Bull, who despite our advice, ended up dying in the sad position of a vile servitor of colonialists and as an enemy of our people and of Africa.

Lately the Portuguese colonialists have resorted to another tactic to try to stop our struggle: dividing the people and setting Africans to fight against Africans. It is an old and much used tactic, both by colonialists and in imperialist colonial wars, but we must denounce it and fight it energetically. so that this new criminal initiative by the enemy results in a telling defeat.

The colonialists invented what they call the 'ethnic congresses' for our country. Their aim is to win over some of our brothers with appointments as chiefs and with honours, but above all to destroy the awareness and national unity which our Party and struggle have already created. By holding the so-called 'ethnic congresses' and promising that each ethnic group should have its own chief, the colonialists are seeking to stir up once more tribal feelings we have already extinguished; they want right now to sabotage the possibilities of a harmonious national existence for our people in the independence which – they know only too well – we are certainly going to win.

By pretending to want to give political authority to the populations they still control, through a few chiefs, what they want to do is to prepare the ground for new conflicts among ethnic groups so that the Balanta should not get on with the Manjaco, the Fula should not get on with the Pepel, so as to spread confusion among us, thus making impossible the life as an African nation we are in the process of building.

With their fake congresses and all their activities, the colonialists – it goes without saying – want to harm our people. But they will not succeed, since our Party exists, since our people are increasingly more aware of their rights and duties as an African people, because no manoeuvre can halt the victorious march of our armed struggle for liberation. And those who, through ambition or opportunism, let themselves be deceived by the lies of congresses, will waste their time and will be branded as willing traitors to the interests of our people and of Africa.

In the same attempt to divide our people, the Portuguese colonialists have for some time been developing a vast campaign against the Cape Verdians on their radio, notably in the vernacular languages of Guiné. Through this campaign, as well as through a certain number of letters they wrote to responsible workers in our Party, with promises of honours and wealth, they state that they are going to expel all the Cape Verdians who are in Guiné in their service and offer the appointments they held to those they call 'the real descendants of Guiné'.

The colonialists know that political and moral unity, the fighting unity of our people in Guiné and Cape Verde, is the principal strength of our Party and our struggle. They also dream of destroying it by trying to arouse hatreds which never existed, spread lies, stir up cupidity and awaken ambition and opportunism among those who, although they do not yet take part in the struggle, are nationalists and want the liberation of our country.

But there also they have failed completely. First, because the true nationalists of Guiné are not racists or opportunists and they know, as militants of our Party, who their leaders are and the value of the unity of the people of Guiné and Cape Verde. In the second place, because the colonialists lie when they say that they are going to expel the Cape Verdians. They could not do it since they need those who serve them in the same way as they need the Guineans who serve them. And the colonialists know well the great service they would render to our Party and the struggle if they really expelled the Cape Verdians from Guiné.

But they are already doing us good service because with the propaganda orchestrated on their radio against the Cape Verdians, they have clearly shown all those who originate from the Cape Verde Islands and serve the colonialists in Guiné that we are right: the colonialists make use of them but do not have the slightest consideration for them. They must, therefore, like the best sons of our people – in Guiné and Cape Verde – take stock of their situation and give their support to our Party and to the struggle for the total liberation of our African country.

In the face of the great difficulties caused by the advances of the struggle and owing to the fact that the young Portuguese soldiers no longer want an inglorious death in our country, the Portuguese colonialists have decided to distribute badges to half a dozen of their African stooges, to call them officers and place them at the head of what they call 'African companies'. They thus seek to prolong their filthy colonial war as long as possible, to feed the war through war and to induce our brothers to fight against us. But they will not succeed in achieving their criminal purposes.

Various members of these companies have already deserted to come over to us and others will do so. They should do this while there is still time. Our brothers armed by the colonialists should cross to our side with their weapons, or they should be prepared to use them against the colonialists themselves, in defence of the interests of our people.

For our part, we must do everything possible to develop contacts with the supposed 'African companies' of the colonialists, so as to agree with them the best way to desert or to co-operate with the armed forces of our Party. They are our brothers, we must do the utmost to prevent them fighting against us. But we must unhesitatingly destroy all those who persist in being armed lackeys of the criminal Portuguese colonialists.

The manoeuvres we have just outlined expose the desperate situation in which the colonialists are placed, while their failure confirms the high degree of political awareness of our militants and the irreversible advances achieved by the struggle. We must, however, strengthen and develop the defence of the gains of our struggle and intensify the combat, since the enemy is determined to use all means, even the most vile and most criminal, to halt the march of our people towards total liberation of the country and independence.

2. Military action by the Portuguese colonialists; an assessment of their balance sheets

For the second time in the course of the filthy colonial war of genocide that they are waging against our African people, the Portuguese colonialists have published a balance sheet of their activities, and the more recent covers the year 1970.

Naturally, the balance sheets of a colonial war represent, to all healthy minds, a confession of crime against mankind, no matter what adjectives and figures compose them, no matter what lies pad them out. No further comment is needed.

But it seems interesting, in view of the conclusions they provide, to take a closer look at the 'figures' and facts contained in the balance sheets of the Portuguese colonialists, whose principal purpose is to deceive Portuguese and world opinion about the real situation in our country.

Clearly, they did not have the effrontery to include in the balance sheets the daily criminal acts they practise against our populations, the number of villages shelled with napalm, the terrorist raids with helicopter-borne troops, the murders of defenceless old men, women and children, the raids and shellings against hospitals and schools, the number of patriots arrested, tortured and murdered, any more than the ignoble provocations and aggressions against the peoples of neighbouring countries.

The colonialists have nothing to say on the facts and results of what constitute the principal aspects of their action in our country: *the shelling with napalm and the terrorist raids with helicopter-borne troops* against the civilian population. Facts which have been widely confirmed by reliable observers, such as journalists, film-makers, writers and other private individuals or organizations of various nationalities, including, most recently, an official Swedish delegation.

While in the 1969 balance sheet, the colonialists limited themselves to losses we had suffered and to material that they had captured, in the 1970 balance sheet, reflecting the new policy adopted by Marcello Caetano in the colonial war, they made extensive reference to supposed 'works of economic and social character' (including several health and school centres) carried out during the year.

The colonialists 'forgot', however, to mention the various mosques they built, and the millions spent on pilgrimages to Mecca, apparently so as not to wound the religious sensibilities of the Portuguese people, who are deeply Catholic. For the latter would certainly wonder why five centuries of the 'Christian civilizing crusade' should end by being changed to a campaign of *Islamization,* with the feverish building of mosques in various urban centres and the official organization of free journeys to Mecca.

For anybody, above all for those who know the reality of recent or current colonial wars in the world, the above-mentioned facts and figures – supposing that they could have any truth– would not deceive anyone. They are rather a confession of the difficult situation in which the Portuguese colonialists are placed in our country.

The construction of aerodromes near the urban centres reveals the preoccupation with solving a problem of logistical character, with the aim of ensuring the supply, reinforcement and evacuation of their troops who, in the remaining occupied urban centres, are besieged and are increasingly the target of attacks from our armed forces. This activity also exposes the criminal intention of the colonialists to do everything possible to strengthen the action of their aircraft and helicopters against our populations and thus to try to prolong the colonial war.

The tarmacing of some stretches of highway in remaining occupied zones or disputed areas aims at the same objectives and above all constitutes an attempt to escape the deadly action of mines and ambushes. But the Portuguese colonialists have nothing to say in their balance sheets about the enormous losses they have already suffered, in material and in men, in the attempt to tarmac certain highways.

The belated carrying out of so-called 'works of social character', with great propaganda backing, comes into the framework of the *policy of smiling and bloodshed,* of carrot and stick, which the colonialists initiated nearly two years ago, with the intention of demobilizing our people. It is an attempt, as desperate as it is vain, to put into practice some of the essential points of the social programme of our Party – and what we have already begun to achieve in the liberated areas. The colonialists are thus seeking to deceive the populations of the urban centres and of the few remaining occupied zones, with the aim of 'proving' that independence is unnecessary and that, as they say in their lying propaganda, 'these populations could benefit from an improvement of their social situation under the Portuguese flag'.

Clearly the colonialists will only succeed in preaching to the converted. The populations are moreover the first to understand this truth: *without our struggle, without our Party, the Portuguese colonialists, who have been so long among us without building schools or health centres or housing,* would never bother to do these things.

For Portuguese and world public opinion, and particularly for those who in any way believed in the myth of the so-called 'civilizing mission' of Portuguese colonialism, the results shown in the balance sheet of the colonialists in the social field would be revealing: after all, during all the time that the colonialist presence has lasted in our country, it is only now that they have understood the need to build health centres, schools and housing. And to do this, it has been necessary to bring us about 40 000 soldiers of all branches. Such social action is therefore seen as one of the clearest results of the victorious development of our liberation struggle.

If the analysis, however brief, of the supposed social achievements of the Portuguese colonialists puts them in a bad light, they will come off even worse when one takes a closer look at the balance sheets of their military action.

For the past two years, they have given the following data about our losses, which they show under the heading 'among other casualties':

1969

Dead		614
Wounded		259
Captured		165
	Total	1038

1970

Dead		895
Wounded		449
Captured		86
Deserters		132
	Total	1562

making 2600 casualties, which we might round off to 3000 (or even more), if we consider that the colonialist balance sheet has only accounted for what it calls 'other casualties'.

And, in an interview given to Portuguese Radio-Television in February 1970, the present military Governor of Bissau declared that 'only some 5000 men constitute the guerrilla force'. Clearly it is a question of the PAIGC guerrilla force, for there is no other among us. This means a guerrilla army whose maximum complement would be 5000 would have lost in two years of warfare 3000 combatants without the struggle being lessened in intensity for this reason, completely the reverse. No comment. But let us look further. According to the reports of the Portuguese staff, our forces would between 1963 and 1966 have suffered 'among others' 10 927 casualties.

As we do not have the secret data covering 1967 and 1968, let us assume for these years the averages of previous years. So we would have for each of them 2618 casualties, or for the two years, 5362 casualties. This, with the addition of the supposed 3000 casualties in 1969 and 1970, would give an overall total of 19 289 casualties among our combatants during the eight years of armed struggle. If we consider the supposed 'other casualties' we could round this figure off to 20 000.

Even the most absent-minded observer or the least sympathetic to the cause of our people's liberation will conclude that these official figures of the Portuguese colonialists are the best propaganda for our Party and our struggle. In fact, in a struggle like ours and in the particular circumstances of our country, a liberation movement which had suffered 20 000 casualties and successfully continued the fight against numerically and materially much stronger forces would accomplish a singular feat, if not a miracle.

But there is more to come. In the interview quoted above, the military Governor of Bissau told Portuguese Radio-Television: 'In the particular case of Guiné, out of its approximately 550 000 inhabitants, fewer than 80 000 have left the national territory or are refugees in the bush'.

Now, one knows that, according to UN statistics, the number of those originating from our country who are refugees in Senegal alone is estimated at about 60 000. And as 80 000 minus 60 000 equals 20 000 we must conclude that, according to the Portuguese balance sheets, secret or published, they must already have killed, wounded or captured all the persons who in our country were refugees in the bush. But further by the logic of figures, these persons would all have been members of our guerrilla force. Where the delirium of lying can lead!

Let us now see what the colonialists say about the material that would have been taken from our forces during the past two years. Both in the balance sheet for 1969 and in that for 1970, they present a long list of weapons, munitions and other material 'taken from the enemy'. Clearly, they do not disclose that the greater part of the material so far taken by the colonialists – in all wars there is taking of weapons by the two belligerents – are old weapons and worthless munitions abandoned by our combatants in old dumps. Whereas the material we are taking from the enemy is wrested from the hands of their soldiers, dead or in rout.

They have shown a total of 99 tons of weapons and munitions, lost by our forces (50 tons in 1969, and 49 tons in 1970).

It is true that war material is generally very heavy. We know it only too well, as we do not possess military vehicles and we must carry it on our back or our head. But we must thank the colonialists for the positive propaganda they are making about our capabilities when they state that in a single year they took 50 tons of materials from us. This means that we are so gifted that we can transport on foot, in the interior of the country, a quantity of material so great that the enemy can take 50 tons in a single year, without this affecting our struggle – a struggle that, completely the reverse, was increasingly strengthened and developed.

Despite the evidence collected in our country by dozens of reliable foreign visitors, the Portuguese colonialists claim that we operate only from the territory of neighbouring countries, where we would have dozens of bases, and they always deny in their interviews and speeches that our Party has liberated and controls a large proportion of our population.

However, in the balance sheet covering 1970, the colonialists report for the first time that 'elements of the population, who were under the control of the enemy, returned to the hand of the Portuguese authorities' *(sic)*. So, for 1970 alone, they show a total of 3000 'returnees'. This would mean that at the very moment when the casualties suffered by our combatants would have reached the figure of 20 000 (with 3000 casualties during the past two years) we would have begun to control elements of the population. This is something that, still according to the view so often expressed by them, had never happened before.

But this would mean likewise that our organization is so firmly installed in the country that we are in a position to control a population so numerous that, in 1970 alone, 3000 of its component elements could have presented themselves to the colonial authorities. This is not merely a confession: it is above all a categorical denial of the colonialistic allegations about the specific situation in our country and the proof that they no longer know what they are doing or what they are saying.

To conclude the balance sheet for 1970, the Portuguese colonialists weakly, but shamelessly, state that among our casualties (dead) 'figure some elements of the army of the Republic of Guinea and four Cubans'. This is a lying provocation by the Portuguese colonialists, whose criminal nature we know only too well. We shall not waste time, however, with the verbal provocations, spoken or written, of the Portuguese colonialists. For as the Portuguese people say in a proverb which their leaders would do well to learn: 'A liar is caught more quickly than a cripple.'

In the course of 1970, the enemy continued to demonstrate their presence above all by aerial shelling and by some terrorist raids against the populations by means of helicopter-borne troops.

The shelling mainly affected the regions of Kinara, Cubisseco, Cubucaré and Quitafine (in the south), Sara, Oio and Canchungo (in the north) and Eastern Boé (in the east). The criminal action of the Portuguese airmen was particularly noted in the zones where the organization of the Party and the dedication of the populations to the struggle are strongest; the raids by helicopter-borne troops, combined with heavy shelling, took place mainly in rice-growing areas (with the aim of burning the crops and terrorizing the populations) and against hospitals and schools.

Several villages were destroyed or burned with napalm, notably at Quinara and Cubisseco (towards the end of the year). But this did not significantly affect the morale and productive activity of the populations. Among the criminal acts perpetrated by the colonialists should be highlighted the shelling of the schools at Iador and Tambico (in the north), which brought 15 dead and 25 injured among the children, the raid on a field hospital in the Tombali zone (in the south) and the shelling of the boarding school site at Boé (in the east), when thirty napalm bombs were dropped by Portuguese airmen.

In Cape Verde, the enemy reinforced repression against patriots; perpetrated crimes against workers in revolt in Santo Antão, tortured our countrymen unjustly imprisoned, and are preparing to drown in blood the legitimate aspirations of the people of the islands to independence.

Almost paralysed and subjected to our attacks during the rainy season, the colonialists have intensified their criminal action of shelling during the dry season. We are facing up to them and dealing them still harder blows.

3. Our action

On the internal level

The enlarged meeting of the Political Bureau of the Party, held from 12 to 15 April 1970, took significant decisions concerning the development of our action in the political, administrative, military and national reconstruction fields.

Responding to the new demands of the struggle and the multiple activities of our organization – whose role is increasingly that of leadership of a state, part of whose territory is occupied by foreign troops – a new structure for the leadership bodies of the Party and the struggle was decided upon. A Supreme Council of the Struggle (CSL) and an Executive Committee of the Struggle (CEL) were created. The Inter-regional Committees were replaced by National Committees of the Liberated Regions (CNRL), which head the activity of the Regional Committees. The functions of those responsible for national reconstruction were more clearly defined, with production being attached to the domain of political action. Organization and action of the security services were strengthened.

On the level of armed struggle, new fronts were defined, with a regular army corps corresponding to each front. Self-defence forces (militia, population and armed militants) were reorganized in the framework of Local Armed Forces (FAL).

Political action was generally intensified, notably in the regions of Quinara, Cubucaré, Tombali (south), Oio (north) and Xitole (east). In the Cape Verde Islands, the advances recorded in 1969 were consolidated and developed. In the Gabu region in the east of the country, which was the fiefdom of certain traditional chiefs sympathetic to the Portuguese colonialists, the development of armed action brought a significant change in the political situation, which is now much more favourable to the struggle.

Moreover, our political action in the liberated areas adjacent to those remaining occupied by the enemy is significantly limited, by virtue of the precarious nature of the means of supply to the populations, who have been attracted by the potential for acquiring in the urban centres the essential items they need. However, clandestine action in these centres has greatly improved.

In the current phase of struggle, it is clear that development and intensification of armed action, notably against the urban centres and the few zones still controlled by the enemy, exert an important positive influence on the political situation. While we continue to develop our political action and national reconstruction, we must however intensify the armed struggle and not let ourselves be dragged by the enemy into the psycho-social war and economic competition.

On the social and cultural level, our activities went ahead normally, despite the shellings and terrorist action by the colonialists. The school year had generally satisfactory results and the education workers went on to the reopening of classes. Nearly a hundred youngsters, boys and girls, left for various foreign countries to attend vocational, middle level and university courses. We have improved certain aspects of medical care for combatants and the populations, but we continue to face serious difficulties in regard to medicaments, notably anti-malarials, antibiotics and dressings.

In all the liberated areas the populations have worked with enthusiasm on agricultural tasks. But a shortage of rain, very pronounced in the months of August and September, caused worrying prospects in regard to rice production, above all in the zones nearest the sea.

Several foreign delegations of various nationalities spent some time in our country during the past year. They prepared reports and films, after having had direct contact not only with the realities of our liberation struggle, but above all with our Party's achievements in the social and cultural domains in the service of better living standards for our people.

On the military level our combatants continue to attack the enemy positions and to cause growing losses by the colonial troops.

All the urban centres, except Bissau and Bafata, were attacked in 1970. The town of Gabu, the capital of the region of the same name, was three times a target of our attacks, including by infantry forces. In this region, the intensification of our action completely upset the enemy plans for 'regrouping of populations'.

On various fronts, but above all on those of Gabu (in the east) and Nhacra (in the north, about thirty kilometres from Bissau), heavy ambushes put out of action several dozen enemy soldiers, destroying an appreciable number of vehicles. An important aspect of our military action in the course of 1970 was the rise in number of senior officers and others eliminated, which sharpened the demoralization of the colonial troops and their chiefs. This is the balance sheet of our principal actions covering the year which has just ended:

Attacks on fortified camps	625
Attacks on aerodromes and port installations	18
Commando operations in urban centres	26
Main ambushes and other important clashes	133

In the course of these actions, and others of minor importance, the colonial troops lost 24 officers and 794 privates and other soldiers (confirmed deaths), with the number of wounded confirmed at 438. Information from reliable sources (in Bissau and Lisbon) indicates that the number of soldiers wounded during 1970 is estimated at about 900. This would give a total of 1718 enemy casualties (dead and wounded).

It should be noted that, according to the same information from Bissau, the military Governor, during a meeting with businessmen at the beginning of January, disclosed to them that during the months of November and December alone the colonial troops had 298 dead.

Our combatants, who seized an important quantity of weapons and other material from the enemy, in addition destroyed 85 vehicles of various types, brought down or damaged 4 aircraft and 7 helicopters, and sank or damaged 34 boats on the rivers. We took 9 fortified camps, including the important posts at Morcunda (in the east), Ganturé (in the south) and Ulencunda (in the north). Three Portuguese soldiers were captured and 8 others deserted from the colonial army.

4. On imperialist and Portuguese joint aggression against the Republic of Guinea

We had an opportunity of dealing with this question of utmost significance in the New Year Message addressed to our people and our combatants. However, it seems to us useful to return to this event in this report. First, because it is a factor of far-reaching implications, not only in the context of our armed liberation struggle but also for the history of Africa and of Portuguese colonialism, and even for the general struggle of peoples against imperialism. Second, because it is a new experience and we must draw from it all the lessons that it provides for the present and for the future of our people's struggle for progress, in independence and dignity. Finally, because it is a fruitful victory for Africa and for all anti-imperialist forces – a victory for our people and our Party, and one of the most shameful, if not the most shameful, defeats of Portuguese colonialism throughout its history.

Obviously for us, as combatants and militants of PAIGC, legitimate representatives of our people, the victorious battles of Conakry and Kundara, in which we had the honour to take part alongside the brother people of the Republic of Guinea, are another episode in our armed liberation struggle, which is entering its ninth year.

In fact we have long been accustomed to desperate acts by the Portuguese colonialists, in their vain attempt to halt our struggle for liberty or even to destroy our Party, in order to perpetuate colonial domination of our country. It is sufficient to recall the battle of Como in 1964, during which for seventy-five days about three thousand colonialist soldiers desperately tried to reconquer this island, but ended by being expelled by our combatants after the former suffered losses estimated at about a third of their complement. The battles of Oio, Cubucaré, Quitafine, Southern Frontier (Balana-Gandembel) and more recently of Canchungo are so many other glorious pages in our struggle, in which the colonialist enemy were defeated, in spite of 'decisive' plans that they had drawn up in detail.

We must, however, admit that although we are accustomed to desperate acts and banditry, to the most abominable crimes on the part of the

Portuguese colonialists, we were none the less surprised by the aggression mentioned that they planned, organized and carried out against the capital of the Republic of Guinea.

It is true that the Portuguese colonialists had already perpetrated many provocations and aggressions against the brother peoples of the Republic of Guinea and Senegal. They had committed innumerable crimes against the peaceful populations of the frontier zones of these countries, shelled and burned villages, robbed and pillaged, under cover of the lie that we had bases in neighbouring territories, from which, according to them, we would attack the Portuguese positions.

But there is no doubt that they excelled all this in perpetrating the aggression of 22 November against Conakry, for which they used their own boats and aircraft, their officers and soldiers, although painted black and diluted among some dozens of African mercenaries from the colonial army, and renegades and criminals originating from the Republic of Guinea. They thus showed, more clearly than ever, just how far their contempt goes for international laws and ethics of our times. They revealed categorically to Africa and to the world the deranged and criminal character of Portuguese colonialism. With the previous authorization of the Government of Marcello Caetano, and certainly with the consent of the allies of colonialist Portugal, the military Governor of Bissau and commander-in-chief of the colonial occupation troops in the urban centres and a few fortified camps in our country drew up detailed plans for aggression against the Republic of Guinea, with the collaboration of their staff, notably *Commodore Luciano Bastos da Costa e Silva,* navy commander. These plans were submitted by the Governor himself for the approval of the head of the Portuguese colonial government, who was given an assurance of success for the enterprise and who, two weeks before the operation, received in private audience Commodore Luciano Bastos and *Captain Guilherme Almor Alboim Galvão* who was appointed to command the aggression against Conakry.

As the colonialists did not have sufficient confidence in the efficiency of the renegades originating from the Republic of Guinea, the majority of the latter (about two hundred) was reserved for the mission of attacking Kundara. Only a minority (some dozens), intended mainly to serve as a guide force, was used in the Conakry landing.

In this action, the Portuguese colonialists deployed the following personnel and transport material:

Two detachments of special fusiliers, the 21st and 22nd, the first of which was commanded by *First Lieutenant Raul Eugenio Castro e Silva,* from the special service squad, assisted by *Second Lieutenant Eduardo Madureira Veiga Rico;* and the second was commanded by *Fusilier Second Lieutenant Alberto Rebordão de Brito,* assisted by *Second Lieutenant Benjamin Lopes Abreu,* both from naval reserve.

Captain Galvão's special escort group, composed of elite elements of Portuguese naval fusilier detachments.

One of the 'African commando companies', in which were included socially rootless elements and traitors to our people, recruited by some of the most faithful stooges of the Portuguese colonialists, including *'Lieutenant'* João Januario Lopes, who was captured by the Guinean militia.

Some dozens of those originating from the Republic of Guinea, whose treason to their people and to Africa was more than ever shown by the fact that they agreed to serve as dogs of the Portuguese colonialists.

In all about 350 men, well equipped and provided with the most modern weapons.

Six naval units, including two LFG type, 'Alfange' class, each able to carry about 150 to 180 men, and armed with 20mm artillery, and four others of the LF type, 'Argos' class, of 180 tons displacement, armed with two 40 mm pieces. Each unit was commanded by two officers who were, like all the crew, of Portuguese origin.

In addition, fighter bombers of the Fiat G-91 type, paratroops transport aircraft and a number of Alouette III helicopters were standing by to intervene, in the event of the operation being successful. Men and material were to be used in the interior of the Republic of Guinea to occupy the principal urban centres (notably Kindia, Labé, Kankan, Boké), while the mercenaries of that country, taken from Bissau through Gabu, would occupy the region of Kundara, starting from Buruntuma.

As everyone knows, the forces of aggression against Guinea set off from the Island of Soga in the Bijagos archipelago, where for several months the renegades from the Republic of Guinea had been trained. Before their departure, they received a visit from the military Governor, who reaffirmed to them his certainty of success for the operation which, in his own words, 'was the only way of putting an end to the war' in our country, meaning to put an end to our liberation struggle.

At dawn on Sunday, 22 November, the operation was started. Thus began the execution of one of the most ignoble and craven crimes perpetrated against Africa. The Portuguese colonial troops and their mercenaries landed at various points of the city of Conakry and its suburbs. Their plan was to attack and occupy 52 objectives, including the palace and the residence of the President of the Republic of Guinea, the main ministries, military camps, ports, airport, radio station and other official organisms of the Guinean state, as well as the installations of the secretariat of our Party, including the pilot-school and kindergarten where there were hundreds of youngsters and children. An abominable plan which, although abortive, showed the monstrous, cynically anti-African and racist nature of the

Portuguese colonialists.

The world now knows the unfolding of events during the days following the landing. By responding promptly and bravely to the appeal of President Sekou Touré, the armed forces, the people's militia and the population of Conakry inflicted on the aggressors a defeat as great as the crimes they had committed. The colonialists and their lackeys had to retreat hastily, abandoning dozens of prisoners and more than a hundred corpses. In the region of Kundara, where about two hundred renegades of the Republic of Guinea, incorporated in elements of the Portuguese colonial army, had penetrated, the aggressors were completely crushed.

The United Nations, the Organization of African Unity and anti-colonialist world opinion in all continents unanimously condemned the craven aggression by the Portuguese colonialists, whose criminal culpability was amply proved by the facts and by the inquiry made by the United Nations Special Commission. Even the most faithful allies of the Portuguese colonialists could not fail to condemn the aggression and to demonstrate their sympathy towards the Republic of Guinea.

The criminal figure of Portuguese colonialism, defeated and isolated before world opinion, was thus more clearly defined than ever as a historical aberration which it is vital and urgent to eliminate by all the necessary means. The crime was transformed into a mistake, and the imperialists themselves, allies of the Portuguese colonialists, will not forgive them this mistake, precisely because they failed.

It is very important for us to understand as clearly as possible why the colonialists made so serious a mistake and why they failed.

However mad the Portuguese colonialists might be and however meglomaniac their representative in our home might be, they would not have committed themselves to such an undertaking if they had not been sure of two conditions: *tacit or declared support from their imperialist allies* and *success of the operation.*

The Government of Portugal knows how much its colonial wars depend on the political and moral support of its allies. The latter, by not opposing the criminal aggression against the Republic of Guinea, nurtured a hope, desired to carry out an old dream, which is very dear to them: *to destroy the popular, democratic and anticolonialist regime of that free and independent African country,* whose fruitful example constitutes a permanent obstacle to the recolonisation of the continent. They also agreed that the Portuguese colonialists, whose difficult situation they know, should serve as the tool to carry out the crime of aggression against the Republic of Guinea.

The Portuguese colonialists, in their turn, had and have sufficient reasons for taking part in any undertaking which would give them, in the desperation they are experiencing in our country, the hope of succeeding in destroying our Party, halting our liberation struggle and totally recolonizing our people. The imperialist dream of destroying the Guinean regime and replacing it with another which would be amenable to neo-colonialist domination is likewise the dream of the Portuguese colonialists.

In fact, having been obliged for a long time to admit that in spite of their crimes they cannot halt our struggle in the interior of the country, they were convinced that the destruction of the Guinean regime – our principal prop in the exterior – was, as the military governor of Bissau declared 'the only way of putting an end to the war in Guiné'. This turns out to mean eliminating our Party and halting our armed liberation struggle. That is why the Portuguese colonialists served as the desperate but willing tool of world imperialism, in their aggression against the Republic of Guinea.

In an effort to mask their crime, the Portuguese colonialists used in turn, both in the attack on Conakry and in the frontier region of Kundara, some groups originating from the Republic of Guinea in the service of imperialism. They allied themselves to the worst enemies of Africa in order to satisfy their political ambitions, and gave definitive proof of their character as renegades, as criminals, as enemies of the people of the Republic of Guinea and of all African peoples.

The plans of the Portuguese colonialists

It is worth underlining that the supposed revision of the Constitution proposed by Marcello Caetano and the aggression against the Republic of Guinea, organized and carried out by the Portuguese staff, are two sides of one coin, constituting the projected solution to put an end to their colonial wars in Africa by definitively eliminating the liberation struggle of our people and of the peoples of Angola and Mozambique.

The plan, necessarily approved by the imperialists, was the following. In a first stage, to replace the current Guinean regime by another, sympathetic to Portuguese domination in our country and an evolution by steps (whose timetable would not be set), leading to a certain internal autonomy, but without any promise of independence. Once this pro-colonialist regime was installed in the Republic of Guinea, to eliminate our Party thus eliminating our struggle, which according to them would be greatly facilitated by the assassination of the principal leaders of our organisation.

In a second stage (which would closely follow the first, with the purpose of diverting international attention from the crime perpetrated against the Republic of Guinea), to announce the revision of the Portuguese Constitution, establishing the 'principle' of internal autonomy for the 'overseas provinces', which would only really affect Angola and Mozambique. As one knows, the latter two territories are settlement colonies with a large population of European origin. The number of settlers would be increased at an accelerated rate, with about one million settlers, either Portuguese or whites originating from other countries.

In a third stage, which would coincide with the development of *dialogue* and of *diplomatic relations* between some African countries and the colonialists and racists of southern Africa, military operations on a grand scale and a new and vast political campaign in Africa would be brought into play in order to eliminate what remained of our own liberation movement, but above all those of Angola and Mozambique, certainly demoralized and sapped by the fall of the Guinean regime and by the destruction of our Party. For this final stage, the colonialists were counting, with or without reason, on the support of some African states.

It is in the framework of this overall plan, minutely drawn up, that we must understand both the (apparently absurd) choice of Conakry for the first attack, as well as the objectives of the operation against the Guinean capital. Occupation of Conakry, from the first phase of aggression, would allow the domination of the entire Republic of Guinea, since, from the viewpoint of the colonialists – and this unhappily corresponds to reality in numerous cases – anyone who dominates the capital of an African country dominates the whole country. It was, therefore, essential and urgent to begin with Conakry which, moreover, according to the information available to the aggressors, would be a very easy target to take. The invasion of the Kundara region, after the Conakry defeat, was an act of desperation rather than a consequence of impetus already acquired by the aggressors.

The principal aims of the Conakry landing were the following: to assassinate President Sekou Touré and thus to ensure the irreparable loss of the principal author of the Guinean revolution; to destroy the Guinean regime, if necessary by killing all the other leaders; to put in power the renegades of the Republic of Guinea, some of whom were waiting in boats, out to sea from the capital, and others in political prisons; to assassinate the Secretary-general of our Party and possibly other leaders who might happen to be in Conakry; to destroy all the installations of PAIGC; and subordinately, to free the Portuguese prisoners of war.

A comparative analysis that takes into account imperialist strategy and policy as well as the interests of the national movement for liberty and of Africa generally shows that one aim of the aggression outstrips all the others: *elimination of the Guinean revolution and assassination of its leader, President Sekou Touré*, who is its incarnation. Once this deed was done, all the rest would be easy, according to the logic of the Portuguese colonialists. This logic explains the savagery with which the aggressors hurled themselves on the residence of the Guinean leader, where according to information they had he usually spent Saturday nights.

We are already accustomed to the manoeuvres and lies of the Portuguese colonialists, particularly to those of their current representative in our country. But we must confess that in the case of the aggression against the Republic of Guinea they outdid all they had invented before in barefaced lying. The people of Portugal are unlucky to have leaders capable of lying so much, and so craven as to try by the most underhand means to deny their proven responsibility for an action which they planned down to the smallest detail, organized and carried out. Even on the subject of the prisoners, the only 'positive' result of the operation, they invented a whole rigmarole to try to flee from their responsibility.

But they went still further in regard to their African stooges killed or captured during the operation. They invented requests for political asylum on the part of those originating from the Republic of Guinea (those who managed to regain the boats), denied the reality of the identification of African soldiers to whom a short while before they were offering badges and decorations. And they reached the point of regarding as a *deserter* and *murderer* one of the 'lieutenants' of their African companies, João Januario Lopes. The Portuguese colonialists thus prove once more that they are veritable gangsters or bandits without the slightest scruple, able to commit the most savage crimes and to put forward the most shameless lies.

Obviously history does not speak of the weak. However, it seems to us worth while to mention, even briefly, the Africans originating from our country or from the Republic of Guinea who took part in the operation alongside the soldiers from Portugal, at the service of the colonialists. The latter, who did their utmost not to leave behind a single Portuguese corpse, wounded or prisoner, abandoned their African stooges to their fate, as soon as they saw that they were defeated. They thus reduced these Africans to their true condition: wretched dogs whom the master abandons hastily when he is caught in the act of crime and must run away.

The causes of the colonialists' failure

But why did the Portuguese colonialists fail in their aggression against the Republic of Guinea?

Obviously, it was the prompt and courageous response of the brother Guinean people and of their armed forces who inflicted on the Portuguese colonialists and on imperialism this now historic defeat. But it is also necessary to discover, within the Portuguese mentality itself, the *internal cause* that motivated their adventure, and hence crushing defeat. It lies basically in the centuries of scorn that the Portuguese colonialists have always manifested towards the African.

This scorn, which is eloquently exposed in the celebrated phrase of Salazar – 'Africa does not exist' – is amply shown by the history of the relations of Portugal with Africa, and by the facts of Portuguese colonialism and the behaviour of the Portuguese towards the African.

From the epoch of the so-called 'discoveries' or 'findings' to that of the slave trade and the crimes of slavery, from the wars of colonial conquest to the golden age of colonialism, from the first overseas 'reforms' to the genocidal colonial wars of our times, the Portuguese colonialists have always shown a superstitious mentality and primitive racism towards the African, whom they regarded and regard as naturally inferior, incapable, of organizing his life and defending his interests, easily fooled, without culture and lacking civilization.

It is in the general framework of this tradition of scorn for the African and of belief in the congenital incapacity of this 'big child' (as the Portuguese say), that the Portuguese colonialists planned and carried out the aggression against the Republic of Guinea. They believed that they would be facing a weak people, unaware and disorganized.

Convinced of their *natural* superiority, they were sure that the African in the Republic of Guinea was incapable of knowing where his true interests lay and of defending them effectively. Just as they are still convinced that they can fool our populations with the lie of their 'better Guiné'.

The Portuguese colonialists (even the Portuguese generally) never remember that the African is a human being. It is costing them dear, and will cost them more and more dear, to learn that we are *men*.

The shameful defeat suffered by the Portuguese colonialists on the occasion of their craven aggression against the Republic of Guinea is one of the most brilliant victories won by an African people in the struggle against imperialism.

The people of the Republic of Guinea, under the leadership of their great Party, the PDG, and of its leader, President Sekou Touré, with the conquest of their sovereignty, opened the path of independence for African peoples. They have just made another extraordinary contribution to the elimination of colonial and racist domination from our continent by repelling the criminal aggression of the Portuguese colonialists.

Given the honour to fight alongside the armed forces and people of the Republic of Guinea, some of our militants and combatants acted with efficiency, gave evidence of courage and determination and maintained the high reputation of our people and our Party. Here I pay deeply felt homage to the comrades who fell on the field of honour, and to the wounded, and I hail enthusiastically all the members of our Party, militants and responsible workers, men and women, who with weapons in hand or in the accomplishment of other tasks of the moment were able to bear themselves worthily in the defence of the sacred interests of Africa.

This is how we should bear ourselves and this is how we did bear ourselves. In fact it is already in the tradition of our combatants to fight with courage and determination, to strike hard against the colonial enemy, not letting them implement their aims. For we are all aware of the fact that our cause is just and our victory is certain, whatever sacrifices have to be made.

With their acts, the Portuguese colonialists have clearly shown how desperate they are in our country, but they also provided a demonstration that the advances made by our struggle are irreversible and that nothing can halt the march of our people towards independence. They contributed effectively to strengthening the awareness of Africa – and of all sincere Africans – in relation to the need for strong union of all the anti-colonialist forces so as to eliminate Portuguese domination from our continent. The results of the OAU Conference in Lagos (Nigeria) prove this rise in awareness and will certainly bear fruit.

With their aggression, the colonialists, in a frankly unexpected way, increased the interest of Africa and the world in our people, our struggle and our Party. They opened up new prospects for the isolation of Portuguese colonialism at the international level, where the constantly growing importance of our fight for liberty has been more clearly defined. And, no less important, they strengthened in all of us the certainty of victory in our struggle, our determination and the very efficiency of our combatants, who during the last two months of the year inflicted heavy losses on the enemy by stepping up their action on all fronts.

We have, therefore, sufficient reason to start another year of struggle with optimism, determined to improve our work at all levels and to strike constantly harder blows against the Portuguese colonialists, in order to defend the conquests by our people who are every day more master of their own destiny. This, whatever the manouevres, lies or crimes of the Portuguese colonialists might be.

5. Some words on the revision of the Portuguese Constitution

A few days after the ignoble aggression against the Republic of Guinea, the head of the Portuguese Government announced before the National Assembly and in the context of 'revision of the Constitution' reforms concerning the Statute for African territories still occupied by Portugal. The latter will accede, gradually and under a timetable that neither the law nor the Portuguese colonialist leader venture to predict, to a certain autonomy 'in their character as *autonomous regions* within the whole of the unitary Portuguese State'.[1]

It was Marcello Caetano himself who explained that these reforms not only did not represent anything new at all, but further sought to perpetuate the racist policy of so-called *spiritual assimilation*, to 'homogenize' the metropole and overseas, which can only mean the oppressive denial of the right of our African peoples to have their own history and culture, freely to decide their own destiny. We quote:

> I know that for many persons, impressed by the intensive propaganda aimed at integration, the idea of autonomy for the overseas province is shocking. But without reason.
>
> In the present text of the Constitution, faithful on this point to what had been established since 1930, the autonomy of the overseas provinces is recognized, and it is there determined that they should have a 'politico-administrative organization adapted to the geographical situation and the conditions of the social environment'.

[1]Title VII, 2nd part.

Moreover, it could not be anything else. It is understandable that one should unfailingly follow a policy of spiritual assimilation, in such a way that the metropole and overseas should constitute a more homogeneous unity every day.

To prove that nothing would change at bottom and that the Portuguese would continue to decide the destiny and the affairs of our peoples, refusing us any of our own personality, the head of the Portuguese Government did not omit to specify the framework in which a certain autonomy would be granted to the 'Portuguese regions' of Africa. We quote:

> The overseas provinces need to maintain a politico-administrative organization like that which the Constitution guarantees them: with laws voted for each of them by their own legislatures, with a government of their own assuring the current flow of public administration, with their own finances enabling them to pay local expenses from revenue collected on the spot, according to the budget drawn up and approved by their elective assembly.
>
> The sovereignty of the single and indivisible State will not for this reason cease to be asserted over all the territory of the Nation, by means of the supremacy of the Constitution and of the laws emanating from the central bodies (where the provinces will increase their representation), as well as by the appointment of Governors delegated from the central government, whose rights of inspection and supervision will remain untouched.

In such a perspective, Marcello Caetano alluded to Angola and Mozambique, but was silent concerning our country, Guiné and Cape Verde. And with reason. As he is aware of the realities of our country, he knows on the one hand that we are not only autonomous but also sovereign over more than two-thirds of the national territory, and, on the other hand, that there is not a sufficient European population in our country to ensure the 'Rhodesianization' which the Portuguese colonialists hope to see established in Angola and Mozambique, as the only acceptable solution to put an end to their colonial war.

Such a prospect, which announces, even sketches in, the creation of new Rhodesias in southern Africa and the perpetuation of the domination of the white minority over the native majority in Angola and Mozambique is not applicable in our case. It is, however, as regards these African territories, and despite the torrents in the speech by Marcello Caetano on the subject of autonomy and 'multi-racial societies', the only *novelty* contained in the new Constitution.

The supposed revision of the Portuguese Constitution ignores and scorns once more the inalienable rights of our people to dispose of themselves in freedom and independence. The so-called 'reforms' concerning the African territories occupied by the colonial armed forces are not only an attempt aimed at masking the advances of the liberating struggle of the African peoples. They also have the aim of trying to deceive Portuguese and international opinion, to demobilize certain African states in relation to the potential or real support they grant to our struggle, and above all to obtain more moral, political and material support on the part of the allies of the Portuguese colonialists for the genocidal colonial war they are waging against Africa.

However, it must be acknowledged that the reforms introduced in the Portuguese Constitution by Marcello Caetano are the result of a great effort for *change* in face of the hostile immovability of the 'ultras'. The mountain has, however, given birth to a mouse – and it is certainly not for this that our people and those of Angola and Mozambique are fighting. Moreover, Marcello Caetano knows it only too well.

Prospects

The prospects for the liberating fight of our people are frankly favourable, despite the difficulties we face and which are part of the specific historical, economic, social and cultural circumstances of our country.

On the internal level, the successes won during the past year and the objective factors we have already established and consolidated enable us to look to the future with confidence. We must, however, realistically strengthen and consolidate the positive factors and gradually, but radically, eliminate negative factors which have grown up in the framework of the struggle. The pace of our struggle depends basically on our capacity for analysis, decision and initiative, and on efforts and sacrifices we are determined to make.

While developing and intensifying armed action, we must always and in all our activities – including the war – bear in mind the fundamentally political character of our struggle. Consolidate and strengthen the organic structures of the Party and the struggle. Act so that each organism really plays its part, so that every militant should constantly feel more responsible and necessary for the purposes of the struggle. Further develop democracy, the spirit of criticism and self-criticism from the bottom to the top of our organization. Carry out and make others carry out the watchwords and all the directives of the Party. Improve the return on the work of each organism and every militant. Strengthen the fight against sloppiness, slackness, opportunism and all moral or political deviations from the line drawn by the Party. Gradually sweep away the obstacles to the carrying out of this major objective of our struggle: namely, that our people should take totally into their hands the political power that our combat has already conquered over more than two-thirds of the national territory. Those are the fundamental tasks of the struggle enabling us to ensure and later to transform the favourable prospects for our liberating fight.

Carrying the heavy burden of their colonial war, after the defeats that we inflicted on them in 1970 and after their shameful defeat suffered on the occasion of their criminal aggression against the Republic of Guinea, the Portuguese colonialists are not merely desperate in our country: *they know they are lost.*

So they are also capable of making new manoeuvres, perpetrating new and more abominable crimes, trying new adventures, no matter how absurd, to attempt some way out of the situation in which they are placed. So – and this is one of the lessons of the aggression against the Republic of Guinea and against the installations of our Secretariat in Conakry – we must reinforce vigilance on all levels, constantly take new and vigorous initiatives, be ready to fight victoriously against the colonialist enemy, wherever we might be.

To bring the advance of the struggle in accordance with the favourable prospects it has, we must reap the utmost profit from the defeats and failures of the enemy, strengthen our action, mainly armed struggle on all fronts, establish precise and limited but meaningful objectives, which we must carry through to the end, and bring the struggle forward each day with more energy.

In the light of the objective situation of our people, the development of our liberating fight does not depend solely on the internal factors which condition the struggle: it depends equally on external factors, notably on the moral, political and material support which can be granted us in the framework of African and international solidarity.

On this level, the prospects resulting from our action, notably in 1970, are also favourable.

The few African countries which grant us direct aid have decided to reinforce their support. The Liberation Committee of the OAU has made and continues to make considerable efforts to develop its aid to our Party. The Extraordinary Session of the Council of Ministers of the OAU (in Lagos, from 9 to 12 December, 1970) unanimously adopted a resolution deciding on reinforcement of material aid to our organization.

We hope that, faithful to the OAU Charter and the interests of African peoples, independent Africa will spare no effort or sacrifice to develop practical support to our struggling people, whether directly or through the intermediary of the OAU. In this perspective, we must develop relations with all the independent states of Africa opposed to Portuguese colonialism and racist domination on our continent. We hope that African countries which have never helped us may decide to do it now in the service of the total liberation of Africa.

It goes without saying that the march of our struggle depends also on that of the heroic struggles of the peoples of Angola and Mozambique. There, too, the prospects are favourable, since these peoples, under the leadership of their fighting organizations, MPLA and FRELIMO respectively, have won significant successes during the past year.

According to various reliably impartial testimonies, the struggle of the Angolan people, through intensification and extension of the action of MPLA combatants, has won significant success, notably in the eastern, south-eastern and central regions of the country. Moreover, it was the

Portuguese authorities themselves who had to confess the failure of their general offensive, aimed at eliminating the struggle of the people of Mozambique, as the FRELIMO combatants had inflicted heavy human and material losses on the common enemy.

We must continue to strengthen the ties of fraternity and combat which unite our Party to MPLA and to FRELIMO, intensify our struggle and seek closer contacts for the urgent elimination of Portuguese colonialism.

We are likewise encouraged by the fact that the socialist countries have decided to develop their aid to our Party. We hope that they will spare no efforts or sacrifices for this purpose, and that those who do not help us or have suspended their practical aid may likewise decide to show evidence of their internationalist spirit by developing their solidarity with our Party, in the service of the common struggle against imperialist colonial domination.

As for the mobilization of anticolonialist opinion of western peoples, the Rome Conference opened up new prospects for our action on the international level.

Such action, which we wish to develop incessantly, is however considerably restricted by the fact that it turns out to be very expensive, as the expenses of journeys and accommodation are generally at our own cost. We must nevertheless do our best, with the help of our friends, to develop and implement in these countries a vast campaign in support of our struggle, notably in those countries which are allies of Portuguese colonialism.

As for Sweden – whose exemplary attitude in regard to our struggle should inspire the countries which, like it, maintain significant relations with Portugal – we must do everything possible to develop and consolidate existing contacts in the framework of active solidarity between our peoples and with the Social Democrat Party and all the Swedish anticolonialist organizations.

As in the past, we must continue to play an active part in the action of the peace, Afro-Asian solidarity and Tricontinental movements, and to develop our contacts with the other democratic and anticolonialist international organizations (of workers, of youth, of students and of women).

In conclusion, we can state that in the light of the prospects for our struggle and the criminal obstinacy of the Portuguese ultracolonialists, the immediate main tasks of our Party are the following:

On the internal level

Improve the organization and strengthen the effectiveness of our armed forces (regular army and local armed forces)

Intensify and step up attacks against the colonial troops, notably against the urban centres still occupied by the enemy, with a view to striking harder blows against them and causing them more human and material losses

Do everything possible to develop further the struggle in Cape Verde

Conserve and develop the political, administrative, economic, social and cultural bases of the new life we are in the process of building in the liberated areas
Improve supply of essential items to the populations in these areas
Reinforce vigilance and security against the enemies of our Party and our people.

On the external level

Strengthen relations with the independent states of Africa, whatever their politico-economic options, particularly with the countries neighbouring on our territory, as their security is also that of our struggle
Extend and develop the contacts of friendship, solidarity and co-operation with the socialist states and Sweden
Develop and consolidate relations with the democratic and anticolonialist organizations of the capitalist countries
Develop the action of information and mobilization of anticolonialist opinion in the Western countries and the world, with a view to isolating the Government of Portugal from its allies and to neutralizing or removing the support of the latter countries for the Portuguese colonial war
While we reinforce vigilance against manoeuvres aimed at deviating our struggle from its real ends, remain, as always, open to any initiative which could favour the solution of the conflict which sets us against the Government of Portugal and speed up the the accession of our people to independence.

Raising high the glorious banner of our Party and in intransigent defence of the principles of freedom, justice and genuine independence, which are those of our organization, let us develop and intensify the fight against the Portuguese colonialist hordes. Let us strengthen political action and the work of national reconstruction, and let us constantly improve the political awareness of our populations as well as our individual behaviour as militants. Let us wage in tandem armed liberation struggle and vigorous political action, in the interior of our country and on the African and international level, in the service of our people.

24. The situation of PAIGC's struggle in January 1973[1]

I

1. The situation in our country is generally well known. In the course of ten years of armed struggle and of intensive political activity very significant progress has been made.

We have liberated more than two-thirds of our national territory. We are in daily combat against the positions still occupied by the enemy, notably the urban centres, including Bissau (the capital) and Bafata (the second city), which have been attacked repeatedly by our combatants. In the Cape Verde Islands, the organization of the Party and the mobilization of the people have made significant advances which demand the passage of the struggle to a new phase, with a view to the total liberation of our country.

The political action of the Portuguese colonialists is currently characterized by demagogic concessions aimed at dividing and demobilizing the people. As this policy has so far not given the results counted on by the enemy, the latter are stepping up police repression against the patriots in the urban centres and developing their criminal action against the populations in the liberated areas.

Military action by the colonialists, who are making desperate efforts to induce Africans to fight against Africans, is mainly characterized by intensive aerial shelling and by terrorist raids on the liberated areas. The massacre of populations (when they can do this), the use of napalm, the destruction of villages, cattle and crops are the main actions by the enemy who are developing plans to use toxic chemicals, herbicides and defoliants against our cultivated fields and our forests. In addition, the enemy are stepping up provocations and aggressions against the neighbouring countries, among which the aggression of 22 November, 1970 against the Republic of Guinea and the invasion of Senegal by an armoured cars unit last 12 October were the most elaborate examples.

Our military action is mainly characterized by systematic attacks against the enemy fortified camps, using artillery and, where it is already possible, infantry. We are developing commando actions against the urban centres, where moreover, we have just carried out acts of sabotage (in Bissau, Bafata

[1]This report was part of a dossier prepared for presentation to the Council of Ministers of the OAU, which was due to meet in its XXth ordinary session in Addis Ababa from 5 to 9 February, 1973. Its first draft was finished a few hours before the assassination of Amilcar Cabral by agents of the Portuguese colonialist government.

and Bula mainly). Our combatants are also operating energetically against the enemy on the remaining communications routes used by them: certain highways and the rivers.

In the liberated areas, where a state is now developing under the leadership of our Party, we have succeeded in creating a new (political, economic, social and cultural) life, while still facing the bombs and some criminal raids from the Portuguese colonialists. Our political activity is intensive in the liberated areas where, in parallel with the consolidation of Party organization, we have developed our own administration, built schools, set up field hospitals and health centres, peoples's courts, a system of barter trade (the people's stores) and various other services. Dozens of reliable observers of various nationalities have provided testimony about the situation in our country.

The United Nations Special Mission, which made a one-week stay (from 2 to 8 April, 1972) in our liberated areas, gave irrefutable testimony before the international community, both of this reality – the existence of vast areas liberated and controlled by our Party – and of the abominable crimes committed by the Portuguese colonialists against our people. In its report, the Special Mission declares, among other conclusions:

> That the struggle for the liberation of the territory continues to progress and that Portugal no longer exercises any effective administrative control in large areas of Guinea (Bissau) are irrefutable facts. . . It is also evident that the population of the liberated areas unreservedly supports the policies and activities of the national liberation movement, PAIGC, which, after nine years of military struggle, exercises free *de facto* administrative control in those areas and is effectively protecting the interests of the inhabitants in spite of Portuguese activities.

The recent creation after general elections by universal and secret suffrage of Regional Councils and the first National Assembly of our country is further evidence and a major factor of the sovereignty of our people and opens up new prospects for the development of our liberating fight.

In the areas not yet liberated, we are developing the clandestine organization of the Party and have begun to operate directly against the enemy, within the very heart of the urban centres. In the Cape Verde Islands, the events which occurred on 21 September in the capital (Praia, Santiago Island), in the course of which the population of the city violently opposed the forces of colonial repression, mark a new phase in the development of the struggle. The colonial authorities had to declare a state of emergency throughout one week, to arrest various persons, above all young people, and to threaten the population with new and more violent reprisals. These events which brought several injured among the population and among the forces of repression give a measure of the growing political tension that reigns in the main islands of the archipelago.

2. The Portuguese colonialists no longer hide the situation of defeat in which they are placed in our country. The military Governor has already on many occasions declared *that they cannot win the war.* Marcello Caetano, the head of the Portuguese Government, goes so far as to speak of the 'threat of Amilcar Cabral to destroy our economy'.

In fact, after a mandate for four years extended for two more, the military Governor, who had promised to eliminate our Party and our struggle in six months, must now confess, in the face of the growth of the struggle and the strengthening of our organization, that a long period is needed to triumph over the resistance of our people and it will be possible to do this only 'through reason'. Moreover, not only does Portugal no longer exercise colonial exploitation of our country, but also, according to a Portuguese economist, about twenty per cent of the Portuguese gross national product is consumed annually in our country without any economic return.

Before such a situation, which grows worse every day at all levels, one might wonder why the Portuguese Government, which is aware of the difficulties it faces and will go on facing, continues to insist on its absurd and criminal policy of seeking to perpetuate the domination of African peoples through colonial war. It is not difficult to recognize the main reasons for the inflexible continuity of Portuguese colonial policy:

The substantial and multiform (political, material and financial) aid that the colonialist government of Portugal receives from its allies in NATO, from the racists of southern Africa and from other countries – aid which constitutes the principal factor enabling that government to carry on the genocidal colonial war against the African peoples

The chronic and characteristic underdevelopment of Portugal which does not have a viable economic infrastructure, and shows itself incapable of imagining a process of decolonization, in which the interests of the Portuguese ruling class would be safeguarded

The inhibiting effects of almost half a century of the Fascist regime over a society which, throughout its history, has never really (or significantly) known what human rights, freedom and democratic practice are

The imperialist mentality of the Portuguese leaders and the ignorance, myths, beliefs, prejudices and narrow nationalism that characterize the culture of the broad strata of the population, subjected down the centuries to the doctrine of the *superiority of the European* and the *inferiority of the African* as well as the myth of the 'civilizing mission' of the Portuguese in regard to the African peoples deemed to be 'savages'.

In spite of the fancies of the Portuguese colonialists concerning 'the creation of multiracial societies', such a doctrine, to which they have lately added the bogey of 'Communist subversion', ends in the crystallization of a *primitive racism* often lacking any clear economic motivation.

The racist character of Portuguese domination is amply shown by contempt for the cultural values of Africa as well as by the most abject crimes committed by the administration and by the Portuguese settler during the golden age of colonialism. It is shown today by the acts of cruelty which are typical of the colonial troops. But there is a tendency now, in the face of African resistance, to demonstrate it through paternalism and the false concern with 'achieving the social advancement of the African in the framework of the Portuguese nation'.

Portuguese racism, which is one of the subjective causes of the pursuit of colonial wars, reaches a peak in the upper echelons of the ruling class. Thus it is that General Kaulza de Arriaga (one of the most conspicuous personalities in the Portuguese colonial leadership, commander-in-chief of the colonial troops in Mozambique and candidate for the post of President of the Republic) when tackling the question of Portuguese strategy, declares: 'Subversion is a war above all of intelligence. One must be highly intelligent to carry on subversion, not everyone can do it. Now the black people are not highly intelligent, on the contrary, they are the least intelligent of all the peoples in the world.'[1]

In the same 'Lessons', the author, who takes the view that 'the export of African slaves to Brazil was a good thing' and that 'the tribal condition of the black populations is favourable for Portuguese strategy', reveals in all its cruelty the principal objective of current Portuguese colonial policy: *to maintain white domination over the black populations.*

After noting that the danger lies in the rise of 'evolved blacks', Kaulza de Arriaga declares: 'We shall be able to maintain white domination, which is a national objective, only if white settlement is carried out at a rate that keeps pace with and overtakes, even slightly, the production of evolved blacks. Because if the opposite happens, if white settlement is overtaken by the production of evolved blacks, then two things will inevitably follow: either we set up apartheid which would be terrible and which we would not stick to, or we shall have black governments with all the consequences that this entails (break-up of the overseas provinces, etc.).'

The master racist goes on to explain the appropriate tactics for avoiding such a situation: 'White settlement does not aim at balancing the black demographic potential, it aims at balancing the evolved blacks...And as, thank God, we cannot possibly bring about the evolution of all the blacks, it is possible, almost certain, that we can place whites there (in Africa) in such number as will balance out the blacks who become evolved.'

On this basis, after underlining that 'we shall not be too efficient in producing evolved blacks, because we must advance them, true, but one must not exaggerate', the General, who is a candidate for the Presidency of the Republic, reveals the key line of current Portuguese strategy in Africa:

[1] Volume XII of *Lessons in Strategy for the High Command Course,* 1966-7

'First, growth of the white population, then limitation of the black population.' Faced with the difficulties of the question and believing the myth of the high fertility of the African, he suggests, albeit in a negative fashion, the practice of scientific birth control: 'Clearly this is an extraordinarily difficult question, since we cannot distribute a contraceptive pill to every black family. . . with the result that what we can do is not to encourage too much the growth of the black population.'

One of the main aims of the Portuguese colonial wars in Africa thus becomes clearer: since it is at present impossible to limit the birth-rate to ensure white supremacy, recourse is had to the physical elimination of the population by constantly more intensive use of aerial shelling, of napalm and of other means of mass destruction of the African, through the deliberate practice of genocide.

Moreover the Portuguese Government wants at all costs to defend the myth according to which the colonies are integral parts of Portugal, 'overseas provinces'. Now the elimination of the Portuguese colonial presence from our country, through the path of negotiation, as the result of our armed struggle, would mean the end of this myth with all the consequences that would flow from this.

The Portuguese Government is convinced that the elimination of the Portuguese colonial presence from our country, which is a trading colony, would sound the death-knell of Portuguese domination in Angola and Mozambique, which are settlement colonies with hundreds of thousands of white settlers and which are counted among the richest countries of Africa. In order to try to block the way to such an evolution, the Lisbon Government intensifies the genocidal colonial war against our people and against those of Angola and Mozambique. At the same time, it adopts a new strategy with the supposed creation of autonomous states in the latter two 'provinces', in the hope of transforming them into new Rhodesias before our country should accede to independence.

The Portuguese Government is convinced that time is on its side, in regard to the aid from its allies whose strategic and material interests in the Portuguese colonies in Africa, notably in Angola and Mozambique, as well as the Cape Verde Islands, are constantly growing.

Finally, certain of their economic and financial supremacy, both in men and material, and knowing well our limitations in these fields, the Portuguese colonialists hope that, by holding out at all costs – even at the price of increasing human and material losses – they will end up by putting our Party and our people in difficulty, even eliminating our struggle.

II

1. However, the impetus of the struggle and the determination of our people are constantly greater. In the course of 1971, which saw the first attacks against the Portuguese positions in the main cities (Bissau, the capital, and Bafata), we inflicted on the enemy heavier losses in men and in material than in previous years. These losses are even greater in 1972, when we put out of action more than 3500 enemy soldiers, including 623 confirmed deaths. We destroyed 63 military vehicles, sank 24 boats and launches on the rivers, brought down 2 aircraft and 2 helicopters, and recovered a significant quantity of material. The attacks carried out against the international airport at Bissalanca (9 kilometres from the capital, on 9 March) and against the new 100 kilowatt medium wave broadcasting transmitter, located 25 kilometres from Bissau and inaugurated in April by the Portuguese Minister for Overseas, are two events of note in the whole of our action which is intensified each day.

The success of the visit of the United Nations Special Mission to the liberated areas of our country, in spite of the terrorist repression launched by the Portuguese colonialists against the liberated south, with the aim of preventing the carrying out of the mission, is further evidence of the politico-military advances of the struggle and of the unshakable determination of our African people to win freedom and to accede to independence under the leadership of our national Party, the PAIGC.

In this perspective, it is interesting to recall here what we have declared many times, in accordance with the principles of our struggle. For us, the prospect for the struggle is to continue to fight until victory. We are determined on everything. We have the necessary means to strike ever harder blows against Portuguese colonialism. However, we are not warmongers. We love peace, we detest war, but we want to be free. We are not against Portugal. We have already said this a thousand times. We are against Portuguese colonialism. We want to have the best possible contacts with Portugal after independence.

We have never confused Portuguese colonialism and the people of Portugal. The people of Portugal are our ally; the people of Portugal are today aware of the fact that the colonial war is a crime, not only against our people but also against themselves, and that we are doing all we can, through this struggle, to strengthen our solidarity with that people, who have lately decided to use even violent methods against the Portuguese colonial war machine.

We are for dialogue. But, up till now, the Government of Portugal has only wanted dialogue by means of weapons. However, at any moment we are ready to negotiate with the aim of obtaining full sovereignty of our people, in the context of a free and independent African nation. Just lately, after the crushing defeat it has suffered on the international level, the Lisbon

Government has developed a campaign of diversion, as demagogic as it is vain, declaring itself ready for talks with the OAU or with the African states on the future of the 'overseas provinces'. At the same time as we reaffirm our confidence in the commitment of the OAU and each African state to our liberating struggle whose clearly defined aim is the conquest of national independence, we repeat that if the Government of Portugal wants to discuss or negotiate over the situation in Guiné and Cape Verde, it must and can do this with our fighting Party.

We look with the closest attention and sympathy at any initiative on the part of the OAU and African states that aims at bringing the Lisbon representatives to negotiations with our Party. But we remain firmly convinced that neither the OAU nor any African state will ever agree to take the place of our Party – hence of our people – in the search for a solution to the conflict which sets us against the colonial-racist Government of Portugal.

Like other peoples in Africa we want to construct – at the price of our efforts and sacrifices, but in co-operation with other countries – the progress of our people in independence.

2. It goes without saying that our people and their national Party face enormous difficulties in order to develop the liberating struggle and consolidate the results already obtained against the criminal action of the particularly retrograde Portuguese colonialists. It is enough to recall the precarious material living conditions of our people to estimate how many sacrifices we have to make at all levels to bring to fruition what constitutes the sacred task of our people in the present stage of the history of Africa: to free our country from the foreign colonial yoke.

It is thanks to the fierce determination of our people and of our combatants to follow the example of other countries in Africa that freed themselves from the colonial yoke that we hold on and will hold on until victory. Thanks also to African and international solidarity which, to a constantly greater extent, grants us appreciable aid for the development of our struggle.

Bearing in mind that the Portuguese colonialists are effectively supported by their allies – who supply them with all the war material and with significant economic and financial aid – it may be imagined how disproportionate is the aid we receive in comparison with that granted to the Government of Portugal. It is clear that we need appropriate assistance developed at all levels – moral, political, material and financial – in order to face effectively the difficulties that we confront and to achieve the liberation of our people as soon as possible.

The truth is that we have now in the liberated areas to face the genuine needs of an independent country, but we are not in a condition to satisfy them. In fact we cannot collect taxes from our people, whose poverty does not allow them to give more than they are giving for the struggle: enormous efforts and sacrifices, their children, food for the combatants. Knowing this reality only too well, the Portuguese colonialists centre their psycho-social action on intensive propaganda concerning the material difficulties of our populations, trying to shift the struggle to the economic and social levels. They are convinced that in this domain time is on their side. This represents a challenge, not only for our people, but also for the OAU and every independent state in Africa, for all the anti-colonialist forces.

In a classified secret document, drawn up for presentation to the Council of Ministers, we indicate in detail what are the main strengths of the Portuguese colonialists which allow them to continue the war against our people, in spite of the losses they suffer in men and material, in spite of the political and military successes we have won. We have also shown what are our weaknesses in the confrontation with the colonial armed forces of Portugal. Finally, we show the fundamental needs of the struggle and the aid we need.

Bearing in mind the particular (geographical, economic, social and cultural) circumstances that characterize our liberating fight against the Portuguese colonialist hordes; considering the successes won by our combatants in the course of nine years of war, supported by our African people who have made and are making enormous sacrifices; in the light of the reality of the existence of a developing state in our country, on the basis of a strong political organization, mobilization of the masses, and all the instruments of sovereignty we have already created – it seems no exaggeration to assert that our armed liberation struggle is not only the most advanced in Africa, but also one of the most advanced in the general framework of the struggle of oppressed peoples against imperialism and colonialism.

Substantial, appropriate and developed aid, that would enable us to overcome our difficulties and our main weaknesses and to neutralize or eliminate the main trumps of the enemy, would be a decisive contribution both for the speeding up of the total elimination of Portuguese colonialism from our country and from Africa, and for the consolidation of the sovereignty, security and peace of the independent African countries. It would achieve the desire formulated in the OAU to see at least one African territory totally liberated from Portuguese colonialism 'in the next three years'. Furthermore: the speedy achievement of the liberation of our country – a hypothesis that even the colonialists regard as viable – would sound the death-knell of Portuguese colonial domination in Africa. It would also open a new and shining era in the general struggle of African peoples against imperialism, colonialism and racism.

III

1. In the context of this substantial, appropriate and developed aid that we expect from the OAU and from every independent state in Africa, political aid deserves particular attention and is becoming increasingly a determinant element for the achievement of the liberation of our people. Since, on one hand, the struggle for independence, whatever form its development takes, is essentially a political fact; on the other hand, our liberating fight has reached a state which demands, in parallel with the intensification of armed action, new initiatives on the political level, both in the interior of the country and in the international arena, with a view to speeding up its development, which can only lead to the conquest of independence by our African people.

In this context and in such a perspective, the action waged by the OAU at the international level in recent years, with a view to enlightening world opinion and isolating colonialist Portugal from its allies, takes on a transcendent dimension. Moreover, the striking success of the International Solidarity Conference with the Peoples of the Portuguese Colonies, held in Rome in June 1970, as well as the audience which His Holiness Pope Paul VI granted us immediately after the closure of that conference, exerted a very favourable influence on world and Portuguese opinion and on the position of certain governments more or less tied to the Government of Portugal, and opens up new prospects for our action at the international level and for the recognition both of the legitimacy of our combat and of our Party as the sole true and legitimate representative of our African people.

The United Nations Organization has recognized the legitimacy of the struggle we are waging against Portuguese colonialism and invited its specialized agencies, including UNESCO, to co-operate with our Party for the improvement of material and cultural living conditions of the populations in the liberated areas, which the latter institution has already begun to do by granting us teaching material aid and publishing school textbooks which we had drawn up. The UN likewise appealed to member states to grant all possible aid to the liberation movements, hence to our Party, for the development of the just struggle against colonialism and racism.

Countries which have relations for economic and/or military co-operation with Portugal, such as Sweden, Norway, Denmark and Finland, took the decision to grant significant humanitarian aid to our Party – which they regard as the legitimate representative of our people – for the improvement of the living conditions of the populations in the liberated areas. In the Netherlands and in Belgium, traditional allies of Portugal, we not only have available the support of political parties and of anti-colonialist mass organizations, but the governments also are showing increasing interest in supporting our Party and the just cause which it defends. In other countries of Europe and America, organizations and personalities – including those within government circles – who recognize the legitimacy of our fight are increasingly numerous and, in the light of the advances made by our struggle, they regard our Party as the sole, true and legitimate representative of our people. This is added to the hard fact of the unreserved support of the independent states of Africa, of socialist countries and of other third world countries, who have always supported our fight and regarded our Party as the organization of unity and struggle of our people, whose leader and spokesman it is, expressing their most legitimate aspirations for freedom, independence and genuine progress.

The visit of the United Nations Special Mission, of historic dimensions, both for our people and for the international organization itself, confirmed a reality which had already been attested to by dozens of visitors (journalists, film-makers, scientists, representatives of governments, of national and international organizations, etc.): *the sovereignty of our African people over the greater part of their national territory,* the existence of a state in the liberated areas and the fact that we are in the process of creating a new economic, political, social and cultural life in those areas. Moreover, on the basis of the observations made by the Special Mission, the UN Committee on Decolonization decided, in a resolution unanimously approved, to recognize our Party as the sole, true and legitimate representative of our people.

On the subject of this recognition, the Special Mission declares in the conclusions of its report:

> The Mission was impressed by the enthusiastic and whole-hearted co-operation which PAIGC receives from the people in the liberated areas and the extent to which the latter are participating in the administrative machinery set up by PAIGC and in the various programmes of reconstruction. Accordingly, the Mission believes that the Special Committee's recognition of PAIGC as being the *de facto* and the sole and authentic representative for the aspirations of the people of the Territory should be taken fully into account by States and the specialized agencies and other organizations within the United Nations system in dealing with matters relating to Guinea (Bissau) and Cape Verde.

While it is true that this recognition is the observation of a truth and confirms the position of the OAU in the matter, it is none the less true that it opens up new prospects for the political action of our Party and of Africa at the international level, in favour of speeding up the total elimination of the Portuguese colonial presence from our country. The confirmation of this recognition by the United Nations General Assembly, in its 27th session and by an overwhelming majority (105 votes for and 5 against, including Portugal, South Africa and Spain), gives an international dimension to the initiatives of our Party, notably to the general elections held in the liberated areas and to the creation of the People's National Assembly.

We are firmly convinced that the time has come to take new initiatives with a view to reinforcing the political battle against Portuguese colonialism in our country, while reinforcing armed action on all the fronts of struggle.

We are likewise convinced that the OAU and every African state has a primordial role to play in this political battle. This decisive role was amply demonstrated by the success of the co-ordinated and effective action of African states during the course of the 27th session of the United Nations General Assembly, an action which led to the granting of observer status to the liberation movements as well as to the resolutions both in the General Assembly and in the Security Council which unreservedly condemn Portuguese policy and colonial war, and demand of the Lisbon Government that it initiate negotiations with the liberation movements.

2. For our part, to respond to the demands of the struggle and in accordance with the specific situation prevailing in our country, we have taken certain initiatives aimed at overcoming the political and criminal obstinacy of the Portuguese colonialists and resolving this crucial contradiction in the situation of our people: *we are sovereign in the interior of our country, but we have no juridical personality at the international level.* In fact, as many observers have been able to note: *our situation is that of an independent state, part of whose national territory, notably the urban centres, is militarily occupied by a foreign power,* which practises police repression against the population it still controls and commits daily armed aggressions against the population of the liberated areas. Having reached this stage, at the cost of enormous efforts and sacrifices, our people are firmly determined to assume all their responsibilities.

It is in this historic perspective, determined by the gains of the struggle and by the particularly retrograde character of Portuguese colonialism, that the recent creation of Regional Councils and, most especially of the first National Assembly of our people, lies. We have just held general elections for the representatives of the people of Guiné-Bissau to their first National Assembly. These elections were held in September – October 1972.

Our People's National Assembly will be called on to take decisions of historic dimension, including chiefly:

a To proclaim the existence of our state, of which our Party, the PAIGC, is the guide and the principal driving force
b To endow this state with an executive body which will function in the interior of the country, so is neither provisional nor in exile
c To promulgate a fundamental law for our African nation, the first Constitution in the history of our people
d To study and adopt, on the proposal of the national leadership of the Party, the most appropriate steps towards strengthening and developing our action both in the country and externally, for the urgent and total elimination of Portuguese military occupation from Guiné and the Cape Verde Islands.

As the legitimate representative of a sovereign people, our state will immediately take necessary steps, with a view to establishing and/or developing relations of solidarity and co-operation with African states and all states desirous of freedom and justice, regardless of their economic and social systems, with a view to putting an end to Portuguese colonial aggression and its sequels, for the total liberation of our people.

It is clear that to take and to develop successfully the initiatives we have just outlined, our people and our Party need the fraternal solidarity of independent Africa. We need the practical support of the OAU and of every African state that truly desires the urgent elimination of Portuguese occupation from our country and of the Fascist colonialism of Portugal from Africa.

Thus, bearing in mind this essential condition for the political battle we must wage in conjunction with Africa, we have the honour of carrying out the duty of submitting to the present session of the Council of Ministers of the OAU the following proposals:

1. That, considering the particular situation prevailing in our country, where the highly advanced stage of the struggle enables us to envisage realistically the immediate elimination of the Portuguese colonial presence, the Council should decide to hold at least one session to be concerned exclusively with our case, with a view to studying and discussing, with the participation of the representatives of our Party, the essential aspects of the situation in the country, with the aim of deciding on the most appropriate steps to adopt to speed up the Portuguese defeat and the national liberation of our people.

2. To adopt a specific resolution on Guiné and Cape Verde, which should contain:

a An assessment of the results of the visit of the United Nations Special Mission to our country as well as the implications of the recent resolutions adopted by the General Assembly of the international organization in its 27th session (recognizing our Party as the sole, true and legitimate representative of our people) and by the Security Council (demanding that Portugal withdraw its troops from our country and initiate negotiations with our Party).

b A reference to the juridical consequences that necessarily flow from the observations made by the United Nations Special Mission concerning the situation of our people, who are free and sovereign over the greater part of their national territory.

c An observation of the fact that the illegal presence of the Portuguese colonialists in our country is henceforth that of an aggressor who occupies by force of arms and police repression a part of a territory subjected to aggression.

d A recommendation to be presented to the Conference of Heads of State, which aims at:

the recognition of our Party, the guide of our people, as the sole, true and legitimate wielder of state power in our country; consequently, the recognition of the right of our people to occupy, within the OAU and through their legitimate representatives, the place that is their due as an African nation, as soon as the existence of their state has been proclaimed and the state endowed with an executive body which will function in the interior of our country.

e An Appeal to the independent states of Africa that, on the basis of the principles of the Charter and resolutions of the OAU, they should grant all possible moral, political and material aid, including military resources to our state, in order to help it in practice to eliminate the remnants of occupation of our national territory by the Portuguese colonial troops.

f An appeal to the United Nations and to all states desirous of freedom and justice to support the candidature of our African nation to the international organization so that it should there occupy the place due to it by right, after the proclamation of the state.

Unreserved support of this OAU Council and of every independent state of Africa for these proposals would constitute decisive aid for our people in the combat they have waged for ten years against the Portuguese colonialists at the expense of enormous efforts and sacrifices in the service of total liberation of our continent. Bearing in mind the circumstances and factors that condition both our struggle and the intervention of Africa in the conflict, this political support is perhaps the most important aid that the African states could, without sacrifice, grant us. It would strike a mortal blow against Portuguese colonial policy and would speed up the development of our struggle, whose outcome can only be the accession of our people to full national and international sovereignty.

GENERAL WATCHWORDS[1]

25. Be aware at every moment of the situation of the struggle

Hope for the best but be prepared for the worst.

In Guiné as in Cape Verde, our struggle has made considerable advances (we might say great strides) since the First Party Congress, held in one of the liberated areas in the south of Guiné in February 1964.

In Guiné, with the elimination of various errors which had been committed on the political level, with the strengthening of our human and material resouces and with the creation of our People's Army and strengthening of our guerrilla forces, the armed struggle has been spread to new areas (Boé, Gabu, S. Domingos) and we are inflicting new defeats on the enemy, who have gone on to the defensive. We have implanted guerrilla warfare in the 'Manjaco Territory' and we have taken control of new areas of the country. A great part of the decisions of our Congress (on Party reorganization, developing of production, supply to the population, the founding of schools, health assistance, the creation of a People's Militia, etc.) has been put into practice and we have seen some very encouraging successes.

In Cape Verde, where difficulties specially geographical (namely, communications and co-ordination) have not allowed a more rapid advance in the struggle, important steps have been taken in the last two years. The organization of the Party was strengthened, mobilization of the population reached a high level, notably in the main urban centres and in some rural sectors. On the other hand, new efforts made by the Party leadership, ably helped by conscientious militants who had begun to devote all their activity to the Party and to the struggle, have brought results which are today translated into a full ripening of the political situation in the main islands.

This situation thus demands the shift of the struggle into a new phase, in which we must lay hold of all the available means to eliminate colonial domination from the islands. Our Party and the mass of the people of Cape Verde have been energetically preparing in all the domains needed to unleash armed struggle in the archipelago.

We must do this, but we must do it under the most favourable

[1]These eight directives giving theoretical and practical guidance for Party workers were written by Cabral in 1965 after the First Party Conference of PAIGC held at Cassaca in February 1964, and were published in Portuguese in November 1965.

circumstances and bearing in mind the particular characteristics of armed struggle for liberation in this very special geographical environment. We must move quickly, but not run, without opportunism, without such enthusiasm that we lose sight of specific reality. It is better to begin the armed struggle with an apparent delay, but with guarantees of being able to continue, than to start at some premature moment, before we have established all the conditions to ensure its continuity and victory for our people.

We have to be thoroughly aware that there are still many failures and errors in our action, as much on the political level as on the military level. An important part of the things we should have done was not done in time or was not done at all.

In various regions, and generally in all regions, political work in the midst of the people and our armed forces was not carried out appropriately. The responsible workers either did not know how or were not able to establish the permanent work of mobilization, training and political organization, decided upon by the higher leadership of the Party. In various areas of the country and even among the responsible workers, there is a very bad tendency towards slacking, towards not carrying out the duties of the Party and the struggle, and even towards a certain demobilization which has not been fought and stamped out. Some responsible workers, even in higher grades, have forgotten that our struggle (even in its armed form, of war) is a political struggle and that this work – in the midst of the people, among militants and combatants, and in the heart of the enemy – is the fundamental (vital) aspect of our daily action.

On the military level, many projects and objectives established by the higher leadership of the Party were not brought to fruition. With the means at our disposal we could have done more and better. Various responsible workers could not properly understand the role of the army and the guerrilla forces, did not properly co-ordinate the action of these two forces and, in some cases, let themselves be obsessed by a preoccupation with defending our positions, forgetting that for us attack is the best form of defence – the offensive, the constant development of our armed struggle. It reached the point of disagreements between responsible workers within the same area, which is reprehensible and must not recur. Moreover, along with excessive waste of ammunition and sometimes incorrect use of some weapons, we have seen that some responsible workers gave no evidence of initiative, spirit of decision and necessary courage, which was also a failing of many combatants. In some cases we were not able to take full advantage of attacks made, while in other cases we allowed the enemy some movements and operations (destruction of bases, for example) which we must no longer permit. In addition to this, as a result of the failure of effective political work inside the armed forces, there has begun to be apparent a certain obsession with 'militarism', which led some combatants and even responsible workers to forget that we are *armed militants* and not *the military*. This tendency must be fought and urgently stamped out inside the FARP (People's Revolutionary Armed Forces). In other aspects of our struggle and our life (teaching, health, trade, etc.) errors have been made which can be explained by our lack of experience but which none the less should be eliminated through all the means necessary.

We must constantly be more aware of the errors and mistakes we make so that we can correct our work and constantly do better in the service of our Party. The mistakes we make should not dishearten us, just as the victories we score should not make us forget our mistakes.

Our situation today is comparable to the situation of a state which still has part of its national territory, mainly the cities and towns (the urban centres) occupied by foreign forces. Our responsibilities towards the Party, the people, Africa and the world are therefore greater. We have to work better on all levels, carry out our duties, to rise to the level of our responsibilities.

In the African context, the prestige of our Party, our people and our struggle grows higher each day. All the African states know and recognize that our national Party is the organization of unity and struggle of our people in Guine and Cape Verde. Africa gives us useful aid through the Liberation Committee and, even if this aid is insufficient, it is a mark of solidarity.

In the world, both in anticolonialist countries and circles and among the allies of our enemy, we enjoy greater respect and everyone admires the work and the victories scored by our people under the leadership of our Party. Our friends, whether in Africa or in the rest of the world, have been developing their aid and thus encouraging our struggle.

We have therefore good reason to be pleased and hopeful. It was never so certain that our victory depends mainly on our action. The enemy know this as well, and are constantly more demoralized and are making desperate efforts to hold on. But they know that their days are numbered and for this reason will attempt greater crimes against our people and against our goods and wealth.

So in the light of favourable prospects for our struggle, we must study each problem thoroughly and find the best solution for it. Think in order to act and act in order to be able to think better. We must as always face the present and the future with optimism, but without losing sight of realities and particularly of the special difficulties of our struggle. We must always bear in mind and carry out the watchwords of our Party: *hope for the best, but be prepared for the worst.*

26. Continually develop and strengthen political work and Party organization

To carry on the victorious development of our struggle, we must:

A. Develop and constantly strengthen political work in the midst of the people, militants and combatants of the Party.

1. In the liberated areas, take all the necessary steps to normalize political life for the population of these regions. The committees at section (villages), zone and regional level must be consolidated and function normally. Hold frequent meetings with the population, to keep them in touch with the struggle, the watchwords of the Party and the criminal intentions of the enemy.

2. In areas still occupied by the enemy, strengthen clandestine work of the Party, mobilization and organization of the populations, and prepare the militants to act and to support as they should the actions of our combatants. In particular, in urban areas (cities and towns), provide watchwords for the strengthening of militants' work, re-establish liaison where it was suspended, prepare members of the Party, especially workers, for action against the enemy and for defence of our material goods.

3. Within the armed forces (army and guerrillas) wherever they are, develop political work, holding frequent political meetings, demanding serious political work from the political commissars. Put into operation the People's Army Political Committees, constituted by the political commissars and by the commander of each unit. Combat the obsession with *militarism* and make each combatant an exemplary militant of our Party.

4. Strengthen political and propaganda activity within the enemy forces. Make posters, tracts, letters, write slogans on the roads, send messages, etc., to inform the enemy forces of the policy of our Party. Establish discreet contacts with elements of the enemy forces who want to be in touch with us, act with boldness and great initiative in this field in order to persuade these elements to serve the Party and our struggle against the criminal colonial war. Do everything possible to help enemy soldiers to desert, ensuring them safety through all the means necessary, in such a way as to encourage them to take the decision to desert.

5. Carry out political work among Africans who still serve the enemy (civilians and soldiers), to persuade these brothers to change course, to serve the Party in the heart of the enemy or to desert with their weapons

and ammunition to join our forces. But act firmly to eliminate all those who knowingly betray our people, all those who insist on taking up arms on the enemy side against our Party and our people.

6. Do everything possible to reinforce our fraternal relations with neighbouring countries, with the people and the authorities of those countries. Do not allow any member of the Party to meddle in the internal affairs of those countries: be watchful in respect of elements of those countries who seek to meddle in our life or make use of our struggle. Act with firmness against enemy agents who orginate from the neighbouring countries. Post on the frontiers only responsible workers who are completely trustworthy, honest, dedicated and dutiful. In particular, take all available steps urgently to improve our relations with the Senegalese authorities, to establish close co-operation with those authorities, in defence of our interests.

B. Carry out urgent reorganization of the Party, in accordance with the demands of the struggle in the new phase it has reached. Improve the work of existing bodies and create all those that need to be created, mainly in the liberated areas.

1. Respect the geographical boundaries of the inter-regions (north and south), while not forgetting that our country is one entity. Strengthen frequent liaison between the north and south of the country.

2. Respect the areas corresponding to Regions and Zones or Sectors, and the characteristic of each section (one or more villages), without making sealed compartments.

3. Strengthen or establish (where they do not yet exist) leadership bodies of the Party, which must be made to operate normally in the liberated areas. Apply the principle of collective leadership in all bodies.

4. The Inter-regional Committee is the leadership body in the Inter-region, directly linked to the higher leadership of the Party. It must meet at least once a month. The Regional Committees are the leadership bodies in the Regions. They are directly subordinate to the Inter-regional Committee and must meet at least once every fifteen days. The Zone Committees are the leadership bodies in the Zones, are subordinate to the Regional Committee and must meet every week. The Section Committees (villages) are subordinate to the Zone Committee and must meet at least once a week.

5. All leadership bodies and all responsible workers must be subjected to frequent control on the part of bodies senior to them and of the higher leadership of the Party. Keep the work of each responsible worker under constant assessment and dismiss from their post each and all responsible workers who do not properly fulfil their duty or who commit serious errors in regard to the Party line.

6. Strengthen and develop the organization of the people's militia which should be constituted from the best militants (men and women between fourteen and thirty years old) from the villages, if they are not enrolled in the guerrilla force or in the People's Army. The militia is the organization of the Party for civil defence and security in the liberated areas. The militia within a given area is subject to the Party Committee of that area, through the intermediary of the responsible worker for security. The people's women, particularly, must be the main element in the formation and development of the militia.

7. Throughout the country, prepare the militants for the holding of the next Congress; explain to the populations the themes that will be discussed at the Congress.

27. Constantly improve organization of our armed forces

Act and continually strengthen our action.
To carry on the victorious development of our struggle, we must:

A. Reorganize our armed forces in accordance with the demands of the struggle in the new phase we have reached. Re-define the role of the guerrilla force and the People's Army.

1. The guerrillas are the principal force for armed struggle, must operate within the region or zone to which they belong, in constant close co-operation with the people and with the People's Army. The guerrilla warfare in each area is led by the Party's leadership body for that area. So in the zone it is the Zone Committee which leads the guerrillas whose bases have at the forefront as responsible workers a base chief and a political commissar. For a region, all the guerrillas of the zones are led by the Party Regional Committee, which is subordinate to the Inter-regional Committee.

2. The army must be constituted by units with their own commands and in this phase we must not form units bigger than the bigroup. Each bigroup must have a commander and a political commissar and comprises two groups. Army units are directly under the orders of the Party Inter-regional Committee, which co-ordinates the action of the army with that of the guerrillas, through the intermediary of the Regional

Committees or the special military Commands which will be increased to the extent that this becomes possible. The People's Army must operate wherever necessary, not being permanently tied to any region or zone in the country. It must have clear, precise and programmed missions to accomplish.

3. In the liberated areas there are guerrilla forces and there may be army forces whenever needed. In regions as yet unliberated army units operate with the purpose of engaging the enemy, liberating new stretches of the country, implanting guerrilla warfare and carrying out work of mobilization and political organization of the population. In conjunction with the guerrilla force, the army must ensure the defence of the population against enemy forces.

4. Increase the number of the guerrilla force and the number of men in each base in all areas where it is necessary to do this. Cut out the non-essential bases to avoid a broad spread of weak bases, but concentrate the guerrilla forces in strong bases, well cited and in close liaison with each other. Place the bases mainly at strategic points in such a way as to paralyse the enemy and to threaten them on all sides, wherever they are. In locating bases, bear in mind the need to defend our populations and their goods against the crimes of the enemy. Urgently establish guerrilla bases in all zones as yet unliberated, as soon as there is a minimum of local support. In establishing bases, give preference to militants from the particular zone, but avoid the leadership of bases and their formation being influenced by any tribal or tribalist consideration. Put at the head of bases the best, bravest, and most disciplined combatants who wield authority and inspire confidence in others.

5. Improve the organization of existing army units, close down the sub-sections and transform them all into bigroups. Establish new bigroups to the level needed to carry out properly the missions to be fulfilled. Put the best combatants at the front of army units, and only put into the army experienced guerrillas, demanding from all the swearing of loyalty to our People's Army.

6. In the liberated areas the main armed forces must be the guerrillas who are responsible for all offensive or defensive actions in these regions. Only send army units to the liberated areas in case of absolute necessity and always as a temporary measure (to help in frontier defence, attacks which require reinforcement, a defensive situation, etc.). In zones still occupied by the enemy, army units must be deployed in sufficient number, with clearly defined missions to accomplish and a timetable mapped out for their accomplishment. To the extent that we control an area and implant guerrilla forces there, let us withdraw from there the army units, who must go and carry out other missions in other parts of the country.

7. To the extent that the organization of people's militia is developed in

the liberated areas, begin to arm their members little by little and give them practical tasks to carry out in military and economic security (above all on the frontiers) and in vigilance in regard to enemy forces. To arm the militia, use above all light weapons (rifles) captured from the enemy and weapons which will least be missed in our forces' action. Establish special caches of munitions for the militiamen who may use them in case of justified need.

8. The Inter-regional Committee, directly linked to the higher leadership of the Party, must carry out the role of *General Command* in the inter-region. It should have auxiliary members, mainly for liaison and co-ordination of the struggle on the various fronts and for the recruitment and training of combatants. As soon as possible (availability of new, appropriately trained cadres) we must establish *General Commands* subordinate to the Inter-regional Committee, but who will devote themselves exclusively to the armed struggle.

B. Continue to carry out better and better the watchwords of the Party in re-guard to the general strategy of our armed struggle. Develop our tactics in accordance with the new stages in the struggle. Derive the greatest return from every action, avoid great losses to our forces in human lives, protect our populations and their goods (homes, crops, cattle). Strengthen our military action from all aspects and throughout the country.

1. Implant the struggle in all areas where there is as yet no struggle. We should energetically prepare to unleash armed struggle in Cape Verde.

2. Further isolate the enemy, cutting them off from all possibilities of supplies or reinforcements in men and material by land, rivers or air (aircraft). Constantly eliminate more live enemy forces, do everything possible to cause heavy enemy casualties and to capture colonialist soldiers. Always fire on boats and aircraft, with all the means at our disposal. Post patrols by the rivers, equipped with special weapons (machine guns, bazookas, artillery) so as to prevent boats passing and to sink them. Form special groups of marksmen against aircraft (with light weapons) and place batteries against aircraft and boats at all strategic points.

3. Do not let the enemy relax in their barracks, attack them with light and rapid sorties, with scattered fire, with firing on sentries, with mortar shelling, with light weapons raids, with bazookas, etc. Do not let the colonialist soldier have even one quiet night's sleep in our land. Surprise the enemy at time of roll-call, meals, exercise, religious services (mass), force him to be constantly on the alert and to feel in danger at every moment. Provoke the enemy, force them to go out of barracks, mount heavy ambushes to destroy the enemy, maintain vigilance patrols to keep on top of all enemy movements. Trick the enemy with false news, make them fall into traps so that we can destroy them in large numbers.

4. Study and prepare as well as possible each important attack, in such a way as to derive the greatest return and the best result from it. As has already been said, lay hold of all available means of gaining specific intelligence of a military nature about the enemy forces. Every day and for every action against the enemy, know how many men and what weapons we are going to have to face. Avoid going into any action blindfold, without knowing the enemy strength. Try to find out, both about the barracks and about the area in general, what is the mood of the enemy forces, their morale, their capability, their will to fight. Try to find out if it is a question of experienced soldiers who have been in our land a good while, or if they are newcomers who have just arrived. Try to find out if there are quarrels or conflicts in the barracks, what is the authority of the officers. Know as much as you can about the weapons the enemy possess, their means of transport, their fuel stores, where they obtain their drinking water, etc. Each responsible worker must remember that acting against an unknown enemy is like going into a dark room, full of obstacles, but without being able to turn on a light.

5. Keep close liaison between political work and action by the armed forces. Develop the spirit of initiative, the capacity for swift decision and action by responsible workers and combatants. Every responsible worker must be able to take initiatives within the framework of his assignments and wield the greatest authority over the men who are under his command. Develop the courage of all, establish prizes and rewards for the bravest. Always remember that courage is something that we have to have within ourselves, since we cannot receive it from outside, in crates like weapons. Dismiss all those responsible workers who show signs of lack of courage, punish cowardly combatants fairly. Always keep the initiative, not letting the enemy have the initiative over us.

6. Intensify, develop and spread the struggle throughout the country. Use to their full our means of action, demand a greater spirit of sacrifice and more courage from all combatants. Carry the armed struggle to every point where it does not yet exist, force the enemy to fight on all sides and to feel constantly threatened with death in our land. Develop all the branches of our People's Revolutionary Armed Forces.

7. Set in train new and ever new areas of struggle, rapidly develop our action in all areas as yet unliberated. Along with intensive political work to be carried out by those responsible for political action and by the armed forces, persuade the people of these areas to take up arms bravely, as guerrillas, to defend their territory and to destroy the enemy forces. Study carefully the implanting of struggle in new areas, and do this only with the certainty that there will be continuity and that we shall be able to impose a new and victorious situation which will strengthen the courage, enthusiasm and dedication of our people to the cause of our Party.

8. Urgently carry the armed action to our urban centres (cities and towns)

to sow insecurity among the enemy and to show the population that we are determined to liberate all points of our country, to prove in fact the proverb 'The bush has caught fire; there is no place to hide'. Shell the enemy barracks, even shell the market places of towns and cities, create conditions which paralyse any commercial activity, make swift and energetic raids, carry out acts of sabotage against camps, offices, petrol stocks, water reserves, troop carriers and administration transport, etc. But for the time being avoid any act of terrorism against the unarmed European or African population. Attack soldiers, officers' clubs, and as far as possible kidnap soldiers, Portuguese agents. Shell airfields, carry out ambushes there, attack aircraft as they land or take off. Form special commandos to operate in the urban centres. The struggle must make itself felt in all the cities and towns in our land and particularly in Bissau.

28. Know well our own strength and the enemy strength

Ensure liaison and information.
To carry on the victorious development of our struggle, we must:
A. Know well our own strength, at every moment have a perfect understanding of the things we can do and the things we cannot yet do. Carefully assess our potential in each area, in each unit of the armed forces, always act in accordance with these potentials and do everything possible to improve our strength and capability both in men and in material. Never do less than we can and should do, but never attempt to do something which we are not yet really in a condition to do. Make and keep every day in every area an inventory of our strength in men and material.
1. Know at every moment the number of armed men, whether in the guerrilla force or in the army or in the militia or by individuals. Know the number of men we could arm as soon as we acquire the material for this. Know each responsible worker and each combatant as well as possible (their qualities, their failings) to improve what is good and to fight and end what is bad.
2. Know precisely at all times the number of weapons and the kinds of weapons in the hands of combatants and those in the armouries. Make a list at every guerrilla base and at every army unit with the names of the combatants and in front the type and the number of the weapon which has

been distributed to them. Always have a list of the quantity of weapons and munitions held in the armouries. Generally every weapon should be in the hands of a combatant or a group of combatants; keep munitions in well guarded armouries, under the reponsibility of completely trustworthy comrades.

3. Take all necessary steps, in close collaboration with the higher bodies of the Party, to ensure the supply of weapons and munitions to our forces. And in cases where the material comes from far away, ensure safe passage of this material along the route it has to follow, and for this it is essential to control the transit zones for material and to form special groups for escort and protection of material. Achieve voluntary co-operation from the people for the transport of material, keeping them informed of our needs of weapons and munitions for defence and enabling them to understand the value of their help. Detach combatant groups from areas of low activity for temporary duty in transport of material. But act firmly, and fairly against all and any elements of the population or a combatant who refuse to co-operate in the duty of transport of material. Calculate for each area and each front of struggle the long-term needs in material, above all in munitions, in such a way as to be able to ensure reserves of material so as to avoid difficult situations.

4. Be sparing of munition and look after weapons and their accessories carefully; train personnel for the duty of repairing weapons. Make each man or woman responsible for the correct maintenance of weapons issued and demand an account of munitions used at the bases, in units and per combatant. Do everything possible to capture weapons and munitions from the enemy, either during operations or through raids designed to obtain material.

5. Do everything possible, as always, to ensure food supplies to combatants, on the basis of production of our country and of our people. The people must help the struggle by providing food for the combatants, but the latter must help the people whenever possible to carry out their agricultural work or other tasks (rebuilding of homes, taking care of cattle, fighting the effects of storms and floods, etc.). Furthermore, combatants, both guerrillas and army members, must till their own fields in the areas where they are to ensure at least a part of their food needs. In the liberated areas, establish collective plots for the supply of the armed forces, where the population and those forces will work together in order to meet this basic necessity of the struggle. Only in very exceptional cases can the Party help combatants to obtain food supplies: in areas where there is no real agricultural potential or no local population, or in some frontier zones where the presence of our forces would be essential and there would be difficulty in obtaining food from our own production. But even in such cases, steps must urgently be taken to obtain the necessary food from our land since the Party will not be able to provide aid over a

long period. For supplies to zones less favoured in food, provisions must be sent from more favoured areas, and this is within the direct competence of the responsible worker for supply to the armed forces in the inter-region. At all costs we must ensure food supplies to combatants from our own production in our country.

B. Pay the closest attention to the question of information, liaison and co-ordination of the struggle.

1. Develop on all sides intelligence networks about the enemy. This task is mainly within the competence of those responsible for security, but the collective leadership bodies of the Party must pay this their closest attention. We must constantly be gathering information about the enemies' circumstances, number of men, quantity of armaments, principal characteristics of the camp and barracks, siting of barracks, of heavy weapons, location of officers and NCOs' housing, of the magazine, of the sentry, the system of vigilance at mealtimes, roll-call, habits of soldiers and officers, contacts with Africans who live outside the camp, etc., etc. We have to be able to infiltrate agents into the heart of the enemy forces to give us information, capture enemy elements to obtain information, to establish contacts with those who are against the colonial war to obtain information from them. Make planned operations with the main aim of finding out the circumstances of the enemy (existing strength, fire-power, fighting spirit, siting of certain weapons, position of shelters, etc., etc.).

2. Do not let the enemy begin a movement without our knowing. Never let the enemy take us by surprise. Strengthen patrols, all the patrols needed, to be watchful and always have fully in mind that the best vigilance is achieved by daily and permanent action against the enemy.

3. Ensure by all available means (men, women, children, long-distance signalling-horn, talking drum, radio) liaison between the leadership of the struggle and the different sectors of the struggle, and between different units in action within a given area. Do everything possible to co-ordinate our action, both in defence and attack and whatever the type of action to be launched.

4. Keep the various struggle fronts informed about what is going on in each front, about our actions and chiefly about the victories scored against the enemy. Form special groups for liaison, communications and co-ordination in the struggle. Put capable responsible workers at the head of these groups in all regions and zones and under the direction of the leadership body in the area. Frequently carry out combined (co-ordinated) operations within a single zone, between various zones of a region and in various regions. Maintain permanent liaison with the higher leadership of the Party and between the various leadership bodies of the Party and the struggle.

5. Urgently install radio communications within the country, both in the inter-region and between north and south, and with the higher leadership of the Party, for which all that is needed is to install the apparatus we possess and to choose the men or women capable of using this apparatus properly. Do not forget the use of codes in communications by radio and insist that such communications should be brief and made only when absolutely necessary.

6. Each responsible worker should constantly keep in mind the truth that no one can fight well if he feels isolated. Moreover, the leadership of the Party cannot carry out its duties properly if it is not always up to date with progress of the struggle in all areas of the country.

29. Strengthen security and discipline in all sectors of the struggle

To carry on the victorious development of our struggle, we must:

A. Develop and strengthen internal and external security of the Party, install and put security bodies into operation, persuade responsible workers to devote themselves to security, form security networks in all areas, and particularly in frontier regions and in enemy contact zones. Strengthen vigilance against enemy agents and opportunists in all sectors of the Party and in our armed forces. Pay special attention to security for responsible workers of the Party, both in the framework of struggle within the country and in their travels abroad.

1. Develop and constantly strengthen the best possible relations between the armed forces and the people. Every combatant must be aware that he is a son of the people serving the people. Every element of the population must be aware that our combatants are sons of the people who with weapons in hand defend the sacred interests of our people against the Portuguese colonialists. No combatant or responsible worker has the right to use our weapons in order to terrorize the people or in order to obtain personal advantages against the interests of the people. The combatant must live in the midst of the people as their son and defender, and the people must be the main and vital support for every combatant.

The people, for us, are any descendants of our land who support our armed struggle against Portuguese colonialism, and who co-operate overtly or covertly with our Party. Those who are against the struggle and against the Party, those who serve the Portuguese colonialists or in any way try to destroy our Party – they do not deserve to be counted among our people. All or any combatants who fail to respect the people, who do not defend the people's interests, who try to use their authority and the weapons in their hands for personal advantage – they do not deserve to be part of the armed forces of our Party and they are not militants of our Party.

2. Turn our armed forces even more into the willing instrument our Party created, organized and leads in order to serve liberation and the building of progress for our people. This is a duty for every combatant, militant or responsible worker in our armed struggle for national liberation.

3. Restrain with speed and justice all acts against the interests of the Party and struggle, hence against the interests of our people. Whether such criminal acts are perpetrated by militants, combatants or by elements of the population not connected with the struggle, they must be unhestitatingly restrained, with clarity and justice and on the base of specific proof. (As a Party and as a developing state, we have at our disposal now effective means of stopping those who commit crimes. The fundamental characteristic of a state is its ability to restrain those who act against the interests of that state. Our interests, the interests of our Party which leads our state are the interests of our people: total liberation and the building of peace and progress in Guiné and Cape Verde.)

4. We must therefore exercise restraint of all criminal elements, whatever their social condition. We should not allow, either from individuals or from groups of individuals, acts against the struggle, the Party and the people. But we should practise justice; judge each case with all the care needed, apply just penalties and always explain to the populations the crimes committed and the reasons for punishment of those found guilty.

5. We must in every region establish and support a *people's court* (constituted by elements of the population who have prestige and the Party's trust) which will have the collaboration of responsible workers of the Party. These courts must operate under strict control by the Inter-regional Committee.

6. Strengthen frontier control to put an end to enemy manoeuvres in these zones, to stamp out the criminal action of traffickers, to control the movements of our own combatants. Entrust groups of guerrillas and militiamen with frontier control and strengthen this control with army units whenever necessary. Armed forces on the frontier must always be operating against the enemy because action makes for the best control. Put at the head of frontier forces reliable comrades, devoted to the Party

and aware of the meaning and duties of this post, and who will not be tempted to make sorties into the neighbouring territory. Do not allow sorties by our combatants whatever the pretexts offered. Army units posted to the frontier must periodically be rotated, and a unit should spend a maximum of three months on the frontier. Increase control over the movement of so-called *refugees,* not allowing any more folk to leave our country, except in very exceptional cases. Do not allow more cattle to leave the country. Control the emigrants who are returning to the country but let them return and go on their way as long as they are neither making trouble nor enemies. Avoid any kind of dispute with the authorities of the neighbouring country, but insist on respect for our rights and courageously defend the interests of the Party, the people and the struggle. Punish justly all militants of the Party who make trouble with the neighbouring country but be watchful against provocations or criminal actions by elements who come from the neighbouring country, whether they are descendants of our land or not.

7. The guerrilla, army and people's militia force are the instruments we possess to take action against those who commit crimes against the struggle, the Party and the people. Prisons, labour camps and even the death penalty are forms of exerting restraint in the service of our struggle. We must be able to apply them with understanding and courage. Before a death sentence can be carried out, it must be confirmed by the higher leadership of the Party.

B. Inside the armed forces strengthen military discipline, which must be strict and fair for responsible workers and for combatants in general. War is an uncommon situation and demands uncommon behaviour from all, notably from the men and women directly engaged in it.

1. Every member of the guerrilla force or the army must show clear evidence of obedience to the orders of heads, of permanent respect for the rules and laws which govern our struggle, of comradeship, of spirit of sacrifice and of deep devotion to the Party and the people. Every combatant must have twofold discipline: he must have the discipline of a conscientious militant of our Party and the military discipline of a member of our armed forces.

2. Responsible workers must always set the example of discipline, and we have to act strictly against all responsible workers who commit faults in discipline, whatever their own category and the value of the work they have already done for the Party. We must not tolerate indiscipline from any combatants and fair penalties must be exacted from all those who commit errors. We have the means for this and no opportunist interpretation of the needs in manpower can shield from punishment those who commit faults.

3. Act promptly and with the greatest severity against an attempt at desertion and against deserters. If up till now we have been understand-

ing over some cases of individual or collective desertion which have already occurred, and which caused serious harm to the struggle, from now onwards we must no longer be tolerant. The deserter or those who try to desert must be disarmed, arrested, tried and punished. In the case of collective desertion (many persons) we must try patiently to find out who is or who are to blame for desertion (the ringleaders) and punish those to blame with all the necessary severity. From now on the individual deserter or the person or persons mainly to blame for a collective desertion must be tried, condemned to death and executed. If they manage to flee, they should be dealt with where they are found. Those who desert unwittingly because they are misled by others should be disarmed and interned in labour camps under strict watch.

4. The Inter-regional Committee of the Party has competence as a *court martial* to try all cases of indiscipline within the armed forces.

30. Destroy the economy of the enemy and build our own economy

Every responsible worker and every militant of our Party, every element of the population in our land in Guiné and Cape Verde, should be aware that our struggle is not only waged on the political level and on the military level. Our struggle – our resistance – must be waged on all levels of the life of our people. We must destroy everything the enemy can use to continue their domination over our people, but at the same time we must be able to construct everything that is needed to create a new life in our land. While we destroy the enemy, their agents and the things that serve their interests, we have to build for ourselves, to ensure the satisfaction of the needs of our people, to train able men and women, constantly to raise standards of living in our land. Along with political resistance and armed resistance, we must constantly strengthen economic resistance, cultural resistance and physical resistance. Destroy the economy of the enemy and build our own economy, destroy the negative influences of the culture of the enemy and develop our own culture, destroy the physical ills which colonialism has brought us in order to build a stronger and more capable new being.

1. *In the liberated areas* develop agricultural production both by extending the cultivated areas and by improving farming methods, with more care in farming and by increasing the range of crops. Pay special attention to the development of food crops (rice, maize, manioc, potato, beans, vegetables, bananas, cashew nut, oranges and other fruit trees). Pay special attention to the care of cattle and breeding livestock (pigs, chickens, sheep, etc.) to cattle fodder and to the preservation of grazing land. Demand an effective control over fires, to avoid the destruction of our forest and bush. Employ all the spare time of the armed forces with help to farmers, above all at harvest time. Do everything possible to finish the harvest quickly to avoid its destruction by the enemy, and persuade the population to store and preserve food products in the best way possible. Develop craftwork (making of wallets, baskets and panniers, chairs and other furniture, weaving of strips, cloths and other woven goods, pieces in ceramic, pottery, pitchers, etc. – all the useful items that our people can make by traditional methods). Help the smiths to carry on developing their skill, notably in the making and repair of farm tools. Intensify the production of coconut, palm oil and other oils, the manufacture of 'home made soap' and all the other products of use to the population and traditionally made in our country. Make preparations to bring back into operation soon the saw-mills abandoned by the settlers. Develop exchange (mutual aid) between families in one village and between villages. Establish collective farming areas for some crops such as the banana, the pineapple and fruit trees. Form through experience and whenever conditions are favourable simple co-operatives for farm production. Hand over properties (orchards, cattle) abandoned by their owners to a local committee to use and manage them. Establish prizes for the best producers, for those who till most and produce most, for those who take best care of cattle, and build a spirit of constructive competition between the producers. The Party could give the best producers the opportunity of visiting foreign countries to learn new types and methods of agriculture and husbandry (breeding of cattle) and to develop their knowledge.

In zones still occupied by the enemy, sabotage by all available means the production of colonial products, above all groundnuts; sabotage the colonial economy both by passive resistance and armed action. Persuade the population to devote itself exclusively to the production of food crops and to improve this production. Destroy the shops of the enemy, the warehouses and stores of the enemy, all their economic activity.

Strengthen vigilance on all frontiers, to prevent or reduce the drain of useful hands from our economy. Make those who want to flee abroad withdraw with their families to the liberated areas, where our forces can ensure their safety and they can work and serve our people. Confiscate all the assets (houses, orchards, cattle and even savings in cash or in gold and othe valuables) of those who insist on abandoning the country. Place these goods in the safekeeping of the Party and under the management (direction) of committees of the people. Do not allow another head of cattle to leave our country without the previous authorization of competent bodies of the Party. Carry out propaganda among the so-called refugees so that they should speedily return to the country with their families and goods. Raise production, constantly obtain more products from agriculture, craftwork and traditional industry. Persuade the people and the armed forces to produce more, to open new production fronts. Ensure the safety of our production – this is one of the important forms of our struggle for freedom, independence and progress.

2. Take all necessary steps to ensure and develop supplies to the populations in the liberated areas of essential items (salt, sugar, tobacco, cloth, footwear, etc.). Always remember that the people do not struggle for ideas, for things in the heads of individuals. The people struggle and accept the sacrifices demanded by the struggle, but in order to gain material advantages, to be able to live a better life in peace, to see their lives progress and to ensure their children's future. National liberation, the struggle against colonialism, working for peace and progress – independence – all these are empty words without meaning for the people, unless they are translated into a real improvement in standards of living. It is useless to liberate an area, if the people of that area are left without the basic necessities of life.

Install 'People's Stores' in all the liberated areas, form brigades for the sale of essential items to supply the villages. Put at the head of all these trading bodies honest responsible workers, who have not been corrupted by colonial commerce, and do not allow these responsible workers to have political duties.

The 'People's Stores' carry on a barter trade, since we do not yet have a currency and the colonialist coinage does not do. Exchange essential items for farm and craftwork products at fair prices and without ever exploiting the customers.

The 'People's Stores' and all their forms of activity are directly guided by the higher leadership of the Party and through the intermediary of some of its principal responsible workers. The local leadership bodies of the Party – the Inter-regional Committee, Regional and Zone Committees – can monitor the activity of the the commercial sector, but they have no right to interfere in its management, nor can they requisition goods from the 'People's Stores'.

Restrain with strictness and justice all those producers who, if they live in liberated areas, try to sell their products or their cattle to the enemy.

31. Improve our knowledge and defend our health

To carry on the victorious development of our struggle, we must:

A. Set up schools and develop teaching in all the liberated areas. Choose youngsters (boys and girls) between the ages of fourteen and twenty, with at least fourth-year education who can be used in the training of cadres. Combat without violence harmful practices, the negative aspects of the beliefs and traditions of our people. Make responsible workers of the Party and all dedicated militants constantly improve their cultural training.

1. Improve the work in the existing schools, avoid a very high number of pupils which might prejudice the advantage to all. Found schools but bear in mind the real potential at our disposal, to avoid our having later to close some schools through lack of resources. Frequently inspect the work of teachers and the methods they are using. Avoid corporal punishment of pupils and strictly follow the programmes drawn up by the Party for elementary and primary education. Set up special courses for the training and advancement of teachers.

2. Constantly strengthen the political training of teachers, their unlimited devotion to the Party and the people. Dismiss and punish all those teachers who fail in their duties. Persuade parents of the absolute necessity for their sons and daughters to attend school, but organize activity for the pupils in such a way that they can also be useful at home in helping their family.

3. Set up courses to teach adults to read and write, whether they are combatants or elements of the population. On all sides ensure respect for the watchword of our Party – 'all those who know should teach those who do not know'.

4. Pay the closest attention to the recruitment of youngsters for training as cadres. Always remember that our political or military victories will lead nowhere if we do not have national cadres available for the reconstruction and scientific and technical development of our land.

In the choice of candidates for training as cadres, give preference to the youngest, to the best militants of the Party, to individuals (boys and girls) who have given evidence of intelligence and willingness to learn.

5. Combat among youth, notably among the more mature (above the age of twenty), the obsession with leaving the country to go and study, the blind ambition to be *doctor,* the inferiority complex and the mistaken notion that those who study and take courses will have privileges

tomorrow in our land. Do not accept as a candidate for a scholarship any responsible worker of the Party with leadership duties, whatever his level of education. But combat, above all among responsible workers who have devoted themselves to the struggle, ill will against those who study or want to study, the complex that makes them think that all students are dangerous and future saboteurs of the Party. (Winning the battle of the training of cadres, to ensure the cadres needed for the development of our land is one of the most important aspects of the action and programme of our Party.)

6. Protect and develop manifestations of our people's culture, respect and ensure respect for the usages, customs and traditions of our land, so long as they are not against human dignity, against the respect we must have for every man, woman or child. Support manifestations of art (music, dance, painting and sculpture), hold competitions among artists, form groups for dancing, singing and theatre, make collections of works of art, and collect texts of legends and tales told by the people. Combat all particularisms (separatist feeling) prejudicial to the unity of the people, all demonstrations of tribalism, of racial or religious discrimination. Respect and ensure respect for each one's religion and the right not to have a religion.

7. Pay special attention to the life of the children, develop their personality and protect them against abuses, even on the part of parents and relatives. Defend the rights of woman, respect and ensure respect for women (in childhood, as young girls and adult women), but persuade women in our land that their liberation must be their own achievement, through their work, dedication to the Party, self-respect, personality and firmness in the face of anything that might offend their dignity.

8. Teach ourselves and teach others and the population in general to combat fear and ignorance, to stamp out little by little submissiveness before nature and natural forces which our system has not yet mastered. Struggle without unnecessary violence against all the negative aspects, harmful to man, which still form part of our beliefs and traditions. Little by little persuade militants of the Party particularly that we shall end up overcoming the fear of nature, knowing that man is the most powerful force in nature.

9. Demand from responsible workers of the Party that they devote themselves seriously to study, that they take an interest in aspects and questions of life and of the struggle in their essential, basic character, and not merely superficially. Make every responsible worker constantly improve his knowledge, his culture, his political training. Convince everyone that no one can know without learning and the most ignorant person is the one who purports to know without having learned. Learn from life, learn with our people, learn in books and from the experience of other. Constantly learn. (Responsible workers must put

a definitive stop to the spirit of childishness, irresponsibility, carefreeness, friendship based on 'easy come', in order to face up to life with seriousness, full awareness of responsibilities, with a concern for proper achievement, with comradeship based on work and duty done – as genuine responsible workers for our Party and our people. None of this rules out joy at living, love of life and amusements, confidence for the future, which must enliven our action, our struggle and the work of each of us.)

10. Little by little set up simple libraries in the liberated areas, lend others the books we possess, help others to learn to read a book, the newspaper and to understand what is read. Give the widest possible distribution to the Party newspaper, hold sessions for collective reading (in a group) and lead those who are reading into discussion and into expressing views on what they have read.

11. Always remember that a good militant (like a good citizen) is the one who does his duty properly. He is the one who, in addition to doing his duty, succeeds in improving himself each day so as to be able to do more and better.

B. Always bear in mind the truth that health is our greatest treasure and the main strength of our combatants and militants. Constantly improve health assistance to wounded and sick combatants, to active militants who suffer from any illness.

1. Set up new health dispensaries in guerrilla bases, improve the existing ones and always include health technicians in army units. Ensure the supply of medicaments and surgical instruments for the health dispensaries and for army units.

2. Put at the head of health services responsible workers, who are conscientious, keen, good, capable and devoted to the sick and wounded.

3. Make efforts for the great majority of sick or wounded combatants to be treated in the interior of the country, but send abroad really serious cases which cannot be treated in the interior. Make clear to everyone that both the dispensaries in the interior and the hospitals abroad are mainly intended for the combatants; they *are military.*

4. But meanwhile little by little and in accordance with the real potential without prejudice to assistance to combatants, develop health assistance for the populations in the liberated areas. Do not create illusions among the people, who must understand that we can only give worth-while care after the liberation of our land and on the basis of our own work and the taxes that everyone will have to pay in order that we can construct our country on all levels.

5. Do not try to treat chronic cases, incurable diseases and lost cases of contagious disease (leprosy, tuberculosis, etc.). Do not send abroad cases of non-combatants who require operations (ruptures, elephantiasis,

eye disease, cancer, etc.). Be constantly aware of what we can and should do, and do not try to do things impossible in the current phase of our life and our struggle.

6. To the extent possible, use local remedies (traditional medicines) like teas (*buco, macete* and other infusions), balsams, pomades, diets, etc., as long as they are demonstrably not prejudicial to the life and health of the patient. Be as sparing as possible with manufactured drugs, but do not refuse to treat an invalid when we have available the means to treat him.

7. Preserve health and hospital equipment as well as possible. Inspect frequently and strictly the activity of health centres or dispensaries and their consumption of medicaments.

8. Always remember that to cure an injured or sick person, to save a human life is to create a new strength for our struggle, for the present and the future of our people.

9. Make preparations for the holding of a population census in all liberated areas. We have to know the number and the kind of people in these areas, so that we can take better steps for their development, progress and defence. Begin right now the selection of comrades who, because of their knowledge, should form part of the teams for the population census we must begin and complete in 1966. Prepare the people to co-operate fully with the census, showing them all that for the first time in the history of our land we are going to hold a census to serve the interests of the people, the improvement of their standard of living.

32. Apply Party principles in practice

On the application of some Party principles

In the current phase of our struggle and in order to strengthen our organization in the face of the great responsibilities it has, it is not enough to put into operation all the leadership bodies of the Party, it is not enough to do good political work and to operate effectively and victoriously on the military level. In order that the Party should be constantly better and rise to the level of its responsibilities, it is essential to apply at all echelons of our life and our struggle the principles of organization and work which the Party adopted as basic norms for its action. A case in point is the principle of *criticism* and *self-criticism* to solve internal questions and contradictions, the principle of *collective leadership* in *leadership* of Party life, the principle of *democratic centralism* and *revolutionary democracy* in the decisions to be taken at all levels and in the practice of Party watchwords.

1. Develop the spirit of *criticism* between militants and responsible workers. Give everyone at every level the opportunity to criticize, to give his opinion about the work and the behaviour or the action of others. Accept criticism, wherever it comes from, as a contribution to improving the work of the Party, as a demonstration of active interest in the internal life of our organization.

Always remember that criticism is not to *speak ill* nor to engage in intrigues. Criticism is and should be the act of expressing an open, candid opinion in front of those concerned, on the basis of facts and in a spirit of fairness, to assess the thought and action of others, with the aim of improving that thought and action. Criticism is to be constructive, to show proof of sincere interest in the work of others, for the improvement of that work.

Combat severely the *evil tongue*, the obsession with intrigues, the 'so-and-so says', unfair and unfounded criticism. To assess the thought and action of a comrade is not necessarily to speak ill of it. To speak highly, to praise, to encourage, to stimulate – this is also criticism. While we must always be watchful against conceit and personal pride, we must not stint praise to someone who deserves it. Praise with cheerfulness, with frankness, in front of others, all those whose thought and action properly serve the progress of the Party. We must likewise apply fair criticism, denounce frankly, censure, condemn and demand the condemnation of all those who practise acts against the progress and interests of the Party, fight face to face errors and faults, help others to improve their work. Derive a lesson from every mistake we make or which others make, in order to avoid making new mistakes, so that we do not fall into the follies into which others have already fallen. Criticizing a comrade does not mean putting oneself against the comrade, making a *sacrifice* in which the comrade is the victim: it is to show him that we are all interested in his work, that we are all one and the same body, that his errors harm us all, and that we are watchful, as friends and comrades, to help him overcome his weaknesses and contribute increasingly in order that the Party should be increasingly better.

Develop the principle of criticism at all Party meetings, in all committees and within the armed forces. In the guerrilla force or in the army, after every operation against the enemy, we must assess the results of that action and the behaviour of every combatant. Derive all the lessons from this action in order to make new and better actions. In education, in production, in commercial activity, in care – in all branches of our life and our struggle – we must be capable of criticizing and of accepting criticism.

But criticism (proof of the willingness of others to help us or of our willingness to help others) must be complemented by self-criticism (proof of our own willingness to help ourselves to improve our thought and our action).

Develop in all militants, responsible workers and combatants the spirit of self-criticism: the ability of each person to make a specific analysis of his own work, to distinguish in it what is good from what is bad, to acknowledge his own errors and to discover the causes and the effects of these errors. To make self-criticism is not merely to say 'Yes, I recognize my fault, my error and I ask forgiveness', while remaining ready soon to commit new faults, new errors. It is not pretending to be repentant of the evil one has done, while remaining convinced deep down that it is the others who do not understand. Still less is making self-criticism to make a *ceremony* so as to go on later with a clear conscience and carry on committing errors. To criticize oneself is not to pay a *response* or an *indulgence* nor to offer *penance*. Self-criticism is an act of frankness, courage, comradeship and awareness of our responsibilies, a proof of our will to accomplish and to accomplish properly, a demonstration of our determination to improve constantly and to make a better contribution to the progress of our Party. Honest self-criticism does not necessarily demand absolution: it is a pledge that we make with our conscience not to commit further errors; it is to accept our responsibilities before others and to mobilize all our capabilities to do more and better. To criticize oneself is to reconstruct oneself within oneself in order to serve better.

2. *Apply progressively at all levels of the Party leadership the principle of collective leadership.* Do everything possible in order that the leadership bodies of the Party may operate genuinely, not on the basis of one, two or three persons, but of all their members, men and women.

Collective leadership means leadership, an order or command made by a group of persons and not by one person alone or by some persons in the group. To lead collectively, in a group, is to study questions jointly, to find their best solution, and to take decisions jointly, it is to benefit from the experience and intelligence of each and all so as to lead, order and command better. In collective leadership, each person in the leadership must have his own clearly defined duties and is responsible for the carrying out of decisions taken by the group in regard to his duties. To lead collectively is to give to each leader the opportunity of thinking and acting, to demand that he takes the responsibilities within his competence, that he has initiative, that he demonstrates his creative capacity with determination and freedom, and that he correctly serves the teamwork, which is the product of the efforts and the contributions made by all. To lead collectively is to co-ordinate the thought and action of those who form the group, to derive the greatest return in the accomplishment of the group's tasks, within the limits of their competence and in the framework of the activities and the interests of the organization. But to lead collectively is not and cannot be, as some suppose, to give to all and everyone the right of uncontrolled views and initiatives, to create anarchy (lack of government), disorder, contradiction between leaders, empty arguments, a passion for meetings without results. Still less is it to give vent to incompetence, ignorance, intellectual foolhardiness, only so as to pretend that everyone gives orders. Although it is true that two heads are better than one, we must be able to distinguish between the heads, and each head must know exactly what it has to do. In the framework of collective leadership, we must respect the opinion of more experienced comrades who for their part must help the others with less experience to learn and to improve their work. In the framework of collective leadership there is always one or other comrade who has a higher standing as Party Leader and who for this reason has more individual responsibility, even if the responsibility for the group's tasks falls on all the members of the group. We must allow prestige to these comrades, help them to have constantly higher standing, but not allow them to monopolize (take over) the work and responsibility of the group. We must, on the other hand, struggle against the spirit of slackness, and uninterest, the fear of responsibilities, the tendency to agree with everything, to obey blindly without thinking.

Combat the spirit of the *'big man'*, the traditional chief, *boss* or *foreman* among responsible workers. But combat also the spirit of *vassal, subject* in the chief's service, the *blue-eyed worker,* the *servant* or the houseboy between responsible workers and militants. In the framework of collective leadership, the higher bodies of the Party must demand from those below them the strict carrying out of their duty on the basis of willing and constructive co-operation. The less elevated bodies must demand from the more elevated that they provide specific tasks to accomplish, clear watchwords and take decisions on questions within their competence.

Combat the spirit of the group and of sects, closed circles, an obsession with secrecy among some persons, personal questions and the ambition to give orders.

Collective leadership must strengthen the leadership capability of the Party and create specific circumstances to make full use of members of the Party.

3. Develop, respect and ensure respect for the correct application of democratic centralism in the practice of decisions and the carrying out of Party watchwords. Specifically limit the duties of each leadership body and the bodies at the base, thoroughly study each question or each new initiative, take objective decisions and give clear watchwords for every task and the practical achievement of Party watchwords.

Democratic centralism means that the power to make decisions, to formulate watchwords, to define tasks – to lead – is concentrated in central bodies or entities, with clearly defined duties, but that these decisions, watchwords, etc., must be arrived at democratically, on the basis of interests and opinion of representatives of the masses, on the basis of respect for the opinion and interests of the majority. It means that each decision concerning a new question must be taken after a full and free discussion within the bodies affected by it or from the base to the top, if the matter is one which affects the whole life of the Party. After this discussion and in accordance with what emerges from it, the central bodies take a decision which must immediately be carried out at all levels concerned, and without further discussion.

Centralism because the power, the capability to decide and to lead, is concentrated in special bodies and no other body or individual can exercise this power. *Democratic* because the exercise of power by these bodies does not depend merely on the will of those who give orders, but is based on the interests and on the opinions expressed by the majority. In order constantly to improve the practice of democratic centralism we must pay attention to the aspirations and opinions of the mass of the people with regard to every important question of our life and our struggle. We must bring into operation all the bodies at the base of the Party and all the leadership bodies. We must develop criticism and self-criticism and allow constant prestige to the responsible workers and leaders who fulfil their duty. Democratic centralism is a school of discipline, of respect for the views of others, of democracy and the ability to put into practice the decisions taken.

4. *Practice revolutionary democracy in all aspects of Party life.* Every responsible worker must bravely assume his responsibilities, must demand from others respect for his activity and must respect the activity of others. Do not hide anything from the mass of the people, do not lie, fight against lies, do not disguise the difficulties, errors and failures, do not believe in easy victories, nor in appearances.

Revolutionary democracy demands that we should combat opportunism, tolerance towards errors, unfounded excuses, friendships and comradeship on the basis of interests opposed to those of the Party and the people, the obsession that one or other responsible worker is irreplaceable in his post. Practice and defend the truth and always the truth in front of militants, responsible workers, the people, whatever the difficulties knowledge of the truth might cause. Revolutionary democracy demands that the militant should not be afraid of the responsible worker, that the responsible worker should have no dread of the militant, nor fear of the mass of the people. It demands that the responsible worker live in the midst of the people, in front of the people and behind the people, that he work for the Party serving the people.

In the framework of revolutionary democracy, power comes from the people, from the majority, and no one should be afraid of losing power. The leader must be the faithful interpreter of the will and the aspirations of the revolutionary majority and not the lord of power, the absolute master who uses the Party and does not serve the Party. In the framework of revolutionary democracy, we must avoid demagogy, promises we cannot keep, exploitation of the people's feelings and the ambitions of opportunists. We must act in accordance with realities, to give everyone the possibility to progress, to verify through his own action and that of others that the Party is the achievement of us all and that we all belong to the Party, which is the instrument our people created for the winning of their freedom and for the construction of their progress. In the framework of revolutionary democracy and in the specific circumstances of our struggle, we must constantly increase the strength of the people, advance bravely for the conquest of power by the people, for the radical transformation (at the base) of the life of our people, for a stage in which the weapons and means of defence of our revolution will be entirely in the hands of the people.. Do not be afraid of the people and persuade the people to take part in all the decisions which concern them – this is the basic condition of revolutionary democracy, which little by little we must achieve in accordance with the development of our struggle and our life.

Revolutionary democracy demands that there should be at the head of our Party and our people the best descendants of our land. Step by step we have to purge the unworthy elements from our Party, the opportunists, the demagogues (deceivers of the people), the dishonest, those who fail in their duty. So as to clear the way increasingly for those who understand and live in its entirety the life of our Party, to those who really want to serve the Party and the people, to those who carry out and increasingly want to carry out and better their duties as militants, responsible workers and revolutionaries. The correct application of the principles of criticism and self-criticism, of collective leadership, of democratic centralism and of revolutionary democracy is the most effective way for us to gain one of the most important victories, if not the most important, of our life and our struggle, namely: *to act so that our Party belongs more and more to those who are able to make it constantly better; to make of our Party an effective instrument for the construction of freedom, peace, progress and happiness for our people in Guiné and Cape Verde.*

33. The options of CONCP[1]

Like all the peoples in the world, we want to live and work in peace, we want to build the progress of our people. Like all the peoples of the world, we have the right to rebel against foreign domination. Like all the peoples in the world, we have today a legal basis for rebellion, to claim our rights, we have the United Nations Charter. And if the United Nations Charter is not enough, if the United Nations itself is not enough, our peoples are enough with the daily sacrifices they make to expel Portuguese colonialism from the soil of our country for ever.

Our direct enemy

Who is this enemy who dominates us, who obstinately dominates us, in contempt of all laws, legality and international ethics of our times? This enemy is not the Portuguese people, not even Portugal itself: for us, fighters for the freedom of the Portuguese colonies, this enemy is Portuguese colonialism represented by the colonial Fascist Government of Portugal. But obviously a government is also to some extent the result of the historical, geographical and economic conditions of the country that it governs. Portugal is an economically backward country, a country where about fifty per cent of the population is illiterate, a country which in all the statistical tables of Europe always appears in the bottom place. This is not the fault of the Portuguese people, who at a certain moment in history were able to show their valour, their courage, their capability, and who even today possess capable sons, just sons, sons who also want to regain freedom and happiness for their people.

Portugal is a country in no position at all to dominate any other country. Portugal came to us proclaiming that it came in the service of God and in the service of civilization. Today we answer it with weapons in hands: whatever God is with the Portuguese colonialists, whatever civilization the Portuguese colonialists represent, we are going to destroy them because we *shall destroy* any kind of foreign domination over us.

[1]Extract from the speech delivered at the plenary session on 5 October 1965, at the 2nd Conference of the Nationalist Organizations of the Portuguese Colonies, In *La Conférence de Dar-es-Salaam,* published by CONCP (Algiers, August 1967), the part 'Two types of encirclement in war', at the request of the author, did not appear in the published version.

I shall not go into detail about the characteristics of Portuguese colonialism. The main characteristic of present-day Portuguese colonialism is a very simple fact: Portuguese colonialism or, if you prefer, the Portuguese economic infrastructure, cannot afford the luxury of practising neocolonialism.

It is from this starting point that we can understand the whole attitude, all the obstinacy of Portuguese colonialism towards our peoples. If Portugal were economically advanced, if Portugal could be classified as a developed country, we should surely not be at war with Portugal today.

But many folk criticize Salazar, speak ill of Salazar. He is a man like any other. He has many failings, he is a Fascist, we hate him, but we are not struggling against Salazar, we are struggling against the Portuguese colonial system. We do not nurture the dream that when Salazar disappears, Portuguese colonialism will disappear. Hence on the basis of this fundamental characteristic – the incapacity of Portugal to practise neocolonialism – the Portuguese Government has always refused any appeal from us for understanding, has been obstinate in launching a new colonial war against Africa, against mankind, against us in so-called Portuguese Guiné, against Angola and Mozambique, and is ready to do the same in other colonies. We, as peaceful peoples but proud of our love of freedom, proud of our attachment to the ideal of progress in this twentieth century, took up arms with determination and unshakably; we took up arms to defend our rights, given that there was no law in the world which could do it for us. I want merely to draw your attention to the fact that we are peaceful peoples, we do not love war, but war, armed struggle for national liberation, was the only way out that Portuguese colonialism left us for the regaining of our dignity as an African people, our human dignity. And we want to say that we must in a way thank the Portuguese Government. Yes, this entails many sacrifices, but also entails many advantages for our people. We are not the proponents of war and, I repeat, we do not love war, but we see today, and the example is general, that the armed struggle for national liberation creates practical conditions for a future free of certain obstacles, that it can contribute to the growing development of political awareness of men, women and even children. Since, given that Portugal has imposed a war on us to which we respond with our armed national liberation struggle, we must be able to draw all the advantages from this circumstance, this obligation.

The deep meaning of our struggle

But our armed national liberation struggle has a deep significance both for Africa and for the world. We are in the process of proving, of providing the evidence, that peoples like ours, economically backward, living sometimes almost naked in the bush, not knowing how to read or write, not having even an elementary knowledge of modern technology, are able by means of their sacrifices and their efforts, to fight an enemy not only more advanced from the technical point of view but also supported by the powerful forces of imperialists in the world. Moreover, before the world and before Africa, we ask: were the Portuguese right when they asserted that we were uncivilized peoples, peoples without culture?

We ask: what is the most striking manifestation of civilization and culture if not that shown by a people who take up arms to defend their country, to defend their right to life, progress, work and happiness?

We, the national liberation movements belonging to CONCP, must be aware that our armed struggle is only one aspect of the general struggle of oppressed peoples against imperialism, of man's struggle for dignity, freedom and progress. We must be able to integrate our struggle within this framework. We must regard ourselves as soldiers, often anonymous, but soldiers of mankind in this vast front of struggle that Africa is in our times. We, in CONCP, are fighting in Africa because Africa is our birthplace, but we shall all of us be ready to go anywhere at all to fight for the dignity of man, for the progress of man, for the happiness of man.

It is precisely in this framework that we must have the courage, both during this conference and anywhere else, to proclaim and to proclaim out loud our fundamental options, our options in favour of mankind. Moreover, we must be able to define our position clearly in relation to our people, in relation to Africa, in relation to the world. We are going to do it, perhaps we are going to repeat ourselves in our conference, but I can tell you this: we, in CONCP, are committed to our peoples, but we are not struggling simply to hoist a flag in our country and to have a national anthem. We, in CONCP, seek that in our countries, which have been martyred for centuries, humiliated and insulted, the insult may no longer rule, that our peoples should never again be exploited, not only by the imperialists, not only by the Europeans, not only by persons with white skin, because we do not confuse exploitation or exploiters with the colour of men's skins; we do not want any more exploitation among us, not even by blacks.

We are struggling to build in our countries, in Angola, in Mozambique, in Guiné, in the Cape Verde Islands and in S. Tomé, a life of happiness, a life where every man will have the respect of all men, where discipline will not be imposed, where no one will be without work, where salaries will be just, where everyone will have the right to everything that man has built, has created for the happiness of men. It is for this that we are struggling. If we do not reach that point, we shall have failed in our duties, in the purpose of our struggle.

We want to say to you that, in relation to Africa, we in CONCP are confident of the destiny of Africa. We have in Africa itself examples to follow and we have likewise in Africa examples we must not follow. Africa is therefore rich in examples today and if we, tomorrow, betray the interests of our peoples it will not be because we did not know, it will be because we wanted to betray and we shall not therefore have any excuse.

In Africa, we are for the total liberation of the African continent from the colonial yoke, since we know that colonialism is an instrument of imperialism. We therefore want to see swept right away from the soil of Africa all the manifestations of imperialism, we are in CONCP fiercely against neocolonialism, no matter what form it takes. Our struggle is not only struggle against Portuguese colonialism; we want in the framework of our struggle to contribute in the most effective way to driving foreign domination from our continent for ever.

African unity

We are, in Africa, for African unity in favour of African peoples. We regard unity as a means and not an end. Unity can strengthen, can speed up the reaching of the ends, but we must not betray the end. It is for this very reason that we are not in such a rush to claim African unity. We know that it will come step by step, as a result of the fruitful efforts of the African peoples. It will come in the service of Africa, in the service of mankind. We are convinced, absolutely convinced, in CONCP, that the realization as a whole of the assets of our continent, of the human, moral and cultural capabilities of our continent, will contribute to creating a rich human space, considerably rich, which in turn will contribute to further enriching mankind. But we do not want the dream of this end to betray in its accomplishment the interests of each African people. We, in Guiné and Cape Verde for example, openly declare in our Party programme that we are ready to unite with any African people, with only one condition: that the conquests, the gains of our people in the national liberation struggle, the economic and social gains, the gains of justice that we pursue and are already achieving little by little, that none of this should be compromised by unities with other peoples. This is our only condition for unity.

We are, in Africa, for an African policy which seeks to defend in the first place the interests of African peoples, of each African country, but also for a policy which does not at any time forget the interests of the world, of all mankind. We are for a policy of peace in Africa and of fraternal co-operation with all the peoples of the world.

On the international level, we in CONCP practise a policy of non-alignment. It is the policy which most accords with the interests of our peoples in the currrent phase of our history. We are convinced of that. But for us, non-alignment does not mean turning one's back on fundamental questions of mankind, of justice. Non-alignment for us means that we do not commit ourselves to blocks, we are not aligned with the decisions of others. We reserve the right to decide for ourselves and if by chance our options and our decisions coincide with those of others, that is not our fault.

International solidarity

We are for the policy of non-alignment, but we regard ourselves as deeply committed to our people and committed to every just cause in the world. We see ourselves as forming part of a vast front of struggle for the good of mankind. You understand that we are struggling in the first place for our peoples. That is our task on this front of struggle. This involves the whole question of solidarity. We, in CONCP, are in total solidarity with all just causes. That is why for us, in FRELIMO, in MPLA, in PAIGC, in CLSTP, in whatever mass organization is affiliated to CONCP, our hearts beat in harmony with the hearts of our brothers in Vietnam, who give a singular example by facing the most shameful and unjustifiable aggression by the United States imperialists against the peaceful people of Vietnam. Our hearts beat likewise with those of our brothers in Congo who, in the bush of this vast and rich African country, are trying to solve their own problems in the face of the aggression of imperialists and the manoeuvres of imperialists through their lackeys. That is why we, in CONCP, shout out loud and strong that we are against Tshombe, against all the Tshombes of Africa. Our hearts beat likewise with our brothers in Cuba who have also shown that a people, even when surrounded by the sea, are capable of defending their fundamental interests, with weapons in hand, and victoriously, and of deciding their destiny for themselves. We are with the blacks of the United States of America, we are with them in the streets of Los Angeles, and when they are deprived of all possibility of life, we suffer with them.

We are with the refugees, the martyred refugees of Palestine, who were humiliated, driven from their country by the manoeuvres of imperialism. We are at the side of the refugees from Palestine and we support with all our hearts' strength all that the children of Palestine are doing to free their country and we support with all our might the Arab countries and the African countries in general in helping the Palestinian people to recover their dignity, their independence, their right to live. We are likewise with the people of South Arabia, of so-called 'French' Somalia (the Somali Coast), of so-called 'Spanish' Guinea, and we are very seriously and very sorrowfully with our brothers in South Africa who face the most savage racial discrimination. We are absolutely certain that development of the struggle in the Portuguese colonies and the victory we are in the process of winning every day over Portuguese colonialism is an effective contribution to the elimination of the shameful, vile regime of racial discrimination, of apartheid from South Africa. And we are also certain that peoples, like those of Angola and Mozambique, and ourselves in Guiné and Cape Verde, far from South Africa, will tomorrow – a tomorrow that we hope is not far off – be able to play a very important role in the final elimination of the last bastion of colonialism, imperialism and racism in Africa that is to be found in South Africa.

We are in solidarity with all just causes in the world, but we are also strengthened by the solidarity of others. We have practical aid from many sources, from many friends, from many brothers. I should simply like to say to you that we, in CONCP, have a basic principle which is to count in the first place on our own efforts, our own sacrifices. But in the specific framework of Portuguese colonialism, and in the current phase of the history of mankind, we are also aware that our struggle is not only ours. It is that of the whole of Africa, it is that of the whole of progressive mankind. That is why we in CONCP, in the light of the particular difficulties of our struggle and in the light of the context of current history, have been aware of the need for practical help on the part of all the progressive forces in the world and on the part of Africa for our struggle. We accept aid of all kinds, no matter where it comes from, but we never ask anybody for the aid we need. We merely wait for the aid that each one can bring to our struggle. Those are our *ethics* for aid.

We want to say to you that it is our duty to state here loud and clear that we have secure allies in the socialist countries. We all know that the African peoples are our brothers. Our struggle is theirs. Every drop of blood that falls from us falls equally from the body and heart of our African brothers, these African peoples. But we also know that since the socialist revolution and after the events of the Second World War, the face of the world has been definitively changed. A socialist camp has arisen in the world. This has completely changed the relations of power, and this socialist camp today shows itself very aware of its international duties, historic not moral duties, since the peoples of the socialist countries have never exploited the colonial peoples. They show themselves aware of their duty and that is why I have the honour here to tell you openly that we receive substantial, effective aid from these countries, which comes to reinforce the aid we receive from our African brothers. If there are persons who do not like to hear this, let them come as well to aid us in our struggle. But they can be certain that we are proud of our sovereignty.

We shall maintain our position: we receive aid from all. And we shall recieve the aid of the socialist countries with pride because today they show the path that can serve man, the path of justice. In this hall, we have representatives of the socialist countries who have come here as friends. I shall not lose this opportunity of saying to the representatives of the Soviet Union and of China, to the representatives of Yugoslavia and of the German Democratic Republic who are here as representatives of socialist countries, that they should kindly transmit to the working peoples whom they represent the gratitude we express for the practical aid they bring to our struggle.

NATO

And what are they doing, those who do not like to hear us saying that the socialist countries help us? They help Portugal, the Fascist colonial Government of Salazar. Today it is no secret to anyone that Portugal, the Portuguese Government, if it did not have, if it could not count on, the aid its NATO allies bring, would not be able to wage a struggle against us. But we must state clearly what NATO means. Yes, we know. NATO is a military block which defends the interests of the West, western civilization, etc. That is not what we want to talk about. NATO is specific countries, governments, specific states. NATO is the United States of America. We have at home captured weapons from the United States of America. NATO is the Federal German Republic. We have many Mauser rifles taken from Portuguese soliders. NATO, for the time being at least, is France. At home there are Alouette helicopters. But we have begun to bring down the Alouettes. NATO is, too, to a certain extent, the government of that heroic people who were able to give so many examples of love of freedom: the Italian people. Yes, we have captured from the Portuguese machine guns and grenades manufactured in Italian factories. But it is for us very agreeable, very encouraging to hear a friend from Italy, a brother from Italy, speak to us such beautiful words, so feeling and sincere, as those we heard yesterday from our brother who spoke to us on behalf of Italy. I should like to say to our brother who spoke here yesterday that we do not confuse the Italian people with the Italian state which forms part of NATO.[1]

Portugal has still further allies: there is South Africa, there is Mr Smith of Southern Rhodesia, there is the Government of Franco, there are other obscure allies who hide their face because of the shame that this represents. But all this aid that the Salazar Government receives to kill our populations, to burn our villages in Angola, in Mozambique, in Guiné, in Cape Verde, in São Tomé, to massacre our populations, has not been able to halt our national liberation struggle. On the contrary, our forces are more powerful each day. Why? Because for us, our force is the force of justice, the force of progress, the force of history; and justice, progress, history are the attibute of the people. Because our basic strengths are our peoples. They are our peoples who support our organizations, they are our peoples who sacrifice themselves every day to supply all the needs of the struggle, all the basic needs of our struggle. They are our peoples who ensure the future and the certainty of our victory.

The prospects for our struggle

In the perspective of our struggle, this conference comes very opportunely.

[1]The reference is to Giovanni Serbandini ('Bini'), an observer at the Conference on behalf of the Italian Anti-colonialist Committee.

You understand the interest of our conference. We must strengthen our unity, not only within each country but also between us, the peoples of the Portuguese colonies. The CONCP has a very special meaning for us. We have the same colonial past, we have all learned to speak and write Portuguese, but we have an even greater, perhaps even more historic, strength: it is the fact that we began the struggle together. It is the struggle that binds the comrades, the companions for the present and the future. The CONCP is for us a fundamental strength of the struggle. The CONCP is in the heart of every combatant in our country, in Angola, in Mozambique. The CONCP must also represent, we are proud to say, an example for the peoples of Africa. For in this glorious struggle against imperialism and colonialism in Africa, we are the first colonies to have joined together, to discuss together, to plan together, to study together the problems concerning the development of their struggle. This cannot fail to be a very interesting contribution to the history of Africa and to the history of our peoples.

We shall not allow what we have already done in the framework of CONCP to be lost and we assure you here that we are determined to leave this conference with practical results. We are determined to go out of here and strengthen our struggle in a co-ordinated way – hence, to speed up significantly the total collapse, the total defeat of Portuguese colonialism in our countries.

We find ourselves today in a new phase of our struggle. There is an armed national liberation struggle on three fronts. This entails greater responsibilities whether for ourselves, or for each of our parties, or for the CONCP as a whole. But this also entails greater responsibilities for our friends and for our brothers. Africa must take care of the question.

Africa helps us, yes. There are some African countries that help us as much as they can, directly, bilaterally. But in our opinion, Africa can help us much more, if Africa comes to understand precisely the value and the importance of our struggle against Portuguese colonialism: we hope therefore that on the basis of the experience of the two years since Addis Ababa, the next summit conference of African heads of state will be able to take practical steps to strengthen effectively the aid from Africa to the combatants of Guiné, Cape Verde, São Tomé, Mozambique and Angola. Moreover, our friends throughout the world, and particularly our friends from the socialist countries, are certainly aware that the development of our struggle entails the development of their fraternal aid. We are convinced that every day both the forces of the socialist countries and the progressive forces of the West will be able to develop their aid, the political, moral and material support for our struggle, in accordance with the latter's development.

Two types of encirclement in war
Before closing, I should like to put to you a problem we have discussed in our Party. It is perhaps a dream. You all know that the war of imperialism

against the colonial peoples is basically characterized by two types of encirclement. I am not saying anything new, but recalling a well-tried theory. On the one hand the imperialist enemy who makes war from his country encircles our people, and in each position he occupies among us encircles our forces. But on the other hand, in our own country, our people and our armed forces encircle every position occupied by the enemy. However, in this mutual encirclement, the imperialists maintain (or were maintaining) one advantage: that of not being encircled in the exterior, while we are simultaneously encircled from the exterior and the interior.

Now, with the transformations that have occurred in life, in the history of our times, it so happens that colonialists, like the Portuguese colonialists, for example, are increasingly isolated in the world. The whole of Africa stands against the Portuguese colonialists. There is a whole continent which begins to encircle Portugal; in Portugal itself the democratic and progressive forces are beginning to encircle the reactionary and colonialist forces of their country. Then the progressive forces of Western Europe express their view, their opposition to Portuguese colonialists. This is also a kind of encirclement. And in the world, the entire socialist camp is fiercely opposed to Portuguese colonialism.

So the initial situation has changed: the Portuguese colonialists are encircled, whether by our forces in our country, or in the exterior. Then we ask: what is the fundamental contradiction of colonial war? From the political point of view, it is what sets the interests of the colonial peoples against those of imperialism. But this contradiction gives birth to another in the war. In our view, on the military level, the essential contradiction lies in the fact that our people, in Guiné, in Angola, in Mozambique, who suffer not only the losses in human lives but also specific material losses, have the sense of war – every moment, every day, sometimes every hour even. They sense the war at home, while the colonialist aggressor does not sense the war in his own country. This colonial war that Portugal has waged in Angola since 4 February 1961, then in Guiné and in Mozambique, is not sensed by the Portuguese people.

Naturally, we are not happy that the people should sense the war; but we do hope very much to resolve the contradictions so as to put an end to this war. And we think this: will the time not soon come to solve this contradiction in the case of Portuguese colonialists? If Portuguese colonialism, with the support of its allies, is obstinately destroying our countries, yes, we are certainly going to overcome Portuguese colonialism. At home, we have already overcome it. Ask the wounded Portuguese soldiers who are in the Lisbon hospital, for example, read the newspapers and you will see: the Portuguese soliders say that against us the war is lost; even the Portuguese Government, through the voice of its Minister for Foreign Affairs to a personality who was trying to persuade him to negotiate with certain forces in Guiné, declared that they had lost in Guiné and that if they did not flee that country it was because they wanted to remain in Angola and Mozambique; if they were to give up Guiné, they would immediately be lost in Angola and Mozambique too.

So the problem is not of winning the war against the Portuguese colonialists but of speeding up the end of this war.

And we wonder if, in the framework of CONCP, we might not be in a position to solve the contradiction about which I was speaking. The Portuguese Government is aided by its allies; possesses at home a very well established infrastructure, sheltered from the attacks of our forces, which supplies and maintains the war against us. Could the CONCP manage tomorrow, in the framework of co-ordination of our political and military action, to proceed in such a way that the Portuguese Government should sense the war at home? This is the question we are raising for our conference. We are convinced that this is not a dream; it is a feasible act; it must be studied to see if it must be solved and how to solve it. If our allies operate as those of Portugal operate, we believe that the basic strengths of our countries will be sufficient, even with our weak resources, to destroy the infrastructure that feeds and maintains the war by the Portuguese Government against our peoples.

I declare to you here on behalf of our Party, the PAIGC, that we shall press for this question to be studied within CONCP. I am sure that we have available logistical means in the African countries geographically closest to Portugal to be able in a modern way to reach the bases of the war that Portugal wages against us. I swear to you here that if we reach an agreement within CONCP, and if the Portuguese Government persists in seeking to dominate our people and wreak destruction on them, then I sear to you that we shall do everything possible within CONCP to gather the basic strengths of our peoples, to add those of the African peoples and those of the progressive peoples of the word, of the socialist peoples, in all domains where their aid is possible, to make war on Portugal: *we shall transform the colonial war into war pure and simple.*

I shall end by simply saying this: at home, in so-called Portuguese Guiné and in Cape Verde Islands, the colonialist troops are pulling further back each day. Today, if we want to fight the colonial troops, we have to fight them on their ground, in the barracks. But we must go there because an end must be put to Portuguese colonialism among us. We are sure that it will soon be the same in Mozambique. And this is already beginning to happen in certain zones. It will be the same in Angola. And this is already beginning to happen in Cabinda. The Portuguese colonialists are beginning to be afraid of us. They sense now that they are lost, but I assure you that if they were present here – it is a pity they do not have agents here – if they were here seeing us, hearing all the delegations speak, seeing this audience, seeing the fraternal welcome accorded to us by the Government of Tanzania, the fear of the Portuguese colonialists would be even greater. But let us go forward, with weapons in hand, wherever a Portuguese colonialist is to be found. Let us go forward, let us destroy him, and let us liberate our countries quickly from the retrograde forces of Portuguese colonialism. But let us prepare ourselves every day too with vigilance not to allow a new form of colonialism to be established among us, not to allow any form of imperialism among us, not to allow neocolonialism, already a cancerous growth in some regions of the world and of Africa, not to allow that cancer to reach our own country.

34. The people of Guiné and Cape Verde before the UN[1]

Allow me, before reading my speech, to take this opportunity to offer you our respectful greetings and to say how honoured we feel to be here before the Fourth Committee to co-operate with it in the framework of the struggle for decolonization. And at the same time, allow me, on behalf of our people and through the distinguished representatives of member countries here, to offer the fraternal and warm greetings of our African nation and our most sincere wishes for the continued success of the work of this United Nations Committee in the service of the liberation of peoples and in the service, therefore, of peace and genuine progress for the world.

For the second time, we have the signal honour to address the Fourth Committee of the United Nations General Assembly. We do so on behalf of our African people, in Guiné and Cape Verde, for whom our national Party, the PAIGC, is the sole, legitimate and genuine representative. We do so with joy and in full awareness of the fact that you are our companions in struggle. This difficult but inspiring struggle for the liberation of peoples and of man from every kind of oppression, for the advent of a better mankind in a world of peace, security and progress.

Without forgetting the often remarkable role of Utopia in the furthering of human progress, we are, however, quite realistic. In fact we know that there are among you some representatives who, perhaps in spite of themselves, are bound to adopt an obstructive, if not negative, attitude when dealing with questions concerning our own national liberation struggle.

[1]Speech to the Fourth Committee of the United Nations General Assembly (27th Session), October 1972.

We venture to say 'in spite of themselves' since, over and above compelling reasons of state, it is difficult for us to believe that there can be responsible men who deep inside themselves are opposed to the legitimate aspirations of our African people to dignity, freedom, national independence and progress. So as the poet would say, in the era in which we live to show solidarity with those who are suffering and struggling for their liberation 'it is no longer necessary to be courageous, it is enough to be honest'.

The first time we addressed this Committee was on 12 December 1962. Ten years is certainly quite a long and sometimes decisive period in the life of a human being, but it is very little in the framework of the destiny of existence or of the history of a people. However, sweeping, radical and irreversible changes have occurred in the life of our people. Unfortunately it is impossible for us to rely on your memory to compare the sitution of yesterday with that of today, because most if not all the representatives on this Committee are no longer the same. With your permission, we shall briefly recall what was happening then.

It was a crucial juncture in the history of our struggle. The massacre of Pidjiguiti, perpetrated by the Portuguese colonialists on 3 August 1959, against the Bissau dockers and the river transport boat workers on strike, at the cost of fifty killed and more than one hundred strikers wounded, had been a painful lesson for our people. We learned that against the Portuguese colonialists there was no question of choosing between peaceful struggle and armed struggle. They had weapons and had decided to massacre us.

We decided then, at a clandestine meeting of the leadership of our Party, held in Bissau on 19 September 1959, to suspend all the peaceful representations in the cities and to prepare ourselves for armed struggle. For this, it was necessary to have a solid political base in the countryside and, after three years of active and intensive mobilization and organization of the rural populations, we had managed to create such a base, despite the increasing vigilance of the colonial authorities. Feeling the breath of the warning breezes that an English leader called 'wind of change', the Portuguese colonialists had launched a vast campaign of police and military repression against the nationalist forces. In June 1962, more than 2000 patriots suspected of nationalism had been arrested throughout the country. Several villages were burned and their inhabitants massacred. Dozens of our countrymen were burned alive or drowned in the rivers. In the prisons, torture had claimed dozens of victims. The dialectic of repression had stiffened the determination of our people for struggle. Some skirmishes had already broken out between armed patriots and the forces of colonialist repression.

Faced with that situation, we believed then that only an appropriate and effective intervention by the UN in support of the inalienable rights of our people could induce the Government of Portugal to respect the international ethics and legality of our times.

In the light of subsequent events, some might think that we were ingenuous then. We regarded it as our duty and right to have recourse to the international organization. It was in this context that we deemed it essential to approach the Fourth Committee. Our message was certainly the appeal of a people confronted with a particularly difficult situation, but resolved to pay the necessary price to regain their dignity and freedom. Our message was likewise a proof of confidence in the strength of the principles and in the capacity for action of the United Nations Organization.

What did we say then before the Fourth Committee?

First, we clearly defined the reasons for and the purposes of our presence before the UN. 'We are here', we said, 'as representatives of the African people of 'Portuguese' Guiné and the Islands of Cape Verde. Our people place their entire trust in our Party, the PAIGC, the organization which has mobilized and organized our national liberation struggle for the difficult task of eliminating colonialism from our midst. Our people are, as you know, gagged by the total absence of fundamental freedoms and by the Portuguese colonial repression. They consider as their legitimate representatives with the right and duty to speak on their behalf those who, in the course of the last fifteen years of the history of Africa, have defended their interests in every possible way.'

We said further: 'We are not here to make propaganda, nor to extract resolutions condemning Portuguese colonialism. We are here to work with you in order to arrive at a constructive solution to a problem which is as much ours as that of the UN itself: the urgent liberation of our people from the colonial yoke.

'We did not come here,' we went on to say, 'to attack Portuguese colonialism with words. We have often attacked and listened to attacks and condemnation of Portuguese colonialism, whose characteristics, subterfuges, methods and acts are now only too well known to the UN and to world opinion.

'We came here, on the basis of the specific situation in our country and with the backing of international laws, in order to seek with you, including the Portuguese delegation itself, the shortest and most effective path for the urgent elimination of Portuguese colonialism from Guiné and Cape Verde.'

And we added: 'For us, for our people and for our Party, the time has come to put an end to indecisions and promises, to adopt definitive action. We have already made too many sacrifices, but we are determined to make more to recover our freedom and human dignity, whatever the path to be followed.

'. . . It is not by chance that we have only now considered our presence here essential. For action, above all in the framework of the problems which brought us to this body, resources are necessary: legal, human and material resources. It so happens that in the course of recent years, these resources have been gradually accumulating, both for the UN and for our struggling people. We are convinced that it is time to act and that the United Nations and our people can really act.

'To do this, we think that a close and effective collaboration is essential. We have the duty and the right to help the UN to help us win our freedom and national independence. Our help lies mainly in the specific information on the situation in our country, in the clear definition of our position, in the presentation of specific proposals for the solution of our case.'

After describing the prevailing situation in the country, notably regarding the intensified police and military repression, the fallacious nature of the supposed 'reforms' adopted by the Government of Portugal in Spetember, 1961, and the prospects for development of our struggle, we then analysed the question of legality or illegality of this struggle. I will refrain from recalling some passages of this analysis, and resume at the following point: 'The resolution on decolonization did not only commit Portugal and our people to eliminate colonial domination from our midst. It committed the UN itself to do everything possible to end colonial domination wherever it still exists, with a view to facilitating the accession of all colonized peoples to national independence.'

'We are convinced that the Portuguese Government cannot continue with impunity in the obstinate practice of an international crime. We are likewise convinced that the UN has at its disposal all the necessary means to devise and execute practical and effective measures both to ensure respect for the principles of the Charter and to impose international legality in our country and defend the interests of peace and civilization.'

We said further: 'We are not here to ask the UN to send troops to free our country from the Portuguese colonial yoke. Perhaps we could have done this, but we do not believe that this is necessary, as we are certain that we ourselves can liberate our country. We are invoking a right: that of obtaining the collaboration and practical aid on the part of the UN with a view to speeding up the liberation of our country from the colonial yoke, and thus reducing the human and material losses which a protracted struggle might entail.

'We are not only conscious', we said, 'of the legality of our struggle. We are today aware of the fact that by struggling by all possible means for liberation of our country, we are struggling in defence of international legality, for peace in the service of the progress of mankind.

'Our struggle has lost its strictly national character to become projected on the international level. In our country today in various ways is waged the struggle for progress against misery and suffering, for freedom against oppression. While it is true that the only victims of this battle are the children of our country, it is no less true that each of our comrades who succumbs to torture, or falls under the bullets of the Portuguese colonial machine-guns, is identified with the hopes and certainties we have in our hearts and minds, with all men who love peace and freedom and want to live a life of progress in the pursuit of happiness.'

We went on to declare: 'We are not struggling only for the achievement of our aspirations for freedom and national independence. We are struggling, and will struggle till victory, in order that the resolutions of the Charter of the United Nations should be respected. In the prisons, in the cities and in the countryside of our country, a battle is currently being fought between the UN, which demands the elimination of the system of colonial domination of peoples, and the armed forces of the Portuguese Government, which seeks to perpetuate this system in defiance of the legitimate rights of our people.'

And we asked before this Committee: 'Really, who are we? When among us a comrade succumbs to police torture, is murdered in prison, is burnt alive or falls to the machine-guns of the Portuguese troops, for what cause has he given his life?'

'He has given it certainly for the liberation of our people from the colonial yoke, but by this very token he has given his life for the cause of the UN. In struggling and dying for the liberation of our country, we are, in the current context of international legality, giving our life for the ideal which the UN itself defined in its Charter and in its resolutions, particularly in the resolution on decolonization.'

'For us, the only difference between an Indian solider, or an Italian pilot, or a Swedish official who is killed in the Congo and our comrade who is killed in Guiné or in Cape Verde lies in the fact that operating in our own country in the service of the same ideal, we are only anonymous combatants in the cause of the UN.'

We were convinced, we said, that the time had come to take stock of this situation and to make radical changes. It benefited only the enemies of the UN and, in our particular case, Portuguese colonialism. Having rejected the idea of begging for freedom, which was incompatible with the dignity and sacred right of our people to be free and independent, we then reaffirmed our steadfast determination, no matter what sacrifices were involved, to eliminate colonial domination from our country and to win for our people the opportunity to build in peace their progress and happiness.

In such a perspective and on the basis of that irrevocable decision, we then defined three possible ways for the evolution and solution of the conflict setting the Government of Portugal against our African people. These possibilities were the following:
1. A radical change in the position of the Portuguese Government
2. Immediate and specific action on the part of the UN
3. Struggle exclusively by our own means.

As proof of our confidence in the international organization and bearing in mind a certain influence that some of its members could exert on the Portuguese Government, we then took into consideration only the first two possibilities and presented the following specific proposals:

For the first alternative: immediate contact between the Portuguese delegation and ours. Consultation with the Portuguese Government, for an early date to be set for the opening of negotiations between its representatives and the legitimate representatives of Guiné and Cape Verde. Pending negotiations, a cessation of repressive acts on the part of the Portuguese colonial forces and of all actions on the part of the nationalists.

For the second alternative: aid from the UN. Acceptance of the principle that UN assistance would only really be effective if carried out simultaneously on the moral, political and material levels. We therefore proposed the immediate creation by the UN of a special committee for the self-determination and national independence of the territories under Portuguese administration. And we proposed likewise that this committee should start its work before the close of that current session. Finally we declared that we were ready to give the fullest co-operation to that committee and proposed that the latter should have the task of giving practical assistance to our people to free themselves urgently from the colonial yoke.

As our proposals were not favourably received, either on the part of the Portuguese Government or on the part of the UN, the patriotic forces in our country moved into generalized action against the colonialist forces in January 1963, in order to respond with our armed liberation struggle to the genocidal colonial war unleashed against our people by the Government of Portugal.

Almost ten years have passed, and we are once again before the Fourth Committee. But the situation is completely different both within our country and at the international level. This Committee and the UN are now better informed than ever about the situation prevailing in our country. In fact, in addition to regular information (reports, information bulletins, war communiqués and other documents we send to the UN), we have on various occasions during these ten years appeared before the Committee on Decolonization to describe the situation of our struggle and the prospects of its evolution.

Dozens of journalists, film-makers, men and women politicians, scientists, writers, artists, photographers and so on, of various nationalities, have visited our country at their initiative or at our invitation and they have provided unanimous and irrefutable testimony about our situation. Others, very few, have done this on the colonialists' side, at the invitation of the Portuguese authorities. And, with rare exceptions, their testimony did not at all please those authorities. Such, for example, is the case of the French television team who visited all the 'overseas provinces' but whose film was rejected by the Lisbon Government because of the part relating to our country. This is the film we were able to show before the Security Council in Addis Ababa. This is also the case of the group of representatives of the American people, led by Congressman Charles Diggs, whose report on their visit to our country merits careful study by this Committee and by anyone wishing to obtain well-founded information on the situation at home. But the UN currently has available information which is, in our view, even more valuable: the report of the Special Mission which at our invitation and duly authorized by the General Assembly visited the liberated areas of our country last April. It is not therefore because of pressing need for information that we are here.

Furthermore, the daily crimes committed by the Portuguese colonialists against our people are sufficiently well known to the UN and to world opinion. Living victims of Portuguese police and military repression have testified before UN bodies, notably before the Commission on Human Rights. Only last year, during the 26th session, two of our countrymen, one with third-degree napalm burns, the other with multilated ears and bearing obvious signs of torture, appeared before this Committee. Visitors to our country, including the members of the United Nations Special Mission, have been able to see on the spot the horrifying effects of the criminal acts of the Portuguese colonialists against the population and against their material goods, the fruit of our people's labour. But alas, the UN knows as well as we do that condemnations and resolutions, no matter what their moral and political value, will not compel the Government of Portugal to put an end to the crime against humanity that it commits in our country. So it is not to obtain new condemnations and more violent resolutions against the Portuguese colonialists that we are once again before this Committee.

Still less is it to ask you to launch an appeal to the allies of the Government of Portugal to cease granting it political support and material, military, economic and financial assistance – which is the primordial factor in the continuation of the Portuguese colonial war against Africa. This has been done on many occasions without any positive result. We must observe, not without regret, that we were right when, nearly ten years ago, we declared before this Committee that, in the face of the specific reality of the Portuguese economy and the interests of states allied to the Government of Portugal, the recommendation, and even the demand, for diplomatic, economic and military boycott would not be an effective means of helping our people. On the contrary, experience has shown that, in acting or being forced to act as real enemies of the liberation and progress of African peoples, the allies of the Portuguese Government, in particular some of the major powers in NATO, have not only strengthened their aid to the Portuguese colonialists but have also systematically refused, if not boycotted, any co-operation with the majority within the UN, seeking to define legally the political ways and other means which will induce the Government of Portugal to comply with the principles of the organization and the resolutions of the General Assembly.

It was not ten years ago but in quite recent years that the Portuguese Government received from its allies the most significant quantities of war material, jet aircraft, helicopters, gunboats, launches, etc. It was not in

1962, but this very year that the Portuguese Government received some five hundred million dollars in financial aid from one of its principal allies.

If states which call themselves champions of freedom and democracy, defenders of the 'free world' and the cause of self-determination and independence of peoples, thus persist in supporting and giving practical aid to the most retrograde colonialism on earth, it is because they have, at least in their view, good reasons for doing it. Perhaps we should try to understand them – even if these reasons are unavowed and unavowable. We must surely be sufficiently realists to stop dreaming and asking the impossible. For, as our African people would say, '*it is only in stories that you can cross the river on the back of the crocodile's friend*'.

We are here with you before the UN to try, as in the past, to obtain for our struggling people practical and effective aid on the part of the international organization. But, as we have said and as you know, the current situation is in every way different from that of 1962. The aid that we need is different too.

In fact, during ten years of armed struggle and at the cost of enormous efforts and sacrifices, we have liberated from Portuguese colonial domination about three-quarters of our national territory, where we effectively control two-thirds. This means specifically that in the greater part of our country, our people currently possess a solid political organization – that of our Party; a developing administrative structure, a judicial structure, a new economy free of any exploitation of the labour of our populations; various social and cultural services (health, hygiene, education) and other means of affirming their personality as well as their ability to take our destiny in hand and manage their own life.

We possess a military organization entirely composed of and led by sons of our people. Our national armed forces, whose task is systematically to attack the colonialist troops wherever they still are, with the purpose of completing the liberation of the country, and our local armed forces, who ensure the defence and security of the liberated areas, are today stronger than ever, tempered by an experience of nearly ten years of combat. The proof is that the colonialists are unable to recover any stretch of our liberated areas, that we cause them more and more losses, and that we can deal increasingly harder blows, even in the main urban centres, like Bissau, the capital, and Bafata, the second city of the country.

However, for our people and for their national Party, the greatest success of our struggle does not lie in the fact that, in spite of particularly difficult circumstances faced by our people, we have been able to fight victoriously against the Portuguese colonialist troops. The greater success of our fight is the fact that while fighting we have been able to begin to build a new political, administrative, economic, social and cultural life in the liberated areas. Still a very hard life, for sure, since it demands of us much effort and many sacrifices, in the face of the reality of a genocidal colonial war. But it is a life

.

full of beauty, because made up of effective productive labour, of freedom, of democracy in the regained dignity of our people.

In fact these nearly ten years of struggle have not only forged a new and strong African nation, they have also brought the birth of a new man and new woman, human beings aware of their rights and their duties on the soil of our African country. We can even assert that the transcendent result of our struggle, which is at the same time its principal strength, is the new awareness that currently characterizes the men, women and even children of our country.

And no one should be surprised if we venture to assert that we do not feel any special pride in the fact that every day by force of circumstances created or imposed by the Portuguese Government, a greater number of young Portuguese succumb ingloriously in the fire fed by the weapons of our combatants. We, we are proud, certainly, we are very proud of the growing national consciousness of our populations, of the now indestructible unity of our people, forged in the struggle, of the harmonious and coexistent flowering of the cultures of different ethnic groups, of the schools, hospitals and health centres which function in broad daylight, despite bombs and terrorist raids by the Portuguese colonialists. We are proud of our people's stores, which supply the populations better and better, of the increase and qualitative improvement in agricultural production, of the beauty, pride and dignity of our children and our women, who were the most exploited human beings in the country. We are proud to see thousands of adults taught to read and write, to see our peasants use for themselves or their children pills and other very simple medicaments, which they had never before had the opportunity of knowing about. And last but by no means least, we are proud of having trained during the struggle no less than 497 higher, middle and professional cadres, and of the fact that at this very moment 495 boys and girls are taking courses in higher, secondary and professional colleges in friendly European countries, while 15 000 children in the school system are attending 156 primary school and 5 secondary, boarding and semi-boarding schools, where teaching is given them by 251 men and women teachers.

This constitutes the greatest pride of our people and their greatest victory over the Portuguese colonialists. Since it is a victory over ignorance, fear and disease, scourges imposed on our people, on the African at home, for more than a century by the Portuguese colonialists. It also constitutes the most striking proof of the sovereignty of our people.

In truth our people are free and sovereign over the greater part of their national territory. To defend and preserve that sovereignty, and to extend it through the whole length and breadth of the national territory, both on the mainland and in the islands, we possess not only our armed forces but also all the instruments that define a state, which, under the leadership of our Party, is strengthened and consolidated day by day. In reality our situation has for some time been comparable to that of an independent state part of whose territory, notably the urban centres, is occupied by foreign military forces. This is all the more a reality as it has for some years been true that our people are no longer subject to economic exploitation by the Portuguese colonialists, since the latter can no longer practise such exploitation. And we are all the more sure of completing the liberation of our country since it is certain both in the urban centres and the occupied zones of Guiné and in the Cape Verde Islands, our clandestine organization and the political action of our militants are more vigorous than ever.

We want to reaffirm before you this certainty: no power in the world will be in a position to stop the total liberation of our people and the conquest of national independence for our country. We reaffirm likewise the indestructible nature of the unity of our African people of Guiné and Cape Verde, as well as our unshakable determination to free all parts of our national territory from the colonial yoke and Portuguese military occupation.

What in the face of such a situation, and our determination, is the attitude of the Government of Portugal? Up until the death of Salazar, whose archaic mentality could not imagine that even fictitious concessions could be made to the Africans, it was only a matter of radicalization of the colonial war. Salazar, who would repeat to anyone willing to listen to him that 'Africa does not exist' – an affirmation which surely expresses an insane racism, but also perfectly sums up the principles and practice of Portuguese colonial policy at all times – could not in his old age survive this greater affirmation of the existence of Africa, that is to say, the victorious armed resistance of the African peoples in the face of the Portuguese colonial war. Salazar was no more than a fanatical believer in the doctrine of European superiority and African inferiority. As one knows, he died from the sickness of Africa.

His successor, Marcello Caetano, is both a theorist (professor of colonial law in the Lisbon Law Faculty) and a practitioner (minister for the colonies for several years). Caetano who claims – as he has declared many times – 'to know the blacks', has opted for a new policy which, in social relations, must be that of the good master who shakes the hand of his houseboy, and, on the political level, internally is that of the old tactics of the stick and the carrot, and externally is that of using the arguments, and even the very words, of the adversary, to confuse him, while preserving one's own position. Moreover this is the difference between the Salazarism and Salazar and the neo-Salazarism of Caetano. The end remains the same: to perpetuate white domination over the mass of blacks in our country.

Caetano's tactics, which our people call 'the policy of smiling and bloodshed', are for us no more than a result, a further success, of our own struggle, as has been so well noted by several who have visited the remaining occupied zones in our country, including an American Congressman, Charles Diggs, and as the populations of the occupied zones have understood so well, and they in the face of the demagogic concessions by the colonilaist murmur 'Djarama PAIGC' (which means 'Thank you, PIGC').

Despite these concessions, despite a vast orchestrated propaganda campaign, both among us and internationally, this policy is bankrupt in our country. In fact the populations of the liberated areas are more united than ever around our Party, while those of the urban centres and the remaining occupied zones every day give more support to the struggle and to our Party, both in Guiné and in Cape Verde. Hundreds of young people are deserting the urban centres, notably Bissau, to join the ranks of the struggle. Desertions are increasing within the supposed African units, various members of which have been arrested by the colonial authorities.

In the face of such a situation, the colonialists increase repression in the occupied zones, notably in the main cities, and intensify their shelling and terrorists raids against the liberated areas. Having been forced to confess that they cannot win the war, they now know that no stratagem can demobilize our people, that nothing can halt their march towards total liberation and independence. The colonialists are seeking therefore to hold out at all costs, while using to the utmost all the means at their disposal to destroy as many lives and as much of our people's property as they can. It is in this framework that the colonialists have intensified the use of napalm and are actively preparing to use against us toxic chemicals, herbicides and defoliants, of which they have set up huge stocks in Bissau.

The desperation of the Portuguese Government is all the more understandable, since it is certain that the struggle of the brother peoples of Angola and Mozambique is developing successfully and that the people of Portugal themselves are more and more standing out against the colonial war. In fact, despite appearances, the economic, political and social situation in Portugal is constantly deteriorating, while the population is declining mainly by reason of the colonial war.

Allow us here to reaffirm our solidarity not only with the brother African peoples in Angola and Mozambique, but also with the people of Portugal whom we have never confused with Portuguese colonialism. We are more convinced than ever that our struggle and the total liberation of our country serve the best interests of the people of Portugal, with whom we hope to establish and develop the closest relations of co-operation, solidarity and friendship, in independence and in the service of the genuine progress of our countries.

If the Government of Portugal has persisted in its absurd and inhuman policy of colonial war during these nearly ten years, the UN has, in our view, made an appreciable moral and political contribution to the development of our liberating action. In fact, the resolutions proclaiming the legitimacy of our struggle by all means necessary, the appeal launched to member states that they should grant all possible assistance to the African liberation movements, the recommendations to the specialized agencies that they should co-operate with the movements through the OAU, the hearing of representatives of these movements by the Security Council in Addis Ababa, the granting of observer status to certain liberation movements and in our particular case the visit by the Special Mission to our country and the recognition of our party by the Committee on Decolonization as the sole, legitimate and genuine representative of the people of Guiné and Cape Verde – these are a significant help to our struggling people.

We also have the pleasure and honour of thanking the Committee on Decolonization and its highly dynamic chairman, Ambassador Salim, the Fourth Committee and through it the General Assembly and all the member states sympathetic to our cause, for such help.

Does this mean that we do not think the UN capable of doing more in support of our struggle? No, we are convinced that the international organization could and must do more to hasten the end of the colonial war in our country and the total liberation of our people. That is why, in Addis Ababa, we submitted specific proposals to the Security Council when we had the honour of being heard by that body. It is also by reason of this confidence in the UN and in its capacity for action, most particularly in our case, that we are here to submit to you new proposals aiming at closer and more effective co-operation between the international organization and our Party, the legitimate representative of our people.

Before this, we should like to highlight some important, we might say epoch-making events occurring at home in recent months.

We shall not speak of the successes already won by our combatants during this year, although they are very significant. We shall speak first about the visit by the United Nations Special Mission to our country, made last April in spite of terrorist aggression launched by the Portuguese colonialists against the liberated south to try to prevent its taking place. A historic and unique landmark for the UN and the liberation movements, this visit was a great victory for our people, but also for the international organization and for mankind. It brought a new stimulus to the courage and determination of our people and of our combatants who had made sacrifices for its achievements.

While it is true that the findings of the Special Mission are no more than confirmation of the testimony of various reliable visitors, of different professions and nationalities, none the less the findings have a particular value and significance, since they are the findings of the UN itself, made by an official mission duly authorized by the General Assembly, and formed by and composed of respected representatives of three member states of the organization. We should also like to underline before you the transcendent importance of the success of the Special Mission, to thank the General Assembly for having authorized it; to thank Ecuador, Sweden and Tunisia for having allowed their distinguished representatives, their Excellencies Messrs. Horacio Sevilla Borja, Folke Löfgren and Kamel Belkhiria, to take part in it. We again congratulate all the participants, including the secretary,

Mr Cheikh Tidiane, and the photographer, Mr Yutaka Nagata, staff members of the General Secretariat, for having carried out with exemplary courage, determination and conscientiousness the duties of a historic and profoundly humanitarian task in the service of the UN and of our people, hence in the service of mankind.

However, it is necessary to remind you that an act, whatever its motives, will always remain sterile, if it does not yield specific practical results.

In inviting the UN to send a Special Mission to our country, we did not at all aim to prove what is now a reality known to everybody: the sovereignty of our people over vast areas of our country. We deliberately wanted to give the UN a further firm base for the effective development of its action against Portuguese colonialism. The success of the Special Mission created this base. It seems to us just and essential for us to take full advantage of it, since, in agreement with the view of the Special Mission, we are convinced that the political, even juridical, situation of our people cannot and must not be the same as in the past. We are also convinced that the UN will be able to implement the recommendations of the Special Mission and we declare our readiness to give whatever co-operation is needed to that end.

Of course any important event has its lighthearted side. And the success of the Mission could be no exception to the rule. There was the desperate and preposterous oral and written response by the Lisbon Government. On this point, we shall limit ourselves merely to quoting our people's proverb, which says: 'Anyone who spits at the sky will soil his face.'

Moreover, with your permission, I shall here recall to you a very pertinent fact. When, for the first time in the history of mankind, an artificial satellite was launched into the cosmos, a physics lecturer at Lisbon Higher Technical Institute gave an interview to the press in the Portuguese capital to declare that he did not believe that a satellite was really spinning around the earth. And he tried to demonstrate scientifically that this was not possible. All the students in Lisbon and above all those of his Institute, took this decision: to telephone him every day to repeat in his ear the signals of the satellite – *bip, bip, bip*. . .

We shall likewise highlight another event of no less importance: the creation of the first National Assembly of our people in Guiné.

We have the honour to announce to this Committee that we have just held universal and secret general elections in all the liberated areas, for the creation of Regional Councils and our first National Assembly, which will be composed of 120 representatives, of whom 80 are elected from among the mass of the people and 40 from among cadres of the Party. Our people and our Party are firmly resolved to take full advantage of the creation of these new organs of sovereignty. Our National Assembly will be called upon to proclaim the existence of our state and to endow it with an executive which will function in the interior of our country. For this we are assured of the fraternal and active support of the independent African states. We are encouraged by the certainty that not only Africa but also the UN and all the genuinely anti-colonialist states will be able to appreciate to the full this clear political and juridical evolution in the situation of our African nation.

The truth is that at the present stage in our struggle, the Portuguese Government neither can nor should represent our people within the UN or any other international organization or body. In the same way that it could not represent them in the OAU. That is why it is not a question for us of seeking the expulsion of Portugal from the UN or any other international organization. The real question is to know if our people, who are sovereign over the greater part of their national territory, who have just created their first National Assembly, and who are going to proclaim the existence of their state, endowed with an executive, will or will not have the right to join the international community in the framework of the existing organizations and despite the occupation of the part of our country by foreign military forces. The real question that arises for us is to know, yes or no, if the UN and all the anticolonialist forces are prepared to strengthen their support and their moral, political and material assistance to our African nation, in accordance with their practical possibilities.

It is true that the war is still in full spate in Guiné and that we must make further sacrifices to complete the liberation of our country, something which has moreover already happened and is still happening to other peoples who possess their own government and an international juridical personality. But it is also true that, thanks to international solidarity, every day we have more resources and more effective resources to strike harder blows against the Portuguese colonial troops. And that the determination of our people, as well as the courage and experience of our combatants, are greater all the time.

And if we do not assert that Portugal runs the risk of military defeat in our midst, it is simply because it never had any chance of emerging victorious. And the only ones who can suffer defeats are those who had at least a possibility of being victorious.

It is also because we remain, as always, attached to our principles of peace, of pursuit of dialogue and negotiation, as an outcome to the conflict that sets our people against the Government of Portugal.

In Cape Verde, where famine ravages once again, while the colonialists reinforce repression by reason of the progress of our political action, we are determined to promote the struggle by all the necessary means, with the purpose of completely liberating our African people from the Portuguese colonial yoke.

Before you, we denounce the despicable fact that the Government of Portugal is now taking advantage of the famine that ravages the archipelago to export workers to Portugal and to other colonies, with the aim of sapping the vital strength of our people and thus trying to undermine our struggle. We wish to reaffirm that, on the basis of the community of blood, history, interests and struggle of the populations of Guiné and the Cape Verde Islands, we are determined to make whatever sacrifices are needed to liberate the archipelago from Portuguese colonial domination.

We submit for examination by the UN, through the intermediary of this Committee, the following proposals based on the practical reality of the life of our people and on everything we have just said:

1. Approaches to the Portuguese Government with the aim that negotiations should be opened immediately between the representatives of that Government and our Party. We propose that these negotiations should have as their working basis a search for the most appropriate and most effective ways and means for the urgent accession of our people to independence. In the case that the Government of Portugal should respond favourably to such an approach, we could at the same time consider ways of taking into account the interests of Portugal in our country.
2. Acceptance of delegates of our Party, with the status of associate members or observers, in all the specialized agencies of the UN, as the sole and legitimate representatives of our people, such as already happens in the Economic Commission for Africa (ECA).
3. Development of practical assistance from these specialized agencies, notably UNESCO, UNICEF, WHO and FAO, to our people in the framework of national reconstruction of our country. (On this point, before speaking of the fourth proposal, we suggest that the specialized agencies of the UN, which must co-operate or collaborate with the liberation movements, might well overcome any norms, let us say of bureaucracy, of legalism, so that this aid, this co-operation should be as effective as possible.)
4. Moral and political support by the UN for all the initiatives that our people and our Party have decided to take to speed up the end of the Portuguese colonial war and the advent of independence of our African nation, and so that the latter may soon occupy its rightful place within the international community.

In the hope that these proposals will be given serious consideration, we strongly urge all member states of the UN, particularly allies of Portugal, the countries of Latin America, especially Brazil, to understand our position and give their support to the legitimate aspirations of our African people to the freedom, independence and progress which is their due.

We are absolutely certain that the governments of the South American peoples, and particularly of Brazil, will understand very well our positions, since these peoples themselves had to fight to free themselves from the colonial yoke. On this point, I recall that the Minister of Foreign Affairs and the Government of Portugal have the habit of quoting the Brazilian case.

Perhaps they are abusing their belief that others do not know history. Because Brazil came to independence through armed struggle after Don Pedro, a prince of Portugal, but tied to the Brazilian people, on the banks of the river Ipiranga shouted with his companions in struggle: 'Independence or death'. This cry of rebellion has gone into history under the name 'the Ipiranga cry'.

That then was the case of Don Pedro, son of the King of Portugal. But Portugal itself became an independent nation, a state, through fratricidal struggle. More than fratricidal because Don Afonso Henriques rebelled against his mother, Donna Teresa, to go on to win the first independence of the people of Portugal.

But we are not Portuguese, much less sons of the King of Portugal, of the Prime Minister of Portugal, or of the Queen of Portugal.

Before closing, allow us to thank very warmly all the African countries, the socialist countries, the Nordic countries and others who bring to our struggle their fraternal aid to make easier our magnificent task of the liberation of our people.

We should likewise wish here to thank, before you, the international organizations such as the World Council of Churches, the World Church Service, the Joseph Rowntree Social Trust of Britain and other non-governmental organizations which bring their aid to our struggle.

We also have something to say to the states which aid Portugal. We declare that we do not at all believe that this attitude coincides with the feelings of the majority of the peoples of those states. We likewise declare that on the one hand no matter what aid they bring Portugal, we shall never confuse them with Portuguese colonialism, and that on the other hand that aid cannot in any way prevent the total liberation of our people. And the states should know that with our feelings and our African culture we are ready to understand them one day, and we shall be open to healthy co-operation in the service of a life of peace and progress for our people and in the interest also of their own peoples.

I have trespassed on your time, I ask your pardon. I still had many things to say because the struggle is very complex. But I want simply to thank you for your welcome, for your attention, and I put myself at the disposal of the Committee to try to answer its questions. Not without repeating, without reaffirming certainty in the victory of our people in Guiné and Cape Verde in their struggle for independence and progress.

THE STATE OF GUINÉ-BISSAU

35. Creation of the People's National Assembly in Guine[1]

Results and bases of the general elections held in the liberated areas in 1972

The situation prevailing in Guiné since 1968 as a result of the national liberation struggle waged by the people of this country, under the leadership of PAIGC, is comparable to that of an independent state, part of whose national territory, notably the urban centres, is occupied by foreign military forces. Dozens of reliable observers of various nationalities and of different professions have been able to visit our country, at their initiative or at our invitation, and have given irrefutable (oral, written, photographic and cinematographic) testimony about the real situation prevailing there: vast areas have been liberated from the colonial yoke and a new political, administrative, economic, social and cultural life is developing in these areas, while the patriotic forces, supported by the population, are fighting successfully against the colonialists to complete the liberation of the country.

Most recently, in April 1972, a United Nations Special Mission, composed of representatives of three member states of the international organization and duly mandated by the General Assembly, visited the liberated areas of our country, where they stayed for one week. Among the conclusions the Special Mission was able to draw from the now historic visit, the following is highlighted: 'That the struggle for the liberation of the territory continues to progress and that Portugal no longer exercises any effective administrative control in large areas of Guinea (Bissau) are irrefutable facts... It is also evident that the population of the liberated areas unreservedly supports the policies and activities of the national liberation movement, PAIGC, which, after nine years of military struggle, exercises free de facto administrative control in those areas and is effectively protecting the interests of the inhabitants in spite of Portuguese activities.'

Such a situation implies a contradiction that in the light of the criminal obstinacy of the Lisbon Government, which intensifies its genocidal colonial war against the legitimate rights of our people to self-determination, independence and progress, hinders the march of the struggle and puts a brake on the full flowering of the personality of our African nation, forged in

[1]Communiqué released on 8 January 1973.

the struggle. In fact, while our people have for years now possessed political, administrative, judicial, military, social and cultural institutions – hence a state - and are free and sovereign over more than two-thirds of the national territory, they do not have a juridical personality at the international level. Moreover the functioning of such institutions in the framework of the new life developing in the liberated areas demands a broader participation by the people, through their representatives, not only in the study and solution of the problems of the country and the struggle, but also in the effective control of the activities of the Party which leads them.

To resolve the above mentioned contradiction and to answer the need for a broader and more effective participation of the people, the national leadership of the Party, after several discussions, opted for the creation by means of free and democratic general elections of a *People's National Assembly,* the first in our history, which in its character as the supreme organ of sovereignty of the people, will be called upon to proclaim the existence of a national state in Guiné, to endow it with an executive and promulgate a constitution for our African nation.

Thus it is that the meeting of the Supreme Council of the Struggle (CSL), held from 7 to 17 August 1971, decided by acclamation that the Party should immediately take all the necessary steps to hold general elections in the liberated areas in 1972 with universal and secret suffrage, for the constitution of the first People's National Assembly (ANP) in Guiné. On the basis of this historic decision, the process and the method to follow for the elections were defined as well as the critieria for the choice of candidates to the ANP, under norms published in a document entitled 'Bases for the creation of the People's National Assembly in Guiné' (cf. Appendix, which was approved by the meeting of the Executive Committee of the Struggle (CEL) in December 1971.

After eight months (January to August) of an intensive campaign of information, debates and discussions, both in the base institutions of the Party and in public meetings, the elections were held at the end of August to 14 October in all the liberated areas.

On 6 November, during a press conference in Algiers, the partial and preliminary results of the elections were published. We give below the definitive results.

A. *In the interior of the country*

1. Ballots distributed, corresponding to the number of *registered*

Yes	83 000
No	83 000

2.	Voters	77 515	93·39%
	Yes	75 163	96·96%
		(90·55% of those registered)	
	No	2352	3·03%
		(2·82% of those registered)	

B. *In the exterior (militants, cadres, students, including some emigrants who militate in the Party)*

1. Ballots distributed (registered)

Yes	4517
No	4517

2.	Voters	4517	100%
	Yes	4517	100%
	No	0	0%

C. *Overall results (interior + exterior)*

1. Ballots distributed (registered)

Yes	87 517
No	87 517

2.	Voters	82 032	93·73%
	Yes	79 680	97·13%
		(91·04% of those registered)	
	No	2 352	2·87%
		(2·80% of those registered)	

As for voting by region, the highest number of votes cast in relation to those registered corresponds to the liberated north, with 95.30 per cent, and the lowest to the eastern regions, with 87.93 per cent. The highest number of *Yes* in relation to votes cast corresponds to the liberated south with 97.85 per cent and the lowest, likewise to the eastern regions, with 94.49 per cent. In six villages the percentage of *No* was slightly higher than that of *Yes*. In one village in the liberated north, there was a 100 per cent *No* score, by reason of a failure to agree among the population of this village and those of others in the sector concerning the candidature of one representative.

The following numbers of *regional councillors* and *representatives to the ANP* were elected by the mass of the people:

Regional councillors	273
Representatives to the ANP	99

of whom 91 were chosen by the elected Regional Councils, five by the National Union of Workers (UNTG) and three by the National Conference of Youth and Students.

To represent zones still occupied and effectively controlled by the occupation troops, 21 representatives to the ANP were provisionally appointed, that is 3 for Bafata, 4 for the Bijagos Islands, 9 for Bissau Island, including the capital, and 5 for Bolama Island, including the city.

The holding of general elections in Guiné and the creation of the first National Assembly of our people are political facts of historic dimension for the new life we have constructed and for the future development of the heroic struggle by our people for independence. These initiatives, which received the most enthusiastic support of the mass of the people in the liberated areas and had a very promising effect on the populations of the zones still occupied by Portuguese colonial troops, open up new prospects for our liberating fight. They will contribute to the strengthening of the struggle in the Cape Verde Islands, an integral and inalienable part of our national territory, where likewise the first People's National Assembly will be created at the opportune moment, with a view to the formation of the supreme organ of the then totally regained sovereignty of our people and their unitary state: the Supreme Assembly of Guiné and Cape Verde.

After the decision taken by the Supreme Council of the Struggle aiming at the creation of the ANP in Guiné, the United Nations Committee on Decolonization at its 848th session, held on April 10, 1972 in Conakry, recognized our Party, the PAIGC, as the only legitimate representative of the people of Guiné and Cape Verde. The 27th session of the United Nations General Assembly confirmed this recognition.

If these facts do no more than confirm the unshakable position of our people who have always considered our combatant Party as the sole, legitimate and genuine representative of their inalienable interests and their legitimate aspirations to independence, peace and progress, they give a new dimension and an international scale to the general elections and the creation of the ANP on the initiative of our Party. it is certainly a new event, if not a new path, in the context of the struggle of peoples for their liberation from imperialist domination. An event and a path that are entirely in accord with the international law and ethics of our times, with the Charter and resolutions of the United Nations.

The National Assembly of our people in Guiné will hold its first session in 1973 in our country as soon as preparations for its meeting are completed. It will then fulfil the first historic mission incumbent upon it: the proclamation of our national state, the promulgation of the constitution and the creation of the corresponding executive bodies.

In publishing the results of the general elections, our purpose is to inform world opinion and all national and international bodies about this major fact of our history and of the struggle by our people. At this moment we wish to reaffirm our certainty in the victory of our people against the Portuguese colonialists. We likewise reaffirm our trust in the unreserved moral and political support of the independent states of Africa and of all the other anti-colonialist and anti-racist forces of the various continents for the decisions that will be taken by our People's National Assembly, in the just cause of the independence and progress of our people.

Appendix I. Bases for the creation of the People's National Assembly in Guiné

1

In accordance with the decisions taken at the meeting of the Supreme Council of the Struggle, held from 9 to 17 August 1971, on the duly founded proposal of the Secretary-general of the Party and after full discussion, *we must immediately take all the necessary steps with a view to creating as soon as possible the first People's National Assembly of Guiné.*

The People's National Assembly of Guiné (ANP) is created on the basic principle according to which *power* comes from the people and must serve the people. The ANP is the highest organ of the national state that our people have forged in the struggle and are in the process of developing and consolidating more and more. It is the supreme organ of the sovereignty of our people in Guiné. This sovereignty has been conquered at the price of a heroic struggle filled with sacrifice, and it is already wielded by our people in the greater part of our national territory.

The ANP holds legislative power within the framework of the sovereignty of our people. Thus and because it is the supreme organ of the state in Guiné, it controls the application of the political, juridical, economic, social and cultural line defined in respect of Guiné by our Party and discussed and approved by the latter.

The ANP will in due course define its functions and its operating rules as well as other norms pertaining to its activity within the framework of the structures and evolution of the state.

2

The first ANP of Guiné is composed of 120 representatives. They are the representatives of the working people (peasants, labourers, employees and professionals in the liberal professions), of all the living and patriotic forces of Guiné.

Candidature to represent the working people of Guiné is open to any individual born in Guiné or who has acquired Guinean nationality, regardless of ethnic origin, sex, social condition or religious belief, provided that he or she satisfies the following conditions:

Being above the age of eighteen

Being a producer or having a well-defined profession

Not being a collaborator with the Portuguese colonialists, nor having collaborated with them since the launching of our struggle

Not having been convicted of common law crime or crime against the interests of our liberation struggle

Having good moral and civic behaviour

Enjoying prestige, respect, esteem and trust on the part of the mass of the working people.

The following conditions have priority for the candidature:

Exemplary attachment to our people, to the Party and to the national liberation struggle

Having carried out important tasks in the framework of our struggle

Exemplary attachment to productive labour

3

The number of representatives to the ANP by region or front of struggle is as follows:

Liberated areas and fronts in the south – 41 distributed:

Balana-Quitafine	5	
Catio	13	
Cubisseco	8	
Quinara	10	
Xitole	5	41

Liberated areas and fronts in the north – 36 distributed:

Bula-Canchungo	9	
Oio	13	
Sara	9	
S. Domingos-Sambuia	5	36

Liberated areas and fronts in the east – 17 distributed:

Bafata	3	
Boé	7	
Gabu	7	17

Islands

Bijagos	4	
Bissau	9	
Bolama	5	18
	Total	112

To this total must be added eight more representatives elected by the following organized social sectors:

By UNTG   5
By youth and students   3

which brings the overall total to 120 (80 + 40).

4

Each group of representatives elected from a liberated area or from a front of struggle is composed of *elements elected among the masses* and elements elected among *the militant cadres of PAIGC*, in the approximate proportion of two to one.

Thus, taking into account the fact that the representatives of UNTG, of Youth and Students (SEP), are elected among the masses of those organized social sectors, the 120 representatives to the ANP comprise 80 from among the masses and 40 elected from among the Party cadres. This means: two-thirds of the ANP is made up of elements coming from the mass of the working people and students, and the other third of elements coming from the militant cadres of PAIGC: 120 = 80 + 40.

5

In the current phase of our struggle, the representatives to the ANP are elected by *Regional Councils* from among their members, by a two-thirds majority. The Regional Council (CR) is the assembly of the elected representatives of the working people in the various politico-administrative and military sectors, which form the regions and the fronts.

In each sector, the representatives to the Regional Council will be elected by direct, universal and secret suffrage, in a single vote on a single and collective list of candidates. Each candidate elected in the sector – each representative of the people in the sector – will have the mandate of those people to represent them within the Regional Council, and to be a candidate to the representation within the ANP, and to elect the representatives to the ANP.

The election of sector representatives to the Regional Council (elements of the mass of the people and militant cadres of the Party) is thus the first phase of the election of representatives to the ANP. The second phase consists of the election, from among the members of the Regional Council, of representatives for the region to the ANP.

The number of representatives to the ANP to emerge from each Regional Council is of the order of one-third of the total number of members of the Council.

For the occupied zones, where it is not yet possible to proceed to elections (Bijagos, Bissau, Bolama and Bafata), representatives will be provisionally appointed.

Special commissions, to be designated later, will prepare and guide the holding of elections among the militants, the cadres and other persons tied to the Party, but residing temporarily in the exterior. Citizens who live abroad outside the framework of the struggle cannot be candidates to the ANP. Below is shown the number of members to be elected for each council, by region and by sector.

6

Number of members of CR to be elected

Liberated areas and fronts in the south

1.	Balana-Quitafine –	15	distributed:
	Balana	9	
	Quitafine	6	
2.	Catio –	39	distributed:
	Como	6	
	Cubucaré	15	
	Tombali	18	
3.	Cubisseco –	24	distributed:
	Lower Cubisseco	15	
	Upper Cubisseco	9	
4.	Quinara –	30	distributed:
	Fulacunda	15	
	Ndjassani	9	
	S. João	6	
5.	Xitole	15	

Liberated areas and fronts in the north

1.	Bula-Canchungo –	27	distributed:
	Bula	12	
	Canchungo	15	
2.	Oio –	39	distributed:
	Maqué	9	
	Morés	18	
	Nhacra	12	
3.	Sara –	27	distributed:
	Candjambari	12	
	Sara	15	
4.	S. Domingos-Sambuia –	15	distributed:
	Sambuia	6	
	S. Domingos	9	

Liberated areas and fronts in the east

1.	Bafata	9
2.	Boé	21
3.	Gabu	21

Islands

1.	Bijagos	12	
2.	Bissau –	27	distributed:
	City	12	
	Countryside	15	
3.	Bolama –	15	distributed:
	City	6	
	Countryside	9	

7

The election of members of the Regional Councils (CR), which is the first phase in the election of representatives to the ANP, is made in the following way:

1. *The special commission* entrusted with organizing and carrying out the elections in each conjunction of liberated areas and fronts will meet to establish the *plan for electoral action* in accordance with the particular circumstances of each area or front.

2. Each special commission will invite the Zone Committees to a meeting to inform them appropriately about the electoral process and the norms to be followed.

3. In each sector or zone of a front of struggle meetings will be held with the population and combatants for the purpose of explaining the meaning of the elections and the way they will be held. For each sector an electoral commission and polling stations will be created.

4. During the meetings in each sector registration will be opened for candidatures as member of the Regional Council (CR). Only candidates who satisfy the conditions stated in section 2 will be admitted.

5. Delegates of the special commission will meet the electoral commissions of the sectors to verify if the registered candidates satisfy the established conditions and priorities and to draw up the list by sector.

6. The lists will be announced to the population of each sector either by the local Party committees or in the public meetings. The ballot papers will be distributed on this occasion. All the committees and any person

present at the public meetings will have the right to debate the content of the lists drawn up and to propose amendments. The lists shall be regarded as definitive when they have been approved by the majority of the committees and, at the public meetings, by the majority of those present.
7. Subsequently, each sector will proceed, on the date or dates set and previously announced to the population, to the election by direct, universal and secret ballot of members of the CR.

As has been said, the voting will be made in relation to a single, collective list, comprising the exact number of members of the CR. Every elector will vote:

Yes – Green ballot
No – White ballot

The electoral commissions of the sectors, with the assistance of delegates of the special commission, will proceed to the count of the votes, whose results will be transmitted immediately to the *special commission.*

8

The election of representatives of the regions to the ANP, on the bases of the numbers and elements stated in section 6 and which constitutes the second phase of the election for the constitution of the ANP, is made in the following way:

First

The special commission entrusted with the elections will call a meeting of the Regional Council of each region, at which meeting a delegate of this commission will be present. During the meeting, the list of members of CR as candidates to be representatives within the ANP will be drawn up in accordance with the established priorities. The list will be subjected to full discussion by members of the Regional Council.

Every candidature will be submitted to the vote of the Council individually. It will be approved if it is voted for by at least a two-thirds majority of the members of the Council. Voting will be carried out by a simple gesture of raising an arm, with the count being made immediately and its result duly recorded. Candidates for representation have the right to vote for their candidature.

Second

All the records of votes in the different Regional Councils will be sent immediately to the special commission which will make a general assessment of the results of the election.

Third

The results of the general checking will be transmitted to the higher leadership of the Party for publication and divulgation both in the country and abroad.

9

The *electorate* are all Guinean citizens above the age of seventeen, regardless of origin, sex, special condition or activity in the framework of our life and our struggle.

Those excluded from the electorate are individuals who serve or have served the colonialists against the interests of our people since the start of our struggle. Those excluded from the electorate are individuals known to be of bad moral and civic behaviour.

10

The special commission entrusted with preparation, organization and holding of the elections will be formed by the Permanent Commission of the National Committee for the Liberated Areas assisted by a delegate from the higher leadership of the Party and a co-worker. The following comrades are designated as delegates and co-workers:

For the south: Vasco Cabral and Luis Sanca;

For the north: Chico Mendes and Flavio Proença;

For the east: Otto Ba and João Pereira.

In the liberated areas, the electoral commissions for sectors will be constituted by the following members of the Zone Committee: the responsible worker for security, the responsible worker for education, a teacher to be designated by the Permanent Commission of the CNRL and two members of the public.

In the fronts of struggle, the electoral commissions will be formed by three combatants who can read and write fluently, whatever their post and the branch they serve in. These combatants will be designated by the front command.

These 'Bases for the creation of the People's National Assembly in Guiné' have the force of law.

Done on 3 December 1971.

Responsible official for Justice and Population Services
Fidelis C. Almada

Secretary-general of PAIGC
Amilcar Cabral

36. New Year's message[1]

Comrades, compatriots,

At this moment when we are beginning a new year of life and struggle and our fight for the independence of our African people is ten years old, I must remind everyone – militants, combatants, responsible workers and leaders in our great Party – that it is time for action and not words. Time for action in Guiné that is each day more vigorous and more effective, in order to inflict greater defeats on the Portuguese colonialists and remove from them all their criminal and vain pretensions of reconquering our land. Action that is constantly more developed and better organized in Cape Verde to carry the struggle into a new phase, in accordance with the aspirations of our people and the imperatives of the total liberation of our African country.

I must, however, respect tradition by addressing a few words to you at a time when all sane human beings – those who want peace, freedom and happiness for all men – renew their hopes and the belief in a better life for mankind, in dignity, independence and genuine progress for all peoples.

As you all know, in the past year we held general elections in the liberated areas, with universal suffrage and a secret vote, for the creation of Regional Councils and the first National Assembly in our people's history. In all sectors of all regions, the elections were conducted in an atmosphere of great enthusiasm on the part of the population. The electorate voted massively for the lists that had been drawn up after eight months of public and democratic discussions, in which the representatives of each sector were selected. When the elected Regional Councils met, they elected in their turn representatives to the People's National Assembly from among their members. This will have 120 members, of whom 80 were elected from among the mass of the people and 40 from among the political cadres, soldiers, technicians and others of the Party. As you know, the representatives for the sectors temporarily occupied by the colonialists have been chosen provisionally.

Today our African people of Guiné possess another organ of sovereignty, their People's National Assembly. In accordance with the constitution we are drawing up, this will be the supreme organ of sovereignty of our people in Guiné. Tomorrow, with the certain development of the struggle, we shall also create the first People's National Assembly in Cape Verde. The joint meeting of the members of these two bodies will constitute the Supreme Assembly of the People of Guiné and Cape Verde.

The creation of the first People's National Assembly in Guiné is an epoch-making victory for the difficult but glorious struggle of our people for independence. It opens up new prospects for the advance of our political and military action, is the result of the efforts and sacrifices offered by our people

[1]January 1973.

in these ten years of armed struggle, and it is practical proof of the sovereignty of our people and their high degree of national and patriotic consciousness. I wish, therefore, at this moment to address my warmest congratulations to our people, to all the electorate, who as conscientious men and women have been able so worthily to accomplish their duties as free citizens of our African nation, to all the militants, responsible workers and leaders who, in the electoral committees or in other sectors of activity, have contributed their utmost for the success of this venture which will live in the history of our land. With equal enthusiasm, I congratulate the valorous combatants of our armed forces, who by their courageous action have created in all sectors the security needed for holding the elections in spite of all the criminal attempts of the colonialist enemy to prevent their taking place.

But a national assembly, like any organ in any living body, must be able to function in order to justify its existence. For this reason, we have a greater task to fulfil in the framework of our struggle in this new year of 1973: we must put our People's National Assembly into operation. And this we shall do, to implement completely the decisions taken by our great Party, at the meeting of the Supreme Council of the Struggle in August 1971, decisions which were enthusiastically supported by the people.

In the course of this coming year and as soon as it is conveniently possible we shall call a meeting of our People's National Assembly in Guiné, so that it can fulfil the first historic mission incumbent on it: the proclamation of the existence of our state, the creation of an executive for this state and the promulgation of a fundamental law – that of the first constitution in our history – which will be the basis of the active existence of our African nation. That is to say: legitimate representatives of our people, chosen by the populations and freely elected by conscientious and patriotic citizens of our land, will proceed to the most important act of their life and of the life of our people, that of declaring before the world that our African nation, forged in the struggle, is irrevocably determined to march forward to independence without waiting for the consent of the Portuguese colonialists and that from then on the executive of our state under the leadership of our Party, the PAIGC, will be the sole, true and legitimate representative of our people in all the national and international questions that concern them.

We are moving from the situation of a colony which has a liberation movement, and whose people have already liberated in ten years of armed struggle the greater part of their national territory, to the situation of a country which runs its own state and which has a part of its national territory occupied by foreign armed forces.

The radical change in the situation in our land corresponds to the specific reality of the life and struggle of our people in Guiné, is based on specific results of our struggle, and has the firm support of all African countries and governments and of all the anticolonialist and anti-racist forces in the world.

It also corresponds to the principles of the United Nations Charter and to the resolutions adopted by that international organization, notably in its 27th session.

Nothing, no criminal action or conjuring trick by the Portuguese colonialists can prevent our African people, masters of their own destiny and aware of their rights and duties, from taking this transcendent and decisive step towards the achievement of the fundamental aim of our struggle: the winning of national independence and the building, in restored peace and dignity, of their genuine progress under the exclusive leadership of their own sons and daughters, under the glorious banner of our Party.

The epoch-making importance of the formation of the People's National Assembly, of the proclamation of the state in Guiné and of the creation of the corresponding executive bodies, who will be neither provisional nor living in exile, necessarily implies much greater responsibilities for our people and, particularly, for the militants, combatants, responsible workers and leaders of our Party. These historic initiatives demand from us all more efforts and daily sacrifices, more thought to act better, more activity to think better. They demand that we study every specific question that we have to resolve in such a way as to find the most appropriate solution for it in the specific circumstances of our land and our struggle. The initiatives demand that we intensify and develop our political and miltary action in Guiné, without neglecting the important activities we have developed on the economic, social and cultural levels. They demand that we successfully deploy the necessary efforts for the advance of the political struggle in Cape Verde and in order that our people in the islands should as soon as possible move into systematic, direct action against the criminal Portuguese colonialists.

In this perspective, we cannot for one moment forget that we are at war and that the principal enemy of our people and of Africa – the Portuguese Fascist colonialists – still nurture, with the sacrifice and misery of their people and by means of the most treacherous manoeuvres and most savage acts, the criminal intention and vain hope of destroying our Party, of eliminating our struggle and recolonizing our people. For this reason, the greater part of our attention, our energies and our efforts must be devoted to the armed struggle, to war and to practical action by our national and local armed forces. For this reason, we must, in the course of 1973, set in motion all our human and material capacity and potential in order to intensify still further the struggle on all fronts to derive a greater return from the men, weapons and experience at our disposal, thereby to strike harder blows against the colonialist enemy by destroying a greater number of their living forces. For the history of colonial wars and our experience over ten years of struggle have taught us that the colonialist aggressors – and most particularly the Portuguese colonialist aggressors – understand only one language, that of force, and measure only one reality, the number of corpses.

It is true that in 1972 we inflicted heavy defeats and very significant losses on the criminal Portuguese colonialist aggressors. Within a few days our Information Services will publish the balance sheet of our action over the past year, which will be widely publicized by our broadcasting station 'Radio Libertação and by other information media. But we must recognize that the enemy, possessing more aircraft and helicopters supplied by their NATO allies, have significantly increased the shelling and terrorist raids against our liberated areas, have tried and are trying to create difficulties for us with their plans for reoccupying some localities within those areas. But above all we must recognize that, with the men, weapons and experience at our disposal, we could and should have done more and better. This is what we must do and certainly will do in 1973, the more so because we are going to use still heavier weapons and other instruments of war on all fronts.

On the basis of a greater number of better trained cadres and combatants with greater experience, we are going to make more effective use of all the means at our disposal and of those that we shall have, to strike decisive and mortal blows on the criminal Portuguese colonialist aggressors.

At the same time as we intensify armed action on all fronts, we must be capable of developing our action in the enemy rearguard and in the enemy heartland where they feel most secure. I congratulate here the brave militants who, by their determined action, struck important blows on the enemy over the past year, particularly in Bissau, Bafata and Bula. But I draw everyone's attention to the need to develop and intensify this type of action. In fact the time has come when, on the basis of effective and strong clandestine organization, we must destroy the greatest possible number of human and material assets of the criminal Portuguese colonialist aggressors in the urban centres of our land. In reality, we face a savage enemy who do not have the slightest scruple in their criminal actions, who use every possible means of trying to destroy us wherever we are. For this reason, and since we are struggling in our land for the sacred rights of our people to independence, peace and genuine progress, we must at this decisive moment strike against the colonialist and racist enemy – against them, their agents and their assets – telling blows wherever they are. This is an urgent task to which all the responsible workers and militants of this sector of the struggle must dedicate themselves with the greatest attention and most especially those comrades who with courage and determination are active in the urban centres and areas still occupied by the enemy.

I want to mention here an important question of the colonial war we face: the huge attempts the enemy have made to occupy or reoccupy some localities of our liberated areas. I remind comrades of the Party and our people that these attempts, successful or not, such as shelling and terrorist assaults, are characteristic of colonial war and necessarily form part of the action of the colonialist aggressor, especially when the patriotic forces have already liberated the greater part of the national territory, as in our case. We must therefore face this problem realistically and give it its correct evaluation within the general framework of our struggle, without exaggerating or minimizing its importance.

As the comrades and above all the leaders and responsible workers of the Party know, in the context of its colonial war the colonialist aggressor faces a principal and insoluble contradiction, with which it has been taxed throughout the war. It is the following contradiction: so as to feel that it dominates the territory, it is obliged to disperse its troops, placing them so as to occupy the greatest possible number of localities. But by dispersing its troops, it becomes weaker and thus the concentrated patriotic forces can strike harder and mortal blows against it. Then it is obliged to withdraw to concentrate its troops and to try to avoid heavy losses in human lives, so as better to resist the advance of nationalist forces against whom it seeks to gain time. But by concentrating its troops, it abandons its military and political presence in vast areas of the country which are organized and administered by the patriotic forces.

In the current phase of our struggle and of the Portuguese colonial war, the enemy, blinded by despair at the defeats they have suffered and are suffering both in our land and at the international level, are trying, certainly in vain, to make the river Corubal return to the Futa Djalon instead of flowing towards the Geba and the sea. In this attempt, as in that of deceiving our people with the mirage of a 'better Guiné' Portuguese style, as with that of making Africans fight against Africans, they are doomed to failure: they will not be able to free themselves from the principal contradiction of their filthy colonial war.

What is important for us, on the basis of understanding the strategy to which the enemy are forced by the objective laws of colonial war, is not to worry too much because the enemy want to install themselves in Gampara, in Cabochanque, in Cadique or in other localities. The important thing is on the one hand for us to carry on with our plans for struggle and on the other to do our best to eliminate the greatest possible number of living forces of the enemy, when they install themselves or move to install themselves in any locality of our liberated areas. What counts is to strike hard blows at them, to allow them no rest, to turn an occupied position into a graveyard for their troops until they are forced to withdraw, as we have done in Balana, Gandembel and more recently in Cubisseco New Village. This is what we must do and will certainly do in any part of our liberated areas that the enemy occupy. We must also do this in their barracks and fortified camps still existing in our country.

Naturally in 1973 we must continue to intensify our political work among the mass of the people, both in the liberated areas and in the occupied zones of Guiné and in Cape Verde. Without in any way minimizing the value of the work already done in this domain, which led to the failure of the spurious and notorious 'policy of a better Guiné', we must recognize that there are some sectors, if not regions, where political action is still deficient. In the course of this coming year, we have to make all the efforts needed to improve our action in these sectors, since, as we know, however important our armed action, our struggle is fundamentally a political struggle which has a specific political objective: the independence and progress of our land.

While I congratulate the comrades who in Guiné and in Cape Verde have greatly improved political work in the past year, I urge everyone to redoubled efforts to consolidate and develop the political conquests of the Party and the struggle, constantly to raise the political awareness and patriotism of the mass of the people, of militants and of combatants, to strengthen the indestructible unity of our people, the essential basis of the successes of our struggle. In the sphere of security and control, to strengthen vigilance against the enemy and their agents, against all those who because of opportunism, ambition, moral weakness or servility towards the enemy might try to destroy our Party and hence the just struggle of our people for independence.

In Cape Verde, the events of September 1972, which constituted the first clash between the population of the archipelago and the forces of colonial repression, have once again shown the level of tension the political situation there has reached. In congratulating the patriots of Praia and S. Santiago, who acted with courage and determination in the face of provocation by the colonialists and their agents, I urge them constantly to improve their clandestine organization, to operate with security and without enabling the enemy to eliminate the nationalist cadres, and to prepare themselves by every means within their reach for the new phase of our struggle in the archipelago, which is forced by the criminal obstinacy of the Portuguese colonialists. I reaffirm that the leadership of the Party is more determined than ever to do everything possible for the advance of the struggle in Cape Verde.

In view of the progress already made in the islands and the complexity of the particular problems to be solved, it has become necessary and urgent, in my opinion, to make a realistic modification in the structure of the leadership of the Party to give some comrades the possibility of devoting themselves entirely to development of the struggle in Cape Verde. Such a modification will be proposed to the next meeting of the Party leadership.

Still on the political level, I draw the attention of comrades to the diversity of new questions we have to study and solve in the appropriate way, which follow from the new prospects for development of the struggle which will be opened up by the proclamation of the state in Guiné: in the interior, improvement and development of the administrative services, creation of controlling bodies for our activities, a new population census, identification of all its component elements, etc; and in the exterior, organization, control and protection of emigrant citizens, their identification with corresponding distribution of passports, mobilization for the struggle of youth resident abroad, etc., not to mention the type of relations to be established at the international level. They are certainly new but very important questions that we must study thoroughly and solve in due course.

Concern with the war and with political work should not, however, make us forget or even underestimate the importance of our activities at the economic, social and cultural level, as the foundation of the new life we are creating in our liberated areas. We must all, but mainly the cadres who specialize in these matter, give the closest attention to questions of the economy, health, social welfare, education and culture, so as to improve our work significantly and to be ready to solve the great problems we have to face with the new situation the struggle is bringing. In this perspective, we must already face with determination and tenacity the key questions of improvement of supply and the living standards of our populations, taxes and exchequer, the new financial life we hope to establish, the currency we shall use, etc., as well as the type of social welfare we shall develop on the basis of our past experience, school systems and training of more cadres for national reconstruction and the building of our people's progress. So many new problems, but the more complex the more exciting, which we must be capable of solving at the same time as we intensify and develop our vigorous action at the politico-military level to expel the colonial troops from the positions they still occupy in our land of Guiné and Cape Verde. The specialist cadres of the Party must devote themselves attentively to the study and solution of these questions, in order to accomplish their duty towards our people.

On behalf of the Party leadership, I congratulate our agricultural producers in Guiné for the harvests collected last year, in spite of the scarcity of rains. I urge all to do more and better this year, to ensure a good crop for, as we know, this is the principal base of our life and our struggle, which the criminal Portuguese colonialist aggressors try to destroy by every means when they cannot steal from us the fruit of our people's labour.

But it is with sorrow that I recall here that at this very moment the populations of Cape Verde are menaced by famine. This is the fault of the Portuguese colonialists who never managed nor wanted to create the minimum of economic and social conditions in the archipelago to ensure subsistence and a decent life for the populations in years of prolonged drought. Forced by the onward rush of the struggle and by the denunciation made by our Party before world opinion, the colonial Government of Portugal has granted loans and subsidies to Cape Verde in order, as the colonialists say, 'to relieve the crisis', meaning to avoid many folk dying of hunger at one time, but without preventing the weakest, above all children, from dying slowly from specific hunger or even total starvation. I raise my voice once again on behalf of the leadership of our Party to protest against this situation and to denounce the crime perpetrated by the colonial Fascist Government of Lisbon in transferring to Portugal about fifteen to twenty thousand young Cape Verdians, to work in the mines, to sweep the streets in the main cities, for jobs as unskilled labourers, thus causing a great haemorrhage in the vital strength of Cape Verde, with the intention of barring the way to the advance of our liberating struggle. I appeal to Cape Verdian and Guinean patriots resident in Portugal to keep close contact and organize themselves, so that in conjunction with all the forced labourers transferred from Cape Verde they may develop their patriotic action in the service of the Party, our people and Africa, and at the right moment strike the blows the enemy deserves, thus making the fetish turn against the fetishist.

I draw the attention of those responsible for supply to the populations and principally of workers in the People's Stores, to the fact that this year the Party will have available greater than ever quantities of essential items which we must be able to put at the disposal of the populations of all the liberated areas, whatever difficulties we have to face. In fact both from the socialist countries, notably the Soviet Union, and from Sweden, Norway and other countries or humanitarian organizations, we are receiving aid which will enable us greatly to improve the functioning of the People's Stores as well as of health and education institutions. I hope that everyone will make the necessary efforts to make 1973 a year of greater efficiency still in supply to our populations of essential items.

As you all know, 1972 was a year of great and decisive victories on the international level for our great Party and our people. Among the main successes scored I want here to recall only the following: the now historic visit of the United Nations Special Mission to the liberated areas of our land, which brought important consequences for the prestige not only of our Party and our struggle but for all the liberation movements in Africa. In recalling this event, which the Portuguese colonialist aggressors wanted to oppose with their most savage crimes, I hail at the start of a new year the peoples of Ecuador, Sweden, Tunisia, Senegal and Japan, whose brave sons visited our land, as members of the Special Mission. I thank their respective governments for having agreed that their representatives should make such a visit and the United Nations Secretary-general for the determined way in which he applied a historic and transcendent resolution of the General Assembly of that international organization.

The resolution of the United Nations Decolonization Committee, in its April 1972 session, by which our Party was recognized by acclamation as the sole, true and legitimate representative of the people of Guiné and Cape Verde.

The resolutions of the United Nations General Assembly which, among other important decisions, confirmed the recognition of our Party as the sole and legitimate representative of our African people and called on all states, governments and national and international organizations and on the United Nations specialized agencies to reinforce their aid to our Party and always and only with the Party to treat all questions concerning the people of Guiné and Cape Verde.

The historic resolution of the Security Council which, under its first woman president, our Guinean sister and comrade Jeanne Martin Cissé, unanimously adopted a resolution condemning Portuguese colonialism and demanding that the Government of Portugal cease the colonial war in Africa, withdraw its occupation troops and enter into negotiations without delay with the respective patriotic forces, which in our land are represented by our Party. For the first time in the political and diplomatic struggle against Portuguese colonialism, our Party spoke in the UN with observer status, and even the allies of the colonial Fascist Government of Portugal voted as a bloc against it in the United Nations Security Council. This resolution has and will now have prime importance in the future development of our politico-military action to expel the criminal Portuguese colonialist aggressors from our land.

Last but not least, I recall the resolutions of solidarity and unconditional total support adopted by the Conference of African Heads of State and Government in Rabat, at which our Party was once again chosen as spokesman for all the liberation movements in Africa.

The past year was in fact a year of great international victories, the more so as we are sure of moral, political and in some cases material, support from independent African states, in the first place from the neighbouring and brother countries, the Republics of Guinea and Senegal, as well as that from all the genuinely anticolonialist and anti-racist countries and forces. We are receiving or are going to receive in this coming year more material aid from the Soviet Union and all the other socialist countries, as well as from Sweden, Norway, Denmark, Finland, from various parties and political organizations in Europe and from humanitarian institutions like the World Council of Churches, Rowntree in Britain, the World Church Service, French People's Aid, the International Red Cross and from various support committees around the world. United Nations specialized or autonomous agencies, like the Economic Commission for Africa, UNESCO, UNICEF, the World Health Organization, the High Commission for Refugees and the International Labour Organization are developing, and will increasingly develop, co-operation with our Party, and tomorrow certainly with our state.

You all thus understand why the colonial Fascist Government of Marcello Caetano and its representatives in our land have good reason for being desperate. Unscrupulous as they are, with contempt for the interests and rights of peoples, including their own, they will lay their hands on any means, any crimes, to try to halt our struggle. You understand thus why the criminal Portuguese colonialist aggressors and their chief in our land are more enraged then ever, intensify the shelling and step up the assaults against our liberated areas, and make every effort to try to reoccupy some localities in these areas, with the purpose of consoling themselves for the military, political and diplomatic defeats we have inflicted on them, and with the aim of seeing if they can succeed with the new crimes they are committing in demoralizing our forces and demobilizing our populations. The defeats they suffered in 1972, both in our land and on the African and international level, explain the intensified aggression against our liberated areas, in particular against the region of Cubucaré, which was visited in April by the United Nations Special Mission.

The desperation of the colonial Fascist Government of Portugal is the more understandable now that it is certain that the so-called 'policy for a better Guiné' has failed completely, and the Government senses that the lie about a policy for a 'better Cape Verde' will also fail. In regard to Guiné it is the colonial Fascist Government of Lisbon itself which, through the voice of the chief of the criminal colonialist aggressors, confesses this failure, when it declares that what the African man wants is to have – and we quote – 'his own political and social voice'. It is exactly what the African man of Guiné and Cape Verde wants. But we call that *independence,* that is to say the total sovereignty of our people on the national and international level, for them to construct for themselves, in peace and dignity, by the expenditure of their own efforts and sacrifices, marching on their own feet and guided by their own head, the progress to which they have a right like all the peoples in the world. And this in co-operation with other peoples, including the people of Portugal, who in three liberation wars against Castile in Spain struggled to win their own political and social voice, their independence – and won. We, like other people who have struggled and won, will continue the struggle in all its forms as long as it is necessary. Because we are in our land and because we have the certainty of winning.

As you know, while the populations of the urban centres occupied by the colonialists show increasing interest in the Party and the struggle, as is proved by the great number of youth who have abandoned Bissau and other trading centres to join the battle fronts, the situation in Portugal is speedily growing worse and the Portuguese people assert their opposition to the criminal colonial war with increasing clamour. For this reason, the colonial Fascist Lisbon Government and its agents in our land are racing to see if they can succeed in changing the situation before they are completely lost in their own land as well.

But they are wasting their time and in vain and ingloriously are wasting the lives of the Portuguese youth they send to war. They will commit still more crimes against our populations, will make many more attempts and manoeuvres to try to destroy our Party and the struggle. They will certainly carry on various acts of shameless aggression against the neighbouring countries. But all in vain. For no crime, no power, no manoeuvre or demagogy of the criminal Portuguese colonialist aggressors can halt the march of history, the irreversible march of our African people of Guiné and Cape Verde towards the independence, peace and genuine progress to which they have a right.

Forward comrades and compatriots in our heroic struggle for national liberation!

Health, long life and greater successes to our African people, to our brave combatants, to all militants, responsible workers and leaders of our great Party!

Let us proclaim the existence of our state in Guiné and advance with the victorious struggle of our people in Cape Verde!

Let us expel the Portuguese colonialists from Cubucaré as from all the regions of our land!

Long live PAIGC, strength, light and guide of our people in Guiné and Cape Verde!

Death to the criminal Portuguese colonialist aggressors!

CPSIA information can be obtained at www.ICGtesting.com
Printed in the USA
BVOW04s0512181113

336470BV00003B/6/A

9 780853 456254